Ray L Beaumont

Beacon Across the Prairie

Beacon Across the Prairie

North Dakota's Land-Grant College

by

WILLIAM C. HUNTER

NORTH DAKOTA INSTITUTE FOR REGIONAL STUDIES
Fargo, 1961

COPYRIGHT 1961

by

WILLIAM C. HUNTER

Fargo, North Dakota

Library of Congress Catalog Number: 61-63838

Printed at
THE LUND PRESS, INC., MINNEAPOLIS

Foreword

This book is a contribution to North Dakota's observance of the Dakota Territory Centennial. It also helps to recognize the forthcoming one-hundredth anniversary of the First Morrill Act of 1862 which encouraged and made possible the establishment of land-grant colleges and universities.

The appearance of the present book marks the conclusion of approximately the first decade's work of the North Dakota Institute for Regional Studies. A short history of this organization has been given by Dr. Hunter in Chapter XIV of this book. We believe that the Institute is becoming an important part of the emerging University in an era when research doubtless will hold the key to many of our state, regional, and national problems.

Writing local history, especially the history of a college, must rank as one of the more dangerous diversions. The risks are great. It is not easy to compress an account of either a "purge" or an important research find, without some of the still alive participants feeling that important information has been omitted (or should have been). It would be hard to please everyone. Dr. Hunter has performed his task well.

What with fast moving social changes and the rapid expansion of an impressive higher education complex in the Fargo-Moorhead community, the North Dakota State University of the future perhaps will bear little resemblance to the past. But for 70 years it was "North Dakota Agricultural College," and it is of this earlier institution that Dr. Hunter has written. In his 80th year the author has produced not only the account of a college but also a personal document. That he had his own enthusiasms and distrusts, his own heroes and villains, will be apparent to the reader. For "Lum" Hunter was a part of the scene he records. For 38 years he was a teacher of history, chairman of the department of social science, and emeritus professor.

The North Dakota State or "A.C." that Dr. Hunter knew intimately is not exactly the North Dakota State of today, yet is part and parcel of it. Perhaps the student or teacher in a university would like to believe that as a child his institution was a most lusty infant. Dr. Hunter shows that the infant, while it had promising moments, at other times almost perished. It was a struggle to establish the simple but vital practices that are the essence of a university. Here is the story of the people who did it — Bolley, Ladd, Shepperd, the Waldrons, Walster, Stevens, and all the others. And it is the people who will make the future of North Dakota State University great, if it is to continue to fulfill its role as a beacon across the prairie.

The Arts and Sciences faculty is grateful for the support given by many citizens inside and outside the State in our collecting, investigating and publishing programs.

                        SETH RUSSELL
                        Dean, Arts and Sciences
                        Director, Institute for Regional Studies

Fargo, N. D.
August 23, 1961

Preface

In 1950 in connection with the sixtieth anniversary of the founding of the North Dakota Agricultural College and also as a contribution to the influence of the newly organized North Dakota Institute for Regional Studies the author was asked by President Fred S. Hultz and Dean G. Ernst Giesecke to write a history of the College. He was given time away from his teaching duties in the spring term and in summer of that year in order to spend time in research on the project. By June 1952 when he retired as chairman of the department of social science, the manuscript was near completion.

Various factors at that time, however, prevented its publication. In 1959 the Board of the Institute authorized a committee of three faculty members, chosen by the author, to help in the revision and enlargement of the manuscript in order to make it ready for publication. That committee consisted of Dean Seth Russell of the School of Arts and Sciences, Professor T. E. Stoa, chief of the division of plant industry and chairman of the department of agronomy in the School of Agriculture, and Dr. C. B. Cleland, associate professor of sociology in the School of Arts and Sciences.

While the earlier manuscript was partly chronological and partly topical, the present revision is an attempt to integrate the various schools of the College and the Experiment Station and the Extension Service into the history of the College and to show their development and growth in seven decades.

The author hopes this account also will be read in relation to the history of the State of North Dakota and its varying economic and political changes. North Dakota is unique in being the most rural of the states in the United States in its outlook and therefore is peculiarly related to land-grant institutions. Also the author has sought to relate the story of the College closely to the general development of public education on the basis of the educational philosophy of land-grant colleges.

The author is indebted to a large number of officials and members of the College staff. Commissioner A. E. Mead of the Board of Higher Education cordially opened its records for study and information. President Hultz gave his interest and time in the initial encouragement and made valuable contributions to the later revisions. H. Dean Stallings, librarian of the College, and the library staff gave freely of their time and help. Dr. Leo Hertel, the editor of the North Dakota Institute for Regional Studies, was most generous in his patience and criticism in helping with the manuscript and its publication. The three members of the revision committee spent considerable time in reading the manuscript and making suggestions. Professor Stoa particularly was of invaluable help to the author due to his longtime connection with the College. To Professor Cleland the author is indebted for his suggestion of the title of the book. Professor O. A. Stevens and Dean Pearl Dinan read most of the manuscript and contributed valuable advice in regard to the content and style. Many other individual staff members and alumni were contacted orally or by correspondence and deserve recognition.

In conclusion the author wishes to express his thanks for the use of extracts and personal reminiscences published in various publications of the College and in the local press.

WILLIAM C. HUNTER
Emeritus Professor of History

Fargo, North Dakota
March 12, 1961

Table of Contents

FOREWORD	V
Seth Russell, Dean, Arts and Sciences	
PREFACE	VII
I. The Founding and Its Background	3
II. Early Years, 1890–1895	21
III. Growth and Expansion, 1895–1916	31
IV. Research and Extension, 1895–1916	46
V. Student Life, 1890–1916	64
VI. Politics and War, 1916–1920	85
VII. A New Era, 1921–1929	102
VIII. Depression and Decline, 1929–1937	122
IX. The Purge, 1937–1938	144
X. Recovery, 1938–1941	163
XI. World War II, 1939–1945	179
XII. New Advances and New Strifes, 1945–1955	193
XIII. Growth in the Fifties, 1955–1960	212
XIV. College and State	227
XV. The College Becomes a University	247

APPENDICES

I. First Morrill Act	261
II. Hatch Act	263
III. Smith-Lever Act	266
IV. Constitutional Amendment Establishing a State Board of Higher Education	268
V. Members of the Governing Boards of the North Dakota Agricultural College	271
VI. Members of the State Board of Higher Education since 1939	273
VII. Presidents and Directors of the North Dakota Agricultural College	274
VIII. Blue Key — Doctors of Service	274
IX. Faculty and Staff Members Who Have Served Ten Years or More	274
X. Editors and Managers of the Yearbooks	283
XI. Editors and Managers of the *Spectrum*	284
XII. Presidents of The Student Commission	285
XIII. Student Organizations in 1960	286
XIV. Students Who Gave Their Lives in World War II	288
XV. The Buildings on the Campus	290
BIBLIOGRAPHY	292
ILLUSTRATIONS	*Between Pages* 54 and 55
INDEX	297

Beacon Across the Prairie

◄ CHAPTER I ►

The Founding and Its Background

Dakota Territory in 1862 was a prairie sea of wild grass, unsettled and undeveloped. In that year, in distant Washington, the Congress of the United States passed a law that was to have a direct influence on North Dakota and on the future North Dakota Agricultural College. This was the Morrill Act, which provided a means of financing higher education through the sale or rent of land.

The Morrill Act of 1862 allotted a grant of land "to each state equal to thirty thousand acres for each senator and representative in Congress. . . . All moneys derived from the sale of the lands should constitute a perpetual fund . . . to the endowment, support and maintenance of at least one college where the leading object should be, without excluding other scientific and classical studies, and including military tactics, to teach such branches of learning as were related to agriculture and mechanic arts in such manner as the Legislatures of the States may respectively prescribe, in order to promote the liberal and practical education of the industrial classes in the several pursuits and professions in life." [1]

The history of the land-grant college movement has been described by Edward Danforth Eddy in the book, *Colleges for Our Land and Time*. He writes that the Morrill Act was preceded by the emergence of science and the industrial revolution which resulted in the development of industry and vocations. The first colleges in the American colonies were founded by churches to train ministers, and the great majority of colleges established between 1789 and 1860 were denominationally inspired. These classical colleges also trained school teachers, doctors and lawyers. Their curricula were narrow and restricted, consisting of philosophy, theology, Latin, Greek, Hebrew and mathematics. There was little interest in research to improve future teaching. As

3

late as 1850 not a single college had a laboratory, for experimentation was not important in the prevailing educational thought. "The classical college was a vested interest in the midst of a rapidly expanding and almost radical America." [2]

America in the first half of the nineteenth century was experiencing a period of intellectual awakening. The American Lyceum provided a popular education for millions of people throughout the country. It was the forerunner of collegiate extension services of the twentieth century. The first science to be taught in the colleges was taught like literature, without practice in a laboratory. In 1824 Steven Van Rensselaer founded the Troy Institute to apply "science to the common purposes of life." He desired to "qualify teachers for instructing the sons and daughters of farmers and mechanics in the application of experimental chemistry, philosophy, and natural history to agriculture, domestic economy, the arts, and manufactures." [3] The agricultural movement paralleled the scientific development. The farmers of the era of Jacksonian democracy wanted education for their children, but they did not know what it should be.

The first state agricultural college was established in Michigan in 1855. At its dedication in 1857 its first president, Joseph R. Williams, stated:

"First we would begin with the farmer himself; morally, physically, intellectually, he must be a man before he can be a farmer. Because he is also a citizen, he should be able to execute the duties of even high responsible stations, with self-reliance and intelligence. He should be qualified to keep his accounts, survey his land, and speak and write his native tongue with ease and vigor. He should be a chemist, a student of physiology, entomology, mechanics, electricity, and the veterinary art." [4]

Other beginnings in agricultural education were made in Pennsylvania (the People's College) and in Massachusetts, Iowa and Maryland. But it remained for the stimulus of the Morrill Act to bring the agricultural college into being. Justin Morrill of Vermont first proposed the land-grant college idea several years before the bill was finally passed in 1862 and signed by President Lincoln. The act granted to each State for the support of a college that would provide a "liberal and practical education of the industrial classes . . ." 30,000 acres of land for each senator and representative that it had in the United States Congress. The act further provided that the funds realized from the sale of all lands should be retained forever and only the income from them should be used for the support of the institutions to be created. When North Dakota became a state in 1889, 90,000 acres within her own boundaries were designated for this purpose. At the same time the State Legislature passed

The Founding and Its Background 5

a provision that none of the designated land could be sold for less than ten dollars per acre.

But why a *land-grant* college? In the early history of the United States, land was the only source of wealth. To the west lay vast miles of uninhabited territory. Moreover, there was a tradition to use land as a stimulus of education. The Continental Congress inserted in the Northwest Ordinance of 1787 the provision that "there shall be reserved the lot No. 16 of every township, for the maintenance of public schools." In the same year the Bill of Sale to the Ohio Company contained the provision that "not more than two complete townships . . . be given perpetually for the purpose of an University." [5]

During the early nineteenth century indirect educational grants were made; by 1957 sixty million acres of public land had been set aside for the support of the common schools. Also four million acres had been granted to fifteen states to endow state universities. Land was practically the only endowment which the Federal Government could bestow.

There has been much discussion as to the true intent of the Morrill Act. In 1867 and again in 1887 Mr. Morrill set forth his views on the purpose of the Act of 1862. From the wording of the legislation itself and from Mr. Morrill's statements it seems clear that at least three purposes were embodied in the legislation:

1. A protest against the then characteristic dominance of the classics in higher education.

2. A desire to develop, at the college level, instruction relating to the practical activities of life.

3. An attempt to offer to those belonging to the industrial classes preparation for the "professions of life."

The emphasis in the legislation was on the class or group from which students come, rather than the one toward which they were headed. The land-grant institutions were meant to be colleges for those from the industrial group. The clear intent was "that they should provide liberal and technical, including professional, preparation at the college level for the large middle class." [6] The Act itself includes the phrase, "in order to promote the liberal and practical education of the industrial classes in the several pursuits and professions in life."

Mr. Paul Dressel, in an address at the North Dakota Agricultural College in 1960, commented on this quotation as follows:

"While the Act also indicated that agriculture and military science must be taught in these land-grant institutions, the impact of this phrase indicates: first, that there was no intent to debar the institutions from offering study in other fields; second, that it was expected that liberal education be promoted by the institutions; and third, that the purpose in encouraging such institutions was as much to provide for a higher level of education for the industrial and agricultural classes as it was to provide education for the rapidly developing technologies. In one sense, the Land-Grant Act may be regarded as the first attempt at the college level to combine the liberal with the vocational. The charge of the land-grant college, then, might be regarded as that of unifying two of the major elements of human experience; that is, making a life and making a living."[7]

In the years between the passage of the Morrill Act of 1862 and the founding of the North Dakota Agricultural College as a land-grant institution in 1890, beginnings had been made in other states in agricultural research and extension. Fields and stables were used as laboratories by teachers of agriculture, while the machine shop and the forge became the laboratory for the engineers. College doors were opened to women and, in 1890, four land-grant colleges had departments of home economics. The teaching of animal husbandry led to courses in veterinary medicine.

Moreover, scientific research and experimental work had been attempted in sixteen colleges. Such work was greatly stimulated by the passage in 1887 of the Federal Hatch Act, which appropriated fifteen thousand dollars annually for research in agriculture to each state having a land-grant institution. The results of the experimental work were brought to the people by farmers' institutes and short courses. Therefore, the infant North Dakota land grant institution could rely upon some experience in older states to serve as precedents for its own program. In 1890 Senator Morrill secured passage of another act providing for an annual appropriation of fifteen thousand dollars for each state, to be increased by one thousand dollars a year for ten years, when it would continue annually at twenty-five thousand dollars.

These Federal acts made possible an educational institution for North Dakota, which became a state in 1889. They were suited to the needs of new settlers who were practically all farmers or engaged in business directly dependent on farming. The North Dakota Agricultural College was to be a "people's college." In contrast, the University of North Dakota, which had been established in 1883, before the Territory became a state, was modeled by its founders after the classical private institutions of the East. It appealed especially to those who desired to enter the professions of teaching, law and medicine. The numerous local normal schools provided for by the state constitution in 1889 were to be engaged in preparing students for teaching in the elementary schools, usually temporarily. The Agricultural College and Experiment Station were intended to provide a liberal and practical education for the sons and daughters of the farmers and to pursue research for improving farm practices and welfare.⁸ In this way Federal legislation had made provision for higher education for the settlers in the Dakotas. Who were these settlers, and what made them come to the Territory?

Dakota Territory was organized in 1861. At that time it comprised the land between the State of Minnesota and the Rocky Mountains, roughly including the present states of North and South Dakota, Montana and Wyoming. Yankton, in the southeast corner, was designated as the capital. Later Montana and Wyoming were cut off and separately organized. A settlement at Pembina made by the Scotch immigrants who had come from Canada existed at this time in the northeastern corner of what is now the State of North Dakota. This settlement became an important fur trading post on the Red River. There were a few other trading posts on the Missouri, Fort Union and Fort Buford being the most important among them. A military post, Fort Abercrombie, had also been established at the head of navigation on the Red River. All the rest of the Territory was a roaming range for buffaloes, a hunting ground for the Indians and half-breeds and an area for explorers and fur traders. Some trade was carried on by steamboat on the Missouri and Red rivers.

Ten years later the coming of the railroad led to the rapid settlement of the northern half of Dakota Territory. The Northern Pacific Railway reached the Red River at Moorhead in 1871–72 and the Missouri River at Bismarck in June, 1873; the Great Northern Railway entered Grand Forks in 1880 and reached Minot in 1886. The Red River Valley was rapidly opened up to settlement in the seventies and the success of the "bonanza" farms of the Dalrymples, Grandins, Amenia-Sharon Land Co. and Elk Valley widely advertised that rich valley. During this period, J. B. Power, land agent of the Northern Pacific Railway, negotiated land sales in the Red River Valley amounting to thousands of acres.⁹ The "Dakota boom" reached its peak by 1884. In 1885 the Red River Valley had a population of 116,000, and the Bismarck area of 14,000.

Most of the settlers came from Minnesota, Wisconsin, New York and Iowa. The 1890 census showed a high percentage of foreign born — 81,000, or nearly 45 percent of the total. About one third were Norwegian, 9,500 were German and 7,800 Canadian. They came to farm and the individual farmer was tempted to take out a homestead claim or buy cheap railroad land, believing he could harvest a profitable wheat crop in one season. The large bonanza operators who had more capital to start with were usually more successful.

It may seem strange that this frontier state took any interest in education when its chief problem was the economic one of making a living.

But there were Easterners among the early settlers and foreigners as well who wanted to become more than mere "grubbers" of the soil, who wanted to continue or attain an education. However, we would hardly expect these new settlers to be interested in higher education at a time when "an elementary school system was barely developed in Dakota and secondary schools hardly existed." [10] Before 1883 territorial legislation had provided for institutions of learning in the more thickly populated area in the southern half of the territory.

In 1883 Dakota Territory consisted of land which is now North and South Dakota and a part of Montana. The government of the Territory consisted of an appointed governor and an elected legislature of two houses, Council and House of Representatives. The northern part (what is now North Dakota) consisted of three council districts: Grand Forks, Walsh and Pembina counties, the northeast district; Cass, Traill and Richland counties, the southeast one; and Barnes, Stutsman and Burleigh counties, the central one. The rest of the Territory was unorganized. These three districts were represented in the Territorial Council of 1883 by George H. Walsh of Grand Forks, Samuel G. Roberts of Fargo, and Johnston Nickeus of Jamestown.

S. G. Roberts, who in his earlier years had been practicing law in Minnesota, came to Fargo in 1872 and settled a claim on a quarter section lying north and west from the old Fargo National Bank corner on Broadway and N. P. Avenue. In 1878 "Major" Alonzo W. Edwards and Dr. J. B. Hall published the *Fargo Daily Republican*, the first daily paper published in Fargo. Later Edwards sold his interest to Hall with an agreement not to start another newspaper in Fargo; however, after a few months he returned and, on November 17, began publishing the *Daily Argus*. The sons of Dr. Hall who in the meantime had taken over the first paper named their paper the *Daily Republican*. Once one of Edwards' employees attempted to compel Roberts, who was an attorney in the land office business, to advertise in the *Daily Argus*. He refused and later charged the paper with trying to slander the title of his property.[11] Thus in the dominant Republican Party to which the two men belonged two factions arose — the Edwards faction and the Roberts faction. The Edwards faction aligned itself with the corporation interests and particularly with the railroad group, and cooperated with Alexander McKenzie of Bismarck, who was seeking to become political boss in the northern part of Dakota Territory.[12]

In 1882 an attempt was made to suspend hostilities. Edwards wished to go to the Territorial Legislature. Roberts wished to be re-elected to the Council. So it was agreed that Roberts be nominated for the Council and Edwards for the House. As the campaign progressed Dr. Hall's sons were persuaded to publish in the *Daily Republican* certain sensational articles regarding Edwards' connection with the defunct Chicago Protective Life Insurance Company in which he was depicted as a robber of widows and orphans. As a result, Edwards was defeated by Capt. L. F. Alred, a Civil War veteran, of Tower City. Roberts was reelected. Edwards sued the *Daily Republican* for libel; a verdict of one cent damages was rendered in favor of Edwards, but the expense of the defense practically bankrupted the paper. Thus the breach between the two factions was intensified.

Prior to the legislative session of 1883 the University of South Dakota had been located at Vermillion, a penitentiary at Sioux Falls, and an "insane hospital" at Yankton. In 1883 bills were introduced by southern members, appropriating large sums to pay for completing the penitentiary, for reimbursing the contractor for an alleged loss in building the "insane hospital," for completing a building for the university, and for constructing a new building for an agricultural college at Brookings.

When these bills came up for a second reading, Roberts gave notice that he would "oppose some of them *in toto*, and would insist on a scaling down of amounts named in others." He objected on the ground that the northern part of the Territory would have to pay one third of the appropriations in taxes, although the institutions were inaccessible and of no practical benefit to his constituents.

After the Council adjourned the southern members sent a committee to confer with Mr. Roberts, and he, in turn, asked the southern members of the Council if they would support a bill duplicating the southern institutions in the north. They agreed. At a meeting of the three northern members of the Council, the northern institutions were divided into educational institutions, the "insane hospital," and the penitentiary. Lots were drawn. Walsh drew first and chose the university; Roberts, second, chose the penitentiary and the agricultural college; Nickeus got the "insane hospital."

Before any of these bills were reported out of committee Alexander McKenzie of Bismarck, and Edwards and John Haggart of Fargo arrived in Yankton supposedly in the interest of railroad legislation. A few days later Nickeus introduced a bill for a penitentiary to be located at Bismarck, explaining that he was "doing the bidding of Mr. McKenzie." Mr. Roberts claims that he was reliably informed that the scheme to get the penitentiary away from Fargo was that of Edwards, to keep Roberts from becoming too strong politically. Judge Spaulding in his *Autobiography* corroborates this belief and states, "after the election of 1882 Edwards and his associates went to Yankton to prevent

Roberts from securing appropriations."[13] Roberts exonerated Haggart from being a party to the scheme.

During the last days of the session the University of North Dakota was located at Grand Forks, the penitentiary at Bismarck, and the "insane hospital" at Jamestown. An agricultural college was located at Fargo but no appropriations were made for it. Trustees named for the college were: N. K. Hubbard and E. B. Eddy of Fargo, G. W. Vernon of Jamestown and Walter Brown of Larimore. These men, however, never accepted their appointments.

The citizens of Fargo were indifferent toward the school, partly because of political dissension and because they still hoped to secure the "insane hospital" or penitentiary, either of which appeared more advantageous than the college. Also, some of the indifference may have been due to the opposition of those Fargo citizens who were interested in maintaining Fargo College, a Congregational institution, sanctioned in 1882 and to be opened in 1884. It is likely that the wisdom of establishing another college at Fargo was questioned.

However, the big fight in the Territorial Legislature of 1883 was not about the location of the institution but was about the question of relocating the capital of the Territory. Yankton was at the southeastern corner of the Territory and was difficult to reach. Moreover, the legislators were much exercised over the lack of hotel accommodations and the exorbitant charges for the poor facilities available. A bill was finally passed in the House, on March 5, to give the choice of a Territorial capital to a commission to be appointed by the governor.[14]

In order to get the bill passed in the Council the commissioners were named in the bill. They were Milo W. Scott of Emerado, Burleigh F. Spaulding of Fargo, Alexander McKenzie of Bismarck, Charles H. Myers of Redfield, George A. Mathews of Brookings, Alexander Hughes of Yankton, Harry H. DeLong of Canton, John P. Belding of Deadwood and M. D. Thompson of Vermillion County. The nine commissioners met in Sioux City, Iowa, in early April, 1883. The Milwaukee Railroad provided a special train which took the commission to Yankton at daybreak, stopped two minutes, long enough for the organization of the commission, and then went on to Canton, headquarters for several days. Alexander Hughes was elected president, Ralph W. Wheelock secretary and Dr. Milo W. Scott treasurer.

Special trains were furnished to the commission to visit those locations which desired to provide 160 acres of land and $100,000 additional. Various sites in South Dakota were first inspected, then Bismarck was visited. The commission was elaborately entertained. The commission met in Fargo, June 2, 1883. On the thirteenth ballot Bismarck received

The Founding and Its Background

five of the nine votes. Spaulding, a friend of Roberts, consistently voted for Redfield. Hughes gave the deciding vote to Bismarck. It is significant that McKenzie was the only northern member to vote for Bismarck.[15] In the meantime, the earlier political antagonism in Cass County had broadened. The "Old Gang" included not only "Major" Edwards, but also Alexander McKenzie of Bismarck, Alexander Hughes of Yankton, Jud T. LaMoure of Pembina and G. H. Walsh of Grand Forks. The "Anti-Gang" consisted of S. G. Roberts, N. K. Hubbard and B. F. Spaulding of Fargo, and George B. Winship, publisher of the *Grand Forks Herald*.

In the legislative assembly of 1885, which met in Bismarck, Twomey, a member of the Council, introduced a bill to appropriate $45,000 to construct and furnish a building for the North Dakota Territorial Agricultural College at Fargo. The bill was passed, but vetoed by Governor Pierce, who explained his position as follows:

"The educational institutions supported by the Territory are already too numerous and are taxing the people for their completion and maintenance without any adequate return. The University of North Dakota, located at Grand Forks, is but eighty miles from the proposed location of this new institution, and if the latter is started, a rivalry will necessarily ensue not conducive to the welfare or advantage of either."

The vote to override the veto was 0 to 20; the veto stood. Nothing was done in the next two sessions regarding the agricultural college.

In 1888 the Cass County convention nominated N. K. Hubbard for territorial representative, with no opposition from the Edwards group. But before the territorial convention met at Jamestown the Edwards faction chartered a Pullman car, filled it with refreshments and workers, and tried to defeat Hubbard by electing Vincent S. Stone of Fargo. The Roberts-Spaulding faction combined with Hansbrough of Devils Lake and L. B. Richardson of Grand Forks. They were successful in electing Hubbard at the convention.

On January 14, 1889, Hugh McDonald of Barnes County introduced a bill to locate the North Dakota Territorial Agricultural College at Valley City.[16] On January 30, Smith Stimmel of Cass County introduced a bill to locate the agricultural college at Fargo. The two bills were then referred to a committee composed of members of the Council from North Dakota which visited both towns and reported on February 15, 1889. The majority report was signed by the members representing Stutsman, Barnes, Walsh, Pembina and Grand Forks counties and recommended the Valley City bill. A minority report signed by members from Burleigh, Traill and Cass favored Fargo. The majority report was adopted and the bill passed both the Council and the House. At once a committee of Fargo citizens consisting of John Haggart, B. F. Spaulding, John Benton and C. R. Stone went to Bismarck to persuade the governor to veto the bill. Governor Church did veto the bill, along with several others, on the ground that they carried appropriations exceeding the resources of the Territory.

The next step in the story of the location of the agricultural college was the meeting of the Constitutional Convention in July, 1889. The Omnibus Bill, admitting four new states, North and South Dakota, Montana and Washington, had been passed by Congress and signed by President Cleveland, February 22, 1889. The election of delegates to the Constitutional Convention in North Dakota took place on May 14. Fargo elected B. F. Spaulding and H. F. Miller, Republicans, and Jacob Lowell, Democrat. The convention met on July 4, 1889, and was in session until August 17. The principal Republican candidates for president of the convention were F. B. Fancher of Jamestown, representing the Farmers' Alliance, and H. F. Miller of Fargo, representing the opposition. Fancher was nominated and easily defeated the Democratic candidate. Miller was made chairman of the Committee on Public Institutions and Buildings.

There was a very considerable division of opinion whether the location of the public institutions should be made by the convention or left to a legislature elected by the people. Delegates from Griggs, Cass (outside of Fargo), Grand Forks, Richland and Walsh counties opposed decision by the convention, maintaining that the delegates were under the control of the railroad corporations. However, the majority report was passed 44 to 30. This gave Bismarck the capitol, Grand Forks the university and school of mines, Jamestown the "insane hospital," Fargo the agricultural college, Valley City and Mayville, normal schools, Devils Lake, the deaf and dumb school, Mandan, the reform school, Lisbon, the soldiers' home, Pembina County, the blind asylum, Ellendale, the industrial school, Bottineau, the school of forestry, and Wahpeton, the scientific school.

The Constitutional Convention was dominated by the interests looking for favors; the apportioning of public institutions was considered a favor. There were two combinations of delegates at the convention, one known as the Bismarck-Fargo group and the other as the Grand Forks group. The Bismarck-Fargo group considered Bismarck the best spot for the capitol and wanted the agricultural college at Fargo. The Northern Pacific Railway supported the Bismarck-Fargo combine; this support, along with the distribution of the other institutions, helped the winning combination. The Grand Forks group, on the other hand, led by Budge and Griggs, was trying to secure the capitol, the agricultural college, a school of mines and a training school. Jamestown offered little resistance to the Bismarck-Fargo combination with the hope of getting the capitol in Jamestown by a compromise of the two larger factions. However, a group in Fargo was opposed to the location of an agricultural college at Fargo. Roberts explains Fargo's hostility in this way:

"Up to that time the people of Cass County and Fargo, including some of the delegates to the state convention, were unable to visualize the importance and possibilities of an agricultural college, though the people of other parts of the proposed new state gave evidence of having considered its importance and did their utmost to secure its location.

"It was only by the most persistent urging that I persuaded influential citizens from the different parts of the state passing thru Fargo en route to the convention, to become interested in and use their influence in the interest of Fargo.

"The plea of some people in Fargo and Cass County—and with some of the Cass County delegates too—was that an Agricultural College would never amount to anything. That it would be better to abandon any attempt to secure its location and go for something of greater benefit, an Indian school, or a school for the deaf and dumb, or a school of science, something big! This may seem like an attempt at sarcasm but it is not. Such talk actually took place and Fargo actually had the Agricultural College thrust upon it, its wishes to the contrary." [17]

Spaulding in an autobiographical sketch makes the following statement in regard to the location of the institution:

"Many people have wondered why so many of the institutions were located in the eastern part of the state and so few in the western but it must be remembered that at this time there were very few people west of the Missouri River. In fact, of the seventy-five delegates to the constitutional convention, only four were from that territory and two of these were from Mandan." [18]

The action of the Constitutional Convention, notwithstanding considerable agitation in Grand Forks and the neighboring counties, seemed not to be too obnoxious to the voters. The official figures of the vote on the adoption of the constitution were 27,441 for the constitution, 8,107 against it, a total of 35,548, a majority of over eighty percent. The vote in Grand Forks County was 687 for and 1,936 against it. The disinterested localities were satisfied with the action of their representatives. Only a small faction in Fargo, a group in Wahpeton, and the large Grand Forks delegation were opposed to it. The fight was not so much over the location of the agricultural college as it was over the capitol. The agricultural college and the other institutions were secondary in the fight and had been used mainly as pawns with which to bargain.

As was said before, the Constitutional Convention was nominated by interests looking for favors. Most of the delegates were not the political leaders of the state, but men of little political reputation outside of their own localities. The dispute between Fargo and Valley City was settled by giving Valley City a teachers college. The decision to locate the agricultural college at Fargo and the capitol at Bismarck appeased the political bosses, John Haggart of Fargo and Alexander McKenzie of Bismarck. Jud LaMoure obtained the school for the blind for Pembina County; Porter McCumber obtained the school of science for Richland County; Jamestown retained its "insane asylum" by the efforts of F. B. Fancher, president of the convention; Budge and Griggs added the school of mines to the university; and Hansbrough obtained the school for the deaf at Devils Lake. It was maintained that the institutions were located in the centers of the populated area. This may have been true at the time, but it was not the main reason for locating the institutions in their respective places.

There were several men who helped Fargo to get the agricultural college. John Haggart's name looms largest, although he wasn't a member of the Constitutional Convention. "A great many Cass County people feel under kindly obligation to John Haggart for favors. John has given especial attention to our boys and no one has worked more faithfully or harder than he for the success of the combine."[19] S. G. Roberts deserves very considerable credit for his earlier efforts at Yankton and for his continued influence up to the time of the close of the Constitutional Convention. H. F. Miller, as an active member of the convention, was next in importance in gaining the agricultural college for Fargo. He held a vital position as chairman of the Committee on Public Buildings and Institutions. Burleigh Spaulding, although his part at the Constitutional Convention was not so outstanding, was one of the earliest backers of the agricultural college in Fargo. His being the chairman of the "protest" committee to the governor in 1889 will testify to that. Addison Leach, another delegate from Cass County, worked for locating the agricultural college at Fargo, while H. M. Peterson of Horace and R. M. Pollock of Casselton were against it. There were many men working indirectly for the agricultural college at Fargo because of their efforts for the combination with Bismarck to retain the capitol.[20] Those men, however, probably had no real interest in seeing the agricultural college in Fargo.

At any rate, the agricultural college was now definitely located in Fargo. Although few Fargoans at this time saw the future advantages which the institution would bring to them, it has turned out to be a real asset to the city. On the other hand, the location of the school in the largest city of the state proved to be a real handicap. The rest of the state was jealous of any attention and of any appropriations that might go to the new institution located at Fargo. The agricultural col-

The Founding and Its Background

lege was considered a Fargo school, not a state school. The farmers for whom it was established looked at it with alien eyes, while some of the people of Fargo considered it a "cow college," and unworthy of their attention. And so for a long time it was not as fully accepted by either the State or the community as its future development has warranted.

The reason for establishing an agricultural college separate from the university followed precedents set by older states. All four of the states which entered the Union in 1889 followed the example of Michigan, Indiana, Iowa, Colorado and Oregon in setting up two institutions of higher learning, one for classical studies and the other for the more practical subjects of agriculture and engineering.

This usual practice seemed to be in accordance with the intention of the Morrill Act of 1862, which sought to "promote the liberal and practical education of the industrial classes in the several pursuits and professions of life." Mr. Morrill had in mind his own state of Vermont and other older states where the private colleges were based on classical tradition. Moreover, the University of North Dakota, which had been founded in 1883, was staffed by administrators and a faculty who had degrees from old eastern institutions, and who emphasized the classical traditions in education. For years the university was popularly known as Grand Forks College, and was for years little more than a normal school and a liberal arts college. The function of the agricultural college was to give training to those who were engaged in farming, the fundamental business of the state. It was to be North Dakota's land-grant college.

Now that the location of the agricultural college was determined by the adoption of the Constitution, the next step was its establishment by the state legislature. At the first meeting of the North Dakota State Legislature on January 20, 1890, John E. Haggart of Fargo introduced Senate Bill 140 entitled "A bill for an act to provide for the Establishment, Erection and Operation of the North Dakota Agricultural College and Agricultural Experiment Station at Fargo." This bill passed both houses and was approved by Governor John Miller on March 8, 1890. A former bill had been vetoed in 1889 on the ground that at that time the State did not need the institution, nor could it afford to appropriate money for it. The second bill was passed and accepted largely on the argument of securing the Federal Experiment Station appropriation.

The more important provisions of this act passed by the legislators are here quoted:

"There is hereby established and located at Fargo, Cass County, North Dakota, an agricultural college, which shall be known by the name of the North Dakota Agricultural College.

BOARD OF TRUSTEES TO FIX SALARIES. The Board of Trustees shall fix the salaries of the president, teachers, instructors and other employees and prescribe their respective duties. The board shall also fix the rate of wages to be allowed the students for labor on the farm and experiment station or in the shops or kitchen of the college. The board may remove the president or subordinate officers and supply all vacancies.

FACULTY TO ADOPT RULES AND REGULATIONS. The faculty shall consist of the president, teachers and instructors and shall pass all needful rules and regulations for the government and discipline of the college, regulating the routine of labor, study, meals and the duties and exercises, and all such rules and regulations as are necessary for the preservation of morals, decorum and health.

COURSE OF INSTRUCTION. The object of such college shall be to afford practical instruction in agriculture and the nature sciences connected therewith, and in the sciences which bear directly upon all industrial arts and pursuits. The course of instruction shall embrace the English language and literature, military tactics, civil engineering, agricultural chemistry, animal and vegetable anatomy, and physiology, the veterinary art, entomology, geology and such other natural sciences as may be prescribed, political, rural and household economy, horticulture, moral philosophy, history, bookkeeping and especially the application of science and the mechanic arts to practical agriculture. A full course of study in the institution shall embrace not less than four years, and the college year shall consist of not less than nine calendar months, which may be divided into terms by the board of trustees as in its judgment will best secure the objects for which the college was founded.

EXPERIMENT STATION. There is hereby established an agricultural experiment station in connection with the North Dakota Agricultural College, and under the board of directors of said college, for the purpose of conducting experiments in agriculture, according to the terms of Section 1 of an act of Congress, approved March 2, 1887, and entitled, 'An act to establish agricultural experiment stations in connection with the colleges established in the several states under the provisions of an act, approved July 2, 1862, and of acts supplementary thereto.' " [21]

Clearly this act of the North Dakota Legislature followed the wording of the original Morrill Act, for it reads: "The object of such college shall be to afford practical instruction in agriculture and the nature sciences connected therewith, and in the sciences which bear directly upon all industrial arts and pursuits" and actually lists required courses. The wording of the Morrill Act is: "the leading object should be, without excluding other scientific and classical studies . . . to teach such branches of learning as were related to agriculture and mechanic arts . . . in order to promote the liberal and practical education of the industrial classes in the several pursuits and professions in life."

The governing body of the College, known as the Board of Trustees, consisted of five (later seven) members appointed by the governor. The first appointees were: O. W. Francis (lawyer), Fargo; J. D. Wallace (merchant), Drayton; M. J. Sanderson (farmer), Edgeley; J. B. Power (farmer), Power; and E. M. Upson (farmer), Cummings. The Board soon organized, electing Francis president and Power secretary. S. S. Lyon, cashier of the First National Bank of Fargo, was named treasurer.

Mr. Francis was an attorney who dealt in tree claims, other real estate and abstracts. He had the "handsomest law office in the Red River Valley" and owned a fine farm in Traill County. His firm was attorney for the Red River National Bank. J. B. Power was the owner of the Helendale Stock Farm. He had been land commissioner for the Northern Pacific and later the Great Northern Railway. In this capacity he had occasion to act as agent in alloting thousands of acres in the fertile Red River Valley to bonanza farmers.[22]

Mr. Power was instrumental in securing the land for Fargo's Island Park for Fargo from the Northern Pacific Railway. S. S. Lyon was a prominent citizen of Fargo, whose banking connections would prove valuable to a new institution.

The Board of Trustees was more concerned about establishing an experiment station than it was about starting a college. At that time the former was considered of more practical and immediate importance. In addition, the Hatch Act of 1887 provided definite federal money appropriations for experiment stations. The first meeting of the Board was held May 1, 1890, in the office of President Francis. After discussion of the best means of raising funds for commencement of work until the Federal appropriations were available, the meeting adjourned until May 15.

At the May 15 meeting, Dr. Samuel T. Satterthwaite, a retired physician residing in Fargo, was elected temporary director of the newly established Experiment Station. James Holes, a local farm operator residing in Fargo, was made superintendent, and Jacob Lowell, assistant. Dr. Satterthwaite served as director from May 15, 1890, to October 15, 1890, during the period of the station's temporary organization.

In the course of the May 15 meeting the secretary was directed to notify the U.S. Secretary of the Interior and the Comptroller of the Treasury of the action of the Board and to make formal application for the appropriation provided for it in the Act of March, 1887. At the following meeting of the Board on July 7 it was voted to select a botanist and a chemist to make a collection and classification of the grasses and other plants and to make an analysis of the soils of the State. The extreme caution of the Board in inaugurating the first work of the institution was revealed in the terms of the action which provided that the term of employment should be for two months and the compensation not to exceed $100 per month.

The position of botanist was offered to C. B. Waldron, who had recently completed a two year post-graduate fellowship at Michigan Agricultural College, from which he was graduated in 1887. He reported for duty on July 19, 1890, and for the next three months Waldron was the only member on the staff at the College or Experiment Station. In 1941 Dr. Waldron recalled his arrival at N.D.A.C. over fifty years earlier for the *Spectrum*:

"Picture in your mind's eye a field of golden wheat in Section 36, Fargo Township, with no buildings to mar its botanical beauty. When the train arrived in Fargo, railway freight cars lying on their sides as a result of a recent tornado and Indian braves in feathered full dress regalia sitting near the depot were his first impressions. Immediately his thoughts returned to the letter recently received from his mother in Michigan warning him not to go to that 'awful' place of Fargo, with its dangerous tornadoes and the possibility of getting 'scalped' by Indians. He bravely continued on his way, although with some anxiety, to begin a new job in this 'frontier' country." [23]

Waldron's work consisted of classifying, preparing and mounting the native plants collected on field trips from the South Dakota boundary to the Turtle Mountains. The collection made at that time was the basis of the present college herbarium which contains all of the plant species of the State that have been located up to the present time. In the fall seeds of the leading hay and pasture grasses was obtained and sown in 1891 in small plots in the Station grounds, this being the first work started of an experimental nature.

At the meeting on August 7, 1890, the Board voted to offer the position of Director of the Experiment Station and President of the College to Dr. H. E. Stockbridge, chemist at Purdue University, Lafayette, Indiana, at a salary of $2,500 a year, to be increased to $3,000 with the beginning of collegiate work. A motion was passed to authorize Dr. Stockbridge to recommend men for the heads of the different departments of the Experiment Station. On August 20 the Board made the following appointments: H. E. Stockbridge, Ph. D., president of the Agricultural College and director of the Experiment Station; H. L. Bolley, M. S., Purdue University, professor of botany and zoology and botanist of the Station; E. F. Ladd, B. S., of the New York Experiment Station, Geneva, professor of chemistry; C. B. Waldron, M. S., Michigan Agricultural College, Lansing, professor of arboriculture. T. D. Hinebauch, M. S., V.S., Purdue University, was appointed professor of veterinary science on November 1, 1890.

At the first joint meeting of the Board and Faculty October 15, 1890, the above appointments were confirmed. Board President Francis appointed a committee to make arrangements with the Trustees of Fargo

The Founding and Its Background

College for the rental of rooms in one of the college buildings for the ensuing year, these to be used for classroom and laboratory purposes until a building should be provided by the Legislature. Professor Bolley thus described this meeting in 1923:

> "The meeting occurred in a little one-story wooden building owned and occupied as an office by O. W. Francis and was situated at a site approximating the position of the building formerly occupied by the Northwestern Mutual Savings and Loan Association. Following this first board meeting, the morning paper, the *Argus*, then edited by Major Edwards, announced in his characteristic form of editorial news note about as follows: 'The Board of Trustees of the North Dakota Agricultural College — whatever that is — met yesterday and elected a faculty — whatever that is — they will at least increase the population.'"[24]

At this meeting also the first formal budget for the College and the Experiment Station was approved, the amount being $2,500 for each, with an additional sum of $800 to be used as needed. During the year 1890 the first bills for equipment, material and supplies were approved on December 18. They included $475 for a gas engine, $750 for chemical apparatus, $258 for desks for the chemical laboratory, a microscope for the department of biology and several books.

In the meantime efforts were being made to secure a permanent home for the College. Section 36, Fargo Township, was in 1890 public school land. The College desired to secure this section and to transfer an equal amount of land to public school purposes. The consent of the Federal Government to appropriate the section in Cass County for the use of the Agricultural College was obtained on September 3, 1890. The first bill introduced in the Senate in the second session of the North Dakota Legislature was made by John E. Haggart for the appropriation of Section 36 as a site for the Agricultural College. On January 16, Governor Burke signed this bill transferring the title of Section 36 to the Agricultural College. Possession was secured on April 18, 1891.

October 15, 1890, is the commonly accepted date of the founding of the North Dakota Agricultural College. At this time Dr. Stockbridge was confirmed as president, his appointments of Bolley, Ladd and Waldron were ratified and the first formal budget of the College was approved.

FOOTNOTES

[1] George A. Works and Barton Morgan. *The Land Grant Colleges*, (Washington, 1939), 110.

[2] Edward Danforth Eddy, *Colleges for Our Land and Time*, (New York, 1957), 4–5.

[3] Eddy, 10.

[4] Madison Kuhn, *Michigan State, the First Hundred Years*, (East Lansing, Mich., 1955), 20.

[5] Eddy, 21.
[6] Works and Morgan, 11.
[7] Paul Dressel, an address (mimeographed), *General Education in a Land-Grant College,* N.D.A.C., Jan. 14, 1960.
[8] The curriculum listings in the earlier catalogs were obviously liberal too. They listed chemistry, botany, zoology, mathematics, physics, geology, English, German, French, history, logic, political economy and mental science.
[9] Murray, Stanley, Railroads and the Agricultural Development of the Red River Valley of the North, *Agricultural History,* XXXI, 57–66 (Oct., 1957).
[10] Louis G. Geiger, *University of the Northern Plains* (Grand Forks, 1958), 14.
[11] S. G. Roberts in a letter to his daughter, Mrs. G. W. Haggart in 1921. (In the library of the *Fargo Forum*).
[12] David Baglein, The McKenzie Era. Unpublished Master's Thesis, North Dakota Agricultural College, Fargo, 1955, 14.
[13] Burleigh Folsom Spaulding. Autobiography, unpublished manuscript in the North Dakota Institute for Regional Studies. Library, N.D.A.C.
[14] Dr. Louis G. Geiger, in his *University of the Northern Plains* (Grand Forks, 1958) 15, cites Governor Ordway as the chief leader in moving the capital to Bismarck. Further research would indicate that Alexander McKenzie was more responsible for it.
[15] George W. Kingsbury in *History of Dakota Territory* (Chicago, 1915) quotes the *Bismarck Tribune* as follows: "We trusted to our magnificent country, the excellence of our location, the size of our bid, the integrity of the commission, and in God; and last, but by no means least, in the pluck and discretion of Alexander McKenzie. To him we owe all honor."
[16] Kingsbury, II, 1553.
[17] Roberts, letter written in 1921. (In the library of the Fargo Forum).
[18] Spaulding, unpublished autobiography, 126. Library, N.D.A.C.
[19] *Fargo Daily Argus,* Aug. 19, 1889.
[20] Clement Lounsberry, *North Dakota* (Chicago, 1917), I, 400.
[21] *Laws of North Dakota,* 1890, chap. 160, 408.
[22] The so-called "bonanza" farmers were those eastern capitalists who laid claim to extended acreages of Red River Valley land in Territorial days. The majority of them were stockholders or bondholders in the Northern Pacific Railway. When the company failed in the 1873 panic, they exchanged their securities for railroad land and developed large wheat farms. These farms were either operated on a large scale or rented to tenants or in some cases sold in small lots to new owners.
[23] C. B. Waldron, "Old Times at NDAC," *Spectrum,* LV, No. 3, Feb. 28, 1941.
[24] Henry L. Bolley, "Early Days at the A.C.," *College and State,* Nov. 1923, 11.

Early Years, 1890–1895

"With a total faculty barely exceeding an even half dozen, only a man with diversified talents and boundless erudition could perform his appointed tasks, and in the course of a year that same instructor might be expounding to the same students the mysteries of the starry heavens and the heights and depths of the earth and the living things therein, the doings of the Greeks and the Romans, not to mention the Dutch and the Irish, the solemn satisfaction that lies in the solution of different equations and the secrets of the skill by which writers and orators move the multitudes. Whether the early students obtained a liberal education or not, most of the first faculty certainly did and it is safe to say that most of their midnights found their oil still burning. . . ."[6]

Gradually additions and changes were made in the staff. Professor McArdle, who in the spring of 1891 had come as assistant in horticulture, soon became instructor in mathematics. Much of his time for the first two or three years was spent in planting trees. He also helped to construct the first building of College Hall, now known popularly as "Old Main." Edward S. Keene, of the University of Illinois, was employed as professor of engineering and physics in 1892. He found to his surprise that the engineering department consisted of a few sets of tools in a small room in the boilerhouse. Since the students did not know what technical engineering meant, he started practical courses that could meet their requirements. Professor Shepperd, who became professor of agriculture in 1893, said that then men carried a good load of college teaching for 30 to 40 students. In addition they did research in the Experiment Station and served in occasional Farmers' Institutes. The faculty meetings every Friday afternoon were held in the small tower room of College Hall. Shepperd, in addition to his duties as professor of agriculture and agriculturist in the Experiment Station, taught arithmetic in the preparatory department. Ladd taught grammar, and one day he laid down an ultimatum to the president that if he was to continue teaching grammar he had to have an unabridged dictionary, of which at that time there was not a single copy in the institution. He got it.

L. S. Bottenfield, A.M., Drake University, was engaged in 1893 as professor of English and modern languages. W. H. Whalen, Ph.B., was assistant in chemistry and also taught geology and mineralogy. W. H. Hayden was instructor in bookkeeping and accounting. E. E. Kaufman was the first instructor in dairying. The first dairy building was erected in 1894 from funds advanced by the citizens of Fargo, who were later reimbursed from a legislative appropriation. In 1894 Miss Marie Senn, M.S., Kansas City College, was appointed professor of domestic economy.

In 1892 the main building, called College Hall, was completed and equipped, and a small greenhouse and boiler room were built just to the west of it. College Hall provided offices, classrooms and laboratories for the teaching staff. The tower room was the president's office. In what is now the business office the few books which made up the library were housed. The president's secretary was also the librarian. The basement was assigned to Professor Ladd and his chemistry experiments. On the second, or ground floor, Professor Bolley's laboratory occupied the room which is now the dean of men's office. Waldron, Hinebauch and McArdle also used the rooms on this floor. The uncompleted upper floor was used as a gymnasium for students and faculty.

In 1893 the Legislature appropriated money for a mechanical building, which provided classrooms, an office, laboratory and a large hall in the second story used for drill by the military department. This building, west of College Hall, is still in use by the College of Engineering. Also in 1893 a students' dormitory, named Francis Hall in honor of the president of the first Board of Trustees, was built at a cost of $17,000 from bricks dug and fired in Fargo. The southeast quarter of the first floor was a kitchen, laboratory and recitation room for the domestic economy department. The northeast quarter of the first floor housed the College dining room for several years following 1893. All of the students boarded there, as well as Professor and Mrs. Keene, Miss Senn, Professor Kaufman, Professor Shepperd, Mr. Hyatt, the farm foreman and all of the farm help.

The northeast quarter of the first floor accommodated the eight or ten girl students. The bathrooms had wooden tubs lined with copper. The southwest quarter provided a reception room where distinguished guests could meet or hold conferences. Back of that were living rooms occupied by Professor and Mrs. Keene. The second floor housed some fifty men students.

A brief account of the work at the Experiment Station during President Stockbridge's administration is found in his 1892 director's report to the governor. The experimental work is listed by departments. Chief stress was given to a study of crop varieties best suited to different parts of the State, emphasizing wheat and sugar beets, but also including rye, barley, oats, corn and peas. The chemistry department devoted one year to the possibilities of profitable sugar beet culture and the second to the study of soils and the composition of hard wheat. The botanical and horticulture departments made an inclusive collection of grasses and forage plants and gave special attention to two plant diseases, potato scab and wheat rust. An extensive planting of shade, forest and fruit trees, berries and garden crops, took place. A successful control of Rocky Mountain locusts in five counties was accomplished. Sheep diseases and rheumatism in horses were studied by the veterinary depart-

Early Years, 1890–1895

ment. The first *Experiment Station Bulletin*, written by Bolley on the subject of potato scab, was published in December, 1891.

With all their varied duties of teaching and research the faculty found time to play. Professor Bolley was interested in developing athletics but also, while still at Fargo College, he found a kindred spirit in the Dean of Fargo College, Miss Frances Sheldon, who had come from Wisconsin to pioneer in the Dakotas. They were married in 1896, and in later years told interesting tales of their courtship experiences, wearing high rubber boots no matter how deep the snow or mud. C. B. Waldron became the escort and soon the husband of the president's secretary, Lois Hooper. Harry McArdle remained a bachelor until captured by one of his women students, Elita Olson. The *Moorhead Daily News*, December 12, 1893, describes a bobsled party held at H. F. Miller's farm northwest of Fargo, which lasted from six p.m. to four a.m. The guests were "the faculty of the North Dakota Agricultural College and their ladies." Another episode was the combination camping-exploring expedition to study the grasses and soils in western North Dakota. A picture taken at Dickinson in 1895 shows Shepperd, Bottenfield, Waldron and Ladd taking part in this expedition. The *Fargo Forum* of March 20, 1893, refers to them as "drugstore" cowboys and "tough looking hombres."

In general the period of the early nineties was a critical period for all the educational institutions. The year 1890, as well as the previous ones, was a drought year, and outside of the Red River Valley the crops were short. The State Legislature passed resolutions calling for Federal aid, and Representative Hansbrough sought unsuccessfully to secure a Federal appropriation to purchase seed wheat for farmers. During these years the Farmers Alliance increased its voting power and claimed to be the liberal wing of the Republican Party. By 1891 it became the chief nucleus of the People's Party, which stood for free silver, direct election of U. S. Senators, government ownership of railroads, telegraph and telephone. In 1892 North Dakota "went populist." Eli C. D. Shortridge was elected governor by a combination of Democrats and the Farmers Alliance.

Governor Shortridge, soon after assuming office, appointed two new members to the Agricultural College Board to take the places of H. R. Miller and J. B. Power on the grounds that they were guilty of misappropriation of funds. Also it appears that there was friction between the two trustees and Dr. Stockbridge, the president of the College. Miller and Power maintained that it was illegal and unconstitutional for the governor to remove them before the end of their appointed term, which would have ended in 1895. They were charged with using the College as a market for the products of their farms. Lyon was accused of using college money in his own private business. There was a long, drawn out attempt to investigate. The affair finally ended by a court decision that the originally appointed members were entitled to hold office until the end of their appointed term.

The whole investigation was carried on with much rancor on both sides. It did no good for the College. On the one hand it was a fight between the conservative element of the Republican Party, represented by the old board, and the more liberal element represented by the governor. It also claimed to be a contest between Fargo and Grand Forks, for Governor Shortridge was loyal to his home county of Grand Forks. The outcome was a victory for Fargo and at this time seemed contrary to the desires of the farmers whose interests the College was supposed to promote.

The victory of the Board in 1893 terminated the Stockbridge administration. Although serving slightly less than three years, Dr. Stockbridge left a lasting impression upon the College. He was probably more scholarly and better trained than most of those who later succeeded him in the presidency. "Upon leaving North Dakota he moved to Americus, Georgia, to give his personal attention to the old Sumter County plantation which he had purchased a few years earlier." In 1897 he became professor of agriculture at the Florida Agricultural College, serving until 1902. From 1906 to 1922 he was agricultural editor of the *Southern Ruralist,* published in Atlanta, Georgia. In 1922 he became editor of the *Southern Farm and Dairy,* a position which he held until his retirement because of failing health.[7]

J. B. Power, secretary of the Board, was appointed acting president of the College. Mr. Power was born in New York, educated in the common schools of Massachusetts, and later took up the study of civil engineering. He served as surveyor and civil engineer for several railroads, he was deputy state treasurer for Minnesota for four years and became chief clerk and later commissioner for the Northern Pacific Railway. In this capacity he was instrumental in interesting stockholders of the company in acquiring thousands of acres in the rich Red River Valley and as a result in promoting the big bonanza wheat farms. In 1886 he retired and settled on a farm in Richland County, where he developed purebred livestock. He was a member of the Board of Trustees and seemed to be a logical choice for interim presidency at the time of the removal of President Stockbridge.

President Power seems to have had harmonious relations with the staff. Professor Shepperd served as acting director of the Experiment Station. Professors Bolley, Ladd, Waldron and Keene headed their de-

◀ CHAPTER II ▶

Early Years, 1890-1895

THE first years of the Agricultural College, 1891–1895, were a period of real trial for the new institution. The College was under the leadership of a young administrator, Horace Edward Stockbridge, a native of New England, born on his father's farm at Hadley, Massachusetts. His father became the first professor of agriculture and later president of the Massachusetts Agricultural College at Amherst. Horace was graduated from that school in 1878 and then did graduate work in agricultural chemistry at Boston University. In 1881 he was appointed instructor in the Massachusetts Agricultural College. The next year he went to Germany to study at the University of Goettingen, from which he received the Ph.D. in 1884. In the spring of 1885 he was appointed professor of chemistry and geology at the Japanese Imperial College of Agriculture and Engineering, located at Sapporo, Japan, and also for two subsequent years he was Chief Chemist for the Japanese Government. In 1889 he was appointed director of the Indiana Agricultural Experiment Station at Purdue University, Lafayette, Indiana. Stockbridge was thirty-three years of age when he became the first president of North Dakota Agricultural College and director of the Experiment Station. Such a scholar and scientist must have been challenged by the possibilities of teaching and research in a frontier western environment.

President Stockbridge was assisted by a group of young, enthusiastic professors and investigators. Clare Bailey Waldron, twenty-four years old, was raised on a fruit farm in Michigan. He was graduated from the Michigan Agricultural College and taught botany and forestry there for the next two years. His field of teaching and research at the North Dakota Agricultural College was horticulture, forestry and landscaping.

Henry Luke Bolley, twenty-four, the youngest of twelve children, spent his early years in southwestern Indiana. He received his B.S. and M.S. degrees from Purdue University, where he served as instructor in biology and as botanist at the Indiana Experiment Station under Director Stockbridge. In 1923 he commented on his appointment as follows:

"I first learned of the North Dakota Agricultural College and Experiment Station through a short talk with Dr. Stockbridge, who said it was to be located at Fargo, a place, as he expressed it, 'the livest, biggest little city in the whole Northwest,' and he asked me to go along with him as botanist and zoologist of the College and botanist and plant pathologist of the Station."[1]

Bolley concentrated his research upon the diseases of crops, particularly of flax, cereals and potatoes, and upon standardization of pure seed supplies and weed control.

Edwin F. Ladd, thirty-one, spent his early years in Maine and was a graduate of its state college. He had served six years as chemist to the New York Agricultural Experiment Station. His field of teaching and research was chemistry, specializing in the chemistry of foods, paints, linseed oil, and cereal chemistry.

Theries D. Hinebauch, thirty, was graduated from Michigan Agricultural College with a B.S. and an M.S. He also had a V.S. degree from Toronto Veterinary College. He was professor of veterinary science at Purdue University and served as veterinarian at the Indiana Experiment Station. He made his first investigations of the ills of livestock after he came to the North Dakota Experiment Station.

Harry W. McArdle, twenty-four, assistant in horticulture and instructor in mathematics, was a graduate of Michigan Agricultural College and had taught in several Michigan towns before he was appointed instructor on April 15, 1891, at the North Dakota Agricultural College.

Michigan Agricultural College and Purdue University, therefore, contributed the most of the earliest faculty members. Waldron, Hinebauch and McArdle were college chums at Michigan State while Stockbridge, Bolley and Hinebauch were colleagues at Purdue.

In the *Prospectus* of the North Dakota Agricultural College, dated June, 1891, President Stockbridge discussed the function and purposes of the College as follows:

"The North Dakota Agricultural College is both a State and National institution. It was established by act of our first state legislature, approved March 9, 1890. It belongs, however, to the galaxy of so-called land-grant colleges of the country, owing their existence to the provisions of the act of Congress, approved July 2, 1862. . . .

"The field to be occupied by the institution has been fully, thoroughly and maturely canvassed. . . . The men upon whom the work devolves are imbued with the spirit in response to which this and the other agricultural colleges of America were created. Every member of the educational force of the institution received his own training in some one of these land-grant colleges.

"The North Dakota Agricultural College shall be . . . distinctly agricultural in character. But one course of instruction will be offered, and that will be positively agricultural. . . . There is today in the state of North Dakota no immediate demand for instruction in other professions not met by institutions already in existence. . . .

"The end and aim of the institution, however, is not restricted solely to the education of farmers. . . . The object of the institution is not first the making of *farmers*, but rather the making of *men*."

In the same *Prospectus,* President Stockbridge evaluated the resources of the Colleges as follows:

"The College is endowed by State and Nation with 130,000 acres of land located in North Dakota, none of which may, by legislative provision, be sold for less than $10 per acre, at which rate the minimum eventual endowment would be $1,500,000. (The income from this land was to be by legislative action and administered by a legislative committee.) The institution is further supplied by act of the last legislature with a section of 640 acres of land as a permanent site, on which buildings are now being erected and where the regular work of the institution has been laid out. By an act of Congress, approved August 30, 1890, this college receives an annual appropriation from the United States Treasury beginning with $15,000 for the fiscal year 1890, and increasing annually at the rate of $1,000 until an income from this course of $25,000 per annum is reached, at which point the appropriation permanently continues. The last Legislative Assembly of the State also appropriated $25,000 for building purposes, which fund is now being expended in the permanent buildings of the institution." [2]

The first home of the North Dakota Agricultural College, located in the basement and on the main floor of Fargo College, proved surprisingly satisfactory. The chemical and biological laboratories were in the basement. There was also a good recitation room and an office for the veterinarian. On the main floor were a small office for the president and two general recitation rooms. The northwest corner room of the building was used as a joint library for the two colleges.

President Stockbridge announced a special winter course in agricultural and related sciences for farmers in January, 1891. "These courses, though conducted on a scientific basis, will be made preeminently practical, the end constantly kept in view being to impart such beneficial practical information as will find constant application on the farm and enable its possessor to conduct his affairs more understandingly and successfully." [3]

There were offered and actually given 25 lectures by Dr. Stockbridge on the general principles of agriculture; 50 by Professor Ladd on the principles of chemistry, balanced rations, nutritive ratio, dairy products, etc; 50 by Professor Hinebauch on the diseases of horses, cattle and sheep and practical horseshoeing; 50 by Professor Waldron on forestry, fruits and landscape gardening; and 50 by Professor Bolley on plant and animal life, plant physiology and control of diseases of farm crops.[4] This course of studies was the first of the winter "short courses" and was sub-collegiate in subject matter.

Thirty students responded to this first call, coming from various parts of the State. Fargo furnished six, Abercrombie, two; Carrington, two; Hillsboro, two; Milnor, two; Amenia, Buffalo, Dickinson, Ellendale, Grand Forks, Grand Rapids, Hamilton, Hope, Horace, Jamestown, Mayville, Norman, Northwood, Portland, Valley City, and Villard, each one. The average age was 27. Two of them, Robert H. Bosard and Robert B. Reed, entered the regular college class in the fall.

Meanwhile W. M. Hays had been secured to supervise the work of the Station with the title of "Agriculturist." After two years he resigned to accept a similar position at the Minnesota Experiment Station. Later he went to Washington, D. C., as Assistant Secretary of Agriculture on appointment by President Cleveland. At the College he was succeeded in 1893 by his wife's brother, John H. Shepperd, a graduate of Iowa Agricultural College, who had done graduate work in dairying at the University of Wisconsin and who had also been assistant editor of the *Orange Judd Farmer*.

Mrs. Hays, who had a M. S. in domestic economy, offered a course in that subject in 1891, at the farm house at the corner of Tenth Ave. and Seventh St., which the College had rented and where she and her husband lived. Fifty-six women from the leading families of Fargo were enrolled in the course. Among the names were "Mesdames Amidon, Angell, Barnard, Blakemore, Chesley, Clapp, Foster, Francis, Hibbard, Hinebauch, Loomis, Luger, Lyon, Nichols, Nugent, Plumley, Porritt, Tyler and Wood." [5]

The first annual catalogue, dated May, 1892, outlined three courses of study, a winter course of three months each for two consecutive winters, giving instruction in domestic economy, agriculture, chemistry, veterinary science, horticulture, biology, mechanics, mathematics, English, geography and history, open to those over fifteen years of age without examination; a preparatory course of one year for young people whose school facilities at home would not enable them to do the regular work of the College; and a regular course of four academic years leading to a degree of bachelor of science.

Dean Waldron in 1924 wrote feelingly of the trials of the faculty during the initial years of the College:

as a market for the products of their farms. Lyon was accused of using college money in his own private business. There was a long, drawn out attempt to investigate. The affair finally ended by a court decision that the originally appointed members were entitled to hold office until the end of their appointed term.

The whole investigation was carried on with much rancor on both sides. It did no good for the College. On the one hand it was a fight between the conservative element of the Republican Party, represented by the old board, and the more liberal element represented by the governor. It also claimed to be a contest between Fargo and Grand Forks, for Governor Shortridge was loyal to his home county of Grand Forks. The outcome was a victory for Fargo and at this time seemed contrary to the desires of the farmers whose interests the College was supposed to promote.

The victory of the Board in 1893 terminated the Stockbridge administration. Although serving slightly less than three years, Dr. Stockbridge left a lasting impression upon the College. He was probably more scholarly and better trained than most of those who later succeeded him in the presidency. "Upon leaving North Dakota he moved to Americus, Georgia, to give his personal attention to the old Sumter County plantation which he had purchased a few years earlier." In 1897 he became professor of agriculture at the Florida Agricultural College, serving until 1902. From 1906 to 1922 he was agricultural editor of the *Southern Ruralist*, published in Atlanta, Georgia. In 1922 he became editor of the *Southern Farm and Dairy*, a position which he held until his retirement because of failing health.[7]

J. B. Power, secretary of the Board, was appointed acting president of the College. Mr. Power was born in New York, educated in the common schools of Massachusetts, and later took up the study of civil engineering. He served as surveyor and civil engineer for several railroads, he was deputy state treasurer for Minnesota for four years and became chief clerk and later commissioner for the Northern Pacific Railway. In this capacity he was instrumental in interesting stockholders of the company in acquiring thousands of acres in the rich Red River Valley and as a result in promoting the big bonanza wheat farms. In 1886 he retired and settled on a farm in Richland County, where he developed purebred livestock. He was a member of the Board of Trustees and seemed to be a logical choice for interim presidency at the time of the removal of President Stockbridge.

President Power seems to have had harmonious relations with the staff. Professor Shepperd served as acting director of the Experiment Station. Professors Bolley, Ladd, Waldron and Keene headed their de-ment. The first *Experiment Station Bulletin,* written by Bolley on the subject of potato scab, was published in December, 1891.

With all their varied duties of teaching and research the faculty found time to play. Professor Bolley was interested in developing athletics but also, while still at Fargo College, he found a kindred spirit in the Dean of Fargo College, Miss Frances Sheldon, who had come from Wisconsin to pioneer in the Dakotas. They were married in 1896, and in later years told interesting tales of their courtship experiences, wearing high rubber boots no matter how deep the snow or mud. C. B. Waldron became the escort and soon the husband of the president's secretary, Lois Hooper. Harry McArdle remained a bachelor until captured by one of his women students, Elita Olson. The *Moorhead Daily News,* December 12, 1893, describes a bobsled party held at H. F. Miller's farm northwest of Fargo, which lasted from six p.m. to four a.m. The guests were "the faculty of the North Dakota Agricultural College and their ladies." Another episode was the combination camping-exploring expedition to study the grasses and soils in western North Dakota. A picture taken at Dickinson in 1895 shows Shepperd, Bottenfield, Waldron and Ladd taking part in this expedition. The *Fargo Forum* of March 20, 1893, refers to them as "drugstore" cowboys and "tough looking hombres."

In general the period of the early nineties was a critical period for all the educational institutions. The year 1890, as well as the previous ones, was a drought year, and outside of the Red River Valley the crops were short. The State Legislature passed resolutions calling for Federal aid, and Representative Hansbrough sought unsuccessfully to secure a Federal appropriation to purchase seed wheat for farmers. During these years the Farmers Alliance increased its voting power and claimed to be the liberal wing of the Republican Party. By 1891 it became the chief nucleus of the People's Party, which stood for free silver, direct election of U. S. Senators, government ownership of railroads, telegraph and telephone. In 1892 North Dakota "went populist." Eli C. D. Shortridge was elected governor by a combination of Democrats and the Farmers Alliance.

Governor Shortridge, soon after assuming office, appointed two new members to the Agricultural College Board to take the places of H. R. Miller and J. B. Power on the grounds that they were guilty of misappropriation of funds. Also it appears that there was friction between the two trustees and Dr. Stockbridge, the president of the College. Miller and Power maintained that it was illegal and unconstitutional for the governor to remove them before the end of their appointed term, which would have ended in 1895. They were charged with using the College partments without interference. But hard times continued, for the State and for the College. In 1893, another year of drought, the Board of Trustees proposed to reduce salaries ten per cent. The faculty protested, although recognizing the right of the Board to make the reduction. They blamed mismanagement on the lack of Station and College organization to control the amount and character of work that was being done and on the lack of proper supervision in limiting expenses. They maintained that reduction of expenses in other services would be preferable to reduction of salaries. Out of this situation, the faculty adopted a report of a committee to improve public relations as follows: 1. That instead of newspaper advertising, more money be spent on Farmers' Institutes; 2. that a member of the faculty be appointed to furnish news items to the papers of the State; 3. that a representative of the College attend Teachers' Institutes; 4. that public lectures be given at the College; 5. that the president appoint some member of the faculty to contact and to correspond with prospective students; 6. that some members of the faculty be appointed to provide musical entertainment under the auspices of the Athenian Society; 7. that in the winter the faculty hold a reception at the College to which citizens of Fargo, members of the Legislature and other prominent persons of the State should be invited.[8] Quite a program of public relations!

As a result of these suggestions in the spring of 1895 President Power, Professor Ladd and Professor Shepperd reported to the faculty a schedule of definite salaries and proposed expenditures for the following departments: president's office, chemistry, veterinary, horticulture, botany, mechanics, domestic science, agriculture, English, mathematics, dairy, accounting, engineering, and chapel. Chapel met daily, and was addressed by the president or faculty members three times a week.

Acting President Power tendered his resignation in the earlier part of the year to take effect June 30, 1895, the end of the fiscal year. On June 12, at his last meeting with the faculty, he thanked them "for their uniform courtesy during his administration as president." John H. Worst, lieutenant governor of the state, was elected president of the College and director of the Experiment Station. On June 25, 1895, President Power presided at his last public function, the first Commencement of the College. The degree of bachelor of science was granted to Robert B. Reed, Merton Field, Charles M. Hall, John W. Hilborn and Ralph D. Ward, all of them representing the first class to be graduated from the Agricultural College. President Power's remarks were brief but friendly and inspiring. They closed with the following: "Your life is before you, it is for you to make it. Do not be content with simply living it for itself, make it a life that will make the world better because you live in it."

FOOTNOTES

[1] Henry L. Bolley, "Early Days at the A.C.," *College and State*, VII, No. 2 (Nov., 1923), 11.

[2] The North Dakota Agricultural College, Fargo, *Prospectus*, June, 1891 (Fargo, N. Dak.), 12–17.

[3] *N.D.A.C. Prospectus*, 20.

[4] *N.D.A.C. Prospectus*, 21–23.

[5] North Dakota Agricultural College, Fargo, *First Annual Catalog*, May, 1892, 49.

[6] *College and State*, VIII, No. 2 (Nov., 1934), 15–6.

[7] Harlow L. Walster in an address before the Quarter Century Club of N.D.A.C., May 13, 1957, quoting from the *Dictionary of National Biography*, XVIII, 37–38 (New York, 1936).

[8] Faculty Record, September 29, 1894, 145–6.

◄ CHAPTER III ►

Growth and Expansion, 1895-1916

THE early years of the history of the College were a period of drouth and business depression. This atmosphere of indecision was responsible for the failure of the Legislature to support the infant institution adequately. In addition, the political friction arising in the attempt of the Populists to gain control of the Republican Party hampered the growth of the College. Obviously politics was responsible for the dismissal of President Stockbridge and continued to affect the administration of Acting President Power.

With the appointment of John Henry Worst in 1895 as the new president of the College, a new era was inaugurated. The times gradually improved. The national excitement of the national election of 1896 was as much due to a rise in wages with the slogan, "a full dinner pail," as it was due to the increased strength of the Republican Party. The resulting rise in the standards of comfort and prosperity was reflected in an increasing interest in education. At the normal schools and at the university as well as at the Agricultural College, the student enrollment was increasing in such numbers that the facilities for instruction proved inadequate. And so, in the still more prosperous first decade of the 20th century, the people of the State insisted on larger appropriations.

During the hard years of previous decades the people of North Dakota had been content with an economic and social progress that provided the bare essentials. In the more prosperous decade that followed, the State was getting established on the basis of a "surplus economy." Although the governor found it necessary at times to exercise his veto in regard to educational policy, insofar as the Legislature represented the will and purpose of the people, it is evident that there was a popular demand for better and larger schools and for liberal proposals and expenditures for social welfare and education. Liberal provisions were made for additional buildings for the public institutions, and for extension of service.

Fortunately this era of greater prosperity and greater interest in social welfare and education was accompanied in the case of the Agricultural College by a new executive in the person of John Henry Worst, who had been defeated for reelection as lieutenant governor, so he was given the presidency of the Agricultural College instead. His appointment was political, but he was wise enough, as an administrator, to retain the group of able young men who had surrounded his predecessors at the College.

J. H. Worst was born in a log cabin on an Ohio farm, was educated in the common schools of his native state and attended Ashland College, which later granted him an honorary L. L. D. degree. While attending an academy he worked on a farm, and later he alternated college attendance with teaching in a district school. Thus he had gained the foundation of a practical agricultural education. In 1883 he homesteaded in Dakota Territory southeast of Bismarck in Emmons County. He served six years as county superintendent of schools until 1889, when he was elected state senator for two terms. In 1894 he was elected lieutenant governor, and presided over the senate for a session. During these years as a staunch Republican he took an active part in politics. He gave many campaign addresses and gained an enviable reputation as a political speaker. He also identified himself with different lodge organizations; he became a 33rd degree Mason and was a member of the Knights of Pythias and the Elks. These political, fraternal and educational qualifications among others made him an "acceptable" candidate for the presidency of the Agricultural College. He was perhaps selected for the job because the men who picked him wanted a man who was a practical farmer, as well as a professional educator.

Just as the College in those days was in its formative stage, so was the science of agriculture. The value and importance of agricultural research was not as widely accepted then as it is now, for one reason, because it had not proved itself in the eyes of the farmer. Those pioneer farmers had learned the hard way, and banked more on the experience of many generations of farming than on "book learning." They rather resented the idea of advice from professional sources.

President Worst was a patient, kindly man, who could feel and sympathize with this sentiment and he did much to smooth away the difficulty of getting the farm scientist accepted as an important, even as probably the most vital, factor in the building of a successful type of agriculture in this region. He was able to do this partly because he could

Growth and Expansion, 1895-1916

talk to farmer audiences and explain scientific developments in farming without talking down to his listeners.

President Worst became known as the "Father of the North Dakota Agricultural College." He remained president for twenty-one years. His account of the mission of the Agricultural College is found in the Commencement Program of 1911:

"The purpose for which the Agricultural College was established is clearly set forth in the Morrill Act of 1862 and Acts supplementary thereto, and in Section 1106 of the Political Code of North Dakota. No unbiased person need mistake the scope of educational work contemplated by these Acts nor the support that should be given by the state for this type of education. As agriculture and the mechanic arts embrace quite completely the productive interests of the State, logically the scope of educational work contemplated for the Agricultural College is co-extensive with these productive interests. Inasmuch as all professions and vocations depend almost exclusively upon agriculture, the mission of the Agricultural College can scarcely be overestimated.

"There are those who, taking advantage of the name "agricultural college," would limit its mission to teaching subjects relating exclusively to technical activities on the farm. The purpose of the land-grant institution is to afford a "liberal and practical education for the industrial classes in the several pursuits and professions of life." In conformity with law and the general welfare, the curricula of these colleges emphasize such sciences and culture subjects as seem necessary to place the productive man, be he farmer or engineer, on the same intellectual plane as the business or professional man.

"The Agricultural College offers such training to students as will enable them to teach or practice what they learn at school. The scope of educational training is as broad as the arts and their related sciences that have a bearing on agriculture and the mechanic arts, together with the supplementary subjects that naturally associate themselves with a college education. Moreover, the work and influence of the college belong as much to the industrialists of the State as to their children on the campus. College extension, therefore, should be promoted earnestly and systematically.

"Agriculture being the dominant industry of the state, the mission of the Agricultural College is no larger than this industry, together with the mechanic arts or engineering problems that naturally correlate with it.

"The home also is given intelligent consideration. The girls, the future homemakers, are educated with special reference to the duties and responsibilities of the wife and mother. Domestic science has even a larger place in education than many popular courses of study that relate almost exclusively to personal improvement. The home, being the "Heart of the Nation," should not be excluded from the curricula of higher institutions of learning. Here it is given actual emphasis.

"To develop the State's latent resources requires a knowledge of those natural laws which govern plant and animal life, and the ability to direct them for the attainment of desired ends. In such education, the sciences must, of course, occupy a place of preeminence. The study of Nature's laws and forces not only enables men more easily and bountifully to provide for themselves the necessities of life, but it also develops and broadens the mind and is as truly cultural as a study of the classics. Indeed, the trend of modern education is toward the practical and concrete instead of toward the theoretical and abstract.

"North Dakota is preeminently an agricultural state. The cultivation of grain and forage crops and the breeding and feeding of livestock will necessarily occupy the attention of the bulk of our population. From these sources must come practically all of our future wealth." [1]

These statements are quoted because President Worst was, as stated before, to a certain degree on the defensive in stressing the importance of the institution he was heading.

The new administration could start its work with the following completed and equipped buildings. College Hall, later known as "Old Main" and now called the Administration Building, contained the principal recitation rooms, laboratories, libraries and offices of the college and the experiment station. The mechanical laboratory contained the office and recitation room of the professor of mechanics, the tools, machinery and equipments of the mechanical department, and the armory and equipment of the military department. The dormitory, a large building capable of accommodating about fifty students with sleeping apartments, kitchen and dining rooms, arranged with special reference to the department of domestic economy, was heated by steam and lighted by electricity. The barn contained a large class room, well equipped for work in agriculture and veterinary, of sufficient size to house the livestock and feed used for farming and feeding experiments. The farmhouse offered private offices for the professor of agriculture and his assistant, farm foreman, farm hands and the dairy apparatus. Two smaller buildings were the machinery building for storing tools and implements used on the college farm, and the boiler house from which was furnished steam heat for College Hall and the greenhouse.

The Record, of May, 1895, published by Clement A. Lounsberry, has this laudatory comment about the plant of the College:

"The North Dakota Agricultural College is fully equipped for instruction in all lines in which the agricultural, industrial and professional classes can obtain a practical and liberal education, and the institution can place at the disposal of its students an education equal in all respects to that offered by the best educational institutions of the country in such departments of learning as experience has demonstrated are of the greatest practical value to their possessor. The instruction imparted is both theoretical and practical, including agriculture, domestic economy, practical mechanics and the natural sciences related to agriculture. Textbook instruction is supplemented by lectures and practical demonstration, while laboratory, field, shop and kitchen practice is utilized to the fullest possible extent, the theoretical instruction of the class room being given its actual application, the aim being in all departments to inculcate habits of individual thought and independent action."

By 1896 the popular "delusion that the Agricultural College was simply a school where methods of farming and tillage were taught was being dispelled."[2] It was being realized that the land-grant college was a school of liberal education where English, mathematics, military tactics, engineering and the chemical, biological and social sciences were taught as well as the application of science and the mechanic arts to practical agriculture. Four full four-year courses in agriculture, mechanics, science and literature, and domestic economy were now being offered, and in addition shorter preparatory courses were provided.

During the twenty years of President Worst's administration, legislative appropriations gradually provided for more new buildings. By 1897, $22,000 for buildings and maintenance provided for a chemistry building, which later became the old Music Hall. In 1899 a small addition was made to the Mechanic Arts Building. In 1901 the south wing of Science Hall, two new barns (a previous barn had burned down), and a sewer system were constructed. In 1903, $15,000 was appropriated for a new heating plant; in 1905, $50,000 for a new chemical laboratory,[3] and in 1907, $108,000 for an engineering building, a greenhouse, implement shed and the remodeling of the Administration Building and the Armory.

In 1909 money was appropriated for a women's building, a combined dormitory and domestic science laboratory, the results of a campaign of the women students which began in 1905. Francis Hall was overcrowded. Students in the department of domestic science had increased from five to 59. Teachers of domestic science were in demand in the State. Ceres Hall, as the new building was named, could house 125 women, provide a dining room for 200 and provide adequate quarters for a four year course in home economics.

In connection with the name of the women's building, Mrs. Jessamine S. Burgum wrote, on April 20, 1950, this amusing account:

"When the question came up to build Ceres Hall, it was suggested to name it after the first girl student, who had enrolled from Bismarck. It was agreed, and one trustee asked, 'What is her name?' 'Why, Jessie Slaughter, from Bismarck.' 'Oh, then the students will be calling it "the Slaughter house" instead of Slaughter Hall,' so they decided to call it Ceres Hall after the Goddess of Wheat, (instead of meat)."

In the same year, 1909, $30,000 was appropriated for a veterinary building, $12,000 for equipment of the engineering laboratory, $10,000 for an electric light plant and $3,000 for sidewalks. Two years later $65,000 was appropriated for a chemistry building,[3] $40,000 for completion of Ceres Hall, and "$15,000 for the purchase of a half section of land for the use of the government experiment station."[4] In 1913 and 1915, $22,000 for repairs and the relaying and extension of steam mains and

$50,000 for the dairy building and barn were appropriated. Each session of the Legislature provided additional buildings and equipment.

During the legislative session of 1901 a permanent provision was made for the support of higher education. It was realized that the advancement of the schools had been somewhat less in proportion to the increase in property valuation in the State. The Legislature, therefore, provided that a one-mill tax be collected to maintain the university and school of mines, the agricultural college and the normal schools. Of this amount one-fifth of a mill should go annually to the Agricultural College. In the fiscal year 1906–07 the income from this source was $33,849.33.

In 1905 in addition to buildings provided by legislative appropriation, the untiring efforts of President Worst were successful in securing from Andrew Carnegie funds for the construction of a library.[5] In 1897 the library consisted of 3,100 volumes and was housed in one room, which is now part of the college business office. The librarian was Mrs. Ethel McVeety, who was also the first stenographer for the Experiment Station. She continued to serve as head librarian until her retirement in 1944. In 1906 the Carnegie Library was dedicated and 8,000 volumes were transferred from the main building. In the fall of 1913 a new course for freshmen in library methods was introduced into the curriculum.

In 1897 an increase of enrollment made it necessary to convert the boys' dormitory, Francis Hall, into class rooms and laboratories to provide space for agriculture, horticulture, veterinary and household economics. A museum and lecture room were completed. A drill hall 40 by 96 feet, named the Armory, was also constructed at a cost of $1,500. The frame building was later enlarged, and used not only for military training but also for physical education, including basketball, and for convocations and dancing parties. Later, when a new physical education building was constructed, the armory was renamed Festival Hall and reserved for convocations, lyceum programs, and for other student and public gatherings.

President Worst began his administration in 1895 with twelve professors and eight assistants. Since most of the professors had been with the College for several years, the president had an experienced corps of workers to assist him in developing the institution. During his regime numerous changes in the staff occurred, but most of the "tried and true" members of the faculty remained to give the College stability and permanence.

In 1899 Gottfried Hult succeeded Mr. Bottenfield as professor of English. Of Swedish parentage, he had received his A.B. and A.M. degrees from the University of Minnesota, and had three years of graduate

Growth and Expansion, 1895–1916

work at the University of Leipzig and another year at the University of Chicago. He left N.D.A.C. in 1907 to become head of the department of classical languages at the University of North Dakota, where he remained until his retirement in 1946.

In April, 1899, Lawrence R. Waldron, brother of C. B. Waldron, a graduate of the Class of 1899, was appointed assistant in botany. He later took advanced work at the University of Michigan and at Cornell University, where he received his doctor's degree.

In the fall of 1901 Mr. P. S. Rose, a graduate of Michigan State College, was made assistant professor in the department of engineering to take charge of the work in steam and gas engineering — the first time such work had been offered in North Dakota. This service attracted a large number of farm boys. In those early days from 1900 to 1918, steam engines were very common and necessary to power the threshing machines in North Dakota. Mr. Rose said he came to the College "to teach young Dakotans to run steam engines without blowing them up." The seven months he expected to stay at N.D.A.C. stretched out to ten years. In 1907 Mr. Rose met with a little group of men at Madison, Wisconsin, to found the American Society of Agricultural Engineers. Later, as editor of *The Country Gentleman*, Mr. Rose was awarded a medal for distinguished service to agriculture, and in 1940 he received the honorary degree of doctor of agriculture from the North Dakota Agricultural College.

Also in 1901 Max Batt, Ph. D. from the University of Chicago, was appointed assistant professor of modern languages and remained with the department for sixteen years. In the same year J. G. Halland, a graduate of Luther College, Iowa, who had been state superintendent of public instruction from 1896 to 1900, was appointed professor of history and civil government.

In the year 1902 several other changes in the staff occurred. Miss Louise Gastman succeeded Miss Marie B. Senn as professor of domestic science. Miss Senn married Thomas Heath, a graduate of the College.[6] The work in manual arts was started with the appointment of George Tibert as instructor in woodwork and Haile Chisholm as instructor in blacksmithing. Practically all of the decorative iron work found in Fargo homes is of Mr. Chisholm's creation and will long endure as examples of his handicraft. He was given a unique honorary degree, Master of Artisans, by President Shepperd of the Agricultural College, in 1931. Mr. Tibert later became superintendent of buildings and grounds.

Another appointment of 1902 was that of Dr. L. Van Es to the chair of veterinary science. He continued in that position for 18 years, during which time he did a great amount of basic work on the different diseases of livestock, the economic value of which was acknowledged by livestock interests everywhere. Dr. Van Es, born in Holland, received a degree in veterinary surgery from Toronto University, a master's degree from the University of Alabama, and his M.D. from the University of Alabama. After resigning from N.D.A.C. he went to the University of Nebraska as head of the department of pathology and hygiene. He received an honorary degree of doctor of agriculture from N.D.A.C. on July 18, 1946. Professor O. A. Stevens said the following about him: "Dr. Van Es was not only one of the most capable of scientific workers but also a well educated man and pleasing conversationalist. My wife was always amused at how he could use a few 'cuss words' without swearing. Once a group of us were discussing the loco disease and he remarked that a band of locoed sheep was the funniest. Some one asked if they behaved differently from other animals. He said, 'No, I don't know that they act differently, but there are so dom many of them.'" [7]

Charles Monroe Hall, one of the graduates of N.D.A.C.'s first class in 1895, had gone on to graduate work at Johns Hopkins University. In 1902 he returned to become professor of geology and to direct the work of the North Dakota Soil Survey.

In the spring of 1903 there came to the College one of its most colorful figures, C. S. "Doc" Putnam. Earlier he had entered a Philadelphia medical school in 1880, playing in orchestras and singing in choirs in his spare time. He was graduated from Hahnemann Medical College in Chicago in 1883. He came to Minnesota, practiced in Moorhead a year and in Ada eight years. The next five years he spent in Superior, Wisconsin, and in Duluth, where he taught music and directed bands and choirs. In 1895 he resumed the practice of medicine in Casselton, where he directed the town band. In 1901 he established a practice in Fargo. Fire halted his career as a practicing physician in Fargo in 1903, for flames swept through the Edwards building, in which he maintained his offices, destroying an extensive medical library and equipment. His fire insurance policy had lapsed five days before the fire.

A few days later he began teaching arithmetic at the Agricultural College. For five years he taught hygiene, sanitary science, materia medica, therapeutics and other classes when no other instructor was available. Soon he was also assisting with music instruction and directing the college band. "The outstanding activity of the department of music during the thirty-seven years under the same director was the development and maintenance of the college band, which had enjoyed high ranking through the years and has added life and color to all college functions." [8]

In 1904 four other staff members who have given the major parts of

Growth and Expansion, 1895-1916

their lives to the College came to the institution. Alfred H. Parrott, a graduate of the University of Kansas who had taught three years at Michigan State College, was employed to teach mathematics. From 1906 until 1952, with brief exceptions, he served as the efficient registrar of the College. He married one of his students, Pearl Canniff, in 1908. Archibald E. Minard came in 1904 as instructor in English and philosophy. He had received bachelor's and master's degrees from Harvard University, and later studied at the University of Chicago, Wisconsin and Oxford. In 1904 as instructor he taught freshman English and had a total of 25 students. In 1907 he became head of the department and in 1919 dean of the newly organized School of Science and Literature. Irvin W. Smith, a graduate of the University of Illinois, was another addition to the staff. He became head of the department of mathematics and later dean of men. Professor W. B. Bell, Ph. D. from the University of Iowa, served in the department of biology from 1905 to 1916. He supervised the work in the State connected with the extermination of undesirable rodents. He resigned in 1916 to go to Washington with the U.S. Biological Survey.

In 1906 a reorganization of the Division of Agriculture was made by President Worst. Professor Shepperd was appointed Dean and headed three departments: applied agriculture with himself as head, agronomy with J. C. McDowell of the University of Wisconsin at the head, and animal husbandry with W. B. Richards, also of the University of Wisconsin, as instructor. In 1908 Professor R. C. Doneghue, with a masters degree from the University of Missouri, was appointed head of the department of agronomy; both Richards and Doneghue remained with the institution for a decade.

The year 1907 brought two other men to the College who were to make their impression on the lives of its students. A. D. Weeks, who had been professor of English at Valley City for five years, was appointed associate professor of English and in 1917 was made dean of the newly created school of education. A. G. Arvold, at first an instructor in English and speech, later became head of the department of public speaking. He originated and developed the Little Country Theater, which became prominent in the social, recreational and educational activities of the institution. Its influence was not limited to the College campus alone, but through its graduates, its public programs of all kinds became a prominent factor in the social life of the State. In 1907 R. H. Slocum, B.S., University of Illinois, became professor of civil engineering and remained with the College until he retired in 1952.

A year later, 1908, Robert Martinus Dolve, a graduate of N.D.A.C., was appointed assistant in agricultural engineering. He continued with the College, later serving as dean of the School of Engineering from 1928 to 1954. In 1909 Orin A. Stevens, a graduate of Kansas State, was appointed assistant professor of botany in the division of seed analysis. He also showed a great interest in the study of birds, flowers, insects and weeds, which led to many publications.

William F. Sudro, B.S. from the University of Michigan, came to the College as an instructor in pharmacy in 1908. As early as 1886 the North Dakota Pharmaceutical Association had been organized by the druggists of the Territory. In 1899 Professor Ladd was invited to address the association in regard to establishing a pharmaceutical school at the Agricultural College. In 1901 President Worst and Professor Ladd were authorized to give courses in all branches of pharmacy, and complete four year and two year courses for pharmacy students were outlined in the department of chemistry and pharmacy. As a result of increased attendance, in 1908 pharmacy was made a division of the department. In 1919 a separate school of pharmacy was authorized. Professor Sudro became its head and a few years later was named dean of the School of Pharmacy. The school was advantageously located at the Agricultural College, as the food and drug laboratories were also established there. It was soon recognized as one of the best schools of its type in the country.

Other faculty appointments during the regime of President Worst include that of Miss Abbie L. Simmons, assistant professor of English in 1909; of Casper I. Nelson, assistant professor of bacteriology in the department of biology in 1914; of Omar O. Churchill, appointed professor of agronomy in 1904; of A. Pearl Dinan, at first instructor in English in 1911, later assistant and associate professor and dean of women in 1930.

In connection with additions to the staff came expansion of instruction. At a meeting on February 19, 1896, a resolution of the faculty recommending the organization of a summer school was adopted by the Board; 42 students were in attendance the first year. For many years the summer school was an important feature of the College, the student body being made up largely of teachers from the surrounding territory. In the spring of 1897 a summer school was organized to operate in conjunction with the department of education of Cass County, and later included Griggs and Ransom Counties. This was discontinued in 1917 but in 1920 the summer school was reorganized on the same basis as the other college terms and continued until 1930. In 1948 the summer session was resumed, and continues to operate up to date.

Upon the recommendations of the faculty, the Board of Directors in 1911 authorized the establishment of a high school. This took the place

Growth and Expansion, 1895–1916   41

of the preparatory courses that had been given since the College was started. The high school was later given the name of practice school in the department of education. With the greater development of high schools through the state, the need for a high school became less, and it was discontinued in 1937, but at one time, with an enrollment of about 250, it was an important educational feature of the institution.

In 1897 the faculty decided to change the old winter short course in agriculture to suit in a better way the needs of the class of students who would take that work. This course was designed especially for the benefit of active farmers regardless of age, for farmers' sons and for young men intending to farm for a livelihood, who could spare only the winter months for some study. In many respects it resembled a continuous Farmers' Institute, where agriculture, veterinary science, horticulture, engineering, dairying and other subjects were illustrated at length and made thoroughly practical.

A three year course of six months each year in agriculture was outlined in the catalog for 1903–04. This course was offered to young men who were not prepared for the regular course, yet desired technical training and practical knowledge in agriculture and kindred subjects, together with grammar, arithmetic, government and history. This course known as farm husbandry attracted a large number of farm boys between 1904 and 1918, most of whom returned to the farm. Some of them became interested in securing a college degree, but all of them were an important part of the institution's training program during those years. Another of the six months' courses which attracted farm boys was the course listed as power machinery (rural engineering). It was listed under the division of agriculture and taught by various instructors.

The administration of many college matters was in the hands of the faculty. Every year numerous faculty committees were announced; dormitory, discipline, publications, museum, gymnasium, military, library committees already existed in 1895. Later there appeared committees on standing, literary societies, student organizations, public programs, etc. All the members of the faculty, including assistants, were entitled and expected to attend the regular monthly and special faculty meetings.

In 1897 a resolution was adopted, that meetings of the faculty should be governed by the following rules:

All matters of importance for consideration of the faculty shall be submitted in writing.

That no one shall speak on a subject or resolution until it has been moved, seconded, and stated by the presiding officer.

That no person may speak more than twice on the same subject until all have spoken who desire to do so, or until permission is obtained from the faculty.[9]

Another important action was taken by the faculty in 1897, in view of the reported reduction to be made in salaries. Resolutions were formulated by a committee appointed by the president consisting of McArdle, Bolley, Ladd, Keene and Bottenfield "in order that the Board of Trustees may gain a full knowledge of the sentiments of the Faculty." These resolutions included a provision that the work of the Experiment Station might require from one-third to two-thirds of the time of the members of the Station and that their pay would be on that basis. Another provision stated that the teaching staff should consist of professors, assistant professors and instructors, that the maximum salary for a full professorship and head of a department in the Experiment Station should be $2,000 per annum, that the maximum salary for an assistant professor should be $1,000 per annum, and that the maximum salary for an instructorship should not exceed $600 per annum, and that these salaries should be "construed as a temporary arrangement necessitated by the present financial condition of the institution."[10] This action is an illustration both of the low salaries of that period as well as of the influence the faculty had in regard to its status.

At the opening of the college year, 1905–06, there were thirty-four members of the faculty besides the president. In the fall of 1900 requirements for the master's degree were laid down by the governing board of the faculty. A system of faculty advisers was established in 1908 by the governing board, by which professors were to become acquainted with the students in their departments, approve their registration each term and supervise the quality of the work done.

As a means of reducing costs of living for several years (about 1908–11) a group of faculty members organized an informal cooperative by which they purchased staple groceries and canned goods from a wholesale dealer at a much lower price than they would have had to pay at the local retailers. The goods were all sent to one address and kept in the basement of one of the members for distribution.

As an illustration of the kindness and cordiality existing between President Worst and the faculty, an incident might be cited told by Mrs. Bell, widow of the assistant professor of biology. Dr. Worst felt that an instructor should receive a bonus of $200 from the Board whenever a new baby arrived in the family. It was the custom, on a nice spring day, for the mothers to parade the new babies in their perambulators to the main building and to receive the rewards.

Some of the faculty members joined Fargo community clubs, such as the Fine Arts Club and various literary groups composed of both town and college members. In 1910 a few aided in organizing the Commons Club, which included members from town and from the College staff. There was a fortnightly Polytechnic Society organized in 1907 which met on the campus to hear papers or addresses by local speakers, most of them members of the faculty.[11] It remained active until 1925.

In the latter part of the administration of President Worst there developed some friction between the older members of the faculty and the newer and younger members. Throughout his administration the entire staff met regularly for discussion of College affairs. It was a rule that assistant professors could vote after two years of service. Consequently the younger men in time outnumbered those who had been with the institution from its earlier days. As a result, it came to be a practice for some of the older members of the staff, sometimes referred to on campus as the "Masonic group," to meet weekly in the basement of Old Main, in order to discuss college problems. A movement to codify the previously established rules pertaining to faculty participation in college matters culminated in the printing of the *"Blue Book"* in 1915.[12] The expense for the printing came from contributions of various members of the faculty, and this *"Blue Book"* came to be regarded as a kind of constitution for the College.

An explanation of the dismissal of President Worst in 1916 will be given in the next chapter, when the work of the Experiment Station will be discussed. His administration of the College may be summarized by the words of a resolution adopted by the Alumni Association, on June 13, 1916

"Because of his diligence, his patriotic solicitude for the welfare of the youth of our State, his wisdom as a leader in education for agriculture and his generous service for the betterment of social life

JOHN HENRY WORST

merits and receives the enduring gratitude of this Association."

After President Worst left the Agricultural College he served as editor of the *New Rockford State Center* for a year, and from 1919 to 1923 he was state commissioner of immigration. The Sixteenth Legislature of North Dakota, in 1922, passed the following resolution in regard to his achievements:

"Whereas, Dr. John H. Worst performed with honor and fidelity the duty of President of the State Agricultural College of the State of North Dakota, for more than twenty years, and

Whereas, he at all times served the interests of the common men and women of this State and worked for the promotion of their happiness and prosperity, and opposed the speculative interests that prey upon the needs of our people, and

Whereas, he refused to interfere or deny the right of academic freedom of thought or speech, and

Whereas, as a teacher he taught truth without fear or favor, and as President of the Agricultural College administered his office with firm and impartial justice, and

Whereas, his services of this State as President of the Agricultural College, teacher in our schools, and citizen, are worthy of the highest commendation and honor, now therefore

Be it Resolved, by the Senate and House of Representatives concurring, that we petition, recommend and earnestly request the State Board of Regents to create the office of President Emeritus of the State Agricultural College, and to appoint Dr. John H. Worst, President Emeritus thereof, and that a copy of this resolution be forwarded to the members of the Board of Regents, and to Dr. John H. Worst." [13]

In accordance with this resolution the Board of Regents on April 5, 1919, named John H. Worst president emeritus and granted him the position of student counselor and lecturer at a salary of $1,800 a year. However, he did not accept this position. For five years he lived with his son, Clayton, at Dore, N. Dak., after which he retired to live with his daughter in California, where he died at the age of 94.

After President Worst's death in 1945, Professor Arvold paid a tribute to him, of which the following quotation is a part:

"His life of nearly ninety-five years has come to an end. This man certainly had a colorful career — country school master, sheep rancher, legislator, lieutenant governor, college president, editor, effective speaker, and, greater than all these, a friend of man, a public benefactor, a man who saw in the holy earth something sacred and divine. That was John Worst. On these grounds, the library, the engineering, the chemical, the veterinary, the dairy, the science laboratories, Ceres Hall, Festival Hall, Music Hall, the mill, the gardens, the trees, are all monuments to his foresight, his energy, and his power to accomplish what he set out to do. He was more than a builder with stone and brick and mortar. He was a leader who inspired the young and those who associated with him to do bigger and finer things for humanity and the State in which they lived. Unselfish in his ideals, he always associated nature with human nature. He was affable, he was kind, he was big hearted. He loved country people. Like Will Rogers, he never saw a man he didn't like. . . . He left with this institution a vision — a vision of interpreting the life of the people in a great state." [14]

FOOTNOTES

[1] North Dakota Agricultural College, *Seventeenth Annual Commencement*, 1911, 32–38.

[2] North Dakota Agricultural College, *Third Biennial Report of the Board of Trustees*, 1895–6, (President Worst).

[3] Fire destroyed the old chemistry building in 1907 and also the greenhouse and power plant; this explains the vacant area between Old Main and the South Engineering Building.

[4] *Laws of North Dakota*, 1911, Ch. 33, 37.

Growth and Expansion, 1895–1916

[5] President Worst carried on an extensive correspondence with Mr. Carnegie's private secretary from 1902 to 1905. Finally Mr. Carnegie gave $15,000 for a building and later added $3,400 to complete the building. The correspondence is in the N.D.A.C. library.

[6] Leita Davy, "40 Years of Home Economics at NDAC," *NDAC Alumni Review*, XII, 1 (Oct., 1950), 2.

[7] O. A. Stevens, personal interview.

[8] Clare B. Waldron, *History of NDAC*, 15.

[9] North Dakota Agricultural College, Faculty Record, June 19, 1897, 199.

[10] N.D.A.C., Faculty Record, 1897, 200.

[11] At one meeting of the Polytechnic Society the professor of history gave a discussion on economic conditions following the Civil War. After a few remarks by other members the chairman asked Dr. Van Es if he had anything to add. He rose with characteristic deliberation and said, "No, I don't know if I have much to say," going on for 20 or 30 minutes with most interesting remarks on what he had seen in Holland when he was young. He recalled his uncle's cussing the Yankee ships in the harbor which were cutting into home trade.

[12] N.D.A.C., Faculty Record, Oct. 1, 1914, Jan. 15, 1918.

[13] North Dakota Agricultural College Board of Regents, Minutes, Apr. 1, 1919.

[14] A. G. Arvold, "Tribute to a Certain Men," Oct. 30, 1945, Library, N.D.A.C. (John H. Worst papers).

◄ CHAPTER IV ►

Research and Extension, 1895-1916

THE progress made by the Experiment Station during the presidency of J. H. Worst can be best indicated by the research programs and accomplishments of several members of the staff, encouraged by Worst as director of the Station from 1895 to 1913. These first staff members were primarily scientists without the intensive training of some of their successors.

The story of one of these staff members, Henry L. Bolley, is eloquently told by Dr. H. L. Walster in a later appraisal of his colleague: "Henry Luke Bolley . . . in his long years of service to the state of North Dakota as botanist, plant pathologist, and state seed commissioner, was a fearless trail blazer who cut deep and lasting 'blazes' in the forest of ignorance about plant diseases. He waged a constant battle for crop improvement. . . . He is best known as 'the Conqueror of Flax Wilt.'"[1]

At the same occasion Dr. Walster quotes A. C. Dillman, an associate agronomist of the U.S.D.A., in regard to Bolley as follows: "Bolley's work is classical. He was probably the first man in the history of agriculture to submit plants to an epidemic of disease in order to obtain selections resistant to disease. This method made deliberate use of the principle of the survival of the fittest. Today it is basic in all crop improvement. . . . Bolley's work completely altered the outlook for flax production in this country."

"Plot 30 at the North Dakota Agricultural Experiment Station, where Bolley and his associates did their work in disease resistance, is perhaps as important in human affairs as any historic battlefield. Its function, however, has been the saving, not the destruction, of man's resources."[2]

Wilt-resistant flax, however, was but one of the scientific contributions of Professor Bolley. He was interested also in problems affecting the potato crop. Scab was prevalent wherever the potato was grown. In earlier times, scientists attributed scab to some soil condition, rubbish or insects. As a student at Purdue University in 1889, Bolley conceived the idea that scab was caused by a parasite and his work at the North Dakota Agricultural Experiment Station proved this theory. He discovered and demonstrated the use of corrosive sublimate as a treatment and reported about it in *Bulletin No. 4*, issued by the Station in 1893.

Another disease problem tackled by Bolley was wheat smuts, about which he wrote in the first official publication of the North Dakota Agricultural Experiment Station, *Bulletin No. 1*, published in 1891. In this contribution he distinguished two kinds, loose or black smut of wheat, oats and barley, and stinking smut of wheat. He recommended two methods of treatment, the old copper sulphate or bluestone, suggested by a European scientist, which was "liable to retard considerably the germination of the seed," and the recently devised treatment of immersing the seed in hot water for fifteen minutes. In a later *Bulletin* in 1897 he recommended four different methods of treating wheat for the control of stinking smut: corrosive sublimate, hot water, copper sulphate, formalin or formaldehyde.

In 1909 Professor Bolley was appointed State Seed Commissioner. As commissioner he formulated North Dakota's first pure seed law and was responsible for its enforcement for the next twenty years. In connection with his study of plant diseases he spent six months in Europe in 1902 studying the subject of flax production. In 1930-31 he went to South America and brought back 409 samples of Argentine flax. He was one of the original and aggressive advocates of barberry eradication as a means of controlling, if not eradicating, stem rust. And he had a large part in getting a State law, and also a Federal law, requiring the removal of the common barberry. Professor Bolley was an aggressive advocate of his ideas and was successful in promoting his recommendations among the farmers of the State.

Once, when Professor Bolley was introduced at a dinner in his honor, the following story was told of a conversation with a farmer. "Could any man be worth a hundred thousand dollars? Yes, said the farmer, it was possible that a man might be worth that much. Could a man be worth five hundred thousand dollars? The farmer was not sure, but conceded that there might be a few such men. Could a man be valued at a million dollars? Well, replied the farmer, he knew of only one man who could possibly be worth a million dollars — and that was that Professor Bolley down at the Agricultural College — he was easily worth a million dollars to North Dakota alone!" [3]

Another of these early day professors who contributed a life's work to the State was C. B. Waldron. He became "North Dakota's first professor of agriculture, of horticulture and landscape gardening, the State's 'apostle of outdoor beauty.' " [4]

The first activity of the Agricultural College and Experiment Station directly related to the welfare of the citizens of the State began in 1892, when Dr. Stockbridge appointed Clare Bailey Waldron to outline a campaign to control a pest of grasshoppers. With the assistance of the Great Northern and Northern Pacific Railways, a program was put in operation that was credited with checking the menace at that time. In addition to Waldron's work in horticulture, he served as staff entomologist until 1921. It is interesting to note that he brought with him from Michigan more than twenty-four hundred insect specimens, which formed the nucleus of the present College collection. Shortly after his first arrival, as botanist, he started a collection of North Dakota grasses. "C.B.," as he was commonly known, also drew plans for the college grounds, and, with the help of H. W. McArdle, planted the trees which now shade the driveways and walks of the Campus. In 1910 he helped to organize the Fargo Park Board and served as a member of it for thirty-five years. Most of the park area owned by Fargo was largely planned by Waldron.

In other parts of the State he landscaped the campus of the State Teachers College at Minot and the grounds of the School for the Deaf at Devils Lake, the School for the Blind at Bathgate, the State School at Grafton, the Normal and Industrial School at Ellendale. The parks at Wahpeton, Williston, Mandan, Park River and Lisbon also were the result of his suggestions and planning. A number of courthouse grounds in the State indeed are memorials to his talent and interest. In 1905 he prepared a plan for "parking" on the campus of the University of North Dakota.[5]

Lawrence Root Waldron, younger brother of "C.B.," was graduated from the North Dakota Agricultural College in 1899. The next year he and Professor Bolley compiled the first published list of North Dakota plants.[6] After securing his M.A. degree in biology at the University of Michigan, he taught at N.D.A.C. until 1905, when he became superintendent of the Dickinson Branch Station, which was established that year. There he collaborated with Charles J. Brand of the U.S. Department of Agriculture in establishing the hardiness of Grimm alfalfa over twenty-one other strains. He came back to Fargo in 1916 to become the first plant breeder at the North Dakota Agricultural Experiment Station, where he developed high quality varieties of wheat resistant to rust.

Among the founders of the North Dakota Agricultural College and the Experiment Station, Edwin F. Ladd deserves an honored place. Erling Rolfsrud in his *Lanterns Over the Prairies* calls him the "Pure

Foods Crusader."[7] Professor Ladd is perhaps best known for his successful efforts to secure and to enforce legislation to prevent the adulteration of food and drugs. He was designated food commissioner in 1905; he urged law enforcement in regard to the illegal use of chemical preservatives, the illegal use of coal tar products, and the illegal use of labels. As chemist of the Station he early collaborated with Bolley and Shepperd in wheat experiments. In 1907 he was responsible for installing an experimental flour mill, and in starting a thorough investigation of the milling and baking qualities of durum wheat. He was able to show that there was no basis for the prevalent discrimination against durum and that for the production of macaroni, spaghetti and noodles it was the best type of wheat.

Next, he showed that the discrimination at the elevators against velvet chaff wheat was unwarranted. Finally, in 1914 he undertook the most important experiments in testing the so-called low grades of wheat by milling and baking. As a result, he issued the Station's famous *Special Bulletin No. 14*, entitled: "Is the Present System of Grading Wheat Equitable?"[8] His answer was "NO." In spite of this, the U.S. Chamber of Commerce continued the practice of classifying North Dakota wheat damaged from rust as "feed" wheat. In these experiments Ladd had the assistance of Thomas Sanderson, pioneer N.D.A.C. miller, who joined the staff in 1907. Ladd, with his chemical knowledge and flair for getting public attention, to prove his point, had Sanderson mill and bake sample loaves from wheats which millers claimed were inferior for bread making. These loaves eventually appeared as exhibits in court and congressional hearings.

In 1905, after the North Dakota Legislature had passed the paint inspection law, an act to "Prevent the Adulteration of and the Deception in the Sale of White Lead and Mixed Paints," the paint trust went before the Federal courts and asked an injunction to prevent its enforcement. Ladd started the most thorough investigation of paints that had ever been made up to that time. He found paint that was twenty-two percent water, paint containing fish oil, petroleum oil or soya bean oil in place of linseed oil, paint containing clay instead of white lead, paint that resembled real paint only in being colored, and in some cases paint of no lasting quality. Ladd used open air experiments with painted boards to prove his point.

The fight over the paint law was carried through the Supreme Court of the United States. The State won, and the paint users of North Dakota and elsewhere obtained better paint than they ever had before. Also, Ladd's investigations disclosed many things of value to all users of paints. The *Bulletin* issued by the College on this subject was one of the most popular ever published.[9]

Dr. Ladd also acted as a policeman, administering state legislation. Whenever a new law was passed requiring inspection work, the Legislature put the enforcement of the law on his shoulders. For this purpose he had a force of inspectors enforcing the measures, most of which were of direct benefit to the farmer. The fertilizer law, the mixed feed stuffs law, the cold storage law, the sanitary inspection law, and the paint law, all came under his enforcement. He was, all in one, State pure foods administrator, State oil inspector, State hotel inspector, State grain inspector. During World War I, he also served as Federal Food Administrator. In the State, the regulatory department, otherwise known as the State Food Drugs Department, was started by Professor Ladd, who at that time was head of the department of chemistry at the College.

In 1913, about a dozen years after he began waging his campaign for pure food and other pure products, Ladd published an appraisal of what the department of chemistry had done for North Dakota. "In less than three months after I began my work, I drew a libel suit for $100,000, backed by 22 firms, big interests including members who have since sat in the President's cabinet, vice presidents of the United States, U. S. Senators, etc. Then, the whiskey ring took a turn and secured a temporary injunction to make us continue the use of their dope which contained no whiskey. Then the paint men took a hand and fought their case to the U. S. Court with defeat at every turn. Then the meat packers took a hand with an injunction, followed likewise by an injunction from the big milling interests, who would have us eat their bleached flour, made, at times, from damaged wheat, but withal, fate seemed against them. It took work, however, to win, and do you know that for more than two years I did not go to bed a single night without a libel suit or an injunction, or both, hanging over my head, and knowing that on the morrow I must be preparing for my defense? . . ."

"But why dwell on this, for today foods are pure, honestly labeled when purchased from dealers in the state; beverages are what they purport to be, and patent medicines are fast finding their place, although many thousands of dollars have been spent by fake patent medicine venders and are still being spent to have their wicked practices and enable them to continue to drug the American people."[10]

Dr. Walster in an unpublished article makes this characteristic personal observation regarding Professor Ladd: "Edwin F. Ladd was a good trencherman, a lover of good food, but one who insisted on pure food. I can see him now, in my mind's eye, standing at the head of the table, for he was a short man, carving a holiday roast for his family and several fortunate holiday guests. The well filled plate passed to you had been skillfully prepared by his good wife, and you sat up to that table with the assurance that everything that went into the preparation of that food had passed the inspection of a highly competent food chemist." [11]

The work of other early staff members of the Agricultural College was perhaps not so dramatic as that mentioned before, but nevertheless was very important. When Professor John Henry Shepperd came to the College in 1893, grain raising was the industry on the cultivated lands of eastern and central North Dakota, and ranching was common on the western prairies. His investigations of roots of plants made valuable contributions to the methods of the culture of crops. His efforts in crop improvement gave the State many superior varieties of wheat, oats, barley and rye, some of which remained standard for many years, as Dakold (ND 959) rye, for example. He was awarded a gold medal for his plant breeding work at the Paris World Exposition in 1900.

However, livestock was Dr. Shepperd's main interest. His many investigations in the value of North Dakota feeds for livestock are a valuable contribution to the feeding of stock in the State. The character of livestock that he developed and the work which he directed is well illustrated by the fact that it won the grand championship at the International Livestock Exposition in Chicago in 1927. The five steers that won the grand championship at the International Livestock Exposition in 1929 give another evidence of his ability to breed and show livestock. The steers as well as their dams for three generations were bred on the farm at the College. In the same year the College was also awarded the reserve championship on a carload of lambs.

Professor Shepperd's interest in livestock led to his long participation in livestock judging at the International. He served most efficiently as superintendent of the Collegiate Livestock Judging Contest for twenty-seven years (1906–38). In recognition of this, his portrait was hung in the Chicago Saddle and Sirloin Club in 1921.

In 1910 Professor Shepperd was instrumental in organizing and fostering the New Salem Breeding Circuit, which became one of the leading Holstein centers in the United States. The section around New Salem, which had failed in wheat growing before 1910, became one of the most prosperous and well known communities in the development of dairy cattle in the nation through cooperation and wise guidance on his part. He was also associated with the founding and growth of the North Dakota Grimm Alfalfa Association, a cooperative organization which for many years supplied the demand for pure Grimm alfalfa seed.

In order to popularize his scientific writings, a new form of bulletin

writing was developed by Dr. Shepperd, in which the writer made use of the language and practical skills of the herdsman. "Daddy" Geiken, College herdsman for over twenty years, frequently figured in these stories. In an article Dr. Shepperd gave this tribute to his "old friend and co-worker":

"In the language of Will Carleton, Daddy 'never swallowed a grammar nor et an 'rithmatic' and he grew to manhood speaking another tongue than ours. Despite these facts and his frequent statement, 'I am so ignorant,' I will take issue with any man who says that Daddy Geiken is not educated."

"The college has three workers, all in the afternoon of life, who have been educated in the school which Abraham Lincoln attended, the institution which is sometimes called the University of Hard Knocks. I refer to Haile Chisholm and Thomas Sanderson as the two classmates who, with Daddy Geiken, have been schooled in the World's University. Daddy Geiken chose to be a stockman and has never missed an opportunity to gather information which will add to the fund of knowledge of an already clever stockman. He has frequently said to me: 'Mr. Shepperd, I'm particular — I can't stand to see things dirty around the barn.' On another occasion he expressed surprise that a certain stockman slept the night through without seeing to his pigs when a storm came up unexpectedly, saying: 'I could not lay in the bed when I know the livestock are not comfortable.'" [12]

As acting director of the Experiment Station Dr. Shepperd was responsible for calling Bolley's attention to flax experimentation at the University of Minnesota Experiment Station. He also helped to set aside a continuous plot for grain experiments at the North Dakota Agricultural Experiment Station, and refused to see it discontinued even against the orders of the Board of Trustees. On this plot and on neighboring plots Professor Ladd analyzed the soil. His findings among others cleared the flax crop of the charge that flax exhausted the soil of plant food more than did other crops. By 1908 Bolley was able to make the first distribution of two strains of selected wilt-resistant flax seed. Other introductions in later years were made to the great advantage of the flax growers of this country.

Professor Shepperd, with the assistance of Professor O. O. Churchill, organized the North Dakota Experimental Union which aimed to bring about closer cooperation between agricultural students who return to the farm and those working at the Experiment Station. It was organized also in order to further the agricultural interests of North Dakota, to make direct application of the results attained by the branch experiment stations, and to demonstrate to the farmers in the different localities the value of these contributions. Any student of the College could become a member by indicating to the Station that he would carry on at home those experiments outlined by the Station. Free seed of three or four of the most promising grain varieties was furnished to them. Listed among such grains were hard wheat, durum wheat, barley, flax, fieldpeas, corn, alfalfa, clover, grasses, grape, mangels, and rutabaga.

Another of the pioneer experimenters of the North Dakota Experiment Station was Dr. Leunis Van Es. He worked out the tuberculin test for avian tuberculosis, a problem which had puzzled veterinarians for years. He did extensive work in hog cholera prevention through the use of serums, as well as extensive investigations of swamp fever. He was also distinguished for his foresight and planning ability, and was responsible for the organization of a Livestock Sanitary Board, which under a legislative act was largely due to his efforts.

Because of the varied physical and climatic conditions in North Dakota, the matter of establishing branch experiment stations in regions outside of the Fargo area was early considered. In the spring of 1903 the first of these was established at Edgeley with O. A. Thompson as superintendent. Subsequently stations were established at Dickinson, Langdon, Williston, Hettinger and Minot. Much valuable data based upon the work done at these stations have been obtained and published with generally beneficial results to agriculture.

A corollary to the operation of branch experiment stations was the policy of establishing demonstration farms in various sections of North Dakota. These were developed by the Experiment Station with the cooperation of officials of the Great Northern and Northern Pacific Railways, beginning in 1907. Three farms along each railroad line, consisting of twenty acres each, were divided into four acre plots and a five year of crop rotation was worked out for each particular locality. E. G. Schollander (N.D.A.C., 1906) was appointed to take charge of the work. W. B. Porter succeeded Schollander in 1908 and by 1912 twenty-five demonstration areas had been established on privately owned farms. According to *Bulletin No. 163* (May 1921) issued by the superintendent of demonstration farms, Edgar I. Olsen, 20 farms were operating demonstration fields. By the spring of 1925 the number of demonstration farms had been cut to four on account of reduced appropriations. Those demonstration farms were located on the Eastgate Brothers Farm at Larimore, on the Leonard Glans Farm at Tioga, on the Henry Becker Farm at Underwood, and on a farm at McLeod which the Experiment Station rented. Edgar I. Olsen, who was the last superintendent of the demonstration farms, resigned in October, 1925 and thereafter the project was discontinued.

During President Worst's administration very considerable attention was given to extension work done by the staff, including both the teachers and the station workers. They believed that the function of a land-grant college was not only to provide education for the youth by attendance at a college but also by carrying its message to the farmers and other adult workers in the State.

Early in the year 1895 requests began to come to the College for speakers to be used for Farmers' Institutes, which had been established in several localities in the State. The first of these 'Farmer Institutes' in which the College participated was held in Casselton in March, 1894, followed later in the season by meetings in Buxton, Mayville and Larimore. From that time until the organization of the Extension Division in 1914 the work at the Farmers' Institutes was carried on chiefly by the members of the College staff, who were also employed in the Experiment Station.

The account of the work of the Farmers' Institutes in the first twenty years of the College is a story in itself. At first it was entirely a voluntary service on the part of the staff. In January and again in November, 1896, President Worst recommended that the Legislature appropriate $1,000 for the next biennium to defray traveling expenses, primarily to aid the dairy interests of the State. Such an appropriation was made by the Sixth General Assembly in 1899 and the success of the program induced the Legislature of 1901 to increase the appropriation to $3,000 and to set up a board of directors consisting of the president of the Board of Trustees of the Agricultural College, the state commissioner of agriculture, the director of the Experiment Station, the professor of agriculture and the professor of dairying. The attendance at the institutes in the various communities rose from 3,710 in 1899–1900 to 7,251 in 1900–01 and to 9,967 in 1901–02. Professor E. E. Kaufman, professor of dairying, carried the chief load, but was assisted by other members of the staff and by outside speakers.

The interest was so marked that it was deemed advisable to publish the addresses of the speakers and of some of the papers presented. Professor Kaufman began editing a publication called the *North Dakota Farmers' Institute Annual*, published from 1900 until 1916. The early numbers were financed by advertisers, the later ones were in part subsidized by the railroad companies. The 1911 annual was published by the Deere and Webber Company of Minneapolis, Northwestern agents for the John Deere agricultural implements, and "presented" to the farmers of North Dakota. When Professor Kaufman's health caused

Justin S. Morrill
The Founder of the Land-Grant Colleges

John E. Haggart

Senator from the Ninth Legislative District Who Introduced Senate Bill No. 1, Entitled: "An Act Designating and Appropriating Section 36, Township 140, Range 49 West in County of Cass, for the Use of the Agricultural College as a Site for That Institution."

The Governor Who Signed the Legislative Act Establishing the North Dakota Agricultural College and Agricultural Experiment Station at Fargo.

JOHN MILLER
First Governor
1889-1890

O. W. Francis

President of the First Board of Trustees, 1890—1892

Presidents of the North Dakota Agricultural College

Horace Edward Stockbridge, Ph.D.,
1890–1893

John Henry Worst, LL.D.,
1895–1916

Edwin Freeman Ladd, LL.D., 1916–1921

John Lee Coulter, Ph.D., 1921–1929

Presidents

John Henry Shepperd, D. Agr.,
1929–1937

Frank Lissenden Eversull, Ph.D., D.D.,
1938–1946

John Harwood Longwell, Ph.D.,
1946–1948

Fred Samuel Hultz, Ph.D., 1948–1961

Deans of the College

Dean E. S. Keene

Dean C. B. Waldron

Dean A. E. Minard

Dean A. D. Weeks

Deans

Dean H. L. Walster

Dean R. M. Dolve

Dean W. F. Sudro

Dean Alba Bales

Early Experimenters

H. L. Bolley

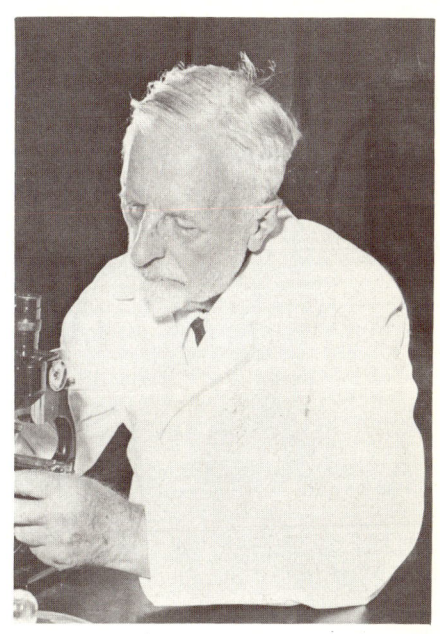

L. Van Es

L. R. Waldron

T. H. Hopper

Early Experimenters

A. F. Yeager

C. T. Nelson

O. A. Stevens

F. A. Munro

Personalities on the Campus

Casey Finnigan

Ethel McVeety

A. G. Arvold

P. F. Trowbridge

Personalities

Haile Chisholm

C. S. Putnam

A. H. Parrott

THE FIRST FACULTY OF THE NORTH DAKOTA AGRICULTURAL COLLEGE

C. B. Waldron

H. L. Bolley

E. F. Ladd

T. D. Hinebauch

H. W. McArdle

W. H. Whalen

Lois M. Hooper

The First Student Body

First Boys to Register—Robert B. Reed, Amenia, N.D.; Robert Bosard, Grand Forks, N.D.; First Girl to Register, Jessamine S. Slaughter, Bismarck, North Dakota.

The First Dress Parade

First Football Team, 1893

Women's Basketball Team, 1898

First College Band

Drill Team, 1914

Athenian Literary Society

Old Main

Francis Hall

Chemistry Building before 1909 Fire

Ceres Hall Upon Completion in 1910

Chemistry Building

Old Science Hall

Steam Engine Race

Ladd's Fence

Early Experiment Plot

Farm Managers' Day, 1951

Barberry Eradication Scouts in 1920

Weaving for Homemakers

Homecoming

Lincoln Log Cabin

Class in Paint Chemistry

Sheep Judging at the Little International

1960 National Champions in the International Livestock Judging Contest at the International Livestock Exposition in Chicago. Members of the Winning Team, Front Row, Left to Right: Richard Knutson, Oakes; Coach Merle Light; and Michael Brandvik, Kildeer. Back Row: James Carr, Baker, Minn.; James Magill, Verona; Paul Brackelsberg, Minot; Ray Kleppe, Dawson; and Keith Bjerke, Northwood.

Memorial Union

Dinan Hall

The Library

Branch Experiment Station in Minot

Branch Experiment Station in Dickinson

Branch Experiment Station in Edgeley

Branch Experiment Station in Langdon

Branch Experiment Station in Williston

Flax Investigations

Experimental Plots

Dickinson Field Day, 1951

Experimental Work in the Greenhouse

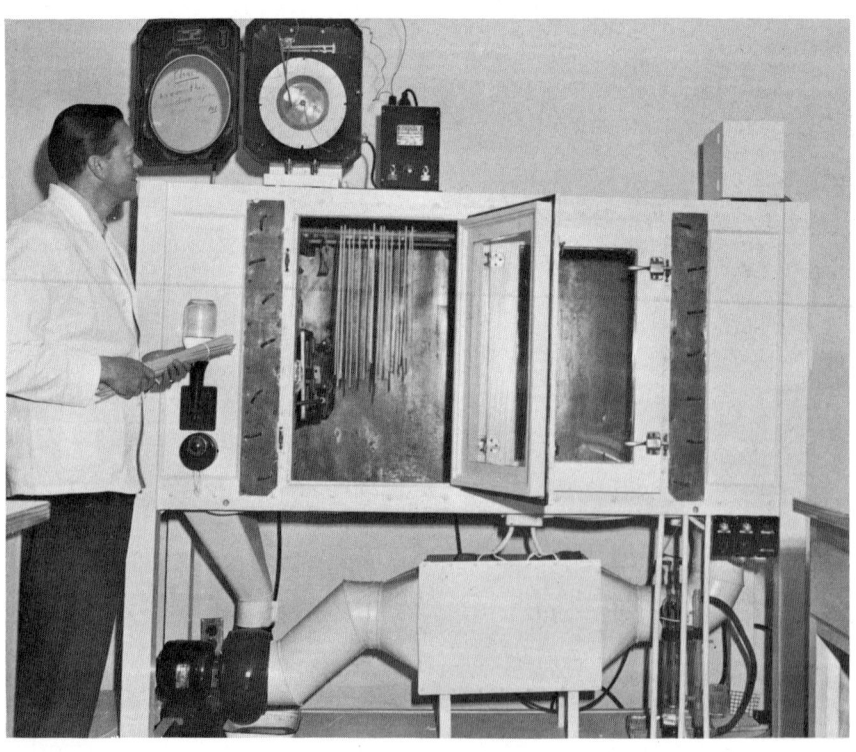

Laboratory Work in Cereal Technology

Entomological Collection

Seminar in
Agricultural Engineering

Morrill Hall

Home Economics Building

Home Management House

Campus after the Tornado of 1957

Choir, 1960

State Board of Higher Education, 1960

From Left to Right: Fred R. Orth, Grand Forks; Mrs. Elvira Jestrab, Williston; Dr. A. E. Mead, Commissioner, Bismarck; Albert Haas, President, New Rockford; Martin G. Kruse, Kindred; Mrs. Mildred Johnson, Wahpeton; Ralph A. Christensen, Minot; Absent—Ray Schnell, Dickinson.

William L. Guy, Governor of North Dakota, 1960 — N.D.A.C. Class of 1941

him to resign in 1907, A. T. Hoverstad of the agricultural sub-station at Crookston, Minnesota, took up the editing of the annual as well as the conducting of the institutes. He was elected superintendent of Farmers' Institutes and given an office in Francis Hall. He had such marked success that he came to be called the "Father of Farmers Institutes."

His contributions are described in the *St. Paul Dispatch* as follows: "He is the farmers' best friend and known all over North Dakota as the tall man with the happy smile and a good suggestion. He was one of the first to graduate from the Minnesota School of Agriculture, in 1890, when such schools were just beginning to dawn. He is not a pumpkin, although he grew up between two rows of corn; and it had to grow some, too, to keep up. Mr. Hoverstad is a delightful companion, and one of the real forces that is building up his state agriculturally." [13]

In 1910 the winter institute season closed April 4 with a record of 95 three-day meetings since November and a total attendance of 45,000. In many cases the businessmen provided free dinners and the Great Northern Railway offered free transportation. Several members of the Station staff, as well as other able leaders from North Dakota, Minnesota and the U.S. Department of Agriculture participated. The great influence of this service, covering a period of twenty years, was and still is highly important. Aside from the material advantages to the State's outstanding industry that accrued from it, the contacts made between the people of the State and the College staff were instrumental in popularizing the College and in creating a feeling that there was an intimate relation between it and the general welfare of the State. In 1909 the farmers' institute program under a different form was incorporated into the newly organized Extension Division of the College.

Another activity similar to that of the Farmers' Institute was known as the Farmers' Excursions. In 1898 President James J. Hill of the Great Northern Railway inaugurated the plan of providing free transportation to farmers to visit the Experiment Station for educational purposes. During the biennium of 1900–02 3,500 farmers and their wives visited the Station. The Northern Pacific Railway furnished transportation at the rate of one half cent per mile. In two years the railroads had brought 5,000 farmers to the campus. For two weeks in July the entire Station staff was busy acting as lecturers and guides.

Another contribution of the railroads was the provision of trains in which staff members exhibited seeds and discussed the results of their experimental experience with various varieties of grains. In 1906 the Northern Pacific Railway provided such a train for six and one half days, the Great Northern Railway for eleven days, and the Soo Line for five days. Altogether, 5,500 farmers were contacted.

In 1910 the Northern Pacific Railway offered the use of a special train, the "Better Farming Special," to be operated along its line for two weeks. Exhibits of farm machinery, plants, livestock and sewing and cooking were carried in it. In 1912 the train was operated for three weeks in June, visiting three towns daily. It consisted of two flat cars for poultry, hogs and sheep with Professors Dynes and Richards in charge; two baggage cars for horses, cattle, trees, shrubs, and vegetables, with Professors Thompson and Waldron in charge; six coaches for dairy, disease prevention, agronomy, tested seed, chemical and home economics exhibits in charge of Professors Martin, Van Es, Shepperd, Donoghue, Ladd, Keene and Miss Hoover. Attached to the train was also a dining car and sleepers for the staff.

In March, 1899, Professor Ladd began the publication of the *Sanitary Home*, a kind of university extension magazine, the only one of its kind in the Northwest. For three years it was published at the College. Later, in July, 1902, it was published under the title, *The North Dakota Farmer and Sanitary Home*, at Lisbon, N. Dak., by W. G. Crocker. It continued under Crocker and Ladd until May–June, 1918, when, due to the wartime loss of staff and pressmen, it was sold to a Fargo firm. During the eighteen years of its publication *The North Dakota Farmer* carried news for the farmer, articles by the college staff, and usually a feature article by President Worst. It was in effect an organ of the College.

A monthly publication, called *The Extension*, appeared for the first time on January 8, 1908, was edited by Professor Weeks and distributed free, primarily to public school teachers. It carried agricultural education news, information about college courses and articles of practical interest to farmers. Members of the staff took turns contributing to it.

The catalogue for 1909–10 included Agricultural Extension in the department of agriculture, with assistant professor G. W. Randlett listed as superintendent. Professor Randlett had attended Iowa State College and Iowa State Teachers College. In 1902 he came to the College under J. H. Shepperd to teach agricultural short courses and in 1908 received from the College his B.S. degree. In 1905 he organized the first boys' and girls' club work in North Dakota.

In 1911 the department of extension was established in order to coordinate the activities described above with Assistant Professor Randlett as director and W. C. Palmer as agricultural editor. The latter was a graduate of the School of Agriculture attached to the University of Minnesota and had worked two years with the United States Department of Agriculture. During this time he had done graduate work at George Washington University and later he had served as dean of agriculture at Winona Lake College in Indiana.

The purpose of the department of college extension as stated in the catalogue for 1911-12 was "to carry to boys and girls, farmers, and teachers, in their home, in a slight degree at least, the opportunities of the resident student." Industrial contests were to be held. High school lecture courses, agricultural, industrial and popular in content, such as soil nitrogen, home sanitation, landscaping, refrigeration, antitoxins, North Dakota birds, were to be offered. The department solicited public school cooperation and promised press service, aid in organizing farmers' clubs, speakers for various occasions and exhibits for local fairs.

The origin of industrial contests in North Dakota seems to have come from corn growing contests among farm boys in Illinois about 1900. At that time seed corn was distributed to 500 farm boys in Macoupin County, who grew and exhibited the products at the county fair. The work was taken up by county superintendents of schools and quickly spread throughout the State of Illinois. In 1905 Randlett adopted the idea as a means of extending the influence of the College beyond the class room and possibly also as a means to enlarge student enrollment. T. E. Stoa, later Experiment Station agronomist, grew and exhibited corn as an industrial contest member when he was a farm boy in Traill County in 1906.

Out of these industrial contests grew the first 4-H Annual Achievement Institute. In 1910 ninety-five boys and girls who were winners of the industrial contests in their counties "met at the Agricultural College where a week was spent in instruction along agricultural lines for boys and domestic science arts for girls. The afternoon of each day was given over to play and social affairs suitable to the ages of those taking part." The 95 who were present "perfected the organization which they chose to call 'the North Dakota Boys' and Girls' Institute.' "[14] Professor Randlett said in that year "if antipass legislation was not too strict he hoped to make the institute an annual affair." Apparently this was about the time that Congress was questioning the railroads' use of passes to influence legislation, and the railroads were probably giving free transportation to the 4-H boys and girls coming to the College. A second institute was held in December, 1911, and attended by 106 boys and girls.

In 1912 local extension schools covering the fundamentals in agriculture, horticulture and domestic science were furnished to a limited number of communities; this service might be called "extension lecture courses." Also package libraries including school orations, amateur plays and discussion materials for civic clubs and literary societies were made available. This last activity reflects the influence of A. G. Arvold of the College. In 1913 two additional members of the Extension staff were secured. Professor A. P. Hollis, former vice president of the Valley City Normal School, was engaged to have charge of the public school end of the extension work and also to handle publicity. Miss Julia O Newton, a graduate of the University of Minnesota, for six years principal of Moorhead High School, later a member of the faculty of Ellendale Normal, was to have charge of extension work in household affairs.

Mr. Hollis continued college extension as a department, using lectures on rural life and education, the rural lyceum and a slide and film bureau, even after the Agricultural Extension Division was established in 1914. Miss Newton spent the first semester of 1913–14 at Cornell University, during which she attended a meeting of land-grant colleges at Washington. In February she went to Ohio State University for conferences of rural leaders and attended a short course for women in a rural Iowa church, where she "learned more in five days than she could at a town school." On September 1, 1914, she started her work at the College in cooperation with Director Cooper, Mr. Randlett, Mr. Palmer and Mr. Hollis. The field work consisted of speaking as a member of a farmers' institute team during the three winter months throughout North Dakota. Train service was primitive, but the friendliness of the people she met on her trips was delightful; Miss Newton had a big share in organizing a home demonstration State program. She left the College to accept a similar position at the University of Minnesota in 1919.

Meanwhile, under private auspices, the Better Farming Association had been organized in North Dakota, on November 15, 1911. This organization was a result of a bankers' convention which met in Minneapolis in 1911 and was attended by bankers, lumbermen, elevator owners from the Twin Cities and North Dakota. President Worst, E. J. Weiser and Alex Stern attended from Fargo. At this meeting Professor Bolley was criticized for publishing bulletins and giving addresses to farmers in North Dakota exposing the diseased condition of the soil and the prevalence of smut, flax wilt and potato scab. This publicity caused Eastern financiers to question investments in North Dakota mortgages. Up to this time Eastern capital could be obtained at six per cent and loaned on North Dakota mortgage security at ten per cent. Statistics show that in 1910 slightly over 50 percent of North Dakota farms were mortgaged, that the average farm debt in twenty years had increased 176.4 per cent, while valuation had increased less.

The Better Farming Association was financed by Twin City railroads, wholesale houses, implement dealers, lumber yards, elevator companies, milling interests, banks and the North Dakota Bankers Association. Funds raised by this association in the various counties would be matched by the state dollar for dollar to carry out the purposes expressed in its name. E. J. Weiser, of Fargo, was president; P. L. Howe, Minneapolis, and C. W. Kelley, Devils Lake, were vice presidents; E. Y. Sarles, Hillsboro, was treasurer. Thomas P. Cooper, a native of Illinois and a graduate of the University of Minnesota, was manager and secretary. John Haw, just out of the "Farm School" in St. Paul, was employed by Cooper as an agent of the Better Farming Association. He was one of some twenty agents in various counties, such as Adams, Barnes, Bottineau, Bowman, Cavalier, Eddy, Grand Forks, Hettinger, Ransom, Stutsman, Ward, and Wells, seeking to bring about a better diversification of agriculture.

According to the articles of incorporation the work was to be: "dissemination of information and instruction in modern scientific methods as applied to agriculture, the promoting of better and more profitable cultivation of the soil, including rotation and diversification of crops, raising of livestock and poultry, and like subjects pertaining to the agriculture of the state." [15]

The plan of work consisted of field demonstrations, livestock demonstrations and advisory farm management. Agricultural experts of broad training and experience were to be placed in counties to develop agricultural interest and induce changes in methods. These agents promoted the raising of alfalfa and corn, the rotation of crops, including grass, the breeding and feeding of livestock. The association supplied dairy heifers, bred gilts, and breeding ewes. In the winter of 1912-13 farmers' clubs were organized to add sociability to the Farmers' Institutes. Haw organized some twenty farmers' clubs. All day meetings included lunch and exchange of crop production experiences. The program of the association was well received, especially by those of Scotch descent, but not so cordially by the Germans in the State.

Many farmers were very skeptical about the Better Farming agents. The majority of them were young men, just out of college, partially paid by bankers, railroad executives and Minneapolis grainmen. In the minds of many farmers these interests had grown rich and fat at the expense of the farmers. In fact, about the time that the Better Farming Association was organized, the Farmers Equity Union, an organization under the leadership of George Loftus and J. M. Anderson, was gaining popularity by fighting the Minneapolis grain interests. Approximately at the same time the Nonpartisan League movement saw the solution of the farm problem in control of the grain market and belittled diversification. And this movement was beginning to cast shadows of what later was to become a bitter fight between the businessman and the farmer.

Into this situation the Better Farming Association agent carried his philosophy of diversification of agricultural production as a means of improving the general welfare of the farmer. While the Better Farming Association agent urged an increase in the production of alfalfa and of livestock and also of better tillage methods, at the same time the farmer's political leadership told the farmer that the businessmen, the grain dealers and the railroad interests were in league against him.

The Better Farming Association agents and the early extension agents pioneered in a field in which the people they contacted were not overly receptive to their ideas. The courage of youth and the firm belief in the soundness of the ideas they carried to farm people enabled these pioneers in the field of adult education to lay the foundation for the North Dakota Agricultural Extension Service, which is now almost universally recognized in the State as a necessary educational service in agriculture.

There were, moreover, many farm leaders who recognized the sincerity of the Better Farming Association agents and the soundness of their ideas, and they became supporters of the work and became their friends. It was through this progressive farm leadership, represented by women as well as by men, and through the friendly businessmen, that the agents persuaded the people of the counties to understand what the aims and purposes of extension service work were.

The *Second Annual Report of the Better Farming Association,* published in 1912, maintained that "the method of organization and forms of work adopted by the Association were effective — that farmers were ready to cooperate along lines that promise results, and that many people find use for a district or county agriculturist who is in a position to give definite advice and help . . . and that succeeding years' work would place the agriculture of North Dakota upon a permanent and profitable basis."

There were 25 agents of the Better Farming Association at the close of the year 1913, according to the 1912 annual report of the Better Farming Association. They reached 40 percent of the agricultural population of the State; they were "coming in daily contact with the people, and the farmers felt a confidence in them."[16] These agents were pioneers in the field of adult education, with little experience and no pattern of educational techniques or professional traditions to guide them. There were compensations which gave the agents a feeling of satisfaction; the eagerness of farm people to learn new practices and better ways and their warm hospitality were sufficient rewards to the agents.

Thus the Better Farming Association, though not connected with the College, was engaged in work similar to the earlier Farmers' Institutes of the College. It was natural that a merger of the two should take place in October, 1913. On July 1, 1914, Thomas Cooper resigned as director of the Better Farming Association and was appointed by the College Board of Trustees director of the Experiment Station, in place of President Worst, and director of the Agricultural Extension Service. During the life of the Better Farming Association, the headquarters and office of the director were in downtown Fargo. When the Extension Service was established by a Federal law, the offices were moved to the College.

The Smith-Lever Cooperative Extension Act became a law on May 8, 1914. It established a Federal agricultural extension service primarily to carry to the people of the several states the results of the investigations of the agricultural experiment stations and the U.S. Department of Agriculture, and to secure the adoption of the information in general farm practice and in the home. The act appropriated to each state $10,000 annually; additional appropriation was to be apportioned to the states in the proportion of the rural population to the total rural population of the United States. Sums other than the basal $10,000 must be matched by state, county or local authorities. The expenditure of funds in North Dakota for the next three years was used largely for four projects: county agricultural agents, home economics, boys' and girls' club work, and farm and livestock management. These projects had already been started. Home economics work was now reorganized in September, 1915, with May C. McDonald as head of the home demonstration department and with Julia Newton as her assistant.

The appointment of Cooper to replace President Worst as director of the Experiment Station was due to political reasons and was not acceptable to Professor Bolley and Professor Ladd, who were required to take orders from and report to Cooper. Ladd refused to accept this order and continued his mill experiments on his own. Bolley complained of the difficulties he encountered with Director Cooper, who objected to the publication of Bolley's bulletins. In 1916, after Professor Ladd became president, Bolley was subjected to a trial.

For a brief time the College in its administration attempted to get along with two independent heads, President Worst of the College and Cooper, director of the Experiment Station and Extension Service. In November, 1914, while President Worst was in Washington attending a meeting of land-grant colleges, the Board of Trustees met and elected Dr. Ladd president and Worst president emeritus of the College. Dr.

Ladd refused to accept the office unless it was agreeable to President Worst, so the matter was to be kept secret until President Worst returned. The president refused to accept the position of president emeritus and the three trustees, Nugent, Hollister and Kelley, who for some time had opposed Cooper, resigned.

Instead of nominating new trustees, Governor Hanna proposed that a new Board of Regents be created to administer the affairs of all the higher educational institutions of the State. In January, 1915, the Legislature passed such a bill. Governor Hanna named to the Board Lewis F. Crawford, ex-governor Frank White, Dr. J. D. Taylor, Emil Scow and Allie Power, son of J. B. Power; all except Taylor being bankers or having banking connections.

President Worst in February, 1916, proposed that the College be divided into three main divisions, teaching, experimentation, and extension. The president of the College to be the chief executive with the directors of the two divisions subordinate to him. However, the Board feared that President Worst might remove Cooper from the directorship of the Station; they again elected Worst president emeritus, but he declined. The Board rescinded its action and held a special meeting in Fargo, where they met with a student committee, with the faculty, and separately with Ladd, Cooper and Bolley. Scow moved that it was for the best interests of the College that Worst be retired immediately. E. F. Ladd was elected temporary president and head of both the College and the Experiment Station.[17] In December, 1917, Mr. Cooper resigned as director of the Experiment Station to accept a position as dean of the Agricultural College and director of the Experiment Station at the University of Kentucky. During his brief directorship at the North Dakota Agricultural College he emphasized the production of livestock and encouraged the raising of more feed crops. Under his direction almost 500 farmers' clubs were organized. Director Cooper believed that relief from serious crop losses due to rust, as encountered in 1914 and 1916, would be attained, if a more aggressive plant breeding program was initiated. He therefore appointed L. R. Waldron plant breeder of the Experiment Station in the belief that he would develop varieties more capable of arresting such disease.

FOOTNOTES

[1] H. L. Walster in *North Dakota Agricultural Experiment Station Bi-Monthly Bulletin*, XII, 6 (July–August, 1950), 187.

[2] *Bi-Monthly Bulletin*, XII, 6, 192.

[3] Erling Rolfsrud, *Lanterns Over the Prairies, Book II* (Brainerd, Minn., 1950), 112.

[4] H. L. Walster, "Faculty Chat — Apostle of Outdoor Beauty," *Spectrum*, LIV, No. 132, (Dec. 9, 1938).

[5] Geiger, 147.

[6] Henry L. Bolley and Lawrence R. Waldron in *North Dakota Agricultural Experiment Station Bulletin No. 46* (Fargo, 1900).

[7] Rolfsrud, II, 113.

[8] *North Dakota Agricultural Experiment Station Special Bulletin, Food Department III, No. 14.* (Jan., 1915), 233-38.

[9] E. F. Ladd, "Practical Paint Tests in 1907," *North Dakota Agricultural Experiment Station Bulletin No. 81*, (Sept., 1908).

[10] E. F. Ladd, "What the Department of Chemistry Has Done for North Dakota," *The North Dakota Farmer*, XIV, 8, (Feb. 15, 1913), 3-4.

[11] H. L. Walster, "Edwin Fremont Ladd, Chemist," unpublished mss., North Dakota Institute for Regional Studies, Library, N.D.A.C.

[12] J. H. Shepperd, papers, North Dakota Institute for Regional Studies, Library, N.D.A.C., containing a clipping from the Bloomington, Ill., *Sunday Pantograph*, Feb. 2, 1930.

[13] *St. Paul Dispatch*, March 4, 1912.

[14] Norbert D. Gorman, "Some Cooperative Agricultural Extension History of North Dakota," unpublished mss. in the office of the Extension Division, N.D.A.C.

[15] Alfred Charles True, *A History of Agricultural Extension Work in the United States.* (Washington, 1928), 75.

[16] Gorman, 34.

[17] Minutes of State Board of Regents, Feb. 19, 26-28, 1916.

◄ CHAPTER V ►

Student Life, 1890-1916

THE preceding chapters have placed emphasis on the administration and the faculty of the College. Before continuing that story, the life and activities of students during this time should also be considered.

The following rules of conduct and student government were adopted at the first faculty meeting of the Agricultural College, held at Fargo College on October 22, 1890, at which President Stockbridge, Secretary Ladd and Professor Bolley were present:

"Students admitted to the College and pursuing any part of its course of instruction are expected at all times to preserve gentlemanly deportment and conduct themselves in a self-respecting manner maintaining respectful demeanor toward each other and toward instructors and citizens. Each student is expected to assume the responsibility of his own actions, and the entire body of students shall act, directly or by representatives, as a court for the trial of offenses against this regulation under such conditions or restrictions as the faculty may impose.

"Each member of the College faculty shall alone be responsible for the conduct of students while in his charge and for the maintenance of discipline within his own jurisdiction.

"In any case of discipline every student shall possess the right of appeal without prejudice to the decision of the full faculty, whose jurisdiction and authority shall be supreme.

"These rules and regulations may be altered, amended, enlarged or restricted at any time by vote of the faculty or by proclamation of the president." [1]

While the College was located in temporary quarters at Fargo College, the students were fed — the term is properly applied — at two large tables of the Fargo College dining room, each, according to rules, presided over by a professor. Hinebauch, Waldron and Bolley, the youngest men of the faculty, voted that job on President Stockbridge and Professor Ladd.[2]

On January 6, 1891, thirty students responded to the first announcement of the opening of the College. The group came from representative communities of the State, including Fargo, Grand Forks, Hillsboro, Jamestown, Valley City, Ellendale, Portland, Amenia, Carrington and Abercrombie. Their average age was 27.

The first girl to enroll at the regular college term in September, 1891, was Jessamine Slaughter, who was awarded a scholarship from Burleigh County. She tells how she was met at the train by President Stockbridge with horses and buggy, and escorted to his home where she met Mrs. Stockbridge, who was to be one of her teachers. She described her attendance at Jones Hall, Fargo College, where she met the other teachers and her three fellow college students, Robert Reed of Amenia, Robert Bossard of Grand Forks, and Carl Lee of Pekin. "We were all bashful sixteen year olds who took our work seriously, at least the 'girl from the west,' as I was called by the Fargo College students where I boarded, for I had come from way out west,— Bismarck. Miss Hooper, who afterwards became Mrs. Waldron, was the president's secretary. One afternoon they took me in their horse and buggy to see the Main Building, then under construction. It was way out of town and the only building on a plowed section, a lonely sight on a level prairie." [3]

In January, 1892, the students were able to move to their own new campus on the northern outskirts of the City of Fargo. It was a bare prairie of dust or mud. College Hall, as it was first called, was a big barn of a building, devoid of surrounding trees or shrubbery. "The upper floor of the new building being uncompleted, was used as a gymnasium, and boxing, wrestling, and 'tugs of war' were popular forms of exercise, where students and faculty met in many friendly contests, and even to this day the old timers delight in reciting the thrilling experiences of the 'matches' between Hinebauch and Bolley, or Whalen and Gibson. These were the days when everybody in school became acquainted with everybody else, and the influence of teacher over pupil was positive and lasting." [4]

Early catalogs give information about how to reach the College: "Follow Broadway north to Tenth Avenue, then follow the sidewalk west and north to the College. During the dry weather the wheeling is good directly west from the north end of the pavement on Broadway." During the winter months the college bus, called the "Black Maria," left the Milwaukee Depot at 7:20 a.m. "for the accommodation of lady students only." It went east, then north, on Broadway. At noon and late in the afternoon it returned.[5]

For a brief time in 1892 before the omnibus was put in use, other arrangements were provided for the girl students. At this time Professor and Mrs. Hays lived in a house at the corner of Tenth Avenue and Seventh Street that had been rented by the College as a farmhouse.

"Here practically all the girls students boarded. In winter Professor Hayes hitched a team of mules, Billy and Juno, to a sled, loaded up the girls and set out for the College. There was generally room for some of the boys, who were useful in the spring when wheels were put on the sled. Sometimes the vehicle would get stuck and the boys would have to carry the girls to comparatively dry land. Fargo citizens used to watch the sled go by, with a major portion of the Agricultural College students on board, and laugh, and then shake their heads and wish they had gotten the 'insane asylum' or the state fair." [6]

The *Prospectus of 1891* outlined the following admission requirements and expenses for students:

"It is intended that the curriculum of the institution shall supplement the public school system of the State and that its course of study shall begin where the best common schools of the state leave off, taking up the work of the latter and carrying it on toward a free fuller development. The advantages of the institution are therefore open to all citizens of the State of either sex over the age of fifteen years, who shall satisfy the faculty of the college, either by examination or by certificate of their proficiency in English grammar, the writing and spelling of the English language, United States history, geography, arithmetic, including the metric systems, and algebra through simple equations.

"Tuition is free to all the students admitted to the regular course. Furnished rooms cost from $3.00 to $8.00 per month. Washing about 55¢ per dozen pieces. Board $5.00 to $4.50 per week. . . . Students will be required to perform a certain amount of farm work as a part of the regular instruction in the course. . . . For this labor students will receive no compensation. . . . For other work on the farm, students so desiring may earn funds toward defraying a considerable portion of the necessary expenses of education." [7]

The estimated expenses, including board, room, books, matriculation fee and incidentals for a college year in 1892 ranged from $117.00 to $214.00.

In 1893 the roster of students included six juniors, two sophomores, twelve freshmen, forty-one in the preparatory class and one special student. With a faculty of twelve and a student body of sixty there was an intimacy that made discipline easy and promoted fellowship. By the end of the decade there were 375 students on the campus.

The rules of conduct formulated at the first faculty meeting were in existence until a student organization was formed in 1898. In 1894 the catalog carried this paragraph:

"It is the policy of the faculty to place the government of the school as far as possible in the hands of the students. To this end an organization has been effected by them, rules have been formulated, and officers elected, who by the advice and assistance of the faculty, are expected to maintain good discipline among the students in their relations to each other, and to the Institution. In addition to this general student organization, a special one exists for the control of the dormitory." [8]

Student Life, 1890–1916

By 1898 a formal student organization was founded "to consider such matters as pertained to the student body." It was composed of the college classes and the senior preparatory class. This organization worked fairly well until 1910, when a plan was put into effect to establish a student council to be composed of five members from each of the college classes, two from each of the academic courses, and one each from the four special courses, making a total of thirty representatives. Its main business was to elect the editor and the business manager of the *Spectrum*, the student published weekly paper, started in 1896, and to appoint the athletic and public speaking boards of control.

Soon, however, there was growing dissatisfaction with the Student Council as a form of government. It was felt by many students to be undemocratic in that it vested power to choose the officers and boards in the hands of thirty students. The new system proposed was in the form of a Student Commission, which provided for a commission of nine members, three to be elected from the senior class, three from the junior class, two from the sophomore class, and one from the freshman class. It also provided for the use of the Initiative, Referendum and Recall, an indication that the students were influenced by the liberal movements in state and civic legislation. The new system was adopted on March 15, 1915. It was claimed that the College was the first school in the United States to adopt the Commission as a form of student government.

During the first few years when the College consisted of only one building, College Hall, the chapel was the center of social life. It was the gathering place for the various joint activities of the students. As in other colleges of that day, chapel exercises occurred daily and were compulsory. This last requirement was difficult to enforce, particularly after the student body grew larger. The programs consisted of scripture reading, prayer, the singing of hymns and short talks by the president or other members of the faculty. Often in the evenings popular lectures for students and the public were given by faculty members or visiting scholars.

The chapel of that day was the front half of what is now the Little Country Theater in the Main Building. An editorial in the *Spectrum* in February, 1900, has the following vivid recollections of early chapel days: "If our chapel walls could talk, what stories they would tell of the fiery streams of oratory and rhetoric that have resounded within its plastered sides; of the trembling persons waiting in their seats or on the rostrum for their turn to appear perhaps for the first time before an audience; of the shouts of command on military drill of former days; of the crash and smash of numerous flag scraps; and the battles that have occurred before their pale faces." [9]

However, daily chapel was soon discontinued. The *Spectrum* of Oct. 15, 1902, announced that since the number of students could not be accommodated in the chapel, daily assembly would be abandoned after November 1, 1902. A general assembly would be held once a week, for which some special program would be arranged. One of the earlier special programs was the celebration of Arbor Day, May, 1897, in the chapel. The program consisted of music by a double quartette, a brief history of Arbor Day observance by Professor Bottenfield, an essay, "Fruits of North Dakota," by L. R. Waldron, a talk, "Plant Life," by Professor Bolley, and reminiscences by President Worst. The audience then adjourned to the campus for a baseball game between faculty and students.

However, before 1897 the chapel ceased to be the center of social life, and the "dorm," the popular name for Francis Hall, took its place. In 1897 Thanksgiving was a gala day. A bountiful dinner was served at Francis Hall by Mrs. Nichol at 2 p.m.; after tea, dancing continued until eleven o'clock.

The girls in the domestic science class often "sneaked out" special delicacies to their special sweethearts. Professor Shepperd, chairman of the dormitory committee, was sympathetic with the pranks played by the boys, and "condoned with the ladies over their lost pies and cakes." He cites the following incidents:

"I remember a class in horticulture that had stolen a cake and finding it impossible to evade Professor C. B. Waldron, boldly marched into his classroom with it. Art Fowler as spokesman and cake bearer said: 'Wasn't it mighty good of Miss Senn to give us this cake, Professor?' The professor took a piece of the cake and as he did so he asked, 'Was Miss Senn half a mile away when she gave you this cake?' ".

"But the climax was reached when Art Fowler and Lee Greene's class stole a roasted turkey from the oven in the domestic science department without being caught. I have seen many dare devil deeds perpetrated by students, but that of stealing a roasted turkey hot from the oven while the cook's back was turned leads all others which have come to my notice." [10]

At commencement time one of the highlights of the season was the inter-society banquet. The banquet in 1899 honored the two graduates by a program of toasts, including one addressed to "Our Seniors"; the irrepressible, mischief-loving Ben Meinecke and the staid, dignified, scholarly L. R. Waldron. The *Spectrum* at this time carried references to Fred Olsen, who boasted that he was "never hampered by petticoats during his college course," to the bobsled ride with the iceman taken by Elita (Tiny) Olson, to Jim McGuigan's teasing Katie Jensen, to Mary Darrow's and Professor Keene's duet in the physics class. Such

Student Life, 1890–1916

references illustrate the friendly and intimate life of the early students.

Two other incidents illustrating student life of this period are found in other issues of the *Spectrum*:

"Forman Beals had finished painting the 20 hitching posts a bright green. A few days later as students came on the campus they saw a band of beautiful yellow around each post. 'Just after classes assembled, a party was noticed in secret council upon the walk between the Administration Building and the Chemical. Professor Parrott had a stern look hidden under a four-inch smile; Dick Kraft grinned in the background; Forman Beals looked stern and smiled by turns while Pat O'Keefe looked on innocently. The party broke up without any result." [11]

"The winter Short Course students were victimized sometimes. They were boys from the farm and many of them had never been away from home nor in a town or city the size of Fargo. One of them, who came in 1909, describes his experiences. The morning after his arrival he went out to the College and stood around for minutes. Two well dressed young fellows came up and asked him for his 'campus ticket.' As he did not have one, they kindly supplied him, charging a dollar for a little piece of green pasteboard. The next Monday, he and nine of the others invested half a dollar in a chapel ticket and later in the day he spent a quarter to enter the library." [12]

Naturally the College staff members became the leaders in various extra curricular activities. This was especially true of Henry L. Bolley. He had "always been interested in athletics." As a boy following his penchant at fishing and hunting while in the rural schools of Indiana, in Michigan he prided himself on considerable skill in wrestling and baseball, at that time the only available sports. Later at Purdue University he made the Varsity team in the three available sports, tennis, baseball and football. While at Purdue University he had the distinction of taking part in the formation of the Inter-collegiate Football League of Indiana, and was quarterback and end on the original Purdue team which in contest with DePauw University put on the first football contest west of the Allegheny Mountains.

Professor Bolley was always a constant advocate of clean, manly sportsmanship; he always strongly maintained that properly systematized inter-collegiate contests were of great benefit to college life and to the future usefulness of the contestants as citizens. For a number of years he coached and managed the athletic teams at the College, being aided in different years by assistant coaches for the football season only.

In 1893 an athletic association was formed by a few loyal members of the faculty and interested students. In 1900 Professor Bolley, still general manager of athletics, recommended to the directors of the association five assistant student managers for football, baseball, basketball, field sports and gymnasium. A Board of Athletic Control, four students and three faculty members, was approved by the faculty in 1910. When the Student Commission as a form of government was adopted in 1915 a student commissioner of athletics became a member of the Board of Athletic Control.

Football was the first form of athletics to be promoted at the College. Professor Bolley was early in communication with M. A. Brannon, botanist at the University of North Dakota and head coach of its squad. The first regularly scheduled games between the University and the "A.C." teams were played in 1894 and were won by the "A.C.," the first at Grand Forks, the second at Fargo. In 1895 the University evened up the score by defeating the "Aggies" twice.

Robert Reed, Ralph Ward, Claude Nugent and Charles Hall were members of that first football team. Reed was quarterback and captain. In commenting on the differences between the way the game was played then and the way it is played now, Mr. Reed says:

"There was no forward pass in the early days and bucking the line was the main feature. Very little kicking was done. The ball was usually forced through the lines and there was some running around the ends. Professor Bolley developed a crisscross play which worked very well and served to confuse the other team.

"We were short of men when we went to Grand Forks in answer to that first challenge, but so were they. They put in their military instructor and we put in Dr. Hinebauch.

"When the University team came down here that fall they were nicely equipped with stocking caps and our boys were bareheaded, but our team had the stocking caps when the game was over (2 to 0) in our favor. They did not forgive us for a long time.

"The spirit of both cities was in the games between the 'A.C.' and the 'U' and it was as much a Grand Forks and Fargo affair as it was a college affair." [13]

The football record for the first fifteen years of the College is found in one of the first numbers of the weekly *Spectrum*. From 1891 to 1899 Professor Bolley acted as missionary, coach, manager and yell master. The teams were coached by Bolley, aided by Ad Leach of Fargo. In 1895 the faculty members withdrew from the team; Mr. Nugent, the genial secretary of the College, was one of the players. In 1900–01 the team was coached by John ("Hinky") Harrison, the crack ex-end of the University of Minnesota; during the two years only one game was lost. The next two years (1902–04) were a banner period. The team coached by Eddie Cochems of the University of Wisconsin, won every game and kept its goal line uncrossed. The first football special train carried 220 enthusiastic Fargoans to Grand Forks to see the "Farmers" defeat the "U."

In 1906 Gilmour ("Gil") Dobie, who had been a star player (quarterback and end) and later assistant coach at the University of Minnesota, took over the College team. Dobie's football team played such teams as

Hamline University and Carleton College; it also beat the University of North Dakota 32 to 0. In the spring of 1907 the faculty of the University discontinued athletic relations with the Agricultural College "in the interest of good fellowship." [14] Indeed for several years the complaint was made that the "A.C." team was unable to schedule any games in the State. In 1907 the team defeated the University of Kansas, the University of South Dakota, and the Haskell Indians by big scores. In his two years as coach Dobie produced championship teams. He was fortunate in having able players, particularly captain Fred Birch, fullback Leo Nemzek, quarterback Victor Hallenberg and George Richardson, an end. The old field was then located between 11th and 12th avenues and 13th street, now a residential district.

In 1913 the College finally secured a football stadium. Dacotah Field was mapped out, north of the Armory, to remain in its original location until 1950, and in the first game on the new playing grounds, the "Farmers" rose to the occasion by beating Wahpeton's "Indians" by the astronomical score of 123 to 0.

In 1914 Coach Howard Wood, who came to the College from Sioux Falls High School, soon learned the abilities of all the men on the team and established a creditable record as coach. He was especially noted for instilling the spirit of fair play in his men. Before the game with Fargo College, he gave his men instructions to "fight to a finish and fight hard, and the first man I see playing unfairly comes off the field." The season of 1914 resulted in winning the state championship for the College, defeating the University. The following period was apparently one of lack of interest on the part of the students, culminating in the decline of enrollment due to World War I.

When the College was founded, basketball was an unknown game. In the *Spectrum* of February, 1898 appeared an article which says: "Some four years ago, there was introduced to the athletes of this school an invigorating, enthusiasm-creating game known as football — now a new child presents himself, but how different he is from his brother who came in his canvas suit, heavy spiked shoes and with hair that would put to shame a cap sheaf on North Dakota wheat shock. This new child, basketball, has found a warm reception . . . even our sisters are falling in love with him. . . ."[15]

A basketball league was organized consisting of the Fargo YMCA, Fargo College and the A.C. A series of nine games was won easily by the Y. The college women also engaged in the sport and in 1901 produced an undefeated team. Basketball at the College was handicapped in comparison with the YMCA and Fargo College, as football dominated the scene in the fall quarter while the other two institutions devoted the major part of the fall and all the winter months to basketball.

There was no organized move for girls' athletics until 1898, when under the leadership of Mrs. Shepperd and Mrs. Bottenfield, the girls organized a basketball team and a physical culture class. They joined the Athletic Association and were given the use of the gymnasium one hour a day. After 1901 they had no connection with the Athletic Association and furnished all their own equipment.

A women's basketball team is mentioned in the *Spectrum* of April 15, 1901. "One thing our institution stands supreme in, and that is an undefeated ladies' basketball team. It has successfully met on the field of athletic honor every form and shape of feminine aspirants for athletic laurels and to them all has it left naught but defeat." There is a picture of this team in the catalog of 1901–02 entitled "Champions of North Dakota." The team included Elizabeth Rice, Professor Bolley's niece, and Emily May, who played for four years according to boys' rules, and who were coached successively by Mr. Parrott, Dr. Bell, Gil Dobie, and Thomas Manns. They defeated Valley City Normal, Mayville Normal, Moorhead State Teachers College, the University of North Dakota and the University of Minnesota teams.

The year 1906 was a championship year for the College. The boys' team "defeated every team with which they played within the state, and made a creditable showing against other teams. The girls' team was the strongest in the history of the institution." Fred Birch was captain of that year's basketball and football teams; Kent Darrow, later a prominent Fargo physician, was captain of the basketball team in 1907.

In 1910 came a resumption of "A.C." and "UND" athletic relations. The first game in four years between the College and the University was a basketball contest in March, 1910.[16] The crowd in the College armory was enthusiastic at the success of the home team; the last score was shot by Frank, "Peewee" Darrow. In 1911 the basketball team played an entire season without a single defeat. Coach Rueber had this to say: "The team has been the most easily handled of any team that I have ever coached. The men realized that they had a chance to make a record for the college and were only too willing to do everything in their power to make the season a successful one." The team consisted of Frank Darrow, captain, of Fargo, a brother of Kent's and later also a successful physician in Fargo; Arthur Bridge, J. Allen Clark, and Scott Drummond, Fargo; Joseph Krafthever, Amenia; Harry McConn, Fairmont; John Nolet, Jamestown; and C. Leslie Wheeler, Fargo.

The 1916 basketball team with eighteen straight victories won the championship of the Minnesota-Dakota conference. "Captain Bruce McKee was one of the best men in this 'neck of the woods.' Bolsinger and McQuillan were two fine guards whose team work was outstanding; "Curly" Movold was one of the fastest and cleverest little men in the entire Northwest; "Dutch" Hauser, the youngest of the quint, was a shark at the fast passing game, which helped to make our teamwork so nearly perfect."[17]

With the coming of World War I basketball as well as football was doomed. The influenza epidemic of 1918-19 affected several members of the squad and wrecked the team.

Throughout the history of athletics at the College minor sports, such as baseball and track, received less attention, because spring season was considered too short to develop sustained interest in intercollegiate teams. The only attention those minor sports received was chiefly through intramural contests or in physical education classes. Baseball and track vied for the available coaching skill and time. A College baseball nine won state championships in 1910, 1911 and 1915. Each time the determining game was with Fargo College.

Although military training was required by the Morrill Act and by State legislation, the College for a time was unable to secure instructors or equipment. Professor Keene organized a company in 1895 by serving as captain and using other faculty men, Professors Hall and Hayden, as lieutenants; equipment was furnished by the State National Guard. Drill was held in the second floor of the Mechanic Arts Building. The next year Professor Kaufman acted as captain with the other officers continuing. In 1897 the U. S. War Department furnished a commandant and equipment. Military instruction was made compulsory for all male students except seniors. An armory and drill hall, now Festival Hall, and a target range were provided.

In 1901 Capt. James Ulio was assigned to the College and served as commandant for over a decade. He organized two companies and held weekly battalion parades which became "a feature of college life attended by crowds which thronged the balconies of the armory." Out of this grew the organization of a "crack squad" made up of eight picked men for exhibition drill. They first appeared at the Tri-State Grain Growers convention in January, 1911 and made numerous other public exhibitions. In 1915 the squad made a ten weeks' tour of the Twin Cities and the West Coast and appeared at the Panama-Pacific Exposition at San Francisco. A splendid advertisement of the Agricultural College!

Among the student activities which were under the control of the student organization was the student paper, the *Spectrum*, started in December, 1896. At that time the editor-in-chief and the business manager were elected by popular vote of the students. Beginning as a monthly with faculty contributions, it became purely a student publication by the end of its first two years. It remained a monthly until 1907, when the student organization requested it to become a weekly. Its policy was to give both sides of any question, thus supplying a forum for student opinion and its own editorials. An extract from the very first editorial, in December, 1896, reads: "We wish to acquaint the people of our state with what we have been doing along the different lines of study. It is also the aim of the management, that by glancing back over the separate numbers of this monthly, we will have before us practically a complete history of the institution for that period."

When in 1907 the *Spectrum* changed from a monthly to a weekly the policy of the paper was reaffirmed. "There is no college or university more capable of supporting a weekly than the Agricultural College of North Dakota. The new paper is designed for two specific purposes: to increase college spirit and patriotism on the part of the students, and to increase the interest of North Dakota farmers and tradesmen in experimental work. . . ."

In 1915 the students adopted the commission form of government and the Student Commission published the *Spectrum*. The Commissioner of Publications, elected by students, appointed the editor-in-chief and was responsible for the publication of the paper. Here is a quotation in regard to the new *Spectrum* from the *Agassiz* of 1918:

"Since 1907, the *Spectrum* has passed through many changes. The form and size has been changed several times. The scope has been widened until the regular issue now reaches fully 3,000 readers every week — the number of papers issued being 1,200 to 1,300 per week. . . . The faculty has authorized the giving of credit for work done on the paper by the members of the staff, and a course in journalism has been started, the first classes having been given last fall."

The first college year book was published in 1907 by the Junior class. It was called the *Agassiz*, in honor of the noted naturalist. It represented a résumé of the year's college events, and contained descriptive accounts of the administration, faculty, student classes, student organizations and the outstanding accomplishments in athletics, dramatics, music, oratory and scholarship. The first issues included literary or humorous sections. In 1923 the name was changed to the *Bison*.

Following the general practice of the nineties and no doubt sponsored or promoted by faculty members, the first student organizations were almost entirely literary. The third *College Catalog*, in 1893–1894, includes the following statement: "The general culture of the students in writing and speaking is provided for in a literary society of which both ladies and gentlemen are received as members, and which is under the direct control of the student membership. Others will be organized to meet the demands of the growth of the school." [18]

This literary society was the first student controlled organization on the campus. It was known as the Athenian Literary Society and made its appearance on December 4, 1892. Its aim was "to develop the art of public speaking and literary work." It presented various programs consisting of "debates, declamations, readings, extemporaneous talks and musical numbers."

A rival society was organized in 1896, called the Philomathian, which after 1910 admitted only male members. Later the Castalian and Hesperian Societies were added. In 1899 the Agricultural Club was formed by fifteen students attending the winter short course, and it became the largest club on the campus and held essay contests and annual banquets with the home economics girls. It sponsored intersociety debates with the Power Machinery Club, with speakers on North Dakota rural life. Although it is no longer active on the campus, it is credited with having exercised a great influence on the rank and file of students, and for years its members, although scattered over the whole country, held fond remembrance of their association with the Agricultural Club.

Allied to the literary societies, and in most cases growing out of them, were the debating and dramatic clubs. In April 1906 a meeting of the Athenian and Philomathian Literary Societies was called to organize an oratorical association. Oratorical and other literary contests had been held in the early years of the College under the auspices of the Western League of Oratory, made up of the North Dakota and South Dakota Oratorial Leagues.[19]

The interest in dramatics and debating received a great stimulus by the appointment of Professor Alfred G. Arvold. He came to the College in 1907, hired "sight unseen" to teach speech. A graduate of the University of Wisconsin, his preparation consisted of several courses in speech at the University, a couple of years' experience as a high school teacher and a "craze for the theater." He took a great interest in the students. At the end of his first year he organized the Edwin Booth Dramatic Club, naming it after his favorite actor. The club was limited to fifteen students whose qualifications for membership were participation in plays, including at least one major role, a scholastic average of at least 85, sophomore standing and an interest and talent in dramatics. The purpose of the club was to create an interest in theatrical entertainment and to promote its practice at the North Dakota Agricultural College. Each spring Edwin Booth's anniversary was celebrated at the home of Professor Arvold.

Mr. Arvold was interested in all the students of the College and tried to help students get acquainted with one another. He promoted the Cyclone Circus, which was held Saturday, March 7, 1908. A parade was staged by the students in downtown Fargo and two performances were given in the Armory. The parade in three sections consisted of bands, floats, Coxey's army, carriages of faculty and marching students. It was headed by Mayor Elliot, President Worst, Major Ulio and Director General Arvold. The afternoon and evening performances included tumbling, wrestling, the "dip of Death," the Dixie quartette, the German band, numerous side shows and concessions. The whole show was voted an "immense success."

The next year, on the night of President Taft's inaugural, occurred the "Big Feed," a banquet attended by five hundred, among them leading Fargo citizens. Professor Arvold, toast master and general manager, was aided by a group of loyal and representative students. The whole affair was a pronounced success in securing student and faculty cooperation.

In 1911 on the night of Washington's birthday a non-partisan political convention was sponsored by the Board of Public Speaking Control in the Armory. The delegates arrived early and ate supper at the Y.W. counter in the Armory. At 6:30 p.m. the convention was called to order by Professor Arvold and a permanent organization effected. During the intermission that followed, a half hour concert was given by the band. The convention presented a platform, heard an address by the permanent chairman and various speeches nominating for the presidency Booker T. Washington, Champ Clark, Theodore Roosevelt, Robert M. LaFollette and Eugene Debs. Clark won out on the second ballot by a slight margin over LaFollette. Most of the credit for the success of the undertaking as a lesson in political methods went to Professor Arvold.

As a climax to the fall quarter of 1911 Professor Arvold promoted a successful festival of the four literary societies, the Athenian, Philomathean, Castalian and Hesperian. Each society staged a one-act play and the four societies competed in a song and yell contest. The evening closed with the "German Village" at which twenty-two kinds of food were served to the members of the literary societies and their friends. Those present declared the evening "the most interesting ever spent at the A.C."

The big event of 1911–12 was the All-College Banquet held in Ceres Hall dining room on March 7, 1912, at which William Jennings Bryan addressed four hundred boosters on "College Spirit." Mr. Arvold presided as toastmaster and called on Governor Burke, several students and others besides Mr. Bryan. The purpose of the banquet was to boost for a bigger and better "A.C." and in this respect it was successful. As the guests passed out of the hall, each addressed and dropped in a mail bag three post cards showing views of the campus, especially printed for this occasion, and stamped.

Finally, in January, 1913, the Student Life Special Train toured the State, visiting thirty towns, to acquaint the State with a picture of student life. The train consisted of two baggage cars containing exhibits illustrating the work of the various departments of the College, a dining car under the supervision of the home economics students and utilizing food produced by the College, a coach car equipped for a moving picture show, a sleeper for the men, and an observation compartment car for the young ladies, chaperoned by President and Mrs. Worst and Clark Kelley, president of the Board, and Mrs. Kelley. The participants numbered seventy, including the band, crack squad, orchestra, "Y" quartette, Edwin Booth Dramatic Club and home economics girls. The tour extended from Monday morning to Friday morning, managed and financed by students, with Professor Arvold as general supervisor. At Devils Lake, Minot and Bismarck evening programs were presented. The Great Northern Railway provided the equipment. It was a successful project both in advertising the College and in promoting loyalty among the students. The train was hailed as the first of its kind in America.

Professor Arvold's chief contribution to the College and to the State was the "Little Country Theater." When Mr. Arvold came to the North Dakota Agricultural College there was nothing like a proper stage on the campus. On the second floor of the Main Building there was a chapel unused for several years. Arvold saw its possibilities. It would take a lot of work, but that did not stop him. Eventually the college carpenter built a stage and proscenium arch. The State Legislature appropriated $3,000 to enlarge the seating capacity. However, this amount was not enough to cover the cost of new seats, stage fixtures and draperies.

Then Arvold decided that this theater should be a laboratory. He would experiment and see just what the people of small country towns or rural communities could accomplish if they were to build a similar theater. Plays and entertainments would supply the money needed to build and improve the theater at the College. The proceeds of all the plays were put back into the theater. "If the profit is only fifty cents, something is bought for the theater with that fifty cents, even if it is only a pot or pan for the kitchen."

Originally the Little Country Theater consisted of the converted chapel in College Hall, as the Main Building was then called. The seating capacity was two hundred. The stage was thirty feet wide and twenty feet deep. It had a proscenium opening ten feet high and fifteen feet wide. The color was green and gold, the gold predominating. The scenery was simple, the kind that could be constructed by anybody in a rural community, and so from a dingy, dull grey chapel there emerged a cheerful country life laboratory where all sorts of programs were tried out — a mecca where people met to discuss ways and means to make life in the open country — in God's garden — more attractive, more interesting and more entertaining. Mr. Arvold said the real purpose of the Little Country Theater "is to use the drama, and all that goes with the drama, as a force in getting people together and acquainted with one another. Instead of making the drama a luxury for the classes, its aim was to make it an instrument for the enlightenment and enjoyment of the masses." [20]

Music had its beginnings in connection with chapel services; Professor H. W. McArdle, as choir master, directed a chapel chorus and developed a male quartette and glee club; he also was instrumental in organizing mandolin and guitar clubs. Although he ceased to be musical director in 1903, he actively participated in the various concerts and operettas sponsored by his successor.

In the spring of 1903 Dr. Clarence S. Putnam began his long career as music director at the College. He came from a talented musical family; his mother was a gifted singer and his father a band director. He said he took up music when he was two years old. "My mother, a member of a choir, laid me behind the organ, and I sang in that choir as long as I was there. At six I carried the alto part alone." As a boy he played snare drums, alto and cornet in a band and at the age of 17 he was directing it. For a while he studied voice and theory and sang tenor in a large church choir.

A separate department of music was organized and in 1903 it offered courses, free of charge, in sight singing, chorus, and playing of band instruments, and for a fee lessons in voice and piano were available. It was no minor department, for the next years saw it develop into a growing concern. Although it was not a conservatory with a graduate course, it had six pianos and by 1908, had 172 music students. In 1906 the old chemistry building was turned over to the music department, which then offered instruction in voice, piano, string, orchestral and band instruments, in addition to training in chorus and glee club. Its staff consisted of Dr. Putnam and Miss Edythe H. Grasse.

Dr. Putnam's long career of music encompassed direction and creation of instrumental and vocal groups on the campus, performance at college and civic affairs, an active participation in community music and in the composition of college and state music. Chief among his musical compositions was the music for "The Yellow and the Green," composed to accompany the words written by Professor A. E. Minard. Professor Minard describes his writing of the song as follows:

"'The Yellow and the Green,' was written, as I recall it now, in the spring of 1908. Professor and Mrs. Bolley, at whose home I was staying, had spoken often of the need for a college song, and one Sunday afternoon some ideas began to take shape. The aim was to weave the college colors, yellow and green, with life and scenery characteristic of the State, for I thought that the verses, if they chanced to have any value, might make a state song as well as a college song.

"I had just come to North Dakota from the East in 1904 and had spent three weeks of 1905 in the harvest field, being No. 50 on the payroll of a big Grandin farm near Blanchard. It was my first experience in the wheat fields. My impressions were rather vivid: the throng of casual labor drifting in on freight cars, the endless yellow fields, the monotonous sweating labor from dawn until after dark and the mosquitoes and the prairie roses, the abundant eating and the wretched beds, all under a sky of marvelous height and sweep with the most gorgeous sunsets I had ever seen. Some of this I tried to embody in 'The Yellow and the Green'." [21]

THE YELLOW AND THE GREEN

Ho! a cheer for Green and Yellow
   Up with Yellow and the Green;
They're the shades that deck our prairies
   Far and wide with glorious sheen,
Fields of waving green in the spring-time,
   Golden yellow in the fall —
How the great high-arching Heaven
   Looks and laughs upon it all!

Here in autumn throng the nations,
   Just to gather in the spoil,
Throng on freight cars from the cities,
   Some to feast and some to toil,
Then the yellow grains flow eastward
   And the yellow gold flows back;
Barren cities boast their plenty
   And the prairies know no lack.

Hushed upon the boundless prairies
   Is the bison's thundering tread,
And the red man passes with him

> On his spoiler's bounty fed.
> But the Norse, the Celt and Saxon
> With their herds increase and find
> Mid these fields of green and yellow
> Plenty e'en for all mankind.
>
> Ho! a cheer for Green and Yellow
> Up with Yellow and the Green;
> They're the shades that deck our prairies
> Far and wide with glorious sheen,
> Fields of waving green in spring-time,
> Golden yellow in the fall —
> How the great high-arching Heaven
> Looks and laughs upon it all! [22]

Dr. Putnam put Professor Minard's words to music and this became the college song of the Agricultural College, sung by students and alumni standing with bare heads. Professor Minard also wrote a song which he entitled, "Our Alma Mater," which, however, did not gain the acclaim which "The Yellow and the Green" received. Dr. Putnam put this to music also and it was sung at various times, including the dedication of the library in 1906 and at the sixteenth annual Commencement in 1918. Dr. Putnam also composed the music for the North Dakota Hymn, the words of which were written by the North Dakota poet laureate, James W. Foley.

In the *Second Annual Catalog of 1893–1894*, there appears the following paragraph headed "religious exercises":

> "No instruction, sectarian in religion, or partisan in politics, is allowed in any department of the College.
> "The daily exercises of the College include a simple religious exercise consisting of reading, usually without comment, of a portion of the scripture, followed by the Lord's Prayer in concert, and the singing of a hymn. All students are required to be in attendance, unless excused by some member of the faculty.
> "Students are given opportunity, and are expected to attend the services of the church of their choice at least once each Sabbath Day. The churches of Fargo include the Presbyterian, Congregational, Methodist, Baptist, Episcopal, Roman Catholic, Unitarian and Norwegian Lutheran, all of which welcome students to their congregations."

A circular of information about the College under the heading, "Religious and Social Advantages," announced already in 1898–99 that a "YMCA is organized at the College. It meets Sunday at 3:00 p.m. and all students are urged to attend." In the *Catalog for 1901–02* this paragraph is found in regard to YMCA activities at the College:

Student Life, 1890–1916

"Preparations have been made to send a student to the Student Conference which will be held next June at Lake Geneva, Wisconsin, for special instruction in the organization and management of YMCA work."

Thomas F. Manns, then engaged in graduate work, was one of the YMCA's active promotors; M. H. Fallis was the first president. The objective of the YMCA, as presented in its constitution, is to "develop the student, morally, mentally, and physically." The first meetings were held in classrooms. Most of the early socials were held in Francis Hall. However, in April, 1902, the organization was granted a meeting room in Engineering Building. The first socials were restricted to members, but later were open to the male student body. To these "stag socials" were soon added freshmen "get-togethers." In 1910 the first joint YM-YW student body receptions were held. Bible classes were held in the college chapel on Sunday afternoons. These meetings, moderately attended at first, became an inspiration to the members of the organizations.

During 1908–09 several joint meetings of the YMCA and YWCA were held. Prominent national figures were invited to speak to the students. Since this received a favorable response, this custom was continued for several years. Leading members of the YMCA during the early period included T. F. Manns, M. H. Fallis, O. W. Dynes and Ray Babcock. Activities included vesper service, deputation teams, bean dinners, "two-bit" dinners, "kiddies' " parties, all college mixers, College handbook, intramural athletics, employment bureau, and a "Red Triangle Auxiliary." The local group began at that time to send delegates to the Geneva Conference and state conventions. Ray Sweetman, prominent in Y history, was resident secretary for many years.

Membership grew so rapidly that quarters in "Old Main" became untenable. The year 1913 is outstanding in "Y" history for at that time, a professional secretary was secured in the person of Ray Sweetman, a man of "tireless energy with a talent for organization." Under his inspiration, a building was contemplated. Contributions of $100 each came from the "visionary twelve," consisting of C. R. Dynes, Geo. W. Gustafson, Dean Mendenhall, Dave Sonquist, Clarence Walter, C. A. Williams, Carl Yerrington, John Horne, George Stewart, Ted Stoa, Clarence Wolstad and Matt Thorfinnson. In 1915 a group of NDAC students started out with the slogan — "Ten thousand dollars or more in six days from the students and faculty of NDAC for a YMCA building!" The sum of $18,000 was raised, and $22,000 was donated by the city of Fargo. Ten thousand dollars more was needed to bring the total to $50,000 in order to receive a grant of $25,000 from the Rockefeller Institute. This was raised by student solicitors traveling throughout North Dakota in "rented Fords." Professor I. W. Smith played a prominent part in the final financial settlement. The building was completed in 1920. After completion, a small operating margin was left for the next few years. Until it was demolished by the 1957 tornado the YMCA building continued to be the meeting place for many organizations, religious and non-religious. It contained facilities for a varied recreational program.

The earliest exclusively women's organization on the campus was the Edith Hill Club, formed in memory of Miss Edith Hill, shortly after the College was organized in 1890. It met on alternate Friday afternoons. "Its object was to help in the social life of the girls and awaken interest along lines that promote general culture and refinement." This organization evolved into the Edith Hill Young Women's Christian Association, which was "organized in March, 1906, by the State Y. W. Secretary of North Dakota, Miss Myra B. Fishback, for the purpose of developing the spiritual, physical, social and intellectual life of the girls on the campus." During its early years it sent delegates to the annual summer conference at Lake Geneva, Wisconsin, held bi-weekly devotional meetings, organized Bible and mission classes, and sponsored personal annual "Big Sister" movements, "YW teas," the YM-YW mixer, the co-ed prom, and the socials at the Florence Crittenden Home.

The YWCA was managed by a student cabinet, aided by an advisory board of faculty women. Its many activities included the annual Big-Little Sister Party, the YW Freshman Party, the YM-YW Kiddies' Party, the YM-YW marriage course, and the "Show Your Religions" series. In addition, many social activities and annual trips to Lake Geneva were carried out.

So far little mention has been made of social fraternities. As long as the College was new and the enrollment small there seemed little need for special groups other than literary societies, departmental clubs and religious organizations. But there was bound to be agitation for fraternal groups with the increase of numbers of students. The movement started at the University of North Dakota and the Agricultural College followed suit.

The Alpha Mu fraternity was organized January 10, 1904, by a few of the men students to form a closer acquaintance and gain general good fellowship. The group was favored by the administration and elected President Worst, Dr. Ladd and Professor Keene honorary members. A room was secured in the Mechanical Building and fitted up for a lounge. The local group had a steady gradual growth in numbers and included the chief social, athletic and scholastic leaders on the campus. On May 12, 1917, it was admitted to Theta Chi, a national fraternity.

The oldest national fraternity became the Dacotah chapter of Alpha Zeta June 8, 1909, through the influence of Professor Doneghue. Its chief emphasis is on scholarship and the study of agricultural problems, yet it seeks to promote bonds of fellowship. The leading members of the agricultural staff belong to it as well as superior undergraduates, so it functions chiefly as an honorary society.

The first sorority, Delta Phi Beta, was organized in the winter of 1908 with nine charter members. It secured as patrons two members of the domestic science staff and was able to meet in a "cozy club room" in Ceres Hall. After a steady growth as a local club it became a chapter of Kappa Kappa Gamma in 1929. In 1912 the faculty adopted a general policy regarding fraternities and other secret organizations of the students. Each such organization was to submit a proposed constitution, which would limit membership to those who attained a standing of 80 per cent, and would admit no students below the sophomore year.

On March 24, 1913, a chapter of Alpha Gamma Rho was organized on the campus, under the sponsorship of the president of the College and members of the agricultural staff. It has opened its ranks usually, but not exclusively, to students in the School of Agriculture. Home economics followed suit in 1915. Phi Upsilon Omicron recognized the local group which had organized under the name of Chi Gamma Psi. This organization, popularly known as Phi U, has done much to promote higher scholarship in home economics; as such it is somewhat of a counterpart to Alpha Zeta, the honorary agricultural fraternity. Several student organizations such as the Lyceum of Engineers (1900), Alpha Zeta for agricultural students (1910) and the Pharmacy Club (1902) were sponsored by faculty members and developed into honor societies.

With the close of President Worst's administration and the outbreak of World War I student life and organization ceased to be closely directed by faculty leadership. The students became more independent, more sophisticated, more inclined to take the initiative themselves. The growing maturity of the College is reflected in the thinking and the attitude of the students of later years.

FOOTNOTES

[1] North Dakota Agricultural College Faculty Record, Oct. 22, 1890, 3–4.
[2] H. L. Bolley, "Early Days at the A.C.," *College and State*, VII, 3 (Nov., 1923).
[3] Jessamine S. Burgum, "Reminiscences," *Spectrum*, LII, No. 6 (Oct. 16, 1936), 6.
[4] "History of the North Dakota Agricultural College," *Seventeenth Annual Commencement Program* (June 2–6, 1911), 18–24.
[5] *North Dakota Agricultural College Annual Catalog*, 1901–2, 9; in the catalog of 1904–5, 7, there is added: "By midsummer, the Fargo and Moorhead Street Railway will be completed and will run cars directly to the College grounds."
[6] Burgum, Reminiscences, 7.
[7] Prospectus, 19.
[8] North Dakota Agricultural College, *Third Annual Catalog*, 50.
[9] *Spectrum*, IV, 78 (Feb. 15, 1900).
[10] *College and State*, VII, 1 (September, 1923), 6.
[11] *Weekly Spectrum*, XV, 3 (Oct. 13, 1908), 2.
[12] *Weekly Spectrum*, XXI, 14 (Jan. 13, 1914), 1.
[13] *College and State*, VI, 1 (Oct., 1922), 9.
[14] Geiger, 240.
[15] *Spectrum*, Feb., 1898, 12.
[16] Geiger, 241.
[17] *Agassiz 1917*, student year book.
[18] *Third Annual Catalog*, 50.
[19] *Spectrum*, Dec., 1896, 3, June, 1897, 9; *Agassiz*, 1908.
[20] A. G. Arvold, *The Little Country Theater — Yesterday — Today — Tomorrow* (Fargo, N.D.A.C. n.d.).
[21] A. E. Minard, papers, North Dakota Institute of Regional Studies, Library, N.D.A.C.
[22] *Spectrum*, XVI, No. 2, 3 (Oct. 8, 1909).

◄ CHAPTER VI ►

Politics and War, 1916-1920

IT is impossible to understand the circumstances surrounding the removal of President Worst in 1916 and the appointment of President Ladd without reviewing the political and economic conditions in the State, as they existed in the first decades of the twentieth century. Throughout this period, adverse weather conditions or plant diseases cut North Dakota's agricultural production below normal, especially in the western part of the State. As a result, when higher prices did come, the farmer often had little grain to sell. His assets, largely in land, were immobile. Taxes and fixed charges were high. Loan companies in general found it difficult to renew mortgages because their money found more profitable investment in war enterprises. Foreclosures were frequent, and loan companies went into receivership. Grain growers felt that unjust tribute was being levied on them by the great grain exchanges and by the rules prevailing in the eastern terminal markets to which all grain raised in North Dakota was sent.

An educational campaign which had been carried on for several years by the College had emphasized the tremendous loss to the State, not only from dockage and mixing of grades, but also from the drainage of the wealth of the farmer to creditors in distant states, with no prospect of return under the system of marketing then prevailing.

Stimulated by the leadership of Senator Robert M. LaFollette in Wisconsin and Theodore Roosevelt in the nation, North Dakota was one of the first states to initiate and adopt a progressive legislative program. In 1911 the Legislature enacted a primary election law. It also took a step toward simplifying government by creating a board of control for the charitable, penal and reformatory institutions, called the Board of Administration. It also created the State Board of Normal School Trustees. The next Legislature ratified the 17th amendment providing for popular election of United States senators; it also provided for the preparation of a budget. The Legislature of 1915 centralized the control of all the state educational institutions in the State Board of Regents by a law passed on March 4, 1915. Suffrage reform provided that the superintendent of public instruction and county superintendents of schools, as well as judges, should be nominated and elected by non-partisan ballots. The same Legislature passed a woman's suffrage act, but attached a referendum clause and the measure was defeated in the general election.

The constitution of the State was amended in 1912 by a measure allowing the Legislature to provide for the erection or purchase of terminal grain elevators in Minnesota or Wisconsin. In 1914 the people were granted direct power of legislation through the initiative and referendum, and the power of amending the constitution by the use of the initiative. A hail insurance department of the state government was set up and a tax commission was created. Thus a series of novel and revolutionary, if not radical, reforms had been enacted by a willing governor and Legislature, both without doubt representative of the people.

In 1914 the voters ratified the constitutional amendment giving the Legislature authority to build, buy and operate a terminal grain elevator in North Dakota. In the 1915 Legislature a bill was presented to provide for a state owned elevator. The debate over its passage brought out that elevators in Manitoba and elsewhere in Canada had been operated by the provinces at a loss, and so the measure failed to pass.

On May 8, 1914, the Federal Smith-Lever Act created the Cooperative Agricultural Extension Service. In North Dakota legislative action was taken in 1915 and with Federal support the North Dakota Extension Division was established on the campus. Director Cooper of the Experiment Station became also director of the Extension Division. When he resigned in 1917, the Extension Division came under the authority of President Ladd, who recalled Gordon W. Randlett, a graduate of the N.D.A.C. in 1908, from South Dakota Agricultural College to be director of the Extension Division. Mr. Randlett had been in charge of college extension work at N.D.A.C. from 1907 to 1914. The extension staff was moved to the second floor of the "new wing in Science Hall," now the central section of Minard Hall.

It was during the time when the Legislature was debating the elevator bill in February, 1915, that Arthur C. Townley conceived the idea of the Nonpartisan League. Townley was a master of organization and he maintained that it was only by organization that the farmers could exert enough pressure to get what they wanted. Townley drew up a program of five planks:

> State ownership of terminal elevators, flour mills, packing houses and cold storage plants;
> State inspection of grain and grain dockage;
> Exemption of farm improvements from taxation;
> State hail insurance on the acreage tax basis;
> Rural credit banks operated at cost.[1]

In order to organize the League, Townley went out among the farmers and by the end of the year the League claimed a membership of about 30,000, with dues paid in advance.[2] The plan of the League was to capture the Republican Party, and in 1916 this was accomplished. By 1917 the executive offices, a majority of the house and a majority of the new senators were elected by the League. However, the League program failed to get through the Legislature because of an adverse majority in the Senate and because of the debt limit set by the State Constitution.

Finally, the election of 1918 gave the League complete control over both houses of the Legislature. At the same time, the people had voted to increase the $2,000,000 debt limit of the State to $10,000,000. The Legislature of 1919, therefore, set up an industrial commission, made up of the governor, the attorney general and the commissioner of agriculture and labor to "conduct . . . certain utilities . . . now hereafter established by law." At the same session a State Bank was chartered, a State Mill and Elevator established and a Home Building Association formed.

It is not the purpose of the writer to discuss the workings of this League program in detail, but only in so far as it affected the management of the College. The result of one of the progressive reforms of the era was the movement toward a greater centralization of administration. It was believed that a greater sense of responsibility on the part of the governor would secure a more efficient supervision of various state agencies.

The College was originally put in the charge of a board of directors, or trustees, who were appointed by the governor. They tended to be more or less local and were subject to the popular opinion of the community in which the College was located. These trustees were able business and professional men, who had only a limited proportion of their time available to give to the management of the institution, and in addition, probably were unable to gain an adequate insight into its affairs. Moreover, the various boards of the individual institutions in the State vied with one another for financial and popular support and duplication resulted. In 1913 the Legislature created a Board of Education to secure greater uniformity by means of classification and inspection. This was a step toward concentration of authority and responsibility by superseding the Board of Examiners and the Agricultural and Training School Board.

In January, 1915, Governor Hanna, a right wing Republican, recommended that a committee from the Senate and House should make a "thorough examination of conditions at the State University, the State Agricultural College and all other educational institutions in order that the charge of extravagance and other charges that have been made may be proved or disproved and the truth made known to the people of the state."[3] He also recommended that a law be passed that should place all the institutions of higher education under a Board of Regents. He held that where there is a board that is representative of only one institution, naturally that board is only interested in that institution.

A report of the Joint Committee on Appropriations, sent to the Senate on February 5, 1915, also recommended the creation of a State Board of Regents "for the purpose of economy, to give the taxpayers more nearly the value of their money, to create a definite system of education, to prevent duplication and competition among institutions." They claimed that salary increases were beyond the financial resources of a pioneer commonwealth, that the state educational institutions were "possibly unconsciously competitors of each other," that they were building up at each other's expense and thus producing "competition, overlapping and duplication," that as a result many thousands of dollars were added needlessly to the tax burden of the State, and that the efficiency of the schools was reduced.[4]

The Board of Regents, appointed by Governor Hanna, met on July 8, 1915, and organized by electing Lewis F. Crawford president and Charles Brewer secretary. A survey of the state educational institutions was required by a law recently enacted by the Legislature. The Board decided to ask the United States Bureau of Education, Department of the Interior, to conduct the survey with the understanding that the Board wanted "all the educational institutions to be state institutions in the broadest sense, rather than local institutions with local rivalries." On October 6, 1915, Dr. P. P. Claxton, U. S. Commissioner of Education, notified the Board that he had assigned Dr. William T. Bawden, specialist in vocational education, for the U. S. Bureau of Education, to assist him in the work of the survey. On October 20 the Board employed Dr. Edwin B. Craighead, former president of the University of Montana, to assist in the survey. On

December 24, Commissioner Claxton appointed Dean Lotus D. Coffman of the School of Education of the University of Minnesota to serve as the fourth member of the survey commission.[5]

The recommendations made by the survey in regard to the Agricultural College may be summarized as follows: "The State Department of Education should be enlarged to supply the demands of the secondary schools of the state for teachers of agriculture and domestic science. The North Dakota Agricultural College should devote its energies and means to instruction in agriculture and its courses in liberal arts and science should be considered only as service courses. Instruction in pharmacy should be continued and expanded. The President of the College should have general control of the Experiment Station and be held responsible to the Board of Regents. The High School at the college should be discontinued. Courses in engineering, and architecture should be limited to agricultural and industrial engineering, and to elementary mechanical engineering." [6]

This report disregarded the provisions of the Morrill Act, which sought "to promote the liberal and practical education of the industrial classes in the several pursuits and professions in life." It also ignored or failed to observe the wording of the legislative act establishing the College which stated: "The course of instruction shall embrace the English language and literature, mathematics, military tactics, civil engineering, agricultural chemistry, animal and vegetable anatomy and physiology, the veterinary art, geology, and such other natural sciences as may be prescribed, political and rural and household economy, horticulture, moral philosophy, history, bookkeeping, and especially the application of science and the mechanic arts to practical agriculture in the field." [7]

On July 7, 1916, Dr. Craighead was elected State Commissioner of Education at a salary of $5,000, effective August 1. An editorial in the *Fargo Forum* of August 5, 1916, complained of the delay in determining the status of the North Dakota Agricultural College. It referred to reports in the Nonpartisan *Leader* and reports from the University that the College was to be "made a secondary institution, devoted almost exclusively to the teaching of purely agricultural courses." This would set up a horizontal line of cleavage by which students might take two years at the College, and then go elsewhere to complete their courses. The *Fargo Forum* advocated the perpendicular cleavage, as was true at Iowa State College, Kansas Agricultural College and Oregon Agricultural College. "The people of Fargo are especially proud of the North Dakota Agricultural College . . .

and do not propose to stand by and see it changed to the shell of its former self."

Meanwhile, in March, 1916, Dr. Ladd was appointed to the presidency on a temporary basis. In an autobiography, B. F. Spaulding in regard to this appointment comments as follows: "When President Worst was relieved of his position as the head of the College, the Board had not found a man they thought would fill the bill. Ladd was accordingly asked to serve as Acting President until a suitable man was found. He accepted on the condition that they would leave off the prefix 'acting', but assured the Board that he would resign after receiving notice that a man with the desired qualifications had been found. It has been reported by thoroughly reliable members of the Board that when the Secretary was about to enter his agreement in the records of the meeting, that a member, Mr. J. A. Power, suggested this would be a reflection on Ladd, and that his word could be safely taken. Humanity is fallible and sometimes forgetful. When the Board was ready to act and called on the Professor, it is said that he had experienced a loss of memory, and had no recollection of having been elected as a temporary president, or that there had been any understanding that he would resign whenever the Board desired to replace him by a permanent president. His activities as described through his publicity agencies had so ingratiated him into the favor of the people, and especially the ladies, that the Board did not deem it politically expedient to make a change, and he was permitted to serve until the Non-Partisans elected him to the Senate." [8]

In what might be termed his inaugural address, on February 29, 1916, Dr. Ladd made it quite clear that "he would let no big or little business run the institution."[9] He was favorably accepted by the students and faculty, as it was well known that he was an ally of the former president. Also, his popularity throughout the State insured his continuation as president of the College.

At its October, 1916, meeting the Board accepted the plan of a college reorganization proposed by President Ladd. The following schools were created: Agriculture, C. B. Waldron, dean; Chemistry and Pharmacy, E. F. Ladd, dean; Education, A. D. Weeks, dean; Home Economics, Katherine Jensen, head; Mechanic Arts, E. S. Keene, dean; Veterinary Science, L. Van Es, dean; Applied Sciences and Biology, H. L. Bolley, dean. The total enrollment at the College on November 10, 1916, was 515, of which 215 were in the college proper, 117 in vocational courses and 113 in high school.

Some changes in staff occurred during the five years of President Ladd's adminstration. Although he remained dean of the School of

Chemistry, Dr. W. T. Pearce, University of Chicago, was appointed to carry on the work of the department of paint chemistry.

Dr. L. Van Es was appointed acting director of the Experiment Station upon the resignation of Director Cooper in January, 1918. His international reputation as a veterinarian, his skill as a linguist and his demonstrated ability as an executive warranted the appointment. President Ladd said that Dr. Van Es was thoroughly trained in scientific methods, with a keen appreciation of the needs and the value of research as applied to agriculture and would devote all his time and thought to the development of this important and essential field as a feeder for college educational work and for the extension workers in the field.

After a few months, Dr. Van Es resigned in April, 1918. In July, 1918 P. F. Trowbridge, A.B., University of Michigan, Ph. D., University of Illinois, who had spent a year in Germany and had served as head of the department of agricultural chemistry and research at the University of Missouri, was elected director of the Experiment Station. He served for sixteen years, after which he became director emeritus.

In 1917 F. W. Christensen of Kansas State College was secured for research and teaching in animal nutrition. In the same decade Harlow L. Walster, Ph. D., University of Chicago, was appointed agronomist, Cap. E. Miller, M.S., Iowa State College, to the department of farm management, E. S. Reynolds, Ph.D., to the department of botany, and C. I. Nelson, to the department of bacteriology. Miss Katherine Jensen, a graduate of North Dakota Agricultural College, who had come in 1912 from Kansas State College as an instructor in cooking, was appointed head of the School of Home Economics in 1916.

After Professor Ladd became president of the College, two members of the faculty, Milbraith and Mercer, who were assistants in botany, accused Dean Bolley of unprofessional acts. President Ladd appointed a committee of Dean Keene, Dr. Van Es and Dean Waldron to investigate the charges. Their report was submitted to the Board. Milbraith and Mercer appeared before the Board and a subcommittee of the Board was named to visit the College, with power to act. Dismissal of the two accusers followed, but the two instructors were given blank recommendations, saying they were capable and conscientious workers.

This action resulted in the organization of a college teachers' organization which became affiliated with the American Federation of Teachers with the understanding that it would be a non-striking organization. Miss Ada Meadows and Professor Casper Nelson were the

College representatives at the meetings at the Labor Temple. This college teachers' union was recognized by the Board of Regents, two of the Board members being quite sympathetic to it.

A *Blue Book*, the code of rules for the governing of the College had been published in 1913. This code, considered a constitution, was revised now by a committee of the college teachers' organization consisting of Messrs. Reynolds, Slocum, Minard, Nelson, Weeks and Miss Dworak; it also had the cooperation of Dr. John M. Gillette of the University of North Dakota in formulating a uniform code. The Board of Regents accepted these revisions.

The outgrowth of this situation resulted in the adoption by the faculty of a constitution previously submitted by Commissioner Craighead with amendments suggested by President Ladd. The motion recommended its adoption by the Board of Regents. This new constitution, still called the *Blue Book*, was approved by the Board of Regents at its meeting on April 16, 1917. The constitution provided for a Council, which was made up of the president, the deans, directors, professors and associate professors, and assistant professors who had gained permanent tenure (three years); the director of the Experiment Station and of the Extension Division were also members of the Council. Beginning with May 17, 1917 the minutes of the Council take the place of the previous Faculty Record.

In 1916 the Nonpartisan League was successful in electing the governor and a majority of the members of the Legislature. Governor Lynn Frazier assumed office in January, 1917, and he and Attorney Aubrey Lawrence maintained that the appointments to the Board of Regents by Governor Hanna were illegal on the ground that he had "appointed the board on March 2, 1915, two days before there was any law for the establishment of such a body" [10] and therefore the new governor sought to oust the members of the Board appointed by Governor Hanna. The House of Representatives passed the Board of Regents bill, known as House Bill 65, which called for the abolition of the existing board and the establishing of a new one. It was strictly a League bill, which, according to the League, was in line with the purpose of placing the College in the hands of a board that was friendly to the farmer. The League was particularly aggrieved against the old board because of the investigations that had resulted in the dismissal of Dr. Worst.

Governor Frazier and the five appointees of a new Board of Regents appointed by the governor called at the office of the old Board and demanded that the office and the records be turned over to them. The Board of Regents refused to relinquish their posts, maintaining that they were appointed for definite terms. Their position was upheld by the Supreme Court and by the Senate, which defeated House Bill 65 by a vote of 26 to 17. When their terms expired, Governor Frazier appointed Rev. C. E. Vermilyea of Valley City to the Board in August to succeed Frank White who resigned. Robert Muir of Sarles and George A. Totten of Bowman were appointed in October. The Board was reorganized and in July, 1918, Muir was definitely accepted as president.

This period of friction was recognized and explained by President Ladd in a statement which appeared in the *North Dakota Farmer,* July 15, 1917:

"I keenly regret that I am forced to make any public statement but duty and loyalty to the College compel me at this time to do so. For seven years the Agricultural College has been the football of politics, kicked about by petty politicians and one group or party in the past has not been one whit better than another. They have not striven for the upbuilding of the college as an educational institution to one-half the extent they have to gain control of its policy or to further their own schemes and ambitions and this to the disgrace of our educational system and state betterment.

"At an adjourned meeting of the board of regents in May a member of the faculty was being, as I thought, unfairly criticized, and I defended, as well as I could, his course, when Mr. Crawford said that if I had been a real president I would have demanded his resignation within 24 hours of the occurrence and my action would have been approved by the board. After further comment and discussion Mr. Crawford asked me to resign as president of the college. . . . No one regrets more keenly than I the dragging of these matters into the public press, but they are beyond my control and will be as long as petty politics dominate and compel subserviency to their demands.

"It is said that I have too much work. I grant I have plenty to do. It is not the work that injures or kills, but petty annoyances and worry because of such annoyances. Besides, I have a devoted body of loyal workers among my associates in the faculty who have aided me.

"There has never been a more loyal and devoted faculty than that of the Agricultural College during the past year. . . . We all come short of what we would like to do. If at times I have seemed unsympathetic, you may now catch a glimpse of the trials that have made it necessary.

"What I am here forced to say is with no feeling of ill will toward any one, and I shall regret it if any one is forced to feel otherwise towards me, but petty politics can never be made to mix with the spirit of true education and research. My work and its results I am willing to leave to the will of the common people whom I have endeavored to serve during these years." [11]

The entrance of the United States into World War I in 1917 had a direct influence on the College, causing a considerable decrease in attendance. Organizations and faculty and staff were depleted by calls from the government, and also by a general scarcity of teachers. Competition with outside institutions forced the Board of Regents to ask for additional funds from the Legislature to make up for higher costs, including increases in salaries.

During World War I there was a desire on the part of the younger faculty members to enlist in the armed forces. Metcalf, professor of zoology, who later was one of the inventors of the Magnovox, secured a commission which paid considerably more than his salary at the College. Others wished to follow his example, but President Ladd obtained an order from the War Department that any member of the staff who wished to enlist should inform him and he would assign him to private military rank and retain his services as a teacher. All the faculty members were put on a twelve months' basis without an increase in salary. One of them finally proved that this order was contrary to his contract and after two years was reimbursed for his extra teaching load.

At the request of the Federal Government and with the consent of the State Council of Defense, the Board of Regents approved the erection of an emergency building for the use of soldiers in training under government direction. The building, now known as Dakota Hall, was constructed in nine weeks in 1918. It covered over 20,000 square feet and provided room for sleeping and feeding of over 400 men. Fargo carpenters, college instructors and students donated time for much of its construction.[12]

In the fall of 1918 one hundred and fifty men were enrolled in the Student Army Training Corps programs as engineers in the School of Mechanic Arts, and instructed by members of that school. Various members of the faculty were assigned to teach the "War Issues" course. Dr. Murphy was to be in charge of the corps for the fall term, Professor Weeks for the winter and Professor Minard for the spring term. Dr. Dolt, Dr. Trowbridge, Professor Waldron and Professor Shepperd were to deliver certain lectures for the fall term. Major Steele was the commandant. The program was interrupted by the Armistice in November.

The close of the war period left the College with certain barracks buildings which were used to increase its dormitory facilities. There was, therefore, no difficulty in caring for the increased attendance following the end of the war. President Ladd at this time published the following circular:

"RETURNED SOLDIERS
HOW TO GET AN EDUCATION

"Every man from North Dakota who served in any branch of war work for the government is entitled to $25.00 per month for each month or part of a

month for which he served. This the State of North Dakota will pay you. The money is to be used for one of the following purposes:
1. To secure an education;
2. To acquire and improve a farm;
3. To build and improve a home.

"If you have served in the Army or Navy, say for twenty months, you are then entitled to $500.00 from the state which may be used for the purpose of securing an education. The Agricultural College invites you to consider the advantages offered at this institution for acquiring an education and for so improving your earning power as to give you greater efficiency and an enlarged income for the balance of your life.

"The State wants you to get the most out of life, to become an efficient and successful citizen. Are you interested in some branch of farming . . . in grain buying . . . in auto mechanics . . . in business and commercial courses? . . . Do you want to fit yourself as a teacher . . . a county agent . . . for pharmacy, or for newspaper work? Then come to the Agricultural College and we can aid you to greater opportunities to a broader life and an enlarged earning power.

"The winter term opens January 5th, 1920".[13]

A considerable number of World War I veterans took advantage of this offer, among them Theodore Martel, who later became State Commissioner of Agriculture and Labor and thus ex-officio a member of the Board of Administration.

In January, 1918, upon recommendation of the State Board of Education, the North Dakota Agricultural College was named as the institution authorized to train teachers in vocational subjects under the provisions of the Federal Smith-Hughes Act. This work has steadily developed until it has become one of the more important features of the State's educational activities. At the beginning of the school year, 1940-41, there were 44 Smith-Hughes teachers in agriculture and 69 teaching home economics in the State. Since the Smith-Hughes teachers in agriculture were employed on a twelve-month basis, their service to the community included advice and assistance to the patrons of the school throughout the year.

On May 9, 1920, the *Fargo Courier-News* carried an article by Sidney W. Hooper in regard to the record of the College Extension Division for services in grasshopper and gopher control, in sweet clover, wheat, corn, alfalfa and seed potatoes demonstrations, in sheep breeding and farmers' exchanges. Such services and possible savings to the farmers of the State amounted to almost seven million dollars, a saving of $32.86 per dollar spent. In addition, boys' and girls' clubs and home demonstration work had been developed throughout the State by the Extension Division.

At the May, 1918, Board meeting Professor H. W. McArdle was elected to the position of secretary of the College, a position which he held until his death in 1933. At the meeting in June the contracts were let for the construction of an addition to the central part of Science Hall. This created classrooms and offices for the departments of English, modern languages, history, education, economics and for overflow classes from other departments. At the April, 1919, meeting of the Board, former president J. H. Worst was unanimously elected to the position of President Emeritus at the request of the Sixteenth Legislative Assembly, as expressed in the following resolution:

"Whereas, Dr. John H. Worst performed, with honor and fidelity, the duty of President of the State Agricultural College of the State of North Dakota for more than twenty years, and

"Whereas, he at all times served the interests of the common men and women of this State and worked for the promotion of their happiness and prosperity, and opposed the special interests that prey upon the needs of our people, and

"Whereas, he refused to interfere or deny the right of academic freedom of thought or speech, and

"Whereas, as a teacher he taught truth without fear or favor, and as President of the Agricultural College administered his office with firm and impartial justice, and

"Whereas, his services to this State, as President of the Agricultural College, teacher in our schools, and citizen, are worthy of the highest commendation and honor, now therefore

"Be is Resolved, by the Senate and House of Representatives concurring, that we petition, recommend, and earnestly request the State Board of Regents to create the office of President Emeritus of the State College, and to appoint Dr. John H. Worst, President Emeritus and that a copy of this resolution be forwarded to the members of the Board of Regents, and to Dr. John H. Worst." [14]

At this same Board meeting he was appointed Student Counselor and Lecturer at a salary of $1,800 a year.

In 1919 the Legislature, following Governor Frazier's recommendation, enacted Senate Bill No. 134, establishing the Board of Administration to supervise and administer "all State Penal, Charitable and Educational Institutions." The Board was to consist of five members: the State Superintendent of Public Instruction, Miss Minnie Nielson of Valley City, the Commissioner of Agriculture and Labor, John S. Hagen of Deering, ex officio, and three other members to be appointed by the governor, Robert T. Muir of Sarles, George A. Totten of Bowman and P. M. Casey of Fargo. The Board of Administration therefore superseded the Board of Education and the Board of Regents.

Opposition to this change in institutional administration came from several sources. It came from political forces opposed to the Nonpartisan League, from the State Superintendent of Public Instruction, and from some of the school superintendents in the State. It also came from teachers' associations influenced by them, from certain professors in institutions of higher education, from Dr. George D. Strayer, professor of educational administration in Columbia University, and from textbook publishers. The most serious of the objections came from Dr. Strayer, who addressed the legislative committee of the State Educational Association at Minot, April 18, 1919, saying:

"The law violates the most fundamental principle of educational administration, that of differentiation between the law control of public education and the professional administration of our schools . . . which should be, and usually is, placed in the hands of a state superintendent of schools or a commissioner of education, together with a staff working with this officer." [15]

The writer of the report of the Board of Administration, presumably its secretary or president, defended the change in institutional administration on the grounds that Dr. Strayer's objections were "lacking in political vision or social justice," that "educators have a tendency to serve the interests of reaction and the existing order with its inherent and inherited evils," and that the State Superintendent of Schools and county and city school officials are elected and may not be the wisest choices. The report further quotes from the first *Biennial Report of the State Board of Administration of Kansas* (5-7) which had also unified the administration of its educational, charitable and penal institutions. [16] However, the policy of placing the educational and eleemosynary institutions under the same board led to political control in Kansas and was subsequently superseded.

At a meeting of the Board of Administration in December, 1919, the matter of salary adjustments was considered in order to bring salaries more nearly in line with the increased cost of all commodities and expenses in general. It was decided that an increase of from fifteen to twenty-five per cent would be necessary to put salaries on an equitable basis. But because of lack of funds not all of these increases could be allowed.

Under the heading of "Wages and Salaries" in the Board's statement of general policies in the *First Annual Report* appears the following:

"It is the policy and purpose of the Board of Administration to pay all its employees not only sufficient to permit a bare living but a decent living. . . .

"A salary of $3,000 is in purchasing power now no larger than a salary of about $1,500 was a few years ago. Incomes, whether from wages, salaries, business enterprise or farming, must necessarily be readjusted . . . two points of serious importance: first, the cost of living has gone up for state employees as well as others, while salaries have remained more nearly stationary, which means in effect an actual diminution in real income; secondly, the state of North Dakota cannot expect to obtain and retain the services of first-class scholars, scientists, engineers and teachers unless it pays them as high salaries as other states pay. . . .

"It may be worth while to call attention to the wrong practice now generally in vogue in American colleges and universities — including our own — of rewarding administrative ability, real and alleged, far more liberally than scientific ability or attainment." [17]

In connection with this situation the report includes a communication, dated June 2, 1919, from the college teachers organization of the Agricultural College, signed by Katherine Jensen, secretary, citing the purposes of the organization to be: the development and maintenance of higher educational standards; increased efficiency in educational institutions; greater democratization of the educational system; development and maintenance of conditions favorable to the accomplishment of the above principles. The organization hoped to affiliate with the American Federation of Teachers in "promoting educational development in a period of crisis in teaching as a profession." [18]

The report also includes a letter from President Ladd, dated October 22, 1919, enclosing salary comparisons of the University of North Dakota, the Montana Agricultural College, the South Dakota Agricultural College and the North Dakota Agricultural College: "We are paying the assistant professors and instructors in proportion to what other institutions are paying, but when it comes to the more important positions, deans, heads of departments and full professors, we are woefully lacking because we have not had the funds in the past to raise the salaries as we should have done."

In commenting on the organization of teachers, the same report says:

"There is an inevitable and natural desire on the part of the teachers at the College to improve their economic status, often painful, since the tremendous increase in prices; but the movement is due also to a desire for a more democratic form of management within the colleges and universities than has heretofore been practiced in the United States."

In August, 1919, the Board met with representatives of the faculty and with President Ladd. Professors Nelson and Slocum stated that assistant professors and instructors had no voice in the administration, that faculty employment was uncertain and that salaries were inadequate. A special meeting of the general faculty was called for December 10, 1919, to elect a committee to confer with the Board of Administration in regard to the proposed restoration of salaries.

Professors Weeks, Nelson, and Minard and Directors Trowbridge and Randlett were chosen.

Some increases in salaries were allowed to members of the faculty after January 1, 1920, ranging from twelve to forty percent, the larger being given to instructors and assistant professors, these being the ones who had suffered most from the increase in the cost of living. This was accomplished by an overdraft, as the appropriations made by the Legislature were insufficient to meet any costs after April 1, 1920. The Board of Administration also recognized an amendment to the *Blue Book*, that the Council, the legislative body of the Agricultural College, should include the president, deans, professors, associate professors, assistant professors and instructors.

In the Republican primary of June 30, 1920, President Ladd, endorsed by the Nonpartisan League, won the nomination for the United States Senator from North Dakota. He was elected in November and on January 28, 1921, he resigned the presidency of the College. In his resignation he said:

"I withdraw from the institution with keen regret but with a full appreciation of the loyal support given me by my associates in the duties which have devolved upon me, to all of whom I tender kindest regards. . . ."

"I shall deem it a privilege to be able to render any and all possible future service to the college, and to the people of the state, believing there are wonderful possibilities for future growth of the college and opportunities for service to the people of North Dakota through the instrumentalities of the college."

"I feel, however, that I should take this occasion to strongly urge the need for providing an assured income increasing with the growth of the college. Such, as established as a mileage tax, would provide for maintenance and a ten year building program to be financed through a bond issue with adequate provisions for a sinking fund and interest to mature at the end of twenty-five years for each biennial issue of bonds." [19]

In some respects the short administration of President Ladd was an interim or transition period in the history of the College. The older group of professors — Ladd, Bolley, Waldron, Keene, McArdle — were no longer as concerned and enthusiastic as when they first came to the institution. Newer and younger faculty members were desirous of a greater share in guiding the policies of the College.

President Ladd himself recognized that the infancy of the College was at an end. In 1917 he wrote, "we now pass from the period of pioneering in college growth to the period of fuller development. We shall need to study the whole educational field of activities to the end that our entire system of education may be brought into harmony with the best thought and needs of our time."

Dr. Ladd was a scientist who placed much stress on details. But that does not always make a good administrator, for a man with such an emphasis often enough is unable, or at least unlikely, to evaluate events or policies with a broad vision. Dr. Ladd's value to the North Dakota Agricultural College is far more related to his work as a chemist in both research and teaching than it is to his heading the administration of the institution for five years. As head of the College he was dogmatic, frequently arbitrary, yet sincerely desirous of furthering the welfare of the faculty and that of the College.

Personally, President and Mrs. Ladd were by nature hospitable. Every September they were gracious hosts to the whole faculty, whom they entertained at a formal reception at their home and afterward at a dance in the Armory. The following week they were hosts to a dance for the student body, at which they asked the unmarried members of the faculty to assist them. Mrs. Ladd was not averse to match-making. Mrs. Ladd in 1919 organized the Faculty Women's Club, which is still in existence. It consisted of women members of the staff and wives of faculty members, and met once a month. The October meeting was a reception for new members, the December meeting honored Extension staff, and in the spring, a tea was held for women in Fargo. Mrs. Ladd was also instrumental in starting a Tuesday sewing circle. A larger and more democratic group was founded in 1909 and later came to be known as the Priscilla Club. Both of these groups met at night, when father could stay at home with the children. Later the Tuesday Club met for luncheon, while the Priscillas met at dinner; each group annually entertained its husbands.

According to Miss Pearl Dinan, there were always extra places at Dr. and Mrs. Ladd's table for guests who might drop in. They lived at the corner of Thirteenth Street and Eleventh Avenue. The story goes that Mrs. Ladd was accustomed to station one of the children at a north window to see whom "Papa" might be bringing home for dinner. President Ladd was a stickler for punctuality — breakfast at seven, office at seven-thirty, dinner at noon.

FOOTNOTES

[1] Lewis F. Crawford, *History of North Dakota* (Chicago, 1931), I, 421.

[2] At first the dues were $2.50 a year, later they were increased to $6.00 and still later to $9.00; Ray Goldberg, *The Nonpartisan League in North Dakota* (Fargo, 1948), 14.

[3] State Board of Regents of North Dakota, *First Biennial Report to the Governor for the biennial period ending June 30, 1916* (Fargo, 1916), 7.

[4] *First Biennial Report*, 8.

[5] *First Biennial Report*, 24.

[6] *First Biennial Report*, 36.

[7] See Appendix.

[8] Spaulding, 49.

[9] *Weekly Spectrum*, March 15, 1916.

[10] Theodore Saloutos, Rise of the Nonpartisan League in North Dakota, *Agricultural History*, XX, 57.

[11] *North Dakota Farmer*, XIX, No. 1 (July 15, 1917), 3.

[12] *Fargo Courier News*, Nov. 10, 1919.

[13] *First Annual Report of the Board of Administration, to the Governor* (Bismarck, 1919), 70-71.

[14] *Minutes of Board of Regents*, Apr. 1, 1919.

[15] *First Annual Report*, 29.

[16] *First Annual Report*, 31-4.

[17] *First Annual Report*, 86, 87.

[18] This hope was realized by the organization of Local 96 of the American Federation of Teachers, which embraced 80 members of the teaching staff.

[19] Minutes of Board of Administration, Jan. 28, 1921.

◂ CHAPTER VII ▸

A New Era, 1921-1929

WITH the twenties another era came in for the College. A new president from outside of the State took over. The institution was growing up, and was viewing wider horizons. With World War I over, staff, students and people generally expected the College to do bigger things. Accordingly, the faculty increased in number, curricula were broadened, a wider clientele of students was served. Geographically, Fargo was becoming more intimately connected with the College, especially after the demise of Fargo College. More Fargoans began to send their children to the Agricultural College. Sororities like Sigma Alpha Iota and Sigma Theta were transferred from the Fargo College campus in town to the College. A new era of athletics developed with the organization of the North Central Conference. There was an increasing demand for a change of name to State College, particularly from students in schools other than agriculture. The College was developing its own distinctive personality.

In November, 1920, Dr. Ladd, endorsed by the Nonpartisan League, was elected to the United States Senate. He continued as president of the College until the following January. In February, 1921, Dean Edward S. Keene of the School of Mechanic Arts was appointed acting president while a successor to President Ladd was being sought.

At this time, the Board of Administration was entirely controlled by the Nonpartisan League. Miss Minnie Nielson and Mr. John Hagan were the members elected in 1920. The appointed members were Messrs. George A. Totten, Robert T. Muir, and Jud Cahill, who had succeeded P. M. Casey. When President Ladd resigned the Board invited the college teachers' organization on the campus to propose names for his successor and to participate in joint discussion with the Board. This "Teachers' Union" set up a committee of twelve, three

A New Era, 1921–1929   103

from each of the four divisions of the institution. A. E. Minard, C. I. Nelson and R. H. Slocum represented the teaching faculty, E. I. Olsen, A. F. Schalk and H. L. Walster the Experiment Station, R. O. Baird, H. L. Bolley and W. C. Palmer the Regulatory Division and John Haw, Don McMahon and G. W. Randlett the Extension Division. The Regulatory Division was set up by President Ladd in 1917 to supervise the work of the State Food Commissioner and later, in 1925, was transferred to Bismarck.

At the first meeting of the Board of Administration and this committee Professor Minard outlined the purpose of the committee and "declared that the thought of the committee was that whoever is chosen to succeed Dr. Ladd should be: from outside of the state, and sympathetic with the work of a land grant college." [1] Three weeks later the committee submitted to the Board a list of desirable candidates. Another joint meeting was held in April and the discussion narrowed the candidates to three: Dr. H. C. Taylor, Office of Farm Management, United States Department of Agriculture, Dean John Lee Coulter, College of Agriculture, University of West Virginia and graduate of the University of North Dakota, and Dean F. B. Mumford, College of Agriculture, University of Missouri.

Dr. Coulter met with the Board on two occasions during the summer. On August 6, at another joint meeting of the Board and the twelve-man committee, several additional names were presented. Two of these, Dr. Hector MacPherson of the University of Oregon, lecturer for the United States Grain Growers, and Professor E. Mean Wilcox of Lincoln, Nebraska, met with the Board and the committee August 20. In a meeting on August 31 the Board limited the choice to Dr. MacPherson and Dr. Coulter. At a vote taken, Totten was for MacPherson, the rest were for Coulter. The faculty committee of twelve had recommended MacPherson, and they had turned down Coulter in their belief that his policies would be too favorable to the business interests of the State.

The choice of Dr. Coulter for the presidency certainly had political implications. The chairman of the Board of Administration in 1921 was Robert T. Muir, who had been commandant of the cadets and National Guard when Coulter was a student at the University of North Dakota, and was determined to secure the appointment of Coulter as president of the Agricultural College. He gained the approval of Attorney General William Lemke, who was a graduate of the University, and of Governor Lynn Frazier, who had been fullback on the University football team. The other members of the Board were agreeable to Muir's wishes, including the ex officio members,

Joseph Kitchin, Commissioner of Agriculture and Labor, and Miss Minnie Nielson, Superintendent of Public Instruction. Miss Nielson, the only member who knew that Coulter was a "liberal" in politics, kept quiet and voted for him.[2]

Obviously Dr. Coulter had certain qualifications. He was born in 1881 in the Red River Valley on a Minnesota farm in Polk County. As a boy he attended a rural school in Minnesota, high school in Grand Forks, and later the University of North Dakota. He worked late in the fall, plowing, and studied nights so that he could enter his university classes at Thanksgiving on a par with the other students. He had a special interest in economics and the sciences, due, in part, to his reading of books in his grandfather's library, which included the works of Adam Smith and John Stuart Mill. He took graduate work at the Universities of Wisconsin and Iowa, receiving his Ph. D. from the University of Wisconsin in 1908. He taught agricultural economics at the University of Minnesota from 1908 to 1910, when he went to Washington to work with the Census Bureau. In 1913 he was sent by President Wilson to Europe for a six months' study of European credit systems, which resulted in establishing a farm loan board and a farm loan banking system. In 1914 he took charge of the Knapp School of Country Life, associated with Peabody College at Nashville, Tennessee. After two years he was made dean of the College and director of the Experiment Station of the West Virginia College of Agriculture. During World War I he was given a leave of absence, was commissioned a major and sent to Europe for seven months in the air service program. He was back in West Virginia again in 1921 as dean and director when he was elected president of the North Dakota Agricultural College.

President Coulter's first published article in *College and State* emphasized that the Agricultural College was a state service institution: ". . . . The land grant colleges were created by the states and chiefly supported by them. Only a small part of their funds come from the federal government or from the students or from special fees for service rendered. . . . We must think of the agricultural college as a 'state institution' organized by the state, supported by the state, and having in mind service to the state. From this standpoint everything done at the agricultural college should have in mind the greatest service to the greatest number of citizens of the state."[3]

This statement was evidently the origin of the slogan — "Our State is Our Campus"— adopted in 1922 by the students, faculty, alumni and business men as a means of developing a greater and more useful Agricultural College. He also declared that the College was not restricted to agriculture, but covered a wide range of subjects. "It should

A New Era, 1921-1929

be the duty of every student, past, present or future, to emphasize this among the people of the state so that the name may not be misleading. . . . A student need not go elsewhere to get a broad, well-rounded out education to fit in with any vocation which he may wish to follow." [4]

A year later Dr. Coulter summarized the four-fold mission of the Agricultural College as follows:

"To search for hidden truths, to build up a body of scientific facts, to test these facts and to prove their practical application;

"To train leaders and to teach them the truths in the many fields of human endeavor represented in college courses, and to help these leaders to see the application of these truths and to aid them to develop the skill to use them;

"To send trained leaders into the farms and homes, to the shops and offices where they may aid our people in the adoption of this useful knowledge that they may prosper and be happy and contented;

"To assist the authorities of government in the enforcement of useful laws by performing useful laboratory analyses and by submitting scientific evidence for their use." [5]

During his presidency Dr. Coulter was frequently called upon to address various gatherings in the State. He never failed to take every occasion to boost the College. One of his favorite themes was that North Dakota is the center of North America:

"North Dakota is the heart of America, the sunshine state, and everyone here has a grouch on. We don't realize that we have here in North Dakota the richest and most resourceful of the states. Fifteen hundred miles to the south of us are the plains of Texas with their lean hungry cattle. Out to the west of us they have to carry every bit of the water they use out to the land, they dig ditches and pump it on; while to the east of us they pay immense sums of money to have the water drained off the land. There is too much water on one side of us, not enough on the other; it is too hot down south of us, and too cold up north. North Dakota is the middle condition between these extremes." [6]

By January, 1923, the first unit of the Agricultural Building was ready for occupancy, the first building on the campus devoted to agriculture alone. This four-story building immediately became the center of this school's activities. Its splendid laboratory facilities, together with the equipment in the farm buildings of the College, were provided to help fit students as agricultural leaders, as farmers and in other capacities. The departments served included agronomy, soils, animal husbandry, poultry, dairying, farm management and economics, horticulture and forestry, agricultural engineering and entomology.

At the dedication of the building, fittingly named Morrill Hall, President Coulter pointed out that this was the first great building venture of the School of Agriculture, "a timely erection in a period of depressed agricultural and business stagnation in this state." [7] Dean Waldron, in closing the dedication ceremonies, said: "The new building will stand for an ideal and will instill the necessary enthusiasm into students of agriculture and put their surroundings on a par with that of any of the students in other departments. This building is dedicated to the agricultural man's ambition, and marks an era in the development and expansion of our state."

A policy of economy was a necessary result of the decade of the twenties. The State was in the midst of a political and economic program initiated by the Nonpartisan League. It had floated bonds for building the State Mill and Elevator. The legislatures of the period were opposed to increasing appropriations and even of maintaining College buildings which were deteriorating in value. President Coulter may be congratulated in using business judgment to make all possible use of the buildings on hand.

A total of $17,000 worth of building and remodeling was in progress in 1923. The more important changes were the enlargement of the Little Country Theater — $3,000; an addition to the greenhouse — $2,500; the making of an office building out of Francis Hall — $2,000; a new central unit for the poultry house — $3,500; redecoration and roof repairing of the Mechanic Arts and Engineering buildings and Music Hall — $5,000 and new sidewalks — $1,000.[8]

The Practice House, or, as it was later called, the Home Management Residence, and now the Alba Bales House, was built during Dr. Coulter's administration. It is a laboratory for students in home economics. It is a ten-room colonial home with laundry equipment in the basement, living room, sun room, dining room and kitchen on the first floor, bedrooms and bath on the second and third floors. Senior girls live there a sufficient time during their last year to learn and practice the various duties of a homemaker under competent supervision.

Also, a rearrangement of offices and classrooms by schools and departments resulted in conveniences for both students and staff, as well as providing room for the anticipated increase in enrollment. The administrators of the Experiment Station and the Extension Division, later known as Extension Service, in 1931 moved to the new wing of Morrill Hall. The offices and classrooms used in teaching science and literature, instead of being scattered in four buildings, were concentrated in Science Hall.

One evidence of the business attitude of the Board during this period was a directive sent out by President Coulter at the request of the Board of Administration made on August 6, 1924. The Board believed that a distinct saving could be made by having all purchases of the state institutions carried out by the purchasing department of the Board of Administration. Therefore it requested that estimates for a period of six months be submitted to the Board so that contracts could be let for furnishing such supplies.

Dr. Coulter was primarily interested in the resident instruction division of the College, for the divisions of the Experiment Station and the Extension Service had their own directors. The resident instruction division had charge of the general supervision of all grounds and buildings, but its chief responsibility was the conduct of all educational work carried on at the College. Its activities were grouped into the following schools and departments:

School of Agriculture, Dean C. B. Waldron
    Department of Agricultural Economics, Cap. E. Miller
    Department of Agricultural Education, E. H. Jones
    Department of Agricultural Entomology, R. L. Webster
    Department of Agronomy, O. O. Churchill
    Department of Animal Husbandry, E. J. Thompson
    Department of Dairy Husbandry, J. R. Dice
    Department of Horticulture and Forestry, C. B. Waldron

School of Mechanic Arts, Dean E. S. Keene
    Department of Architecture and Architectural Engineering, S. A. Smith
    Department of Civil Engineering, R. H. Slocum
    Department of Mechanical Engineering, E. S. Keene
    Department of Physics, E. G. Keene

School of Home Economics, Dean Alba Bales
    Department of Applied Art, Evelyn H. Riebe
    Department of Clothing and Textiles, Minnie Anderson
    Department of Foods and Nutrition, Adah Lewis
    Department of Household and Institutional Management, Alba Bales

School of Chemistry and Technology, Head, W. T. Pearce
    Department of Agricultural Chemistry, T. H. Hopper
    Department of Biochemistry, R. E. Remington
    Department of Inorganic and Qualitative Chemistry, L. L. Carrick
    Department of Organic and Quantitative Chemistry, C. A. Gottschall
    Department of Physical and Industrial Chemistry, W. T. Pearce

School of Pharmacy, Dean W. F. Sudro
    Department of Pharmacy, W. F. Sudro

School of Veterinary Science, Head, A. F. Schalk
  Department of Veterinary Science, A. F. Schalk

School of Science and Literature, Head, A. E. Minard
  Department of Bacteriology (Biology), C. I. Nelson
  Department of Botany (Biology), Dean H. L. Bolley, E. D. Reynolds
  Department of English and Philosophy, A. E. Minard
  Department of Geology and Mineralogy, J. E. Doerr
  Department of History, E. D. Ross
  Department of Mathematics, I. W. Smith
  Department of Modern Languages, Leon Metzinger
  Department of Public Discussion, A. G. Arvold
  Department of Social and Economic Science, A. F. Hunsaker
  Department of Zoology and Physiology, R. T. Hance

School of Education, Dean A. D. Weeks
  Department of Education, A. D. Weeks

Miscellaneous Departments
  Department of Commerce, J. H. Hjelmstad
  Library, Ethel McVeety
  Department of Military Science and Tactics, W. F. Harrell
  Department of Music, C. S. Putnam
  Department of Physical Training and Athletics, S. E. Borleske.[9]

This organization, with modifications and additions, has continued to be characteristic of the College up to the present time.

Soon after assuming office, President J. L. Coulter was authorized by the Board of Administration "to organize the work of Agricultural Economics and to coordinate same in the college, experiment station and extension division, and to secure a competent man to take charge of the work." Later he was "authorized and directed to so coordinate the work of the Agricultural College as to avoid duplication of work as much as possible to reduce the overhead so that the institution can be made to function more as an Agricultural College."[10] This ruling of the Board of Administration was in line with the prevailing conception of that time that the College was predominantly "agricultural"; it was not in accordance with the original purpose of the Morrill Act, or with the intention of the legislative act of 1890.

In 1921 Edward H. Jones, with a master's degree from the University of Wisconsin, was appointed state supervisor and professor of agricultural education. In May, 1924, Dean Waldron was transferred to his former position of professor of horticulture and forestry, which he held

A New Era, 1921–1929   109

until he retired in 1945. Dr. H. L. Walster was made chairman of the department of agronomy and dean of agriculture. Thus began the long administration of this outstanding educator and national leader. The next year saw the curriculum in agriculture greatly broadened. A basic course of 156 units was required, leaving 69 units for electives. Thus not all of a student's time was spent entirely in a narrow specialized field.

In 1926 the curricula in the winter short courses for farmers were reorganized in order to enable them to get special training in agriculture in two winters of two terms each. Among the courses offered were economics, accounting, farm management and marketing.

J. Alexander Munro, a graduate of Ontario Agricultural College with a master's degree from Kansas State College, was appointed professor of entomology in 1926. He was also entomologist for the Experiment Station, where his time was devoted chiefly to injurious insects and apiculture.

The School of Science and Literature also received its share of attention. During President Coulter's administration, with the cooperation of Dean Minard, the ten departments of this school became increasingly efficient in training all of the students in fundamental and necessary subjects. Besides the service courses the school had a considerable number of students of its own who were preparing for teaching or for entering schools of medicine, law or other professional fields. This school was said by Dean Minard to be "the mixing bowl" of the College. Several members of the staff, Kenneth Kuhn, W. C. Hunter, Rudolph Ottersen, Christine Finlayson, Matilda Thompson, Ruby Grimes, and A. D. Whedon, were appointed during this administration and continued with the institution until their retirement. The department of bacteriology was transferred to the School of Agriculture in order to secure greater legislative support.

The School of Chemistry was also largely a service school, but in addition prepared its own students for industry, particularly for paint industry, and for teaching in high schools and junior colleges. Dr. L. L. Carrick, who came to the College in 1920, later succeeded Dr. Pearce as dean.

Before 1907 the School of Mechanic Arts, as it was originally called, was limited to the field of mechanical engineering, with Professor Keene as instructor. In that year civil engineering was made possible by the employment of Professor Slocum. After World War I there was an increased demand for more engineering training. Professor H. S. Rush was appointed in 1921 to teach electrical engineering. Other additions to the school staff in the twenties were Charles L. Swisher in physics and Homer B. Huntoon in architecture. When Dean Keene in 1928 was voted the title of Dean Emeritus, R. M. Dolve was named dean. Dean Keene gradually had developed the School of Mechanic Arts and had served as teacher and counselor to students of the school for many years. He brought the first moving picture machine to the State and was the first to use an x-ray machine successfully in this part of the Northwest.

During the period of Dr. Coulter's presidency the School of Home Economics was greatly strengthened and expanded. The prime mover in this policy was Miss Alba Bales, who came from Montana State College in 1921, and was given the title of Dean in 1926. Four departments were formed: Minnie Anderson heading the clothing and textiles department; Elvira Smith the foods and nutrition department; Lucile Horton the education department and Dorothy Hatch the department of related art. Constance Leeby was placed in charge of home economics research. These departments made it possible for students to prepare for specific vocations. Under Dean Bales the North Dakota Agricultural College was among the first of the colleges to undertake an off-campus teacher-training program. In 1928 a department of institutional management was provided. Also Christine Finlayson was employed to serve as supervisor of home economics teaching in the secondary schools of the State.

The School of Pharmacy had grown steadily under the supervision of Dean Sudro. In 1925 a minimum course of three years was inaugurated, which was soon increased to four years. In 1928 there were ninety men and women registered, 27 of whom finished the course.

When Dr. Coulter became president, he did not abide by the *Blue Book*, which had been recognized by the faculty and the Board as the constitution of the College. At the invitation of Totten and Muir of the Board, the twelve men committee, which was still in existence, authorized Nelson, Metzinger and Minard to go to Dr. Coulter and remind him of the existence of the *Blue Book*. Dr. Coulter agreed to follow it after some changes were made. A special meeting of the College Council was held on May 14, 1923, to "elect one member of the professorial staff to act with President Coulter and the representative of the Advisory Committee in the revision of the *Blue Book*." It was moved that the Council elect a committee of three, which should choose one of its members to sit with the institutional committee. Professors Nelson, Slocum and Christensen were elected.[11]

The American Association of University Professors organized a local chapter and adopted a constitution on December 9, 1927. Officers were elected and a membership of thirty-six secured. Monthly meetings were held at which reports of national meetings were given and problems such as academic freedom, conduct of local chapters, the North Dakota retirement fund, the teaching load, the division of functions of the state educational institutions were discussed. The organization sought to become an organ of faculty opinion.

On the whole, Dr. Coulter's relations with the Council and general faculty were cordial. In 1926 he recommended that ten professors, most of them heads of departments, be changed from the twelve month basis to the nine months without reduction in salary. The Board authorized the change. Dr. Coulter explained this recommendation as one means of bringing about a salary increase. Additional pay would go to such teachers on a nine months basis who were engaged in summer teaching.

In 1921 a summer school was reorganized by Dean A. D. Weeks of the department of education as director and a curriculum committee of seven faculty members. Summer school at the College continued until 1933, but was often a problem and was probably the weakest part of the whole college program. The attendance was small because the great majority of the students of the College wished to utilize the summer months for earning money, or else wished to take advantage of courses offered by other nearby institutions. As a result, the cost of instruction per student was high. School teachers were the chief group from which students were recruited, and they usually preferred the normal schools.

A committee of the Council recommended, on November 16, 1922, that correspondence courses be established. Upon recommendation of President Coulter, the Board, at its meeting of April, 1925, considered the matter and in September of that year T. W. Thordarson was employed as director of correspondence courses. It has more recently been expanded to include all subjects of high school grade and is known as Supervised Study. It has also set up an extensive film library. During the years that Mr. Thordarson has had charge of that work many hundreds of students have been enrolled. At present, although housed in a College building, this unit is directly responsible to another board, and hence is not organized as a part of the College.

The position of dean of women was revived by the Board of Administration at the request of President Coulter. Mrs. Myrtle Gleason Cole, state leader of home demonstration agents, was appointed to the position. Her duties included the supervision of Ceres Hall, securing the cooperation of sororities, women's rooming houses and parents of resident girls. She was also in charge of social regulations and other interests of women students. Mrs. Cole was a graduate of the University of Iowa, where she was in charge of a girls' dormitory and had worked with sororities and other groups of the women students. She continued to devote part of her time to home demonstration work in the State until

1928. At that time, Miss Pearl Dinan, a member of the English department, was appointed Dean of Women.

A new emphasis on research also characterized this period. While this had begun before 1920, it was given further impetus during the Coulter administration. The Experiment Station budget in support of research was separated from the College budget while research personnel was employed jointly with teaching or exclusively for research. Though the president does not have direct supervision of the research program, since this is the responsibility of the director of the experiment station, any research program must have the confidence and full support of the president in order to be effective.

Director P. E. Trowbridge (1918-1934) fostered a program to improve the quality of the station personnel and the research programs by bringing in well-trained men with doctor's degrees and, in cooperation with President Coulter, by encouraging staff members to do further graduate work during sabbatical leaves. H. L. Walster in agronomy, F. W. Christensen in animal nutrition and A. H. Benton in marketing, are examples of new appointees. C. I. Nelson, L. M. Roderick, and L. R. Waldron attained their doctorates during this period.

As to the character of research, perhaps the most important factor in the opinion of the farmers of the State was the need for a variety of wheat which could resist the ravages of stem rust. In 1926 the department of agronomy released Dr. L. R. Waldron's Ceres which soon replaced Marquis on millions of acres in the spring wheat area. During this period, the higher protein content and superior quality of hard red spring wheat flour for bread baking purposes came to be more fully recognized. Also, this period saw the beginning of closer cooperation between the several experiment stations and the United States Department of Agriculture in wheat improvement research programs.

A rust resistant variety of oat and improved varieties of flax were made available to North Dakota farmers. In order to lessen the risks due to plant disease and drought, a more diversified program for agriculture was promoted: more forage was harvested, more intertilled crops such as corn, potatoes and sugar beets were raised and more livestock was fed in order to consume the feed and forage crops.

A new veterinary technique, the Ruman fistula which was a window in a cow's stomach, was developed by Dr. Schalk and his associates in the veterinary department, making possible a closer study and diagnosis of digestive disturbances in ruminants. This department also investigated sweet clover poisoning which resulted from feeding moldy or spoiled sweet clover hay. The new knowledge thus gained was later

A New Era, 1921–1929

used in medicine applied to humans, particularly in treatment of blood clots.

Dr. Coulter, with a Ph.D. in economics, was especially interested in agricultural economics. He realized that during the wartime period the "wheat acreage was advanced almost 2,500,000 acres to the great sacrifice of corn and other phases of a well balanced farm system. Farmers became deeply involved in debt ... and this was encouraged by a most liberal credit policy."[12] Now that a guaranteed price for wheat had been abandoned, it was all the more necessary to take up a program of more diversified agriculture.

In 1920 Rex E. Willard joined the staff of the Experiment Station and was placed in charge of farm management. Mr. Willard had wide experience with the United States Department of Agriculture in the Bureau of Soils and in the Department of Farm Management. He and his assistants made a comprehensive study of costs and agricultural practices under actual farm conditions. He also published a text for rural schools entitled "*Simple Farm Accounts.*" He remained with the Station for ten years.

The marketing of farm products was another phase of the Station's activities encouraged by Dr. Coulter. In 1922 Dr. A. H. Benton, specialist in marketing and rural organization, was brought to the College. Dr. Benton, with a bachelor's degree from the University of Wisconsin, had spent 14 years teaching at the University of Minnesota, at the University of Wisconsin, and at the University of Manitoba. At the Agricultural College Dr. Benton investigated the marketing problem of important farm crops grown in North Dakota, and was particularly interested in the flax situation as it was related to the tariff.

One feature of the work of this department of marketing was the collection and analysis of farm prices, freight rates, marketing costs, taxation and farm indebtedness. For nearly ten years scarcely a month passed that some member of the North Dakota Agricultural Experiment Station staff was not called upon by the North Dakota Railroad Commission, by other state officials, farm producers of flaxseed, potatoes, or grain to assist them in rate cases, tariff hearings, and legislative matters of vital concern to the State. The testimony of Rex Willard, Alva Benton and Dr. Coulter at the State Railroad Commission hearings was an important factor in securing favorable decisions by the Interstate Commerce Commission.

Other experimental work was done during the twenties. In 1924 the State Experiment Station cooperated with the United States Department of Agriculture in an extensive sheep business survey of two hundred farms in northwestern North Dakota. In 1927 D. J. Griswold, a trained and experienced sheep man, was employed on the staff. Experimental studies in animal nutrition were made by F. W. Christensen in cooperation with T. H. Hopper of the agricultural chemistry department. Home economics research in nutrition was carried on by Esther Latzke and Constance Leeby under the provisions of the Purnell Act.

In the field of horticulture Dr. A. F. Yeager introduced Sunshine sweet corn, Red River and Early Jumbo tomatoes and the Dry Weather strawberry.

The Extension Service had only limited attention from President Coulter. Gordon W. Randlett, who had been appointed director in 1918, continued to head the staff, which occupied rooms on the second floor of Science Hall. Harry E. Rilling was appointed State 4-H club leader in 1921. Mrs. Myrtle G. Cole became State home demonstration leader in December, 1920; in 1922 she established Homemakers' Clubs as an educational device. In 1921 the first school of instruction for field extension workers was held in order to acquaint them with the latest developments in agriculture, followed by the annual conferences of extension workers. This program has been continued ever since. The depression of the twenties caused the debt-ridden farmers to vote out county extension agents in many counties. The resignation of Director Randlett in 1926 was followed by the appointment of C. F. Monroe, Director of Extension Service in New Mexico, to the new post. Charley Monroe, a native of Iowa, was graduated from Iowa State College and had done graduate work at Washington State College.

Student enrollment rapidly increased during Dr. Coulter's administration. In the five year period from 1915 to 1920 the yearly average was 254 in the College. In 1920–21 the enrollment was 375; in 1921–22 it was 480; in 1922–23 it was 656; and in 1923–24 it was 804; in four years the enrollment had more than doubled. It is significant that increases were evenly distributed among the various schools. Various reasons for the increase were advanced: the larger number of high school graduates in the State, the increased demand for a college education following World War I, a shifting from the professions such as law, medicine and the ministry to vocations such as agriculture, home economics, mechanic arts, chemistry and pharmacy. Certainly there was no corresponding increase in population in North Dakota. Whatever the causes, there was increasing pressure on the facilities of the College — classrooms, laboratories, instructors — to take care of the students. In the later twenties enrollment increases continued: 899 in 1924–25, 951 in 1925–26, 1,089 in 1926–27, 1,219 in 1927–28, 1,295 in 1928–29.

By 1929 crowded conditions at the College were becoming serious. No buildings had been erected at North Dakota Agricultural College

A New Era, 1921–1929

for ten years, although $5,000,000 had been spent for buildings at other institutions in North Dakota. The number of students in the College had increased from 375 in 1920–21 to 1,330 in 1929. No other institution had grown as rapidly. The Legislature in 1927 did appropriate money for additions to the Agricultural Building and Science Hall, but these bills were vetoed by Governor Sorlie because the appropriations were not recommended by the budget board. Every basement and attic room at the College had to be repaired and put to use, and still the rooms were overcrowded and new buildings were absolutely necessary.

At last the efforts of president, students and alumni were crowned with success. The budget board recommended and the Legislature passed appropriations for a wing to Science Hall, a wing to the Agricultural Building, Morrill Hall, and a physical education building, the bill for the last being introduced and steered largely by Senator Arthur W. Fowler, '01.

Throughout his administration President Coulter had actively encouraged athletics. In 1922 North Dakota Agricultural College entered the North Central Conference and a new era was at hand. In that year also a Letterman's Club was formed. In 1925 Ion Cortright became coach and the Bison, led by Claudie Miller, won the North Central Conference Championship in football. In the same year, under the coaching of George Dewey, the basketball team, captained by Cy Arnold, made an enviable record and in 1926 the team led by Miller, "Cy" Arnold and "Red" Blakely won 21 out of 23 games and in basketball brought the first North Central Conference Championship to the College.

In 1928 C. C. (Casey) Finnegan was appointed athletic director, Stan Borleske returned as football coach and Leonard Saalwaechter continued as coach of basketball. The last named also coached track and his cross country team won a conference title.

President Coulter and Director Finnegan planned an extensive program of intramural and interscholastic activities for every student. In regard to it, Mr. Finnegan made the following statements in the *Spectrum*, March 7, 1930: "The greater emphasis on physical training and exercise is in line with the changing times everywhere. Business men realize its value to themselves and their employees. The shorter working day and week gives more time for play and focuses attention on the importance of the right kind of recreation. Every normal youth has a natural liking for one or more kinds of play. That is the reason that there are more than 160 men participating in our intramural basketball program. . . ."

Interest in other sports was evidenced by the class enrollments: 160

men in boxing, 38 in tumbling, 30 in hockey, 19 in wrestling. More than 600 men participated in some form of athletics.

In May, 1920, the Women's Athletic Association was reorganized on the basis of participation in athletics. In 1925 Dorothy Cole, B.S., Teachers College, Columbia University, took over the work in physical education for women, which included basketball, baseball and soccer, riflery, bowling, tennis, hockey, archery and swimming. A dance recital was held annually and interclass and intercollegiate sports were encouraged.

Military training was subjected to much criticism during the postwar years among the public and in the state legislature, especially by members of the Farmers' Union. The ROTC unit was discontinued in 1921 by the War Department, but the discontinuation was reconsidered due to the efforts of Acting President Keene and Major F. B. Carrithers. The succeeding commandant, Major W. F. Harrell, with the hearty backing of President Coulter, was successful in gaining an honor rating which was awarded to only 23 of the 230 schools of the nation and to only two of the thirty in the Seventh Corps area.

Other student interests were recognized by the Coulter administration. In 1923 the name of the College annual was changed from *Agassiz* to *Bison*. Since the athletic teams at the College were no longer known as the "Aggies" but were the "Bison," Arthur Ostman, editor of the 1924 *Agassiz*, suggested changing the name, which would follow the policy of other large colleges and universities of the nation in calling the yearbook by the same name as the athletic teams. "It is the argument of the *Agassiz* staff and of many other supporters of the change in name plan that Agassiz has no meaning outside the college. Also that it will aid in educating the students to the recognition of the name Bison as applied to Aggie teams and in aiding to make the A.C. battle name a fixture. When commenting, in conversation or writing, on the *Bison* as a publication, people will at once connect it with the Agricultural College, but Agassiz is known only to the elect." [13]

A vote of the students and discussions with faculty members resulted in a decided preference for the new name. Also, President Coulter and other members of the administrative and instructional staff were heartily in favor of the change.

Changes were also noticeable in the registration of students. Rather elaborate plans for freshman orientation were developed; several days were spent in informing the new students of the new way of life and in seeking to bring about a better adjustment to their new surroundings. Tests, both psychological and curricular, were administered by the department of personnel; attempts at guidance were begun.

In 1925 the enrollment reached a new high mark, totaling 1,560 students. During the preceding five years a ten percent increase came each year. Seven foreign countries and fourteen states contributed to the total registration; 224 came from without the State of North Dakota. Every North Dakota county but two sent students to the College. Cass County led with 654, Barnes was second with 53, the others ranged from two to 32.

The year 1926–27 showed even a greater increase: 2,052 students, 346 from outside of North Dakota, 659 from Cass county, 66 from Barnes county, and two to 58 from other counties. In 1929 522 freshmen were enrolled, as compared to 391 the previous year; the largest increase being in the School of Mechanic Arts. In this year a new freshman program was inaugurated for the purpose of acquainting the new students with the institution, the various schools and with one another. Placement tests were given and College rules and practices explained.

Student employment was a necessary consideration during this period of agricultural depression when it was difficult for farm families to finance their children's expenses at college. In 1927, 396 men and 50 women were earning their entire way through college, while an additional 161 men and 33 women were paying their expenses in part. This latter figure meant three fourths of the men and one fourth of the women students acted as clerks in stores, as barbers, table waiters, furnace firemen, draftsmen, collectors, etc.

An employment bureau was set up in the fall of 1928 with Mrs. Psyche M. Gooden as supervisor, who had been in a similar position at Drake University, Des Moines, Iowa. Prospective employers were contacted, suitable students were recommended, and later checked. By December 1928, 300 students were placed with only eight complaints out of 800 jobs. In 1931 seventy-five to ninety per cent of the students were working part time and approximately thirty-five per cent were entirely dependent on their own efforts and work. Board and room jobs were most in demand.

Student government seems to have encountered little friction. The annual elections of commission members occurred regularly. Sometimes the candidates were chiefly athletes, sometimes debaters, sometimes students from one school or another, but nearly always the leading fraternities secured control of the commission. Light votes were the rule. At times only twenty-five per cent of the student body cast ballots.

With the increase of both staff and student body student-faculty relations were less intimate and personal. Each student organization was required to have at least one official faculty adviser who exercised as much supervision as the individual thought best. These advisers were chosen by the student members subject to the approval of the College Council.

As to the intellectual activities of the students, the literary societies were no longer in existence. The *Agassiz* of 1922 was the last annual yearbook to carry a picture and a story of the Athenian Literary Society, the only one still active. Debating and dramatics were under the control of the department of public speaking. Pi Gamma Mu furnished an outlet for social science students. Scholarship was promoted by special honorary societies in each school and by Phi Kappa Phi for the entire college.

Service activities were largely sponsored by departmental organizations in agriculture, engineering and home economics. Blue Key, a national honor society, was established on the campus in 1927. It is a men's service organization committed to work with the faculty and students to further the best interests of the institution. It is composed of superior undergraduates distinguished for character, scholarship, leadership and service; it awards the degree of Doctor of Service annually to a person, usually one of the staff, who has been of service to the College. A limited number of honorary members from the faculty is chosen by the student members. Senior Staff, honor society for girls, was founded in 1923; it is composed of members chosen at the end of their junior year on the basis of scholarship and service to the institution.

The Board of Publications supervised the annual *Bison*, the weekly *Spectrum* and a quarterly alumni publication. When the *Bison* was issued, the day was called Gay Cat Day, a time for celebration and an outlet for spring fever. It was initiated by the Student Commission to increase class spirit, but as the years passed the celebration lost interest and was cancelled in 1929. Weekly convocations stressing non-local speakers and optional attendance were under the direction of Dean Minard. Occasionally they served as spontaneous outlets for athletic enthusiasm.

Another instance of Dr. Coulter's business administration was his aid in making the College YMCA solvent. Eric Thompson, secretary of the YMCA, had grandiose ideas and had run the organization into considerable debt. The Advisory Board of the YMCA was greatly aided by Dr. Coulter, who succeeded in getting their creditors to discount the bills for cash, and by this means the YMCA was able to get out of the "red".

In Dr. Coulter's administration there was developed a much greater interest among the alumni. Although an alumni association had been organized in 1901 it had comparatively little influence in the College or in the State. In 1907 Oliver Dynes started an alumni publication, *Col-*

lege and State. Alumni Secretary T. E. Stoa, stimulated by President Coulter, suggested a consolidation of the alumni and former students associations in 1922. A slogan — "Our State is our Campus" — stimulated growth of the College. In 1923, according to a study made by T. S. Thorfinnson, 46 per cent of graduates of North Dakota Agricultural College were located in North Dakota, 12 per cent in Minnesota, five per cent in Montana, four per cent in Illinois, two per cent in California; the other 31 per cent were in other states, foreign countries or their location was unknown. The next year secretary T. W. Thordarson organized Bison Booster clubs in several counties of the State. Another alumni chapter was organized in New York City. The association sponsored an investigating committee to determine the needs of the school.

In June, 1929, President Coulter tendered his resignation to take effect August 31 in order to accept a position as chief economist of the U.S. Tariff Commission. There was a concerted action on the part of the students and others to have President Coulter reconsider his action and continue at the college.

"The resignation of President John Lee Coulter is a distinct loss to our institution. In the last eight years the college enrollment has increased from less than four hundred to over thirteen hundred, a rate of increase much higher than the rate of the country as a whole. The faculty has had to be increased and salaries, which were below standard, were raised. At the same time the state was facing a period of economic depression that called loudly for lower taxes and reduced appropriations. No new buildings were provided. Attics and temporary structures were pressed into use. Every dollar of appropriation was made to do full duty. It is something of a marvel how the college could grow three-fold with no new buildings and only the most meager increase in appropriations.

"Dr. Coulter's managerial ability and sound economic training enabled him to guide the institution during these critical years and at the same time actually raise the standards of scholarship and college efficiency."[14]

During his presidency, Dr. Coulter did much in the way of public relations to secure more intimate and cordial feelings between the College and the community of Fargo. In an address before the Fargo Rotary Club on "What the State College of Agriculture means to Fargo and to North Dakota" he made the following statement: "The North Dakota State College is a tremendous advertisement for the city and state. It brings the leading talent of the nation and the world to our state. During the past year the leading scientists from practically every country in the whole civilized world visited the agricultural college. In this way the people of North Dakota are kept in touch with the leading thinkers of the world through interviews, lectures and information in general."[14]

At a dinner given him by the Fargo Chamber of Commerce universal regret was expressed at the loss of Dr. Coulter as president of the North Dakota Agricultural College. Dr. Coulter explained that he was leaving because the steady grind of eight years' continuous service as president of the College had been rather strenuous, and that he was tired and wished a change. He felt this call to national service was an opportunity to spend a year or two in Washington at a time when he might be able to be of service to the farming interests of the nations. "I am not leaving because of any differences with the Board regarding salary, or for any other difference with that body", said Dr. Coulter. "My relations with the board always have been pleasant and cordial."

In a personal visit with the author, Dr. Coulter attributed his success as president to several factors: his administration was in a period of good years, of prosperity and increasing salary payments, he largely left student affairs to the faculty, his relations with board members, legislature and alumni were cordial. Having been brought up on a farm, he could talk the farmer's language and also more important, do the farm chores. (He planned to reach a farm at milking time, milk one or more cows himself and eat supper with the family). He joined everything, including the Chamber of Commerce and a church. He spoke, particularly, of the aid accorded him by friends of the College such as Roy Johnson, William Watt, Robert Reed, Art Fowler, Bill Williams, Fred Olsen, Ralph Gunkelman, Ben Meinecke and others; he continued contact with them until his death in 1959.

After serving as chief economist of the United States Tariff Commission for several years, Dr. Coulter in 1934 was named expert assistant to George Peck, special adviser to President Roosevelt on world trade. Later he established a practice as economic adviser to firms engaged in foreign trade in Washington.

Dean A. E. Minard of the School of Applied Arts and Sciences was named acting president from July until September, 1929, when his successor was chosen. Before leaving, Dr. Coulter recommended the building of a home for the president on the campus.

FOOTNOTES

[1] Minutes of Board of Administration, Feb. 26, 1921.
[2] John Lee Coulter, interview, June 20, 1950.
[3] *College and State*, V, No. 2 (Nov., 1921), 4–5.
[4] *College and State*, Nov., 1921, 5.
[5] *College and State*, VI, No. 2 (Dec., 1922), 21.
[6] *Fargo Forum*, Oct. 29, 1923.
[7] *Weekly Spectrum*, XXXVI, No. 15 (Jan. 26, 1923), 1.
[8] *Fargo Forum*, Aug. 18, 1923.

A New Era, 1921–1929

[9] *Catalog,* 1922–23.
[10] Minutes of the Board of Administration, Dec. 24, 1921; May 2, 1922.
[11] *Fargo Forum,* May 15, 1937.
[12] *Weekly Spectrum,* XXXII, No. 16 (Feb. 2, 1923), 4.
[13] This quotation appeared in the *Broadcast,* October, 1929, an irregular publication of the College.
[14] *Spectrum,* XLIII, No. 2 (Sept. 30, 1927), 3.

◄ CHAPTER VIII ►

Depression and Decline, 1929-1937

AFTER a brief period of three months, in September, 1929, Dean Minard turned over his office to Professor Shepperd, who was named acting president by the Board. John H. Shepperd was one of the pioneer leaders of the College. He had served as professor of agriculture in the College and agriculturist of the Experiment Station from 1893 to 1904, then as dean of the School of Agriculture from 1904 to 1915, and from 1915 to 1929 was head of the department of animal husbandry. In 1928 he was granted an honorary degree of doctor of agriculture by Iowa State College. In the long career Dr. Shepperd's various capacities as teacher, dean, experimentalist and writer had given him a wealth of experience that now could be utilized as head of the institution which he so often compared to "All Gaul" with its three-fold divisions of college, experiment station and extension.

Upon accepting office, Dr. Shepperd made the following statement: "I interpret the duties of an acting president of a college to be the carrying forward of the plans already laid out. I shall not, therefore, propose innovations but will attempt to 'carry on' with as little jarring of the craft as possible . . . "I find the college so well organized that complete provision has already been made in almost every quarter . . . I expect to do all that I can to bring about team work on the part of the faculty and staff, with cordial mutual support."[1] This announcement reflected his sound common sense as well as his unsurpassed training and agricultural background which made his choice a fortunate one.

Soon sentiment throughout the State was overwhelmingly in favor of making his appointment permanent. The North Dakota Livestock Association urged such action on the Board of Administration, basing its argument on Dr. Shepperd's success as acting president. The *Grand Forks Herald* praised his long close contact with the institution and his recognition internationally as an authority on agricultural matters. Numerous other recommendations came from various individuals and organizations. One statement seems worth quoting: "There is one very favorable point in favor of the present acting president. Many of the former presidents have been aspirants to be United States senators, or some big political appointment of some form, using the college only as something to lean on, and to step up when the opportunity came. We feel that Dr. Shepperd is so thoroughly wrapped up in the welfare and future of that institution that nothing else would entice him away from it. With him as president the institution would have a man at its head that would be working for the college and agriculture of the state, and not for himself and his political future." [2]

On March 31, 1930, the Board named him president after seven months' service as acting president. The appointment was enthusiastically received at a convocation of the College.

The administration got off to a good start. Dr. Coulter's term had been a successful one. The political complexion, moreover, had veered from an almost complete political control by the Nonpartisan League in the early twenties to a preponderant influence of the independent and conservative Republicans, particularly in the office of the governor. This situation made for greater harmony with the college administration. Two new buildings were constructed near each other, the Men's Residence Hall, erected under the provisions of a legislative act authorizing a holding company; the other a Physical Education Building and Armory combined.

This new fireproof structure, ample enough to insure a practical "athletics for all" program, was dedicated on December 5, 1931. President Sauvain of the Board was introduced by A. W. Fowler, class of 1901, who, as state senator, introduced in the 1929 Legislature the bill providing for the appropriation. Sauvain presented the building to the College and President Shepperd responded. The basketball team, coached by Leonard Saalwaechter, completed the dedication by a well-played game with the University of Minnesota. Although defeated by Minnesota 31 to 18, the N.D.A.C. team later won the Conference Championship of 1932. The old Armory, which had housed athletics and military instruction for almost forty years, was rechristened "Festival Hall" and was destined to serve as an auditorium and community center for many years to come.

The status of the College in 1931 is expressed by President Shepperd in the following statement:

"The remarkable growth in student attendance of somewhat better than twenty-five percent during the past three years—which must be credited to the splendid work of the college Faculty and Staff—brought the favorable consideration represented by the $80,000 appropriation and an addition of about five percent to our maintenance allowance for the present biennium.

"The returning student of the older day will find a changed campus, with a three-eight mile frontage on Thirteenth Street, a Physical Education-Auditorium Building that will seat over three thousand people, Science Hall expanded until it has more floor space than any other college building in the State—exceeding that of the University of North Dakota Liberal Arts Building by a few square feet—and a tile smoke stack at our heating plant towering 175 feet into the air.

"Better than all of these physical appointments, the student of yesterday returning will find an earnest, capable, well trained, hard working faculty and a high class student body numbering over 1,500 young people carrying forward the traditions of the college along the lines they knew of yore." [3]

President Shepperd entered the presidency at a critical time. The years immediately after World War I were a period of hard times for agriculture, although one of prosperity for industry. However, the stock market crash of 1929 represented also a blow to the financial interests of the East. As a consequence, the debtor farmers of North Dakota were also seriously hurt. Their loans were called in, their mortgages foreclosed. Harder times for this area resulted in the thirties. Naturally the College was severely affected by the situation.

As the depression deepened, attempts were made in various ways to reduce the costs of administration. Economy was being practiced by offering some of the courses in alternate years and work in some of the lines of research and extension was reduced. The institution had nine professors and one instructor less than it had a year before. Several professors were paid a smaller salary than they had for the same work the year before. The sum of all these reductions in addition to what the staff donated to the Red Cross and Community Chest amounted to almost a ten per cent reduction in the salaries of the faculty, station and extension staff.

Unfortunately the harmony between the president and the Board of the first years of Dr. Shepperd's administration did not last. In May, 1931, the president of the College and Nelson Sauvain, chairman of the State Board of Administration, were in sharp disagreement over the finances of the State Seed Department.

Already in 1927 "certain political forces, dissatisfied with H. L. Bolley's work as seed commissioner, sought to unseat him; a battle raged in the legislature at that time." [4] Bolley continued in office and on April 24, 1929, was notified by the Board that he had been reappointed for a two-year term beginning July 1, 1929, with the understanding that half of his salary was to be paid by the seed certification fund and the potato grade inspection fund, and the balance by the Experiment Station. Both

Depression and Decline, 1929–1937

Dr. Coulter, then the president of the College, and P. F. Trowbridge, director of the Experiment Station, recommended Bolley, who preferred an appointment for an indefinite period rather than for two years.

As a result of this friction in the Legislature, the secretary of the Board of Administration in a letter to Dr. Coulter on July 1, 1929 introduced him to Mr. E. M. Gillig, who had been appointed state seed commissioner by the Board of Administration. On July 18 the secretary of the Board wrote to Dr. Coulter as follows: "Probably some explanation should be made to you in regard to the appointment of Mr. Gillig as seed commissioner. This appointment was absolutely necessary as the state potato growers insisted that some man be appointed by the board who could give his entire time to the organization of this work . . . Kindly extend to Professor Bolley the thanks of the board for the excellent service that he has rendered and assure him that the change was necessary, not from any lack of ability on his part, but so that the seed commissioner would be entirely divorced from the faculty of the agricultural college."

On July 25, 1929, Dr. Coulter advised the Board that the College would provide offices, with heat, light, gas, telephone and janitor service to the new seed commissioner. Upon recommendations of the seed commissioner the Board ordered the College, through the Experiment Station, to pay "nearly all of the seed commissioner's expense for labor and equipment, to set up a small kingdom within the agricultural college at the expense of that institution over which it had no control."[5]

The Legislature of 1931 reorganized the seed commission with a $60,000 appropriation available immediately, making it unnecessary for the Experiment Station to carry the pay of Mr. Stevens, seed analyst. Since legislative appropriations were decreased as prices for farm products declined, the revenue of the Experiment Station was very greatly reduced. Consequently, on March 26, 1931, President Shepperd recommended to the Board that the seed testing laboratory be transferred to the state seed department on April 1. And that under this proposal the seed department would carry the salary of Stevens, seed analyst, at $3,000 a year, together with a proportionate share of the costs for carrying the laboratory and the overhead institutional charges.[6] A copy was sent to Mr. Gillig.

The Board approved the recommendation on March 28, inserting the sentence: "The Board presumes, of course, that this matter has been taken up with the seed commissioner." On May 11 the Board rescinded its action of March 28 and ordered the payment by the Experiment Station of a large share of Gillig's expenses up to July 1, the end of the biennium. In the vote of the Board Nelson Sauvain, the chairman, J.

A. Kitchen, commissioner of agriculture and labor, and Bertha Palmer, superintendent of public instruction, were for it, R. B. Murphy and W. J. Church against it.[7] This controversy resulted in friction in the Board, as well as friction on the campus and more especially in friction between the College administration and a majority of the Board of Administration.

In 1932 William Langer was elected governor, endorsed by the Nonpartisan League. In 1916 he had been elected attorney general by the League with Frazier as governor. In 1920 he had run against Frazier on the Independent Voters' Association ticket, and was defeated; as a result of this he returned to the League faction.

The period following 1932 was a trying one for the rural population in North Dakota. The farmers suffered because of low market prices for farm products, and of crop failures. This situation was especially acute at the beginning of Governor Langer's administration because many farm mortgages had been based on pre-depression valuations and farmers faced foreclosure and the loss of their life's efforts. To prevent foreclosure Governor Langer declared various farm-mortgage moratoria by executive order. For a time an embargo on agricultural products was in effect, forbidding their shipment from the State in the hope that prices would be forced upward. In 1933 laws were passed outlawing crop mortgages and deficiency judgments.

A public appeal to North Dakota Republicans was sent from Bismarck by O. E. Erickson, chairman, on November 29, 1932 for funds to meet the party's deficit. On December 10, members of the Agricultural College faculty were solicited for contributions by personal letters signed by Erickson and R. N. Smith, secretary, with a letterhead listing 47 committeemen. In the same year petitions sponsored by the North Dakota Taxpayers' Association were circulated in the State calling for initiated measures to reduce and to fix salaries for elected state officials and for appointed state employees, which as interpreted later, would include instructors of institutions of higher education.

In the early thirties the local chapter of the American Association of University Professors continued to be influential as a means of expressing faculty opinion. Its members had increased and cordial relations were established with the chapter at the University of North Dakota. In 1932 when an amendment to the state constitution was initiated which would reduce and fix salaries of state officials, the College chapter of A.A.U.P. issued the following statement:

"The local chapter of the American Association of University Professors believes that, since the proposed initiated measure to reduce and fix salaries of state officers and employees offers such dangers to higher education in the state, it is their duty to inform people of the situation.

"The proposed law is so vaguely worded that it will have to be interpreted by the courts. If the courts rule that the measure applies to the faculties of the educational institutions it will mean that a $2,400 maximum will be placed on the salaries of all professors and administrators of the various state educational institutions. As a result it would be impossible for anyone in North Dakota to receive a first-class college education without leaving the state." [8]

However, the initiated measure to reduce and fix salaries for elected state officials and appointed state employees received the support of the North Dakota Taxpayers' Association and was made a law at the November election. In consequence of it the buying power of the faculty and staff of the College was reduced and individual staff members were accused of instituting a boycott against local Fargo merchants who were held responsible for signatures in the petitions of the Taxpayer's Association. Registrar Parrott sought to explain to the merchants that the real reason for a cut down in purchases was the inability of faculty members to buy in view of actual and prospective salary reductions. Also, in a similar vein, the North Dakota Agricultural College chapter of the American Association of University Professors pointed out that: "A 20 percent reduction in expenditures has already been effected. This saving has been made by a 10 percent reduction in salaries, by the elimination of a number of staff members, and by cutting operating costs. Any additional drastic reduction would seriously handicap the institutions (of the state) . . . "We realize that the burdens of the tax payers must be lightened. We believe, however, that mature consideration of the matter by our state legislature will result in sounder economy without injury to the educational standards of the university and of the agricultural college."[9]

The Legislature of 1933 reduced the appropriations for the College 59 percent, from a figure of $930,206.30 for 1931 to $374,265.67, which was a quarter of a million below the recommendation of the budget board and even below the governor's recommendation. These figures included student fees and other local income. Salaries were radically cut. The president's salary was limited to $3,000 and deans and heads of departments could not receive more than $1,920. Appropriations for the University of North Dakota were cut 55 percent and those of the North Dakota Agricultural College 59 percent. These unprecedented salary slices were put through in the hectic finish of a legislative session in a period of extreme economic depression. Clocks in the state house were stopped while the Legislature worked three days overtime.

Moreover, in May, 1933, a plan to finance *The Leader*, the official

Nonpartisan paper, by requiring state employees to pledge five percent of their annual salary to its support, was credited to Governor Langer. Employees of the State Mill and Elevator were pledged and employees of the University of North Dakota were approached. Also, the College campus was visited by solicitors who signed up employees in the secretary's office and the janitorial staff, but were turned down by the registrar. In July, 1933, President Shepperd sent to the various schools the following copy of the action of the Board: "That it be made public that no employee in any institution which is under the supervision of the Board of Administration will jeopardize his or her position or job, because of failure to contribute 5% assessment for a newspaper and that we instruct the Secretary to so notify the head of the institutions under the jurisdiction of the Board." On January 29, 1934, the staff received the following note from President Shepperd: "An arrangement for college publicity through *The Leader* brings as a phase of the consideration, a year's subscription to you to that journal."

On a Monday morning, September 18, 1933, another of Governor Langer's projects, the sales tax, came to the attention of the College. Chairman Nelson Sauvain, Robert M. Rishworth and Jennie Ulsrud of the Board of Administration conferred with Acting President A. E. Minard (President Shepperd was in Europe at this time). In the afternoon the Advisory Board of the College was called together. It decided to call a meeting Tuesday morning of the entire personnel of the Staff. Steve Hagan, who had recently been appointed secretary of the College by the Board of Administration which included his father, John Hagan, addressed the group, urging support of the sales tax and asking them to go on record favoring it. Mr. Hagan outlined the financial condition of the State, saying that the farmers could not pay their taxes because of drought, crop failures, etc. He felt that the State was in a serious condition financially. Unless money was raised some way he did not know what would happen to the State and its educational facilities. He maintained that this was an economic, not a political, question, that many I.V.A. senators as well as those of the Nonpartisan League favored the measure. E. A. Willson and Dr. C. E. Kellogg, members of the staff, both expressed the sentiment that the College should commit itself.

P. F. Trowbridge, director of the Experiment Station, advised against the practice of the institution's committing itself politically. Dean Minard concurred in this point of view. Professor J. R. Dice of the dairy department moved for adjournment. His motion was passed by a heavy chorus of "ayes." While some sentiment on the campus favored the tax, a decided majority seemed to be against it, largely because they thought

Depression and Decline, 1929–1937   129

the propsoal was politically inspired." A common expression found among faculty members was: "First they cut our salaries and our appropriations for other expenses necessary to our work. Then they make a political job out of the secretaryship and appoint a Langer man. Then they have nerve enough to come around and ask us for 5 percent of what little we are getting as a subscription for the administration paper. And now they want us to pay two per cent of what's left on everything we buy." [10]

Some members of the faculty, dissatisfied with the policy of the local chapter of the American Association of University Professors, thought that they should independently take active steps to obtain economic security. Consequently a local of the American Federation of Teachers was organized on the campus and a federation set up for the State. How much it accomplished cannot be measured. Its membership was criticized for lowering the ideals of the teaching profession by resorting to the tactics of a trade union. However, this organization did not last long, because of political circumstances, and on account of becoming controlled by some staff members who cooperated with the Farmers' Union.

A comparison of salaries paid to the different departments of the State with those paid to the faculties of the institutions of higher education illustrated the injustices felt by the teaching staff. Nine members of the State Mill and Elevator received an average $227 plus a month, twenty beer inspectors received over $150 a month, sixteen in the Regulatory Department received over $150, and sixteen other inspectors received over $150 and averaged at least $175. However, none of the faculty members received over $160. Members of the State Beer Commission drew $3,600, which was $600 more than the presidents of the College and the University received.

The president of the Agricultural College was tied with two other employees for tenth position in rank as measured by the rate of salary compensation at the College. His subordinates who received higher pay than he did received their salaries from the Federal Government.

Men of similar rank in the institution, who had been paid the same salaries for ten years or more and who continued to render similar service, now received very disproportionate pay. Thanks to the Federal Government stepping in, one man received twice as much money as his neighbor across the hall.[11]

As early as February, 1932, President Shepperd defended the previous salary scale of the College as expressed in the following statements:

"Salaries paid to faculty members at the North Dakota Agricultural College are not high compared to other institutions which offer the constant threat of taking the capable men from the local school because of more attractive monetary inducements . . .

"Ohio State University's salaries to deans, professors, assistant professors and instructors are 20 percent higher than the North Dakota Agricultural College pays for similar positions. Iowa State College pays for the positions named 29 percent more than the North Dakota Agricultural College does for the same positions. These two institutions have taken several of the outstanding men away from us recently while Nebraska and other states have likewise shown a disposition to draw away men we can ill afford to lose.

"A cut in salaries will make the inducements of these older institutions even more attractive and each outstanding man taken from us reduces the grade of our standing as an institution and thereby blocks the opportunities of our students." [12]

Later, after the Legislature passed its drastic cut, President Shepperd again protested against it:

"The greatest danger to the college from the depressed financial situation is the risk of losing its 'key men and women' to more favored public and business institutions through overbidding for their services, leaving only the second choice of the force as a working staff.

"So far the morale of this college has held, and the best of our faculty have remained with us, not withstanding the fact that the salaries paid for this biennium range from forty to fifty percent below those received by folks doing identical work at nearby institutions. They are staying simply because of their innate interest in the institution they have helped to build and with the expectation that their status will be improved for the next biennium.

"Most of the Agricultural College faculty members own homes in Fargo, take a prominent part in its organizations, have spent years studying the state and its needs, and will neither drop nor neglect their work by reason of their meager salaries for these two years of stress period." [13]

In the biennium 1932–34 nine members of the staff resigned and secured better paying positions elsewhere averaging $3,680, while the maximum salary of teachers who remained was $1,920. The members of the faculty petitioned the president and the Board of Administration that "their salary schedule of June 1, 1933, be restored on or before May 1, 1934." They based their request on the increased prices for wheat and other agricultural commodities and the large amounts of Federal funds that had come into the State. Salaries of Federal employees at the College had been restored to 1932 levels. Taxes paid into the state treasury had increased while at the same time the cost of living of the College staff members had increased only by ten to twelve percent. "Many faculty members had been forced to drop their insurance, refinance or lose their homes, curtail the education of their children, drop their membership in learned societies and carry over many unpaid bills which they could neither pay nor refinance." Therefore, a very considerable discontent, worry and lower morale was developing.

On November 7, 1933, the Board of Administration officially adopted a plan for reorganizing the College, effective July 1, 1934, as a means of simplifying and reducing costs. There were to be a president, four deans forming an advisory committee, a council and two service officers, a registrar and a secretary. The four divisions of the college would be Agriculture, Engineering which would include Chemistry, Home Economics, and Arts and Sciences, which would include Education and Pharmacy. Also there was to be a dean of students who should serve as counselor for both men and women. There was to be one director for both the Experiment Station and the Extension Service, with a separate budget and staff from that of the resident teaching staff.

According to this reorganization Dr. H. L. Walster, dean of Agriculture, was appointed director of both the Experiment Station and the Extension Service. Dr. Walster resigned as head of the department of agronomy and was succeeded by T. E. Stoa. Dr. Trowbridge devoted his time to special research and C. F. Monroe accepted a position as secretary of the Federal Bank of Cooperatives in St. Paul. Peter J. Olson, agronomist, was appointed assistant dean of agriculture and assistant director of the Experiment Station. Dr. L. W. Roderick was designated chairman of the department of animal pathology and hygiene, formerly called veterinary science. R. M. Dolve continued as dean of the Division of Engineering and Chemistry with L. L. Carrick as associate dean. A. E. Minard continued as dean of the Division of Applied Arts and Sciences with A. D. Weeks and W. F. Sudro as associate deans. In the reorganization the status of the Division of Home Economics was not changed.

This reorganization was severely criticized by faculty members, especially by those whose departments were reduced from their former status and transferred to other divisions, such as chemistry, education and pharmacy. On the other hand the change was defended as a measure of economy, to reduce the number of faculty members engaged in executive duties so that they might devote additional time to research and teaching activities.

The fall enrollment, despite these adverse conditions, increased by over one hundred over the previous year. This increase was doubtless due to the prospects of jobs under the Federal Emergency Relief Administration or other jobs obtained through the office of the employment secretary. Dean I. W. Smith reported that 147 FERA jobs were available. The employment secretary, with the cooperation of business men, merchants and householders in Fargo, provided some 500 part time jobs for students. Bachelor kitchen units were installed at the men's dormitory as a further economy.

In April, 1935, Attorney Eli Weston, who represented the employers in a strike of truckers in Fargo, spoke before the Fargo Kiwanis Club. In this speech he attributed the control and direction of the strike to Communists and in this connection made charges against certain members of the College faculty: "The activities of a group on the payroll of the agricultural college have all the earmarks and resemblances of communism."[14] This charge was indignantly denied by faculty and alumni. When asked by one of the staff members of the College to define the term "communism", Weston hesitated and finally admitted that he could not give a satisfactory definition. Later in May, 1936, E. D. Lum, publisher of the *Richland County Farmer Globe* in Wahpeton, at the 47th annual congress of the Sons of the American Revolution in Portland, Maine, charged that "half of the faculty" of the Iowa State Agricultural College at Ames were Communists, that conditions at North Dakota Agricultural College were "not much different," and that the campuses of the Universities of North Dakota and Minnesota were "hot beds of what we are trying to combat." President Shepperd of the North Dakota Agricultural College, President West of the University of North Dakota and President Coffman of the University of Minnesota emphatically denied the truth of such unsupported statements.

In July, 1935, the Board of Administration increased salaries by seven and a half per cent. In addition, the Federal Bankhead-Jones Act provided sufficient money for land-grant colleges to enable salaries at the North Dakota Agricultural College to be raised so that the president would receive 61.8 per cent of his salary of 1931-32, the deans 64.8 per cent, professors 73.3 per cent, instructors 74.1 per cent, and the rest of the staff even larger percentages.

The period of the administration of President Shepperd, which included the depression years, was naturally also a time for a look toward developing economies in administration and reducing the heavy burden of taxation. The "Peik Report" on the training of teachers in North Dakota, published in 1930 and made at the request of the Board of Administration, pointed out that too many institutions were engaged in teacher training out of proportion to the population of the State and that unnecessary and expensive duplication was in evidence. It recommended that secondary teachers in agriculture, home economics and the industrial arts and the physical and biological sciences be trained at the Agricultural College, but that other fields be taught at the University. The "Peik Report" thus misinterpreted the function of a land-grant college, which, according to the Morrill Act, should provide training and preparation in all branches of learning for the people of the State.

In 1932 the report of the North Dakota Governmental Survey Commission, created by the Legislature in 1931, included chapters on taxation, elections, local government and education. Chapter IX in this report dealing with the institutions of higher education, criticized duplication of curricula which was largely due to local influences to which individual institutions were subjected, resulting in a lack of unified administration and waste. The report recommended an organization of all the state educational institutions under the supervision of a single board of education, appointed by the governor.

This report was followed by much newspaper criticism in regard to the cost of higher education. An article in the *Richland County Farmer-Globe* decried duplication at the University and the Agricultural College. The writer of the article claimed that three schools — Mechanical Arts, Education and Science and Education — at the College duplicated three — Engineering, Education and Liberal Arts — at the University.[15] Doubtless this article was in part the result of a news story in the *Fargo Forum* which pointed out that the Taxpayers Association was disposed to ask the Legislature to move the State School of Science in Wahpeton to Fargo.

A number of articles appeared in the press in August, 1935, in reference to a union of the Agricultural College and the University under one administrative head, as suggested by an interim tax survey commission. This proposal was associated with the "possible shifting of the present administrative head at the State Agricultural College, President J. H. Shepperd."[16] The argument of Dr. Spencer A. Larsen, consultant of the tax survey commission, was that one head over these two institutions, with the support of the Board of Administration, could eliminate any unwarranted duplication of work not in the interests of the students and taxpayers.

The Leader maintained that sixty per cent of the State legislators who had replied to a questionnaire sent out by the tax survey commission favored the merger. Actually, of the 50 out of 168 replying, 30 legislators favored unification, 10 were opposed and 10 were "uncertain." Sample statements in favor of the merger were quoted: "The Agricultural College has degenerated, if the term may be used, into another university"; the Agricultural College had "grown away from its original aim." But in general the plan was opposed on the ground that it was not "practical," that it would not "effect economy," that "endless conflicts, eventually crippling one institution by preference given the other," would ensue.[17]

Of the Fargo legislators Representative Ed Cosgriff favored the union on the basis of good business. Senator A. W. Fowler and three other representatives were opposed claiming that there would be little saving, that it would tend to make the Agricultural College a secondary institution, and that the existing system was working very well.

As to a change in the presidency of the College, Judge J. D. Harris, chairman of the Board of Administration, and R. M. Rishworth, a member, denied that the Board had ever discussed any such change. Even so in certain circles George A. Chaney of Des Moines, Iowa, an educator and lecturer had been mentioned as a successor to Dr. Shepperd.

A long article appeared in the *Fargo Forum* on August 9, 1935: "It is advanced in Bismarck that Dr. Shepperd would relinquish his position 'voluntarily' and step back to his former position as head of the animal husbandry division at the Experiment Station." In defense President Shepperd told the *Fargo Forum* that he had no such plan in mind. "While he had frequently commented unofficially that he would some day like to resume his experimental work and his writings, which have appeared in outstanding agricultural journals, he said Friday that he would much prefer to stay on as president of the College until 'I get things out here a bit more squarely on their feet'. The college has suffered heavily through drastically cut appropriations, necessitating a drastic program of retrenchment on the part of its executive officers."[18]

In the meantime, the complexion of the Board of Administration had changed since July 1, 1935. J. D. Harris succeeded Sauvain as chairman. Other members were R. M. Rishworth, an appointee of Governor George F. Shafer, Mrs. Jennie Ulsrud, an appointee of Governor William Langer, and elected members State Superintendent of Public Instruction A. E. Thompson and Commissioner of Agriculture and Labor Theodore Martel.

The conditions resulting from the legislative acts of 1933 affected all of the educational institutions of higher learning. In May, 1934 the Minot State Teachers' College had initiated a movement to form an organization of faculties of the institutions of higher learning to cooperate in a mutual plan of betterment. The faculties of the University, of the teachers colleges of Mayville, Valley City and Dickinson, and of the School of Science at Wahpeton acted by the first of July and planned a meeting in Valley City to perfect such an organization.

Due to the absence of President Shepperd, who had gone to Europe, and of various faculty members during the summer, the faculty of the Agricultural College did not act on the proposed organization until

October, when it voted to join the Higher Education Association "for the purpose of securing rehabilitation of salary schedules." However, its situation was complicated by the fact that a considerable number of the staff were paid in whole or in part by the Federal Government.

By 1933 Clarence McCulloch, at the request of Governor Langer, was named a special examiner for the College by Adam LeFor, state examiner. He was instructed to make a complete audit of records of the North Dakota Agricultural College, including the Extension Division and the Experiment Station, and also including an examination of the entire departmental set up.

Meanwhile, the State was undergoing a stormy period of political history. Governor Langer was convicted on a Federal charge of conspiracy, arising from solicitation of contributions from State and Federal employees for support of his political newspaper, *The Leader*. He was therefore held disqualified under the State constitution by the Supreme Court and removed from office on July 18, 1934. Ole Olson, lieutenant governor, served the remainder of the term.

In November, 1934, Mrs. Langer was defeated for governor by Thomas H. Moodie, the Democratic candidate, but he was subsequently declared ineligible by the Supreme Court on February 1, 1935, because of insufficient residence in the State. Walter Welford, lieutenant governor and member of the Nonpartisan League, became acting governor. Thus North Dakota had four governors in a little over six months. Later the Federal district court reversed Langer's conviction.

The election of 1936 was to have special influence on the College. In the June primary former Governor Langer ran against Acting Governor Welford for the nomination and was defeated. In the November election Langer ran on the Independent ticket and was elected. In his inaugural address on January 6, 1937, Governor Langer said:

"I sincerely desire to be the governor of all the people regardless of race, creed or political beliefs. I hope to cooperate with you and have each and all of you consult with and advise me at all times. . . .

"On every side we witness conditions of distress and poverty. Poor crops with depressed prices, extending over a period of several years — worst of all last year — have brought before us for consideration and action, a situation which never before existed. . . .

"Our first and most important concern is the participation of our state in giving all necessary aid and relief to those who are in destitute circumstances within the state. Investigation has revealed that 70,000 families are on the relief rolls . . . It is therefore recommended that the legislature make available immediately $1,000,000 to cover the period to June 1, 1937. Old age benefits and unemployment insurance are here . . . I recommend that an unemployment compensation measure be enacted immediately so that this state may qualify for help. . . .

"As you all know, I have continuously advocated reduction of taxes . . . At the same time in this program of reduction of taxes and greater economy in government, I am in favor of maintaining our school system in this state, both the elementary schools and higher education, at its highest possible efficiency. . . .

"Our teachers, whether in rural schools, high schools, or institutions of higher learning, must be competent, and we must be willing to pay them well for the services they render. With the higher costs of living, their scale of wages ought to be higher. In our institutions of higher learning, we cannot expect to secure that competent service, or to retain it as we have it, without paying a wage at least similar to those paid for work in other employments of the state . . .

"Our people are now passing through the stormiest seas of economic depression and worldwide devastation. Our people are looking over the hills to see tomorrow's sunshine of betterment for the protection of themselves, their home, their business and their children. They look to you and to me to cooperate for their interest. . . ."[19]

The favorable attitude expressed in Governor Langer's inaugural address gave rise to hope for an increase in the salaries of the faculty members. The College had been severely crippled by the slash in appropriations in 1933. Since 1930, according to a report prepared by President Shepperd, 57 full-time staff members had left the institution and 27 of the vacancies had not been filled due to shortage of funds. 35 of the 57 left for other positions, thereby bettering themselves financially by an average increase of $1,448 in their annual salaries.

However, the budget board recommended a decrease of $19,083 in the budget below the aproprations of the 1935-37 biennium, at the same time when every other institution of higher learning in the State was given an increase. The Board explained that instructors at the North Dakota Agricultural College would receive money from the fund of the Federal Bankhead-Jones Act, although actually these funds applied only to a minor portion of the staff.

When the legislature convened in January, 1937, President Shepperd was called to Bismarck to meet with the house appropriations committee to go over the coming budget of the College. The real purpose seems to have been to go over the books of the College to see if there was misuse of any funds. This suspicion was quite apparent when the committee directed Steve Hagan, secretary, to bring the College books to Bismarck. Certain members of the committee, coached by Hagan, spent hours trying to find misuse of funds, although other members exerted every effort in behalf of the College and Dr. Shepperd.

On May 25 President Shepperd announced to the alumni board that he was ready to retire from his office whenever a suitable successor could be obtained: "There has been continued and persistent rumors throughout the state since early in the year that a change

Depression and Decline, 1929–1937

is contemplated in the office of the president. If there is to be a change, it would not be personally unwelcome to me. My service as president has been during some of the most difficult years the institution and the state have had to face. It has been a constant struggle. During this time, it has become necessary for me to lay aside almost entirely my work in animal husbandry, always my principal interest. I would be far from reluctant to resume that work where I left off."[20]

Prominently mentioned for several weeks as Dr. Shepperd's successor was E. W. Gillig, connected with the College as State seed commissioner. Other men mentioned were Dr. J. T. E. Dinwoodie, head of the AAA conservation program in the State, and E. J. Tainter of the Park River Agricultural School.

In early July, Mrs. Ulsrud was named chairman of the Board of Administration, and R. A. Kinzer of Valley City was appointed a new member to succeed Rishworth. The North Dakota Holiday Association endorsed H. C. Hanson for president of the College. The *Fargo Forum* on July 25 reported that President Shepperd had submitted his resignation in June or early July.

On July 29th the Board accepted President Shepperd's resignation and appointed John C. West, president of the University of North Dakota, acting president of the Agricultural College. John Hagan, one of the prime movers in bringing about the appointment, said there was no intent to make the Agricultural College "the tail of the kite" of the University. He further said, "On the contrary, this is a move to build up the A.C. or perhaps you could say to rehabilitate it as an agricultural institution . . . as an agricultural institution it has been slipping badly over a long period of years, building up other departments at the expense of the agricultural. The board was looking for an administrator, an executive . . . if he can do for the A.C. what he has done for the university the board will be satisfied."[21] R. A. Kinzer, a Board member, asserted that an act of the Legislature, passed in 1933, guided the Board in its action. This act required the elimination of duplication and a gradual coordination of the courses of study in the state educational institutions.

On July 30th the *Fargo Forum* announced that the State Board of Administration had accepted Dr. Shepperd's resignation and that he had been named president emeritus.

This account of the political unrest and the economic difficulties in North Dakota and the resulting low budgets of the College during President Shepperd's administration explains why only a minimum could be accomplished in the way of original experimentation. However, the record showed that progress was made in the study of crops, of emergency feed for livestock, of animal diseases, of plant diseases and in control of insect pests.

Director Trowbridge resigned as director of the Experiment Station in 1934 and was succeeded by Dr. Walster. Shortly before his death in 1937 Dr. Trowbridge was honored by some 200 friends and fellow workers headed by T. H. Hopper, chairman of agricultural chemistry, by having his portrait hung in the gallery of the National Saddle and Sirloin Club Hall of Fame in Chicago. This was a great honor, recognizing "only those individuals, who have made notable contributions to animal research and livestock industry". Not only was it a tribute to Dr. Trowbridge, but also a reflection of lasting honor and recognition for the College.

The Experiment Station was faced with a new situation in the midthirties. In 1935 a rapid increase and spreading of stem rust in spring wheat developed and heavy damage occurred in fields sown in Ceres, which, up to that time, had been quite rust resistant. Fortunately, lines which could resist the disease were already in production or under development in the wheat breeding nurseries. By 1938, two of these lines were being increased, and by 1939 they were named Rival and Pilot and released to North Dakota farmers; by 1942 they were in wide use. Another wheat line, released in 1944 and named Mida, had still greater resistance to the rust and came into extensive use over a wide area. These three wheats developed by the Experiment Station occupied from one half to two thirds of the spring wheat acreage in North Dakota for the next several years.

The same thing which the plant breeders accomplished in order to afford rust protection in the hard red spring wheats was also accomplished in durum. Two varieties developed in cooperation with the United States Department of Agriculture by crossing durum with emmer ("speltz") were released in 1943 under the names Stewart and Carleton. They had excellent resistance to stem rust and were extensively grown during the next few years.

The successive drought years in the thirties brought along a large increase in grasshoppers throughout the Great Plains. Entomologists of the Experiment Station and Extension Service cooperated in developing a poison bait and supervising its use. Better insecticides were also applied and effected greater control of grasshopper outbreaks.

Unfavorable crop years — low production and low prices — brought urgent requests from western counties to the Experiment Station to develop a more equitable system of appraising land for taxation purposes. Soil scientists from the Station and from the United States

Department of Agriculture made a detailed soil survey in those counties and developed a system of rural land classification which would serve as a basis for the equalization of assessments.

The Extension Service was frequently called upon to assist in alleviating the suffering and distress of the State's farming population. In the depression years of 1931, 1932, 1933 and the drought year of 1936 suffering was severe. The prices of farm commodities were the lowest in seventy years. Debt and past due taxes swept away the life savings of many farmers. Many lost their farms and survived by renting farms they formerly owned. Many were forced to accept Red Cross and Federal relief to clothe and feed their families.

Three devastating periods of drought occurred in the thirties and the first, in 1931, occurred in the midst of a financial depression. This was most severe in the northwest section of the State; in six counties little or no vegetation grew and in nine counties no grain was harvested. The governor called on the Extension Service to play a major role in the relief work. Federal loans were made available. Over 2,000 carloads of hay, 2,900 tons of cotton seed cake and 2,100 tons of dried beet pulp were purchased. The Red Cross bought and distributed 80,000 bushels of potatoes. The work of the Extension Service in emergencies such as the World War, the grasshopper invasions of the twenties, the droughts of the thirties, justified the confidence of the people.

In regard to it Director Monroe's annual report for 1931 makes this statement: "It is noted that during the present depression, farmers are more willing to cooperate with Extension workers than in times of greater prosperity. They feel the need of greater efficiency in the production of their products and are more inclined to welcome the information brought to them by County Agents and other Extension workers. . . . Leadership of the Extension organization and the County Agent in particular, has prevented a great deal of suffering from lack of feed and has contributed materially to the support of many farmers in the drought area."

It was natural that the discouragement of farm people and their determination to get tax relief would cause them to desire to eliminate the expense of county agent work. In addition, taxpayers' associations were active in all counties circulating petitions to discontinue county agent work. The Extension Service made a valiant effort to educate people to vote in favor of retaining county agents, but nine of the 19 counties voted against it.

The passage of the Federal Agricultural Adjustment Act in 1933 helped to bring agriculture out of the worst depression in our history. The Extension Service was given the job of organizing the wheat allotment plan and of training the personnel for administering it. In spite of inadequate office facilities and help the agents carried out their regular duties as well as the special tasks required by the federal program.

Director Monroe resigned on June 30, 1933, to accept a position with the newly formed Bank for Cooperatives in St. Paul and Dean H. L. Walster, director of the Experiment Station, was appointed also director of Extension. Since Dr. Walster was scheduled to take over the directorship of the Experiment Station on July 1, and at the same time retain his position as dean of agriculture, his selection as head of Extension Service in the State permitted close correlation of the educational and research branches of the College. As director of the Extension Service Dr. Walster was to supervise the work of extension agents in 22 counties as well as the activities of agricultural emergency assistants in all counties of the State. He would have charge of the wheat production and the corn-hog adjustment programs of the Agricultural Adjustment Administration in North Dakota.

In 1933 the State Legislature greatly reduced appropriations for the Extension Service. The governor vetoed the Extension state budget passed by the legislature, and directed the Board of Administration to reduce the salaries of the personnel of all educational institutions to a maximum annual salary of $1,920. No state funds were used in the payment of salaries of the Extension staff members, yet they were included in the salary reduction. N. D. Gorman, county agent leader, had this to say:

"After receiving the low salaries for about six months, three members of the staff, E. J. Haslerud, assistant county agent leader, John Dinwoodie, district supervisor, and N. D. Gorman, county agent leader, received offers of employment from the Farm Credit Administration. On the agreement of the three, N. D. Gorman called Geo. E. Farrell, Chief of the Agricultural Adjustment Section of the U.S.D.A. and informed him that unless the salaries of the Extension staff members could be restored within fifteen percent of the 1932 level, the reduction on all federal salaries, the three would be forced to resign and accept the Farm Credit offer. Several days later Mr. Farrell arrived at the Agricultural College and it was agreed that Extension salaries would be restored to within fifteen percent of the 1932 level, as the U.S.D.A. could ill afford to disrupt the Extension organization." [22]

In the year 1934 occurred the most devastating drought in the experience of the people in North Dakota. County and emergency agents organized and directed drought relief programs as well as the

Depression and Decline, 1929-1937

newly formed wheat allotment programs. The Extension Service received no help or encouragement from the State government, although a vast number of farm and business leaders did serve on F.E.R.A. and other Federal agencies.

The year 1936 was marked by the return of 27 counties to the Extension Service fold through the ballot and the passage of the Bankhead-Jones Act, adding $124,104.00 of Federal funds to the Extension budget. The drought was most severe in the southwest counties of the State. The addition of the 27 counties brought a total of 48 counties on an extension cooperating basis. Although the crop situation in 1937 was a vast improvement over the three previous years, more people received Federal help that year than at any previous time. It was estimated that forty-five per cent of the people of the State were receiving some form of Federal grants, relief, National Youth Administration or Public Works Administration assistance.

Up to this point the period of President Shepperd's administration has been described from the standpoint of its relation to the faculty and the Board of Administration. These trying years of 1929-1937 also had their repercussions on the students.

Reduced appropriations in the thirties had an effect on the library budget. Dr. Trowbridge, chairman of the library committee, recommended that the journal subscriptions of the various departments be transferred to the library account, but President Shepperd believed it would be more difficult to finance. However, some departments found it impossible to carry journal subscriptions. Once an order of books by a department was denied on the grounds that the money was needed for more essential purposes.

In January, 1935, a senior student in agriculture wrote to Speaker Crockett of the North Dakota house of representatives, asking the Legislature to enact a law making military drill optional at State schools. He claimed that a majority of students at the College were opposed to compulsory drill, although this statement was challenged by local cadet officers.

The Legislature failed to pass such a bill by narrow margins in both houses in 1935. In 1936 a convocation for peace was addressed by Senator C. W. Fine, sponsored by the American Student Union, and locally by the College Farmers' Union and the International Relations Club. In 1937 a bill to make drill optional was introduced in the house of representatives. Two student members of Scabbard and Blade appeared before the house committee on education to present arguments against the bill. A college convocation of 1,000 students heard a discussion of the issue by student leaders. Over 800 signatures were affixed to petitions requesting the retention of compulsory drill; however, both houses passed the bill and Governor Langer signed it.

Student politics again became reactivated. In 1929 a student "frame" won every office.[23] From then on, frames were the order of the day. "The Hog-It-All" frame in 1932 was defeated by the "Holier-Than-Thou" party, whose chief strength was the independent vote. In 1934 the two frames split and a new alignment, the Progressives (Not-So-Sure) won over the Not-So-Pures. These contests were a means of student expression of political rivalry.

Pageants and spectacles given by Professor Arvold won the attention of many. In 1929 "Covered Wagon Days" was held in El Zagal Park, a large natural bowl which El Zagal Shrine had transformed from a dumping ground into a park and golf course. The whole College celebrated the Bicentennial of Washington's birthday in February, 1932. The program included a dramatization of the Federal Constitutional Convention of 1887, a colonial ball, exhibits of colonial furniture and textiles, a colonial tea, ending in a convocation addressed by Judge Burr of the Supreme Court.

The Little Country Theater had celebrated its tenth anniversary in 1924 by an address by Lorado Taft, the sculptor; it celebrated its twentieth by the dedication of the "Peer Gynt" window and later anniversaries by additional windows, "As You Like It" and "Faust."

A faculty-student relations committee was appointed by President Shepperd to counsel with representatives of student organizations and discuss their problems. It was designed to serve as a clearinghouse of ideas between faculty and students.

The administration of President Shepperd ended with a distinct note of censure against him. The next chapter will seek to show whether that adverse criticism was deserved. The early years of Dr. Shepperd's life as professor and experimenter have already been described. Throughout his career at the College he and Mrs. Shepperd were associated as helpmates and mutual advisers. She served as assistant to Dr. Ladd a considerable number of years and was an active club woman for twenty-five years. John and Adele Shepperd considered themselves as partners in a variety of enterprises. They both entered heartily into the social activities of the faculty and students. President Shepperd's efforts to carry on in spite of economic distress and political opposition should be appreciated. It was his misfortune to have to deal with those who took advantage of his honest and trusting nature.

FOOTNOTES

[1] *College and State*, XIII, No. 1 (Oct., 1929), 7.
[2] *Renville County Farmer*, Feb. 13, 1930.
[3] *College and State*, XV, No. 2 (Jan., 1932), 2.
[4] *Bismarck Tribune*, May 20, 1931.
[5] *Bismarck Tribune*, May 20, 1931.
[6] Minutes of the Board of Administration, March 26, 1931.
[7] Minutes of the Board of Administration, May 11, 1931.
[8] *Spectrum*, Nov. 1, 1932.
[9] *Fargo Forum*, Nov. 9, 1932.
[10] *Fargo Forum*, Sept. 19, 1933.
[11] *Fargo Forum*, Feb. 7, 1932.
[12] Shepperd, (MSS., May 26, 1932), Institute for Regional Studies, Library, N.D.A.C.
[13] Shepperd, (MSS, 1932) Institute for Regional Studies, Library, N.D.A.C.
[14] *Fargo Forum*, Apr. 23, 1935. Mr. Weston based his charges on the sympathy expressed by members of the local A. F. of L. for the strikers.
[15] *Richland County Farmer-Globe* (Wahpeton), Dec. 23, 1932.
[16] *Fargo Forum*, Aug. 12, 1935.
[17] *The Leader*, Oct. 3, 1935.
[18] *Fargo Forum*, Aug. 9, 1935.
[19] *Fargo Forum*, Jan. 7, 1937.
[20] *Spectrum*, May 26, 1937.
[21] *The Leader*, Aug. 5, 1937.
[22] N. D. Gorman, 203.
[23] A frame was a popular term for a combination of several fraternities and sororities, sometimes in cooperation with the independent or non-fraternity students.

◄ CHAPTER IX ►

The Purge, 1937-1938

THE most dramatic and tragic event in the history of the North Dakota Agricultural College occurred in the summer of 1937. As mentioned in the previous chapter, rather unexpectedly, on Thursday, July 29, 1937, the Board of Administration, with all members except A. E. Thompson present, accepted the resignation of President Shepperd and appointed Dr. John C. West, president of the University of North Dakota, as acting president of the North Dakota Agricultural College, to take effect immediately. Explaining the reasons for this action, John Hagan, member of the Board, said that "the Board was looking for an administrator and executive" and that "Dr. West had faced difficult problems at the university with respect to reduced appropriations and made a good record."[1] R. A. Kinzer, another member, said that "the move was made primarily to start gradual consolidation of specialty departments in the two schools." He asserted that "the move would eliminate duplication and would prove to be an economy measure."[2]

Following this action, the Board of Administration sent registered letters of dismissal to seven of the higher ranking members of the College staff. The letters were received by the members on Saturday, July 31, at 9 a.m., and the dismissals were to become effective at noon. Faculty members dismissed by this action were R. M. Dolve, dean of the School of Engineering, a member of the faculty since 1906; Alba Bales, dean of the School of Home Economics, a member of the faculty since 1920; P. J. Olson, assistant dean of the School of Agriculture, a member of the staff since 1924; and I. W. Smith, professor of mathematics and dean of men, a member of the faculty since 1909. Other staff members dismissed were A. H. Parrott, registrar and member of the staff since 1903; N. D. Gorman, county agent leader for the Extension Service and member of the staff since 1924; Jean Traynor, secretary to President Shepperd, who had been employed on the campus for twenty-six years and had served under three presidents. Dr. H. L. Walster, associated with the College since 1919, dean of the School of Agriculture, director of the Experiment Station, and director of the Extension Service, was relieved as director of the Station and Extension and ordered to "confine his duties exclusively to the School of Agriculture."

The letters were signed by A. B. Welch, secretary of the Board, who said that the action removing the seven college staff members was taken July 29 at the Board meeting prior to the appointment of Dr. West as acting president. A. E. Thompson, state superintendent of public instruction and ex-officio member of the Board, was not present at this meeting, since he was representing the Board at summer school commencements at Mayville and Ellendale. Why this important meeting of the Board was scheduled for a time when one member could not be present can only be surmised. However, there remains the fact that the order of dismissal was signed on July 31, although the decision itself was made two days before, on July 29.

As ordered by the Board of Administration, the combination on the vault in the president's office was changed by S. W. Hagan, secretary of the College, who also personally sealed the files in the offices of all the staff members dismissed.

The reasons for this action are subjects for conjecture. Mrs. Jennie Ulsrud, chairman of the Board, said that "the dismissals were made because in the opinion of the Board it was for the best interests of the institution." The Fargo Chamber of Commerce, in a resolution passed August 5, placed the responsibility for the action of the Board on Governor Langer. Of the members of the Board, Mrs. Ulsrud and J. D. Harris were former appointees of the governor. R. A. Kinzer had only recently, on July 1, been appointed by Governor Langer. Thus a majority of the Board were appointed by Langer and, in addition, John Hagan, who was elected Commissioner of Agriculture and Labor, sided with the majority of the Board.

The control of the Extension Service and the Experiment Station by Governor Langer was believed in the State to have been the ultimate objective behind the action of the Board. With the resignation of President Shepperd, the Board was in a position to control all administrative appointments at the College. Two of the seven dismissals involved the two top-ranking members of the Extension Service and the Experiment Station, Director H. L. Walster and N. D. Gorman, state county agent leader. "Administration of the whole setup would involve disposal of a million dollar payroll involving about 3,200 persons, of whom some 600 were practically on a full time basis, and of the distribution of about $20,000,000 annually in benefit payments to farmers for AAA compliance."[3]

On Saturday, July 31, President Shepperd, whose resignation had just been accepted, telephoned the Board in Bismarck and asked that the staff members dismissed be given a hearing. In a prepared statement released for publication on August 4, he commented as follows in regard to the dismissals:

"Relative to the seven members of the staff dropped from the college rolls by the board of administration, following their acceptance of my voluntary resignation, I wish to say that they are efficient workers in their respective lines and all well above the average in similar colleges and universities in the country. The notices of dismissal which they showed me on Saturday morning, July 31, were my first information that such a plan was contemplated. Since there have been no charges preferred nor reasons given for their dismissal, I can only marvel at the occurrence."

"I fancy the board members were not aware of the common practice and usage in terminating the employment of college professors nor of the damaging results to individual teachers of sudden dismissal from their positions." [4]

In answer to Dr. Shepperd's request for a hearing, on Monday, August 2, a wire was drafted by Secretary Welch giving 11 a.m., August 3, as the earliest date when all members could be present for a hearing. This message was reportedly sent to Dr. Shepperd, but he did not receive the wire and there was no record of it found at the office of Western Union.[5]

The Alumni and Former Students' Association of the North Dakota Agricultural College in 1937 was headed by an executive board of ten members, consisting of Glenn Cook, O. Gunvaldson, J. G. Halbeisen, William Guy, Max Hughes, Edgar I. Olsen, Dr. B. K. Bjornson, O. A. Schollander, S. Lynn Huey and R. Worth Lumry. As its first action this group drafted a letter to President West of the University of North Dakota, who had been named acting president of the College, asserting that the Association "questioned the fitness of a man to accept the A.C. presidency unless he demanded that the Board reinstate the dismissed staff members."[6] The Alumni Association also, on August 4, sent the following telegram to Governor Langer:

"Because of the widespread feeling over the state that grave injustice has been done to individual members of the agricultural college faculty and because a fatal blow has been struck against the best interests of the institutions of higher learning of North Dakota, we hereby demand that you secure the prompt re-instatement of all members of the agricultural college staff summarily dismissed by recent action of the board of administration. We respectfully request an immediate statement of your position." [7]

In addition to these communications, the Alumni Association at the same time sent to all graduates and former students an appeal to join in a campaign for re-instatement of the staff members dismissed.

On August 5, Governor Langer sent the following telegram to the Alumni Association:

"In 1933 when the legislative committees voted to close the agricultural college because they believed it failed in its original purposes I saved it by a personal appeal to the legislators and succeeded only in keeping it open by agreeing not to veto a 20 per cent cut in salaries . . . At the recent legislative session the appropriation was only finally secured after a terrific fight and again only after a personal appeal . . . At the recent session of the legislature, spokesmen for the college could not even explain to the appropriations committee what the money was needed for and were hopelessly confused until the committee finally sent for the secretary to straighten out the confusion . . ."

"From my contact with the taxpayers, particularly the farmers, and laborers, I believe they overwhelmingly approve the action taken without my knowledge by the board in the removal of persons they thought should be removed and I also believe that they overwhelmingly approve the appointment of Dr. John C. West which action was taken with my full knowledge . . . In response that I state my position I emphatically say that I shall do nothing to secure the reinstatement of any members of the faculty removed by the board of administration but that on the contrary I shall support, sustain and uphold them in their endeavor to give the people the kind of a school the pioneers of North Dakota intended they should have. It is my belief that you and the Alumni Association are being used by a small coterie of Fargo politicians to mistakenly work against the very best interests of the institution which in my heart I feel you love and want to serve well." [8]

Langer's newspaper, *The Leader,* in an editorial headed "For a Better Agricultural College," followed a line of reasoning similar to that in the governor's statement:

"For more than a decade the A.C. of Fargo has been under an anaesthetic-hold in the throttle-grip of a small clique . . . as an institution for the training of our farm boys and girls in the science of agriculture the A.C. has gone steadily backwards . . . under the dictatorship of a group of men who regarded themselves as untouchables . . . aided and abetted by the so-called Fargo gang of politicians . . . The institution came to be regarded as the sole property of the city of Fargo. Nearly half of the student body was drawn from the city and the immediate vicinity . . . The Fargo crowd set out to make it a second state university, where the teaching of agriculture was very secondary . . . the instruction and graduation of trained agriculturists dropped to practically nothing . . . (there is) a noticeable reluctance for a huge appropriation for an agricultural college that had fallen down on the job . . . In dismissing several staff members the Board has taken the first steps in a program of rebuilding and rehabilitation for the agricultural college." [9]

The charge that the Agricultural College was not living up to its original purpose was obviously an error. The objective of the Morrill Act, upon which the College was founded, was not to train only in agriculture, but to train sons and daughters of "farmers and artisans" for any business or profession, but particularly for agriculture and the mechanic arts. The College had emphasized those courses but had not neglected others. The people of North Dakota are themselves responsible for the curricula which their children elect. And it was not true that the teaching of agriculture and engineering had been neglected.

On August 12, without consulting Dr. West, the Board abolished alumni fees formerly collected at both the College and at the University of North Dakota. Chairman Jennie Ulsrud said the purpose of this action of the Board was to reduce the cost of registration "for the benefit of the students and parents with no intent to hurt the alumni associations."

On August 16 the Alumni Association advised Langer that the usefulness of the Association to the institution was "terminated" by this action of the Board. In the same letter the Alumni Association also took issue with Langer's contention that he had been responsible for saving the N.D.A.C. in 1933.

"In reply to your telegram of Aug. 5 permit us to inform you that a careful perusal of the house and senate journals fails to disclose that any action such as you state for the closing of the agricultural college was contemplated by the legislature of 1933 . . . In 1933 the records show a partial veto of agricultural college appropriations by yourself as governor, in the amount of $96,707. over the heavy reductions which had already been made to all educational institutions in the state.

"With reference to the recent legislature there seems to be no personal appeal by yourself in behalf of the agricultural college. On the contrary the difficulty which the agricultural college appropriations experienced was inspired by a man close to your administration . . . the secretary of the college to whom you refer, arrived in Bismarck and there ensued, largely behind closed doors, a campaign to discredit heads of the agricultural college which terminated in the recent action by you and the board of administration when these educational leaders were removed from the institution, thus placing this and all schools in the state into politics." [10]

Meanwhile, Dr. John C. West arrived in Fargo on August 6 to take over his duties as acting president. He said that his job was to prepare for the opening of the College, confer with members of the faculty, handle the pay roll, etc. At a dinner with a joint committee representing the Fargo Chamber of Commerce and the College Alumni Association, he indicated that there would be no immediate replacement of any of the staff members, at least while a hearing for them was under consideration. At this dinner he was asked to urge the Board to hold a hearing for the dismissed staff members, but he refused by saying that his appointment required him to cooperate with the Board of Administration.

In a personal letter released for publication, Dr. West revealed certain plans for the College, among them:

"That an expanded rather than a restricted curriculum is anticipated."

"That rural electrification studies and engineering work are under consideration as special fields. That no plan is contemplated to move the school of pharmacy to the University of North Dakota at Grand Forks. That N.D.A.C. will continue as an accredited institution if it is in my power, and I think it is, to keep it so."[11]

Dr. West also sought a conference with the representatives of the Federal Government, representing the United States Department of Agriculture. On August 12, C. W. Warburton, chief of the Extension Division, R. W. Trullinger, acting chief of the Experiment Station and H. W. Gilbertson, regional agent in charge of extension work in the central states, met with Dr. West, and Mrs. Ulsrud, chairman, R. A. Kinzer and John H. Hagan, members of the State Board of Administration. Their purposes were to discuss "the relationship between Federal and state government in operating the extension division and experiment station," to iron out any difficulties that might arise from the dismissal of the seven staff members, and to discuss the future of the new administration. The Federal representatives were concerned with the type and training of the men whom the Board might select for the key administrative positions, and they asked for assurance that the administrative officers handling Federal funds would not be under political domination.

The State Board of Administration, consisting of Mrs. Ulsrud, Kinzer, Hagan and A. E. Thompson, on August 13 named Dr. Herbert C. Hanson, botanist of the College since 1930, director of the Experiment Station. Mr. Trullinger advised the Board that he would remain in Fargo to "check in" Dr. Hanson. At this time no one was named head of the Extension Division, but "it was understood that the entire division was sifted over in search of a qualified and 'accepted' appointee."

On August 14 the appointment of George J. Baker, extension animal husbandman at the College, as acting director of the Extension Service was announced. The action had the approval of C. W. Warburton, chief of the Extension Division. Dr. West announced that the Federal officials were given the absolute promise of the State Board of Administration that both Baker and Hanson would be free to recommend their assistants and appointees without "political consideration, and that there would be no interference permitted for political purposes in either department." Dr. West also said that both appointments were on an "acting" basis.

Upon the recommendation of President West, on September 3, 1937, Miss Alice Haley was appoined dean of Home Economics at a salary of $3,000. At the same meeting Professor W. F. Sudro, associate dean in the Division of Applied Arts and Sciences since July 1, 1934, was made Dean of Pharmacy, with pharmacy as a full college division. Dr. E. A. Helgeson was appointed acting chairman of the Botany Department in place of Hanson, who was granted a year's leave of absence while acting as director of the Experiment Station. Dr. L. L. Carrick, associate dean in the Division of Engineering, was made Dean of the School of Chemistry. Professor H. S. Rush was appointed acting Dean of Engineering. R. C. Olson was appointed extension animal husbandman in place of G. J. Baker. President Emeritus Shepperd was assigned to the position of associate animal husbandman in the College, Experiment Station and Extension Service. C. A. Sevrinson was named Dean of Men. President West submitted to the Board a general program for appointments and dismissals of College employees which recommended discussions with all superior officers and department chairmen, deans, and the president, and then formal recommendations to the State Board of Administration.

In the meantime what became of the staff members who had been so summarily dismissed? Dean R. M. Dolve secured a position as assistant professor of mechanical engineering at the University of Minnesota. Dean Alba Bales left Fargo. Dean I. W. Smith was appointed an actuary for the Pioneer Life Insurance Company. Assistant Dean P. J. Olson was appointed agronomist of the College of Agriculture at the University of Manitoba at a salary greater than he had received at N.D.A.C. County Agent Leader N. D. Gorman was appointed supervisor of the Federal North Dakota wheat insurance program by the Federal Crop Insurance Corporation. Registrar A. H. Parrott left Fargo to reside in Seattle, Washington.

In October, 1937, Dr. A. F. Yeager, head of the department of horticulture and internationally famous for his work in plant breeding, resigned from the staff of the North Dakota Agricultural College, effective January 1, 1938. At the time of his resignation he said, "To anyone familiar with the situation at the College, my reasons should be obvious." Before leaving to take up work at Michigan State College he gave an explanation of his action, which is quoted in part:

"The real reason why I resigned is fundamentally that the Board of Administration wrecked the merit system at the College.

"Let me explain what I mean by the merit system . . . It . . . is a system under which men work for more than just financial rewards, which haven't been very large at any time at N.D.A.C.; they work for the love of working and for the satisfaction of jobs well done . . .

"We all (at the College) went through the time when the top pay was $1,920 a year. If we had been working only for money, that would have ruined our spirit and our morale. But it didn't . . . Dr. Olson sat up nights worrying where to find money to run his departments, and where to use it most effectively. Then he was fired on three hours' notice without a hearing.

"Dr. Walster is criticized in the audit because he was engaged in so many activities. He did not go about hunting for that extra work. Those extra jobs came to Dr. Walster because it was well known he'd accept a burden when it was shoved at him and do his best at it.

"The institution has been suffering from 'Fargoitis' for years. That's my own term, but I think it fits. Because it happens to be located in Fargo, it is made the goat because of a politically manufactured unfriendly feeling toward Fargo. The way to be popular in some political circles has been to attack Fargo.

"The institution's appropriation for years has never been based on what the institution is worth to the state but always on a trade-off of votes. Almost every legislature has had its attack of Fargoitis, and the peculiar thing about it is that in Fargo there is a large group of people who don't care a thing for the college; in fact, they disdain it.

"If the merit system is not immediately restored to the North Dakota Agricultural College, there will be little left. What it has achieved up to now has been with very limited budgets, plus a high spirit of morale. Place it all on a mercenary basis, and the future looks anything but bright for it." [12]

In February, 1938, Dr. L. M. Roderick, professor of animal pathology and hygiene, resigned to become head of the department of pathology at Kansas State College. Dr. Roderick's research was fundamental; among others he found the cure for sweet clover poisoning of livestock, which occurred under certain conditions. His departure from the College was a distinct loss to the Experiment Station and to North Dakota.

In the meantime, two months had passed since the dismissals had taken place. The dismissed staff members still had not been given a hearing. Five of them had engaged legal counsel, Conmy and Conmy, who on August 5 asked Chairman Jennie Ulsrud for charges to be revealed and a date set for hearings. The Board wired back on August 8 that it would hear the dismissed staff members the following day at 9:30 a.m. in Bismarck. No reference was made to charges. The telegram reached Fargo at 3 p.m., after the westbound train had departed, and therefore the members could not reach the meeting in time for the hearing. The staff members' counsel wired the reason for their non-appearance and again asked for charges. No reply was received, for obviously the Board had no charges, or else was waiting for charges to be formulated.

On Monday, August 2, auditors had been employed by the Board at College expense to check the books and files of the dismissed members. M. H. Chernick, Bismarck special examiner, named by Governor Langer, and F. F. Burchard, Grand Forks, collaborator, were employed for the purpose. On October 10 Board member R. A. Kinzer announced the imminent publication of the auditors' report, saying that it would explain the "reasons for dismissing seven faculty members at the college!" and that when the audit is revealed there might be "further changes . . ."[13]

On December 10 the report, consisting of 323 pages, was filed with the Board of Administration and five days later was released to the press. On December 13 the Board voted (four to one) that the auditors' bill of $1,100 be paid, fifty percent from the Board's emergency fund and fifty percent from the N.D.A.C. emergency fund. The auditors' statement with regard to the scope of their investigation was as follows: "Our work covered an examination of the Office of the Secretary and Business Manager, the registrar, the Extension Division, the College Division, Experimental Station Division, Student Activities, Athletic Association, and a number of miscellaneous branches involved."[14]

Much of the report was devoted to reproduction of correspondence in faculty files. Letters between Dean Dolve and his nephew, Samuel Dolve, were cited as evidence of Dolve's efforts to promote the closing of the colleges at Mayville, Ellendale and Bottineau. The report also charged many cases of "nepotism" and criticized Dean Walster for being connected with twenty-seven governmental activities.

Many departments were criticized for lax handling of finances and inefficient bookkeeping, but no evidence in support of such charges was shown. This report declared "we believe changes that have been made in personnel and policy are a step forward." The audit failed to mention I. W. Smith, A. H. Parrott or Jean Traynor, and only indirect reference was made to Alba Bales. Considerable mention was made of P. J. Olson and N. D. Gorman, but no acts justifying dismissal were cited.

To the audit report the investigators added this statement: "Some

The Purge, 1937–1938

of the conditions uncovered at the institution were so rotten that in the opinion of the examiners they should not be made public. These phases of the investigation will therefore be covered in a supplementary report made privately to the members of the board . . ." [15]

This confidential supplementary report to Governor Langer and the Board of Administration came to light and was published on April 7, 1938, in the *Normanden*, a Scandinavian language newspaper published by O. Gunvaldson. The following statements are extracts from this "confidential" report:

"We are satisfied from various leads we received that there is a certain amount of conversion of personal property belonging to the State of North Dakota that is not reported to the proper executive of the school. We were informed that a check-up was made several years ago that substantiates this rumor. We were unable to acquire a copy or submit copies of two checks, one for $180.00, a second for $84.15 that were believed to be evidence of lax bookkeeping. Mr. Shepperd was being paid by the Animal Husbandry Department for writing for various magazines and farm papers. The main reason which caused Mr. Yeager's resignation was his failure to cooperate with others in his department and to stay within the funds allotted to him . . .

We believe that the activities of the Extension Business Office are a waste of time and money . . . a consolidation of accounting should be immediately put into effect.

"We call attention to numerous "Purported reports" of immoral practices according to police reports. We were informed that one of the deans was the owner and operator of a saloon or drink parlor in the city of Fargo . . .

"The records kept prove conclusively that they (the officials of the college) were either inefficient or the system was used to cover up improper acts." [16]

On April 7, 1938, in a meeting in Chicago, the North Dakota Agricultural College was removed from the accredited list of the North Central Association of Colleges and Secondary Schools through the association's commission on institutions of higher learning. This action was based on a preceding investigation of two months, initiated by the association and conducted by President Charles Finley of Iowa State College at Ames, President Thomas Barrows of Lawrence College, Appleton, Wisconsin, and Dean A. J. Brumbaugh of the University of Chicago. Announcement of the action taken by the association at its Chicago meeting was made in a letter to Dr. West, signed by George A. Works, secretary of North Central's commission on institutions of higher learning. The following reasons were given for the removal of the College from the accredited list:

"The evidence indicated undue interference by the board of administration in the internal administration of the college.

"The morale of the faculty has declined to a point where the quality of instruction is seriously jeopardized.

"There is no concrete assurance that the legal structure and organization for the administration of North Dakota Agricultural College and other institutions of higher learning in the state provide a stable and constructive leadership and a sufficient degree of autonomy to the individual institution to guarantee a satisfactory level of performance." [17]

The North Central Association is a mutual, voluntary, cooperative accrediting association of schools and colleges in the Midwest, banded together to improve educational standards, standardize the best methods and practices, exchange information, encourage research and experimentation and adopt certain standards to which any school is free to subscribe, if it can. It was founded in 1905. The North Dakota Agricultural College sought and received accreditation in 1916. This meant that at the time of acceptance and in the following years the College voluntarily met the standards of the association in respect to organization, policies, administration and academic standards, and on account of this was admitted to membership within the organization.

The meeting at which the North Dakota Agricultural College was removed from the accredited list of the North Central Association was attended by a member of the College Alumni Board, who assured the officials of the association that removal of the College from the list of accredited institutions was the only way by which the dismissed staff members could regain their positions.

The action of the North Central Association was a blow to faculty and students alike. President West was away when the news came. C. A. Sevrinson, assistant to the president, dismissed classes for the rest of the week. The students held mass meetings, paraded through the streets of Fargo, and burned the four members of the Board in effigy. Committees were chosen to work with Dean Sevrinson to explain to the students the meaning of the removal of the College from the accredited list and to seek as soon as possible a reinstatement, which President West had requested. C. A. Williams of the Class of 1914, a Fargo business man, suggested that the students attend classes regularly and cooperate with the alumni association and the Good Government League[18] to secure signers for an initiated measure to be presented to the State at the next election. This measure was a proposed amendment to the constitution withdrawing control of the institutions of higher education from the Board of Administration and vesting the control in an appointive Board of Higher Education, a non-political body, subject to removal by impeachment only.

In order to secure signatures for the measure a student steering committee of eleven members was chosen by the student body. Those so chosen were Orville Goplen of Fargo, Maurice Benidt of Lidgerwood, James McGregor of Page, John Lynch of LaMoure, Millard Borke of Billsboro, John Clason of Akeley, Minn., Mercedes Morris of Wahpeton, Reuben Arnason, Dale Hogoboom, DeLawrence Nelson and Florenz Dinwoodie of Fargo. Support in the June primary for the initiated constitutional amendment was also solicited over a statewide radio hook-up. College students home for the Easter recess planned to contact voters personally. A College convocation was held, at which Dr. West declared that he was bending every effort to secure the acceptability of the College's credits at other institutions. He praised the self control and orderliness displayed by the student body. A total of $320 was raised by voluntary student contributions to promote the campaign.

The State Board of Administration, through *The Leader,* defended their policy by attempting to discredit the North Central Association and by minimizing the importance of its action. Some of the statements made in the paper were:

"A small clique of outside educators (who probably have never seen North Dakota and know nothing of the state's problems) got together in a Chicago hotel and dropped the A.C. from the North Central.

"The North Central Association ruling against A.C. will have little effect, the 1938 class is not hit. Iowa State and Minnesota will recognize their credits.

"For forty years and more Fargo politicians have been playing politics with the Agricultural College (and everybody knows it) . . . The student demonstrations in Fargo were all part of a carefully worked out plan — a plan conceived in the minds of men who are masters in the art of political strategy and men who know the psychological value of the dramatic in appealing to the public mind. The demonstrations were staged productions from start to finish — planned, organized, financed and executed by politicians.

"The A.C. has not closed its doors . . . in spite of the criminal attack by the academic royalists of Chicago and the crafty engineerings of Fargo politicians who propose to kick the college around as a political football in the coming campaign."[19]

On May 9, 1938, Steve W. Hagan, secretary-treasurer of the College, advised President West that he intended to resign, effective June 1. It was assumed that this resignation was requested by the advisory committee of the Nonpartisan League in view of his father's candidacy for governor. On May 29 the Board of Administration voted to "remove S. W. Hagan from the payroll on June 30, 1938, and that his services as Secretary-Treasurer be terminated as of May 21, 1938." The real reason of the removal was that while Hagan was secretary of the College, he tried for three years, 1934-1937, to obtain a degree in engineering from the College. He submitteed diplomas from nonexistent institutions, or diploma mills, in his efforts to be awarded this degree. He tried to influence several deans to aid him in obtaining the degree, but the committee of deans denied his request.[20]

On May 10, 1938, Governor Langer brought suit in the Federal Court of Illinois against the North Central Association and its officers seeking to enjoin them "from removing the University and State Agricultural College of North Dakota from the list of accredited colleges, or from interference with or obstructing the administration, operation and maintenance of the public school system of the State of North Dakota, and from counseling, conspiring, scheming and conniving with political agencies and other persons in the promulgation and exercise of any functions which defendants may claim to possess . . . and for a mandatory injunction directing the defendants to expunge, annul and avoid any order or recommendation with reference to removing the State Agricultural College from the list of accredited colleges."

The case came before Judge Walter C. Lindley of the District Court of the United States for the Eastern District of Illinois at Danville. "The Association as defendant, contended first, that the court had no jurisdiction in the matter as the controversy was one solely between members of voluntary organizations, and second, because the College's remedy under the Constitution and rules of procedure of the Association must be exhausted before there is any remedy in court . . ."[21]

Judge Lindley listened to the presentations made by the plaintiff and the defendant and then took the case under advisement. On June 16, 1938, he rendered his decision, denying the motion for a temporary injunction and dissolving the temporary restraining order which had previously been issued.

Meanwhile, the campaign to secure the adoption of a constitutional amendment providing for a new Board of Higher Education was successful and the measure passed at the primary election on June 18, 1938, to become effective July 1, 1939. The seven members of the Board were to be appointed by the governor from the list of three names for each position, selected by the joint action of the President of the North Dakota Educational Association, the Chief Justice of the Supreme Court and the Superintendent of Public Instruction, with the consent of the majority of members of the Senate. Much of the success for this measure was due to the efforts of the eleven students from the College who formed the steering committee, reinforced by the demands of an aroused citizenry who did not wish to see the schools used by power-seeking politicians.

Dr. W. E. Peik, dean of the College of Education at the University of Minnesota, who in 1929 had made an exhaustive survey of North Dakota's educational system, praised this new law in 1938. He said it would go a long way toward reconciling the North Dakota Agricultural College with the North Central Association. He said that it removed the administration from politics but provided for both appointive members and laymen.[22]

On May 17, 1938, a meeting of the deans of the College was called by Dr. West to consider his recommendation in regard to a new administrative committee. Those present were Deans Walster, Rush, Haley, Dinan, Carrick, Sudro, Minard and Sevrinson. It was decided that the committee be composed of the deans of the various schools. the dean of men, the dean of women and two other members elected by the Council from the body of professors, associate professors and assistant professors who had served three years or longer.

The duties of the administrative committee were to cooperate with the deans in enrolling students, to exercise the functions of the Council in questions of scholarship and attendance, to co-ordinate outside activities, methods of recording class standing and credits, examination and recitation schedules, vacations, and the institution catalog and calendar, and to pass upon all student petitions and administrative details, except in cases involving general Agricultural College policies. The discipline committee, the library committee, the curriculum committee, and the committee on standings were subordinate to this administrative committee.[23]

The Council adopted this recommendation with instructions to revise the *Blue Book*, which was the popular name for the previous constitution. President West appointed Professor A. G. Arvold and Dr. C. I. Nelson members of the administrative committee. On June 4, 1938, the revised constitution of North Dakota Agricultural College was presented to the Council by Dr. West. It was considered article by article and, after several minor amendments, was adopted.

Throughout his temporary administration of the affairs of the college Acting President West should be commended for his conduct of its business. All appointments were made on an acting basis and no policies initiated by him that might interfere with the welfare of the College.

On July 16, 1938, Dr. West recommended to the Board of Administration that the Agricultural College should have a "full time executive," skilled in administration and "having experience or training in extension and agricultural experimentation." In support of it Arthur F. Thompson, superintendent of public instruction and ex-officio member of the Board, made the following statement: "I believe the board of administration should proceed to select a full time president and cut down the excessive number of 'acting' appointments. I am satisfied this will give greater stability. I fully believe that if this suggestion is followed, the College will shortly be restored to membership in the North Central Association."[24]

Monday, August 1, 1938, Dr. Frank L. Eversull, president of Huron College at Huron, South Dakota, and a vice president of the North Central Association, was appointed president of North Dakota Agricultural College. Dr. Eversull, a native of Ohio, earned a Ph.B. degree from the University of Chicago in 1920 and a Ph.D. in school administration from Yale University in 1934; he had also studied at McCormick Theological Seminary and Washington University. He was ordained into the Presbyterian ministry in 1917 and served two pastorates. Later he served as principal of several high schools and was instructor in education at Yale University in 1933-34. Dr. Eversull was a Mason and a Shriner, a member of the National Education Association, of Phi Delta Kappa and of Pi Gamma Mu. In Illinois he was engaged in Farm Institute work, and as president of Huron College he supervised 35,000 acres of farm land owned by the school.

Upon receiving the appointment, President Eversull said he would "take immediate steps to reinstate the college on the North Central Association's accredited list . . . My objective is to make the Fargo school a grand agricultural college—the best in the northwest. I do not believe that there is a possibility of getting reinstatement of the college on the North Central Association accredited lists this fall but I intend to start action toward that end at once."[25]

Reports appeared in the *Fargo Forum* and *Bismarck Tribune* that "Governor Langer asked for the resignation of the three appointive members of the Board of Administration because of their appointment of Dr. Eversull without the consent of Langer, who favored the appointment of E. M. Gillig, State seed commissioner. Also that John H. Hagan, ex-officio member of the Board and Republican candidate for governor, felt that the situation at the College constituted a handicap to him in his race for the governorship and that he wanted it cleaned up before the fall campaign began. Langer later withdrew his request."[26]

The September registration at the College resulted in 1,353 students in attendance, a loss of 229 from the previous year, while all the other schools in the State showed gains of from 17 to 119 students.

The November election in the State resulted in the choice of John Moses, Democrat, for governor over John Hagan, Republican. On December 12, 1938, President Eversull requested permission of the Board to apply on behalf of the College to the North Central Association for admission and for an inspection. On February 21, 1939, the Board by a vote of three to two turned down the request. Harris and Superintendent Thompson voted yes. Chairman Ulsrud, Kinzer and Math Dahl, the new commissioner of agriculture and labor, voted no. Chairman Ulsrud said that an inspection for accrediting would cost the State about $400 and she voted "no" because "these accrediting agencies do not offer any constructive criticism, are taking and have taken too much money of our educational institutions for the service they render, and their main interest is tenure in office. With the present financial conditions of the state, I feel this money would not be wisely spent." Kinzer declared he voted "no" because the "North Central Association will require the restoration of dismissed instructors and help before an application for being accredited will be considered."[27]

Governor Moses overruled the Board and ordered President Eversull to present his application for reinstatement of the College on the accredited list of the North Central Association. He said he personally intended to appear before the North Central board to plead the case of the College. Dr. Eversull reported that the student body was willing to put up thirty cents apiece to provide the necessary money. Also, several Fargo alumni had asked to help if the $400 were needed. Math Dahl, who had voted "no" with Mrs. Ulsrud and Kinzer, said he would change his vote and thus a majority of the Board would favor the application.

Although the law initiating the new Board of Higher Education had carried, the Board of Administration was still in authority in March, 1939. Even when the new Board was to take over, state institutions other than the schools of higher education would still be under the old Board. In the meantime hearings were held for Mrs. Ulsrud and R. A. Kinzer. Three charges were brought against them, accusing them of being guilty of malfeasance in office and neglect of duty and of gross incompetence in connection with the administration of the State Hospital at Jamestown, the State Prison Twine Plant at Bismarck, and the 1937 discharge of seven employees of the State Agricultural College.

The last charge read as follows: "The said defendants in July of 1937 caused the discharge of seven employees of the state agricultural college at Fargo, said employees including three deans and one assistant dean; that said employees had served said institution for an average of 15 years; and said dismissals, in several instances, were made upon trivial complaints and that in all cases such complaints were based largely upon rumors and gossip; that no charges of any kind were made or filed against said dismissed employees and the said employees were denied a hearing."[28]

The governor found that "the dismissal action was taken contrary to the provisions of the charter of *Blue Book* of the said institution, which charter of *Blue Book* had been approved by the Board of Regents and for many years had been recognized by the Board of Administration, and the provisions of which *Blue Book*, with reference to tenure and dismissal, had been used and referred to in securing instructors of the said college, and with the knowledge, consent and approval of the state board of administration." Consequently, Mrs. Ulsrud and Mr. Kinzer were removed as members of the Board by Governor Moses. Mark I. Forkner and R. H. Sherman were appointed instead.

At the March 23, 1939, meeting of the Board of Administration thus reconstituted the following resolution was moved by A. E. Thompson and seconded by Math Dahl:

"Whereas, the Board of Administration did dismiss seven members of the staff of North Dakota Agricultural College on July 29, 1937, at a special meeting attended by Mrs. Ulsrud, R. A. Kinzer, J. D. Harris and John Hagan and,

"Whereas, the seven members were not given adequate opportunity to present their cases to the Board before dismissal, and

"Whereas, an audit of files was made to give reasons for their dismissal, and

"Whereas, allegations in the audit do not show adequate reasons for their dismissal

"Therefore, be it resolved, that the Board of Administration recommend to President Eversull that he give consideration to these persons, where, in his judgement, they may be employed or until adjustments made in finances are provided by the legislative assembly of North Dakota." [29]

A motion was also passed that the Board of Administration was favoring in principle the constitution of North Dakota Agricultural College as submitted to the faculty by President Eversull. Present at this meeting were two representatives of the North Central Association, Dr. John Hale Russell of the University of Chicago and Dr. Charles Henry Oldfather of the University of Nebraska.

These two representatives of the North Central Association, accompanied by President Eversull, went to Chicago and presented their report, which was accepted by the association and therefore the North Dakota Agricultural College was readmitted to membership in the North Central Association. This action was taken with the understanding that the dismissed staff members would be reinstated. N. D. Gorman was the first to be reappointed to his old job, on May 9, 1939.

The new Board of Higher Education appointed by Governor Moses January 31, 1939, assumed control on July 1, 1939, under the initiated amendment to the constitution adopted in June, 1938. They consisted of P. J. Murphy of Grafton, Howard I. Henry of Westhope, Merle Kidder of Towner, Mrs. Matt Crowley of Hebron, Lars O. Fredrickson of Pekin, F. J. Traynor of Devils Lake and Roy Johnson of Casselton. At its meeting at the College on August 1, the Board passed the following resolution:

"Whereas, the state board of higher education has been requested by the North Central Association to express the general policy which it plans to pursue with regard to the government of the institutions of higher learning under its control.

"Now, Therefore, be it resolved that the board unanimously makes the following statement:

(1) It will be the plea and purpose of the state board of higher education to clearly and definitely divorce the institutions of higher learning from so-called "political" domination or interference.

(2) The board is further determined that reports and recommendations regarding faculty changes shall come through the regular channels and will be considered on their merits.

(3) The right of faculty members to have a hearing on any charges filed against them will be respected."

The board, acting on the recommendations of President Eversull, in addition ordered: That Dr. H. L. Walster be restored to his former position of director of the Experiment Station, Dr. Hanson to be retained as vice director; that R. M. Dolve, appointed professor of mechanical engineering at the University of Minnesota, be restored as dean of Engineering, and H. S. Rush, as assistant dean; that A. H. Parrott be restored as registrar, and Viola Borderud, as assistant; that Jean Traynor, former secretary to the president, be restored to a secretarial position; that P. J. Olson, appointed agronomist at the University of Manitoba, be restored as assistant dean of the School of Agriculture and professor of agronomy."[30] (He chose to retain his position in Canada.)

N. D. Gorman, named supervisor of North Dakota Crop Insurance Program in May, had already been reinstated as county agent leader. I. W. Smith had been made dean emeritus at his own request. Miss Bales indicated that she would return to the College in 1940.

FOOTNOTES

[1] Minutes of Board of Administration, July 29, 1937.
[2] *Fargo Forum*, July 30, 1937.
[3] *Fargo Forum*, August 1, 1937.
[4] *Fargo Forum*, August 4, 1937.
[5] Minutes of the Board, Aug. 2, 1937.
[6] *Fargo Forum*, August 2, 1937.
[7] *Fargo Forum*, Aug. 5, 1937.
[8] *Fargo Forum*, Aug. 6, 1937.
[9] *The Leader*, Aug. 5, 1937.
[10] *Fargo Forum*, Aug. 17, 1937.
[11] *Fargo Forum*, Aug. 10, 1937.
[12] *Fargo Forum*, Jan. 2, 1938.
[13] *Fargo Forum*, Oct. 16, 1937.
[14] Minutes of the Board, Dec. 13, 1937.
[15] *The Leader*, Oct. 28, 1937, *Fargo Forum*, Jan. 4, 1938.
[16] In the archives of the College in the Library, N.D.A.C.
[17] *Fargo Forum*, Apr. 12, 1938.
[18] The official name of the "League" was the Good Government Cooperative Association, headed by O. Gunvaldson, Executive Secretary, organized to secure the passage of the initiated amendment.
[19] *The Leader*, Apr. 14, 28, 1938.
[20] *Fargo Forum*, Mar. 1, 1939. Testimony of A. H. Parrott and R. M. Dolve at the hearing in connection with the removal of Mrs. Ulsrud and R. A. Kinzer.
[21] *North Central Association Quarterly*, XIII, 3.
[22] *Fargo Forum*, July 14, 1938.
[23] *Faculty Record*, C, 455.
[24] *Fargo Forum*, July 23, 1938.
[25] *Fargo Forum*, Aug. 2, 1938.
[26] *Fargo Forum*, Aug. 9; *Bismarck Tribune*, Aug. 10, 1938.
[27] *Fargo Forum*, Feb. 21, 1939.
[28] *Fargo Forum*, Mar. 1, 1939.
[29] Minutes of the Board, Mar. 23, 1939.
[30] Minutes of the Board, Aug. 19, 1939.

◄ CHAPTER X ►

Recovery, 1938-1941

PRESIDENT EVERSULL assumed the presidency of the North Dakota Agricultural College under trying conditions. The school was under a cloud of political disturbance; as mentioned in the previous chapter it had been removed from the accredited list of the North Central Association, and the Board of Administration, which had dismissed seven competent staff members of the College, was still responsible for its control. The new president, though an experienced traditional educator, had had little experience in the administration of an agricultural and technical college. For several years he had been president of Huron College, a church affiliated liberal arts college in South Dakota, but he was not familiar with the political and economic conditions in North Dakota. In addition, as an ordained minister he could encounter difficulties in gaining the confidence of practical business men and farmers. As an educator, however, he had an advantage in being a vice-president in the North Central Association.

At once he set out to make the Agricultural College "the best agricultural school in the Northwest." He sought to win over both the farmer-legislators of the State and the business men of Fargo. A few weeks after he came, on September 29, 1938, he addressed the Fargo Chamber of Commerce and outlined a ten-year development program for the College. In this outline entitled "Looking Ahead with the Agricultural College" he proposed to secure more adequate physical facilities:

"A $300,000 Federal building 'to be provided by Federal funds if possible, to house all agencies supported by the Federal government, a new farm folk school and a new library, a health center, more adequate quarters for engineering and chemistry, a new dormitory for girls, and a student union building to provide a center for student activities', which he hoped might be in the nature of a memorial.

"However, I am thoroughly convinced that buildings do not make a college. A college can be no better than its faculty. So I am thinking of this ten-year program in terms of a valiant faculty that will be adequate and carefully selected ... I want to have this state feel that this college is prepared and willing to assume a large part in solving problems, and in given direction to all enterprises which will help make life more and more significant in North Dakota.

"I earnestly yearn for an opportunity to re-sell N.D.A.C. to the people of this state ... I am devoted to the policy that this is the college for the entire state ...

"I present this ten-year program with the sincere hope that we can rebuild the A.C. into the minds and hearts of the citizens of this state ... Our motive is solely to serve the youth of this state and to make life happier and better for all our fellow-citizens." [1]

On October 28, 1938, for the first time in the history of the College, the new president, Dr. Eversull, was inaugurated at the Field House with very considerable display of an academic ritual, with a procession and convocation of college delegates, the Board of Administration, the faculty, students and citizens of the State and community. The president of the Board, Mrs. Ulsrud, presented him, and Dr. Eversull's brother, Harry K. Eversull, president of Marietta College in Ohio, gave him the charge. In response the new president dwelt on the life and works of Justin S. Morrill, especially his contributions to the cause of education in founding the land-grant colleges, with its emphasis on a scientific, classical and practical education. In closing he said:

"North Dakota Agricultural College, along with the other land grant colleges, stands at the threshold of a new day. It needs the support of the mothers and fathers of all youth. The leaders and directors of this commonwealth must see to it that educational opportunities are undiminished and that their activities increase with the growing needs of this great state ... When dawn comes to North Dakota may our children be awake and prepared to lead North Dakota and America out into the everlasting Peace and Prosperity that can come only when God's children serve Him and serve their fellow man, therefore, let us keep the ideal which was envisioned by Justin Smith Morrill and let us keep faith with our State, our Nation, and our children." [2]

This inaugural was a part of the homecoming program for 1938. "Service to the State" was the theme. The football game between the Agricultural College and the University was played in the recently dedicated stadium, which was built by the Works Progress Administration through the Athletic Board of the College. The W.P.A. spent over $25,000 in wages to 43 men in the community employed for ten months. It also spent over $2,000 for material for construction. The Athletic Board of Control, in addition, spent $20,000 for material and equipment. Not only was the stadium and its stands built, but a new cinder track was installed, the football field leveled, the old bleachers demolished, and the grounds landscaped.

President Eversull at once took steps to secure the re-accrediting of the College with the North Central Association. As indicated before, he was successful in this regard. However, credit for achieving that goal must go to thousands of students and citizens of the State, to Governor Moses and to the group that met with the College committee in Chicago. Behind them lay the work of the North Dakota Bar Association, the North Dakota Education Association, hundreds of community clubs throughout the State, thousands of individual workers, including candidates for State office, members of the Alumni Association and Fargo business men and all those who secured the passage of the initiated measure establishing the Board of Higher Education.

Immediately after his inauguration President Eversull made public relations his chief concern. He addressed many meetings and he endeavored to popularize the Agricultural College in Fargo, throughout the State and in the Legislature. He made careful preparations for these talks and spent many hours familiarizing himself with conditions in the State. In this endeavor he was probably most effective in educational and religious fields, in which he had most of his training and experience.

In 1938 he brought to the campus Dr. Otto J. Beyers to become director of student guidance, personnel and placement. Dr. Beyers had worked with Dr. Eversull before and had acquired a reputation in modern educational research methods and practices. President Eversull wished to acquaint the faculty with the newest and best educational methods, and in 1939 he organized a seminar in higher education for members of the staff. In the fall quarter Dr. Beyers discussed "Guidance Problems in an Agricultural College" in five different sessions; in the winter quarter Dr. Eversull led five discussions on the "Art of Teaching in an Agricultural College;" in the spring quarter five sessions were led by different staff members on the historical, educational, philosophical, moral and scientific aspects of the College. He encouraged faculty members to address various groups and was instrumental in arranging and listing a speakers bureau for commencements, institutes, general meetings, special occasions and forums.

A leadership training conference on "Forum and Discussion Methods" was held on the campus for representatives of agricultural, labor, civic, religious and other groups two days in February, 1940. Leaders in various fields participated. In 1941 a Farm and Home Week was sponsored by members of the three divisions of the College: the instruction, extension and station staffs. A "Religion and Life Conference" came to the campus in January, 1940. Twelve nationally prominent leaders chosen by the University Christian Mission were in attendance for a week, speaking at convocations, meetings and dinners and luncheons with groups of students and faculty and leading afternoon seminars. Plans were in charge of a "Committee of One Hundred" under the leadership of President Eversull and the Y.M.C.A. executive secretary, Richard E. Sweitzer.[3]

Dr. Eversull's administrations stimulated the activities and the work of every department of the College, which took on new life. The students felt that their efforts had brought about re-accrediting and a more effective policy on the part of the Board of Higher Education. Enrollment greatly increased in 1938-39 and continued to increase until the outbreak of World War II. Athletics was strong again. In 1938, the revamped Dacotah Field saw one of the College's all time football thrillers. North Dakota Agricultural College with Ernie Wheeler playing superbly, edged out the University of North Dakota, led by their great Negro star, Fritz Pollard. In basketball the next year, 1935-40, a starting five — "Swede" (Arnold) Johnson, Larry Tanberg, Cliff Nygaard, John Abbott and Jim Fletcher — proved superior to all previous teams. In 1940-41, they won the North Central Conference championship.

In 1940 the National Youth Administration furnished $22,520 to 250 students who "worked at jobs requiring everything from janitorial service to experienced retail salesmen." This NYA work was under the direction of Murray Schaetzel, '39, director of student employment. A survey in 1941 showed that fifty-seven percent of the students were employed outside of NYA, another twelve percent had earned something during the year, and nineteen and a half percent were receiving NYA aid. Dakota Hall was refitted as a dormitory with a kitchen and dining room. The whole program was under the direction of Dean Sevrinson. A total of $7,155 in NYA funds was allocated to the College for the year 1942-43; selections were based on need, character, ability, scholarship, class attendance and capacity to work.

The former short courses given for many years, which had been omitted for several years, were revived and reorganized into the Farm Folk School by Dean Walster. Courses were outlined in agricultural economics, agricultural engineering, entomology, agronomy, animal husbandry, bacteriology, chemistry, dairy husbandry, English, public discussion, social science, home economics, horticulture, plant pathology, poultry husbandry and physical education. Forty-four young farmers from as many North Dakota counties attended the 1940 winter session. Their attendance was made possible by a grant by Sears-Roebuck and Co. North Dakota Agricultural College was the second college in the United States to be selected for such an experimental course. Professor William Promersberger served as principal. The boys were chosen by leading agricultural workers in their counties; they learned of problems they had never faced before and found sources of information in regard to modern farm practices. They gave half time to rebuilding and refurnishing the old barracks of the Student Army Training Corps, later known as Dakota Hall. The second floor was divided into rooms, new hardwood floors were laid, and the building was rewired.

The benefits of the Farm Folk School were realized in December, 1939, when it was learned that sixty-two percent of former students were working on their home farms. Eighteen percent of the former students included in the survey stated that the Farm Folk School training had aided them in obtaining other than farm employment.[3] These figures show that "the students are receiving beneficial farm training and that the training is also of such nature that it helps materially when they leave the farm," said Principal W. J. Promersberger. The course in "farm shop" was voted the one students valued most. Farm machinery, English, arithmetic, forge shop, foods and feeding, animal husbandry, and poultry production were also popular.

For a number of years it was realized by the staff and students of the Division of Agriculture that a publication was needed to do for its students and those of its sister division of Home Economics what the *State College Engineer* had been doing for the School of Mechanical Arts. In 1938 Alpha Zeta, national agricultural honor fraternity, sponsored such a magazine, the *Bison Furrows*.

In the first issue of *Bison Furrows* Dean Walster thus described what he believed its purpose should be: "It is my hope that the power which drives *Bison Furrows* may plow its way into every farm home in North Dakota. That power is love of home land and faith in the efficacy of truth. Let us have truth and yet more truth about the soil, about trees and flowers, about grass and grain, about wild fowl and poultry, about fish and streams and ponds and lakes, and about better livestock. I charge *Bison Furrows* with the job of holding up a mirror to every new thing happening on this campus, in its fields, laboratories, barns and paddocks with the job of catching that image and reflecting it to the people of the state."[4]

Always interested in betterment of farming methods, Sears-Roebuck and Company awarded twenty scholarships of $125 each to freshmen in the School of Agriculture in 1938-39. These awards were made on the basis of past scholastic records, interest in agriculture, and leadership in the community. The recipients in the first year ranged from sixteen to twenty-three years in age and all paid most of their expenses themselves. The *Bison Furrows* in 1939 carried the following item: "Each year Sears-Roebuck picks one student from the freshman scholarship students who is awarded a $200.00 sophomore scholarship which includes a trip to Chicago and a chance to compete for a $250 Junior and a $500 Senior scholarship."[5]

A similar contribution was made by the Danforth Foundation and the Ralston Purina Mills. Each year a junior is selected from each of the agricultural colleges in the United States and from the Ontario Agricultural College to receive a similar fellowship. Two weeks are spent at St. Louis and at the Purina experimental farm studying nutritional problems, commercial research and operation of successful industries, and two weeks at the American Youth Foundation camp at Shelby, Michigan, where Mr. Danforth personally challenged the group to "Live Tall, Think Tall, Stand Tall and Smile Tall."

In 1939-40 Dean Walster could say that there were 464 regular students in the College who were enrolled in agriculture, and in addition there were eighty-seven students in the Farm Folk School. The enrollment in the School of Agriculture outnumbered any other school on the campus. A division of animal industry was created in the School of Agriculture in which all livestock could be handled upon a broad basis. Dr. J. H. Longwell was appointed in 1941 to head the new division. He was a graduate of the University of Missouri with a master's and doctor's degree from the University of Illinois. He was a specialist in animal nutrition and breeding, an effective teacher and research member of the faculty until he was chosen president of the College in 1946.

During Dr. Eversull's administration two men who had recently passed away, Dr. Clarence S. Putnam and Dr. Walter Lee Airheart, were honored at the May, 1944, Commencement. Dr. Putnam's connection with the college has already been told. Dr. Airheart's deserves a more extended account.

During the administration of President Coulter in the twenties there was started an organization which was to become a unique contribution to higher education in North Dakota. Colleges and universities supported by public funds are not permitted to have departments of religion. This is in keeping with the practice of separation of church and state. The founders of the College recognized, however, the need of some religious instruction and education among the students. At chapel, scripture readings, prayer and the singing of hymns took place. Students were urged to participate in worship in the churches of Fargo. The YMCA and the YWCA were encouraged to organize on the campus. Individual faculty members took an active part in all of these extra-curricular religious activities. In time student foundations were set up by various denominations. Religious clubs were organized among the students and fellowships were established in connection with Fargo churches.

In 1921 Wesley College, a Methodist school affiliated with the University of North Dakota, established a branch at the North Dakota Agricultural College. It was affiliated with the College under provisions similar to those at the University, to be recognized as a separate institution, authorized to teach religious education and grant degrees. Its credits were recognized by the College and could be counted toward a degree. Professor Walter Lee Airheart was transferred from Wesley College to take charge of the College branch and he carried on the entire work of the school in a makeshift building located on several lots belonging to Wesley College on Thirteenth Street across the campus from Ceres Hall.

After maintaining the school for several years Wesley College withdrew its support due to financial difficulties during the depression years. Professor Airheart, who had become an influential man in the Fargo community, realizing the value of a religious school in connection with the College, contacted a number of prominent citizens in an effort to secure the continuance of the school. Consequently, on June 4, 1932, there was organized a voluntary, nonprofit, nonsectarian and self-perpetuating corporation known as the Fargo School of Religious Education. The membership of the corporation was at first seventeen but was later increased to twenty-five. Officers consisted of a president, vice-president, secretary and treasurer. Walter L. Stockwell was elected president and held the office until his death in 1950. Since it was the purpose of the Board to represent a cross section of the religious interests of the community, no more than five members of any one denomination could serve on the board at one time. No minister or priest could be chosen. The board members consisted of Roman Catholic, Jewish and Protestant laymen.

The new organization paid the delinquent taxes of Wesley College and signed a 99-year lease on the Thirteenth Street property. In 1937 a new building was dedicated and a home for the director was remodeled. S. Fred Knight of Fargo, founder of the Knight Printing

Company, contributed the main cost of the building. After 1932 the current expenditures consisting of the director's salary and the upkeep of the building and grounds were met by annual voluntary contributions of the citizens of Fargo. Professor Airheart secured his doctorate from the University of North Dakota and taught until his death in February, 1944. For the next year, during the war, direction of the school was under Dr. W. C. Hunter, chairman of the history department of the College, who had been a member of its board of trustees since its founding. Besides heading the school, he also was an active member of the YMCA Board of the College and advisor to the Student Inter-religious Council; he continued as director of the School until 1956. In that year Stafford Studer, pastor of the Moorhead Presbyterian Church was chosen director, who later resigned to become dean of Emporia College, Kansas. The present director is Corwin Roach with a Ph.D. degree from Yale University.

The Fargo School of Religion supplements the work of the church related foundations, concentrating on the teaching of religion. Many of the city ministers have taught one or more classes, and the clergy have made use of the building. It fills a definite place in the life and curriculum of the Agricutural College. It is an active institution which strives to strengthen the ties of the individual student with his church by broadening his field of religious knowledge and experience and by developing in him high character and an appreciation for the ethical standards of a Christian society.

During his administration Dr. Eversull was able to secure one of the projected new buildings, a Student Health Center. This was the culmination of the efforts of several staff members for a long period of years. During the first half of the history of the College health was considered a personal responsibility; the faculty and students had to assume the expense of illness through their own endeavors.

After 1913 the administration's policy was to hire the service of a local Fargo physician who would be willing to devote an hour a day to student "sick calls." His office was established in the College Mill. Office hours were from one to two p.m. He was paid $1,000 from administration sources (State funds) for his services. These usually consisted of bandaging wounds, examination of sore throats and quarantining of those afflicted with contagious diseases. Little use was made of the doctor's service, largely because of the inaccessibility of the office and the time of service. No service was given on Saturday.

The first World War and the development of the Student Army Training Corps at the College brought attention to the tremendous importance of adequate medical attention to the student body. The epidemic of influenza in 1918 was made worse by the increased incidence of epidemic pneumonia. In the crowded military quarters on the campus the mortality from secondary pneumonia rose to an alarming height. This made the College realize that a really efficient student health program was needed.

In the year 1919 Professor McArdle, who as secretary of the College had been so closely connected with the influenza epidemic, proposed that a charge of thirty cents per student per term be collected with the general fee paid at the beginning of each term. Money so collected was to be used as a trust fund from which worthy students might borrow money at a nominal interest rate, the loan to be paid back after graduation. Only those might borrow whose continuance in college was jeopardized by illness or surgical attention. A faculty committee was organized to check requests for loans and references. The original committee consisted of Professor McArdle, G. E. Miller, biology, and C. I. Nelson, bacteriology.

As the trust fund grew the committee became more lenient in the granting of loans, sometimes maybe too lenient. Many of the outstanding loans became difficult to collect until the uncollected amount was a considerable part of the total fund. The committee then decided to speed up collections and restrict the loans as originally intended.

In the year 1921 President Coulter called a general assembly of all the students. His message concerned the danger of an epidemic of influenza which was rising to an alarming height. He warned them that the best prevention measure was to avoid large group gatherings. Following this student meeting Dr. Nelson and others from the bacteriology department composed a letter which they sent rather jokingly to President Coulter asking if in calling such a meeting he had not committed the very action he had preached against. Dr. Coulter immediately replied that since these gentlemen had shown such a keen interest in student health they were thereby appointed to investigate and recommend a new student health program.

The program suggested by the committee was a change from a student loan policy to a student health program. A more efficient arrangement was made for the doctor at the College Mill so that the student could receive better medical attention.

At the end of World War I, other quarters were found for a doctor's office, consultation rooms, and even two or three beds, in the Men's Residence Hall. The physician's office was on the first floor of the east wing and adjacent to it was a well equipped clinic with separate waiting rooms for men and women. The health unit as a whole was secluded from the rest of the building. The doctor was in attendance from 4:30 to 6:00 p.m. Monday through Friday and from 11:00 to 12 a.m. Saturdays. A nurse was procured to give full time service.

In order to facilitate a health program further a dispensary was established in connection with the School of Pharmacy. This was to serve a two-fold purpose, first, to enable the college students who received medical aid and treatment from the College physician to have their prescriptions filled at the College Dispensary, and second, to furnish practical instruction in prescription compounding for senior students enrolled in pharmacy.

While the regular State funds were still assigned to pay the doctor, only student funds were available to pay the nurse. Thus the trust fund was of necessity restricted for use in the regular student medical service, less and less being loaned out as originally intended. Eventually only that portion of the student trust fund outstanding on individual loans, which were difficult to collect, plus a small part of the total ($2,000) was allocated to a special Student Health Loan Service. It was put under the management of a special faculty committee. The balance of the student trust fund was allocated to a regular student health committee. In this way a student health movement evolved from a movement which was originally of quite a different nature.

The service was financed from two sources. The state paid $600 yearly towards the physician's salary. Each student paid a fee of thirty cents per term toward expenses he might incur, including his physical examination. This money was used to hire a nurse for ten months and to supplement the doctor's salary. Only 29 out of 1,500 students were ill with contagious disease during the year 1935-36. It was no accident that during this time the cases of scarlet fever, mumps, smallpox and chicken pox did not spread throughout the campus. In that year 306 sick students visited the doctor and nurse; there occurred 389 smallpox vaccinations, isolation of exposed persons, and a rigid program of throat spraying, especially in the dormitories.

By 1939 a fund of approximately $20,000 was accumulated from student fees for a new health program. During the administration of President Eversull the present Student Health Center was constructed from these funds (about $10,000) supplemented by WPA funds (about $15,000). Paul Jones, Fargo architect and former faculty member at the College, drew up the plans, and T. L. Hanson, head of the department of architecture, supervised construction.

The health Center is a building of one story and basement, 60 x 40 feet; it is built of brick and is fireproof throughout. It has a waiting room, a four-patient men's ward, a four-patient women's ward, a doctor's office and a nurse's office and living quarters. The interior is finished in natural wood; glass brick is used in some walls and most rooms are air-conditioned.

President Eversull began his administration with an elaborate system of faculty committees and detailed instructions. In announcing them to the Council he stated that, in making up these committees, it was intended to include as many members of the staff as possible in order that the resources of the group might be widely used. Each committee had sufficient work to do to warrant at least a monthly meeting. In February, 1941, owing to the varied practices of different committees, the personnel committee appealed to the Council for an opinion regarding its functions, responsibilities and authority. The matter was placed on the table. The following September Dr. Eversull submitted a diagramatic plan of a functional organization of the College which showed the relationship of the different parts of the College to each other and the channels of operation for the different college units and committees. The plan was approved by the Council.

Several new members of the staff were appointed during the Eversull administration. Upon the resignation of Dean Carrick in 1943, Dr. Ralph E. Dunbar, who had come to the College as an instructor in 1937, was made dean of the School of Chemistry. A graduate of Dakota Wesleyan University, Mitchell, South Dakota, with a master's degree from Columbia and a Ph.D. degree from the University of Wisconsin, he was an associate editor of the *Encyclopedia of Chemical Reactions,* author or co-author of several text books and a frequent contributor to national journals of chemistry. Professor Knute Henning, who had come to the College in 1930, was advanced to the chairmanship of the department of architecture in 1943.

Miss Bales returned as dean of Home Economics in July, 1940, and served the next two years. September 1, 1942, she retired after nineteen years of service at the College. These years witnessed many changes in the School of Home Economics and a steady increase in enrollment. Sixty girls had been enrolled in 1920 as compared to approximately 316 in 1942. One of Dean Bales' outstanding innovations was the Home Management House for senior students, where she also made her home. The dietetics program, the correlation of art to home training and the increased emphasis on health were inaugurated during her administration. Her fine philosophy of life contributed to the development of the School of Home Economics and won for her a host of friends.[6]

Succeeding Miss Bales as acting dean was Miss Lucille Horton, who had come to the campus in 1929 as head of the department of home economics education. She had her bachelor's and master's degrees from the University of Minnesota. Her work at the College was largely with seniors, who spend five weeks practice teaching under her guidance.

Two years later, in 1944, Dr. Leita Davy was appointed dean. She had received a master's degree from the University of Iowa and a doctorate from the University of Wisconsin. Preceding her appointment she had been head of the department of home economics at the University of Louisville. Later she took special medical courses at the University of Texas. She was a member of Sigma Xi and a fellow of the American Association for the Advancement of Science. Formerly, she also was in charge of public health and nutrition for the State of Ohio.

After the death of Dean Weeks, the department of education was combined with agricultural and home economics education under Professor E. H. Jones, who was succeeded in 1939 by Professor E. C. Darling, a graduate of North Dakota Agricultural College, with a doctorate from the University of Iowa.

By 1941, the department of education prepared fewer high school teachers in academic fields (history, English, mathematics and science) than formerly; only about thirty were graduated each year. But there was a decided increase in the number of vocational teachers graduating, amounting to about sixty. No teachers were prepared for grade school positions. The department did not duplicate the program for training superintendents and principals offered by the University of North Dakota. It did provide a program for schoolmen in rural or consolidated high schools, where men were needed who understood the problems of farm people, and who were prepared to teach in several basic high school fields.

Dean I. W. Smith, after being dismissed in 1937, secured a position with a local insurance company and did not return to a teaching position. He, as chairman of the department of mathematics, was succeeded by Professor Householder, who in 1943 was succeeded by A. Glenn Hill, of the class of 1927, with an M.S., from the University of Wisconsin in 1932; he still continues as chairman.

Mr. Hill and Miss Matilda B. Thompson of the department of mathematics were invited by the State Department of Education to participate in writing a syllabus for mathematics to be used in the secondary schools of North Dakota. They also published a mathematics manual for college students in home economics.

In 1938 an attempt to meet the growing need for additional library facilities was made by President Eversull. A proposal for a new library, estimated to cost $200,000, was formerly submitted to the office of the regional P.W.A. director at Omaha by S. W. Hagan, secretary. This project was one of many submitted in the hope that some way could be found to provide additional funds to pay the State's share of the financing. The proposal included the following paragraph:

"Library facilities at N.D.A.C. are woefully inadequate. According to standards established for modern educational institutions, the facilities here can accommodate, properly, no more than a school of 250 students, whereas they must be made to do for a student body of from 1,300 to 1,800. The library seating capacity is about 75. It should be 400." [7]

The proposal failed to receive the sanction of the P.W.A. administration and so the agitation for legislative appropriations continued. On the basis of a probable new building, Elliot Hardaway, formerly on the staff of the Library of Congress, was chosen to succeed Mrs. Ethel McVeety, who resigned in June, 1944.

By 1938 the library collection amounted to 60,000 volumes and several thousands of pamphlets. Of this number, 16,713 volumes were in departmental libraries and offices. To show the growth of the library: in 1910 the library numbered 22,272 volumes; in 1920, 30,455; in 1930, 47,292, not including government documents; in 1940, 63,337; and in 1960, over 138,000.

Since 1897, when the College Library consisted of two rooms in the administration building, Mrs. McVeety had seen the growth of the library directly, and college life indirectly, through the years of the Spanish-American War, of the first World War, of a boom period, of a depression, and part of another World War. She had watched a fluctuating student enrollment, close to 190 in 1897, later rising into the thousands. It had been a long job; it had been a big job. To thousands of students Mrs. McVeety was identified with the library; they remember her "Sh-Shushing" their frequent attempts just to visit. During her years of faithful service she had a number of assistants. Miss Harriet Pearson, 1916-36, was one of the ablest; she served as an instructor in library methods, as well as being a consultant to the faculty.

Mr. Hardaway, the new librarian, a graduate of Vanderbilt University, with a master's degree from the University of Illinois, who arrived in 1944, was especially trained in the field of technical libraries. He accepted the appointment at the College on the understanding that a new improved library building would be erected. When the North Central Association restored the North Dakota Agricultural College to the accredited list, it criticized the inadequacy of library facilities. Plans for the building were drawn by Professor Henning and Mr. Hardaway. Provisions were to be made for a modern rectangular building which would include reading, reference and seminar rooms. A microfilm reading room and listening rooms for radio and record player were to be provided. However, the funds for such a building were not appropriated until after Mr. Hardaway's resignation.

Director Baker of the Extension Service died in 1939. He was succeeded by E. J. Haslerud, who had carried the duties of the county agent leader's office; he is still serving in it efficiently and acceptably.

In 1939 the twenty-fifth anniversary of the signing of the Smith-Lever Act, creating the co-operative extension work on a national scale, was celebrated. On May 8 members of the School of Agriculture presented the National Farm and Home Hour program over a coast-to-coast network of the National Broadcasting Company, reviewing the accomplishments of the period. Director Haslerud appointed a committee consisting of W. C. Palmer, Harry Rilling, E. G. Parizek and Miss Julia Brekke to outline plans for observance of the anniversary in the State. Programs were set up by some of the county Extension agents. A brief account of 4-H club work in North Dakota was written by former Extension director H. L. Walster, and a more complete account was published by H. E. Rilling. Miss Grace DeLong, State home demonstration leader, wrote a narrative of the development of home demonstration work in North Dakota and presented a brief statement of the history of Home Economics Extension in North Dakota.

Early in his administration Dr. Eversull inaugurated the practice of having quarterly commencements for those seniors who had completed their work during the college quarter. This was in line with other schools of higher education in the State. Members of the staff were invited to be commencement speakers at the end of the fall, winter and summer quarters. He also initiated the practice of honoring eminent men at the time of the June Commencement. In 1939 Dean Bolley and Dean C. B. Waldron were accorded honorary degrees — Doctor of Agriculture — the first honorary degrees granted by the North Dakota Agricultural College. In 1940 the College celebrated its fiftieth anniversary by awarding five honorary degrees, one degree for each of the ten years that the College had existed. Of the five men honored, two received the honorary degree of Doctor of Science, and the others the honorary degree of Doctor of Agriculture.

One of the five, Arni Helgason, born in Iceland, previously had received a B.S. in mechanical engineering from North Dakota Agricultural College and an M.S. in electrical engineering from the University of Wisconsin. He later became chief engineer, part owner and general manager of the Chicago Transformer Corporation. Since his student days he had been a serious and able student of Scandinavian literature and in 1939 was decorated by the King of Denmark and Iceland for promoting science and Scandinavian culture.

George F. Will, the son of a pioneer North Dakota seedsman, who had graduated from Harvard University with a major in anthropology and ethnology, was another recipient. An authority on the Plains Indians, he was author of several publications on their culture, and of many articles on botanical and horticultural subjects. He had been active as a plant breeder, particularly in the improvement of corn, squash and beans. He also made extensive tree-ring studies, using timbers from ancient Indian lodges and from specimens growing in the Bismarck area; the results of these studies were published in an Experiment Station bulletin.

Phillip S. Rose, a graduate of Michigan Agricultural College, taught agricultural engineering for ten years at the College. He helped to organize and became president of the American Society of Agricultural Engineering. He was probably best known as editor of *The Country Gentleman*.

M. L. Wilson became Montana's first county extension agent, and was later professor and head of the department of agricultural economics at Montana State College. In 1932 he entered the services of the U. S. Department of Agriculture as assistant secretary and director of extension work.

Henry H. Kildee had a B.S.A. and an M.S.A. from Iowa State College, and became head of the department of animal husbandry, vice-dean and finally dean of agriculture at that institution. He was internationally known as a livestock judge and was active in promoting the work of the Dairy Science Association.

On October 22, 1942, Haile Chisholm was the guest of honor at a birthday banquet in the Log Cabin and Little Country Theater. Mr. Chisholm first joined the College staff in 1902 as an instructor in forge and metal work. He retired in 1937 at the age of 85. In 1944 bronze busts of Professor Bolley and Dr. L. R. Waldron, sculptured by Ida Bisek Prokop Lee, were presented to the College by the man who had so often weeded Plot 30, A. M. Christensen of Minot. In 1945 a bronze bust of Dean C. B. Waldron, executed by I. B. Prokop Lee, was presented to the College by the North Dakota Horticultural Society.

FOOTNOTES

[1] *Fargo Forum*, Sept. 30, 1938.
[2] *North Dakota Agricultural College Bulletin*, XXIX, No. 4, Oct. 28, 1938.
[3] *Spectrum*, Jan. 5, 1940.
[4] *Bison Furrows*, I, Spring Quarter, 1938–39.
[5] *Bison Furrows*, III, Fall Quarter, 1939, 10.
[6] *Spectrum*, Oct. 23, 1942.
[7] *Fargo Forum*, Sept. 29, 1938.

◂ CHAPTER XI ▸

World War II, 1939-1945

WHEN World War II began in Europe in 1939 there was not too much concern about it in the Middle West, although in the Eastern States defense preparations developed and in the fall of 1940 Congress passed a Selective Service Act. At first enrollment at the North Dakota Agricultural College did not seem to be affected by the war. In the year 1940-1941 there was an enrollment of 1,479; in 1941-1942 it increased to 1,682; and in 1942-1943 to 1,735. The Japanese attack on Pearl Harbor in December, 1941, and the resulting declaration of war by the United States in the same month also did not seem to have an effect on registration until 1943. In the fall of that year however only 586 enrolled in the College and in the next year only 550, nearly all of them women. Not until 1945, after the war was ended, did the registration come back to an enrollment of 1,457.

With the entrance of the United States into active participation in World War II, President Eversull was faced with an array of new problems. A war adjustment conference, made up of school men, teachers and community leaders, was called for March 23 and 24, 1942, and met on the campus, heard addresses and participated in forums on a number of topics. Another conference in July of the same year was concerned more particularly with the problems facing higher education.

The total facilities of the College were mustered to meet the needs of the nation in its war effort. The teaching program was accelerated, special wartime courses were added and a "war council" formed to direct activities. The school year was divided into four full quarters of ten weeks each. New courses included human nutrition, nurses' training, war economics, problems of democracy, contemporary history, international relations, aeronautical training. The "war council" consisted of eleven students and eleven staff members. Committees were organized dealing with forums, a speakers' bureau, student morale, sale of war bonds and stamps, defense, civil air patrol, student recruitment, and the Red Cross.

World War II changed public opinion as to military service at the College. The State Legislature of 1943 reestablished compulsory military training and so the R.O.T.C. was revived at the College.

On September 21, 1942, an officer candidate school was opened at the College with 335 candidates to become officers in military administration. The Field House, Men's Residence Hall, Dakota Hall, Festival Hall, Ceres Hall cafeteria and the north wing of Science Hall accommodated the school. In addition, the Army rented the Theta Chi and Alpha Gamma Rho fraternity houses as post headquarters and the College YMCA as a recreational center. The College furnished housing and mess facilities. Instruction in the school was given by regular Army officers. A unit of 335 candidates was to be admitted every four weeks; the courses lasted for twelve weeks. By April, 1943, approximately 1,300 young men, after completing the course, had been commissioned second lieutenants.

They were a fine group of men who had a beneficial influence on the campus and the community. They were loud in their praise of Fargo people, Fargo hospitality and the facilities of the College, especially of the meal service. When the school was discontinued in June, 1943, 2,139 had graduated from it. At the last graduation of officer candidates, June 23, 1943, Major General James A. Ulio, was given an honorary degree of Doctor of Science in Military Science. General Ulio, a native of Fargo, was the son of an early commandant at the College. After June the officer candidate school was replaced by an army administration school for enlisted men.

In the summer of 1943, 400 Army engineer students arrived at the College for training; others came later. Instruction work was under the direction of the College faculty; mess facilities and housing were also provided by the College. This meant that a total of 1,800 Army men were stationed at the College in the fall of 1943, besides the regular students, mostly women.

In January, 1944, the Army administration school was closed; only a unit of an Army Specialized Training Program with about 600 men remained. Already some of the veterans of World War II were being enrolled as regular students. The ASTP program was discontinued March 15, 1944.

Before the opening of the fall quarter of 1944 the staff members of the College at the call of the president, were engaged in a post war planning workshop. From September 11 to September 19 the mornings were devoted to individual presentations of different phases of the institutional program by the proper staff members. The afternoons were given over to planning workshops. Members of the divisions of resident instruction, Experiment Station and Extension Service participated. A conclusive evaluation of the series stressed the value of increasing cooperation among the three divisions and the several schools and departments, and advised the participation of representative students in future conferences dealing with vital student problems. This conference was successful in giving the staff an overall picture of the institution and a greater appreciation of the abilities of various staff members. In January, 1945, a new school, School of Veterans Education, was set up with Charles A. Sevrinson, dean of men and assistant to the president, as dean. The new school worked in cooperation with the six established schools on the campus, but did not give its own degrees. It was hoped that veterans might obtain the training they needed or desired with a minimum of delay and red tape. Dean Sevrinson had been with the College since 1928 and had worked with the Army programs of 1942-44.

In connection with the establishing of this new school a faculty committee on curriculum and post war planning headed by Dr. J. H. Longwell, chief of the division of animal industry, worked closely with Carl H. Schmidt, director of personnel. Plans for study and work among various types of veterans were made; every encouragement was offered to induce them to complete a college education. The College was to keep in close touch with the United States Armed Forces Institute at the University of Wisconsin, in order that veterans might receive credit for work done in any training post of the armed services.

A post war education planning conference was held on the College campus April 30 to May 1, 1945, to aid the Board of Higher Education in its policies. This conference, promoted by Dr. Eversull, was "designed to offer opportunities for full and free discussion of the problems which confront higher education in teacher-training, recruitment, veterans' education, faculty security, curricular revision, and other pertinent topics." The conference sought to evaluate the basic factors underlying a State program of higher education.

During the next months in 1945 returning veterans arrived in increasing numbers, swelling the College enrollment. The problem of housing became acute for both students and staff. Eighty-eight trailers, ranging from $25 to $30 per month in rental, were secured and located on vacant spots on the campus, and equipped with water and electricity, some of them with College heat. Other privately owned trailers were allowed to locate on the campus. Married men and fathers soon became a commonplace among the students and they proved to be serious and able contributors to campus morale.

In March, 1946, the State Board of Higher Education received a recommendation from President Eversull setting the retirement age for the teaching staff at 70 years and that of administration officers at 65 with positions of satisfactory rank held until 70. The Board passed the recommendation, setting a salary for limited service at $1,200 yearly. "Limited service" was possible only "when the State Board of Higher Education finds that some demonstrated need exists within the institution which makes such assignment desirable to the success of the educational program."[1]

A spirit of unrest had been brewing for some time, inspired largely by the veterans who had returned to the College. They felt the standard of training they were receiving was inadequate, in view of overcrowded class rooms and underpaid and overworked instructors. They did not openly criticize President Eversull but they felt that the administration was not doing enough to correct the situation. Opinion came to a head over the question of a Student Union building, to supply the needs of all students, and especially veterans, for social activities and to supply a place where they could "dance, eat, play games, or just sit around and talk in an affable atmosphere." President Eversull suggested that the YMCA building be remodeled to house the union, but this plan met with the objection that the building was endowed for the Y. Another proposal was to build a "modest edifice" exclusively for Student Union purposes.

An "open forum" student commission meeting was held Tuesday, April 30, 1946, at the Y which 35 representatives of various campus organizations attended and in which the following resolution was adopted: "Due to the general dissatisfaction with the present administration, we hereby resolve to unanimously pledge ourselves to work for an improved education program and an enlightened, progressive, democratic administration."[2]

A. F. Arnason, who had been elected commissioner of the State Board of Higher Education, visited the campus on May 6 and 7 and announced that he would recommend a special meeting of the Board with the president, with members of the advisory committee, with the Alumni Association, with a special faculty committee, and with representatives of the student commission.[3] The faculty met Wednesday, May 8, and elected a nine-man committee representing all schools on the campus, including the Experiment Station and the

Extension Service. This group was instructed to work with student groups "on actions deemed advisable for the general improvement of the college and preparation of plans looking toward enhancing the prestige of N.D.A.C."[4]

The State Board of Higher Education met on May 14 and interviewed representatives of the student commission, the Alumni Association, Fargo business men and the nine-man faculty committee. A special convocation was called on May 23, 1946, at which a student committee proposed a plan of action. This included the securing of a full time publicity director to be paid by the College and Alumni Association, and an intra-state student action committee to be made up of four representatives from each of the institutions of higher education in North Dakota. This joint committee would contact State legislators and make them aware of the need for larger appropriations. A publicity campaign was to make the people of North Dakota more aware of the value of education and the need of funds to maintain the desired standards of these institutions.[5]

It was explained that the causes of the recent maladjustments were the sudden termination of the war and the resulting inadequacy of legislative appropriations for salaries and retirement of the staff. The faculty committee proposed a reorganization in administration which was approved by the Board and the president. A date for the first meeting of the intrastate student conference was set for June 18-19 at the campus of the Agricultural College. Its purpose was to support and broaden education in the State, and in contrast to events in 1938 this time this progressive movement was not confined to the campus of the Agricultural College.

In summarizing the administration of President Eversull, one must be fair to both the administration and the public. Dr. Eversull made strenuous efforts to win over the community and the State. He accepted all invitations to address a variety of audiences and he made some excellent and thought-provoking speeches. Perhaps he excelled in those which were religious in approach or idealistic in nature. He appealed to the idealist more than to the practical business man. He was a promoter, and as such he was prominent in organizing the Fargo-Moorhead Executives Club. At the beginning he was a real force in the community; he made many promises but unfortunately his promises frequently failed to materialize. In the State he was less effective, particularly among the farmer legislators, who failed to be impressed by his educational philosophy. Often enough he failed to get along with the politicians, with the Fargo business men, with the students and with the faculty. In 1946 he may have come to realize that his period of service to the Agricultural College was approaching an end, and so he resigned on June 11 to accept a position as an educational adviser for the U. S. Department of Defense in Korea.

The Board accepted his resignation and passed the following resolution:

"President Frank L. Eversull having presented his resignation in order that he might assume new duties in a larger field of educational activity in the service of the United States in foreign lands, the Board takes this opportunity to express appreciation of the many accomplishments effected by him in his administration of the College.

"He came to the institution when its educational standing and morale was at the lowest ebb, but his inspiration and personality put new life and vigor in the school and its educational standing and morale was brought to the highest point in the school's history. It had been reaccredited and held its head high among agricultural colleges.

"Largely through his personal efforts and influence, army programs were instituted and conducted through the war, and these brought high commendation from the armed forces command. The war over, he brought about the task of providing housing facilities for returned service men and obtained excellent results.

"The Board releases President Eversull for greater service in behalf of our nation's efforts to bring about better conditions throughout the world, educationally and otherwise, with confidence that great and worthwhile tasks will be accomplished by him." [6]

After the resignation of President Eversull, Dean Sevrinson was appointed acting president, a logical choice, for he had been assistant to the president ever since 1939. Roy Johnson, Howard Henry and Commissioner Arnason were chosen to meet with the College advisory committee to appraise and to recommend candidates for a new president.

During the summer of 1946 a special convocation was held to award an honorary degree of Doctor of Agriculture to Dr. L. Van Es, a former faculty member of the College. At this time Dr. Van Es participated in the annual meeting of the North Dakota Veterinary Medical Association. In presenting the citation Dr. Walster described him as "a man of outstanding character in the field of science, as physician, veterinarian and bacteriologist."

On July 24, 1946, Dr. John H. Longwell was appointed president to succeed Dr. Eversull.[7] He had received his B.S. in agriculture from the University of Missouri and his master's and doctor's degrees from the University of Illinois. He had taught at Washington State College, West Virginia University and the University of Illinois. He came to the North Dakota Agricultural College in 1941 as chief of the division of animal industry, and became associate director of

World War II, 1939–1945

the Experiment Station in 1945. In that year he was elected president of the North Dakota Academy of Science. President Longwell appreciated the circumstances surrounding his choice as president. In personality and philosophy he was almost a complete antithesis of his predecessor and sought to give the College a safe, sound and conservative administration. In one of his first published statements, entitled "Present Situation at North Dakota Agricultural College," he made these sensible comments:

"The state's young people today are entitled to educational opportunities equivalent to those enjoyed by former students as well as the opportunities offered by other states. Likewise, the agricultural and industrial interests of the state deserve a research program that will provide for the maximum development of the state's resources.

"If the institution is to perform these services its development must keep pace with the changing needs of the state. This college is owned and supported by the citizens of the state. Its development will depend upon the support which the citizens feel they are justified in giving . . . During the years of drought and depression, followed by the war, financial support to the college was considerably restricted. This has resulted in low salaries, reduced size of staff, and deterioration of the physical plant. Now, with the largest enrollment on record, and a greater number of problems calling for solutions by the experiment station, the college is not in a position to render as effective service as it should."[8]

At his inauguration on November 6, 1946, in Festival Hall, Dean Walster presided and made it a simple and informal occasion. A dinner and reception followed. Dr. Clyde L. Bailey, Dean of Agriculture at the University of Minnesota, an alumnus of the College, was the chief speaker at the dinner.

In his speech of acceptance, President Longwell related science to the development of a democracy. He advocated for the College "an adequate program of instruction and research" which would require a staff of well trained and experienced teachers and investigators. He said that salaries should be commensurate with the training and experience of the staff members. Satisfactory retirement and opportunities for professional improvement should be provided for the staff. Old buildings should be repaired and additional buildings erected. Added laboratory equipment was needed; closer relationships between college and alumni should be developed; student welfare departments should be established.

When Dr. Longwell was named president of the College, he was succeeded as chief of the division of animal industry by Professor M. L. Buchanan, a graduate of Oklahoma Agricultural and Mechanical College with an M.S. degree from the University of West Virginia. His department greatly profited by the half section of land northwest of the campus which had been presented to the College by the merchants of Fargo for the expansion of livestock work. Dr. R. L. Bryant, a graduate of the University of Kentucky with advanced degrees from Cornell, was secured in the winter of 1947 for the department of poultry husbandry to succeed Professor O. A. Barton, who retired. Professor Barton was on the staff of the College for 36 years, serving as 4-H Club Leader and professor of poultry husbandry. He was widely known for his skill as a poultry judge, for his promotion of the turkey industry, and for his enthusiasm as a teacher.

In entomology, Dr. R. L. Post came to the College in 1946. He was a graduate of Michigan State College and received his Ph.D. from Oregon State College in 1947. He added over 10,000 specimens to the insect collection started by C. B. Waldron and increased by R. L. Webster, J. A. Munro, and O. A. Stevens.

The department of horticulture was greatly strengthened by the appointment of Dr. Joseph H. Schultz, a native of North Dakota, a former student of the College, who had received his B.S. and M.S. from Michigan State College and a Ph.D. degree from Washington State University. His work at Michigan was largely specialized research in the use of vegetables, at Washington, in the use of fruits.

Agricultural economics advanced under the leadership of Dr. Rainer E. Schickele, who came to the College in 1947, a former member of the Iowa State College faculty and later employed by the U. S. Department of Agriculture. He received a doctorate from the University of Berlin in 1931, did post-doctorate research at Iowa State College and Harvard University and had published a book entitled "*Agricultural Policy.*" In 1955 he resigned from his position at the College to join the Food and Agricultural Organization of the United Nations with headquarters in Rome, Italy. While at the College he revised the curriculum and secured able instructors and investigators in his field. He did much to increase the interest in agricultural economics on the campus by conducting a senior seminar open to faculty, advanced students, and others interested in the subjects discussed.

In 1947 Dr. Glenn S. Smith was named associate dean of the School of Agriculture and associate director of the Agricultural Experiment Station, succeeding Dr. C. C. Volkerding, who resigned. Dr. Smith spent most of his childhood at the Dickinson Branch Experiment Station, where his father was Federal agronomist. He was graduated from the North Dakota Agricultural College, with a major in agronomy, and later was awarded a Ph.D. degree in plant breeding from the University of Minnesota. He is best known for his breeding of rust-resistant durum wheats while doing research at the North Dakota Agricultural College.

In 1947 P. J. Iverson, with a Ph.D. degree from the University of Cincinnati, was appointed head of the department of education and psychology, succeeding Dr. Darling. He had been brought to the College by President Worst as principal of the Manual Training High School, which was used until 1937 as a laboratory school for high school teachers. He emphasized particularly the use of visual aids in education. The field of psychology was strengthened and the emphasis on summer and night classes had resulted in renewed interest in graduate study among the teachers in the Fargo-Moorhead area.

When in March, 1947, Mr. Hardaway, the librarian, resigned, he was succeeded by H. Dean Stallings, with a bachelor's degree from Leland Stanford University and a master's degree in library science from the University of Illinois. Before coming to the College he was librarian at South Dakota State College.

In 1947 Willard D. Pye, with a Ph.D. degree from the University of Chicago, became head of the department of geology. He showed a great interest in the recent petroleum developments in the State and wrote some illuminating articles about it for newspapers in the State. Also Professor J. A. Oakey was made chairman of the department of civil engineering and Professor A. W. Anderson, who had been at the College since 1934, became chairman of the department of mechanical engineering.

In April, 1948, fifty-seven staff members who had served the institution for at least a quarter-century each were honored at a dinner sponsored by the North Dakota Farm Bureau. They were presented with brass plaques mounted on walnut, bearing the inscription: "In grateful appreciation of over a quarter century of unwavering loyalty to North Dakota Agricultural College and to the cause of American Agriculture." At this recognition dinner the Quarter Century Club was organized, A. H. Parrott being elected president, O. O. Churchill, vice president, and Pearl Dinan, secretary. The club has met annually since 1948, honoring those who have served twenty-five years at the College.

At the June, 1948, Commencement, Professor O. A. Stevens was awarded the honorary degree of Doctor of Science. The citation by Dr. Walster called him a "plant scientist, a plant lover who has been as greatly interested in the humble weeds with their inconspicuous bloom as in the resplendence of the many-hued flowers of our prairies," a true apostle of conservation, an authority on bees and wasps, "the bird man at the A.C.," the author of a "long list of popular and scientific articles in three distinct sciences: botany, entomology and ornithology."

During the administration of President Eversull and continuing during the succeeding administrations there was a real effort on the part of the faculty to obtain a satisfactory constitution for the College. Previous to 1920, when the Board of Regents was the governing body, the so-called *Blue Book* was in effect. Under the Board of Administration this code was rarely, if ever, consulted. Dr. Coulter utilized the services of the College Council, which met monthly. The purge of 1937 was a lesson in mal-administration which an accepted constitution could have prevented.

In May, 1946, a committee of the faculty was selected to work with the students regarding the matter of improved conditions for the College. This committee was asked by Commissioner Arnason to propose a revision of the College constitution. The result of their efforts, formulated in weekly sessions during the summer and fall, was submitted to the Council on November 14, 1946.

The chief criticism of the proposal was that it failed to include the Experiment Station and the Extension Service. The draft was discussed by the Council at length. Consequently a new committee was elected which spent more hours on the composition of a new constitution. Finally the Council did pass it and referred it to a general staff meeting, which endorsed it.

In 1947 criticism was directed against certain departments which had announced increased offerings in their curricula. In order to make clear the policy of the State Board of Higher Education regarding "expansion of offerings" Commissioner Arnason wrote the following directive to President Longwell, which the latter read to the Council on December 17, 1947:

"Whenever an institution seeks to initiate or establish a new department, division, school or vocational training program; or plans to increase course offerings in any field to a minor; expand a minor to a major, or add options to a curriculum, no action or announcement of plans or intentions shall be made until such plans, accompanied by objective evidence, justifying the proposed expansion, have been submitted to and subsequently approved by the State Board of Higher Education. All new courses are to be submitted to the Commissioner of Higher Education for approval.

"All recommendations within the scope of this policy shall be submitted at least 90 days before the opening date of the term at which the courses or expanded offerings are to be offered." [9]

Dr. Longwell and his staff made plans for increasing the physical plant, basing their requests from the Legislature on the needs of

World War II, 1939-1945

an ever increasing number of students, for the post war enrollments increased not only from normal reasons but also from the G.I. Bill, which financed veterans. The last buildings erected on the campus had been built in 1930, when enrollment was about 1,400. In 1947, 2,350 students crowded classroom and laboratory space to the limit. Proposed building needs included a library, a maintenance building, an agricultural engineering building and a home economics building and additions to Morrill Hall and the engineering building. There was a pressing need for a larger teaching staff and also for an expanded research and Extension program, which would require more space and a larger staff.

The budget board approved appropriations for a new library, an agricultural engineering laboratory, a livestock building, a maintenance building and further addition to Old Main. The Legislature of 1947 appropriated money for all these buildings and additional appropriations for repairs, for grounds and for student welfare.

During the two years of President Longwell's administration, the students showed a renewed interest in athletics. World War II had resulted in bringing back to the campus a number of veterans. One of these was Cliff Rothrock, who in 1946 was named center on the Little All-American team selected by the Associated Press. Twice before this honor had come to the North Dakota Agricultural College, in 1933 to Fritz Hanson and in 1939 to Ernie Wheeler. The team in 1946 under the coaching of Stan Kostka and C. P. (Chalky) Reed won over Concordia College, Morningside College, South Dakota State College and the University of North Dakota, but was defeated by Iowa Teachers College and the University of South Dakota.

In basketball "Chalky" Reed's squad was slow in developing a winning team; North Dakota Agricultural College was sixth in the conference, but at the end of the season defeated the University of North Dakota, which ranked second. Paul (Red) Brostrom was the spark plug for the team. Despite the ability of the director of athletics, Casey Finnegan, a gradually decreasing interest in athletics could be explained by the continuing difficulty of securing and retaining coaches, and by the competition of larger universities in seeking athletic talent.

In May, 1947, the students voted overwhelmingly for the creation of a Student Union building fund. This vote of 821 to 89 on June 4 meant that a special assessment of $5.00 per quarter would be added to the student activity fees. A committee of two faculty members, three students and two alumni members was announced by President Longwell to plan for the solicitation of gifts, develop a budget and make plans for construction. Four graduate students in architecture prepared initial plans for the building. Merle Nott served as corporation representative for solicitation. Five thousand brochures were distributed, which told the story of the Union and its purpose. In his report in September, 1948, Merle Nott listed three chief sources of funds for the construction of the Union: "Gifts from alumni, and other friends of the College; student fees from students at the rate of $5 per term; public sale of bonds, to be retired over 20 years by fees, with the building maintained by concessionaire income, bowling fees, and other returns from public services housed therein."[10]

One of the chief problems facing the post war administration was that of housing. Over 2,300 students were enrolled in 1946-47, of whom 1,500 were veterans, many of them married. Women students were housed in Dakota Hall, single men in the Field House basement, but the big demand for housing came from the married veterans. To help them, 92 trailers were secured; 65 quonset-style houses were built north of the Field House; 30 pre-fabricated units were purchased by a faculty housing corporation and rebuilt north of the College Y.M.C.A. Another housing project, some 146 family units, was provided by Federal money on Thirteenth Street north of the Field House; later this development was called North Court. Students and faculty owning private trailers were permitted to locate them on certain parts of the campus.

In the fall of 1946 Lt. Colonel Frank T. Balke became the R.O.T.C. commandant. He had served with the National Guard during the thirties, had entered the regular Army in 1940 and spent the war years in active combat. Under his command the advanced air courses were reactivated, open to veterans of more than one year of service. In March, 1947, Scabbard and Blade was reactivated and seven new members pledged. In 1948 Colonel Balke announced that the chief source of commissioned officers would be the R.O.T.C. and therefore the R.O.T.C. program in the colleges was of vital importance. A direct commission as a second lieutenant in the regular Army or Air Force could be secured by "distinguished" rating. This honor was to belong to "those R.O.T.C. graduates who rank in the upper third of their class in R.O.T.C. subjects, who possess outstanding leadership, aptitude and moral qualities, and who are selected by the school's professor of military science and tactics and the dean of men."[11]

On June 5, 1947, graduates, former students and instructors who gave their lives in World War II were honored by an observance in the College stadium. A. H. Parrott, the College registrar, was chairman

World War II, 1939–1945

of the program; speakers were Brigadier General Clinton A. Pierce of the War Department, President Longwell and Major Carl Almer, chaplain of the Army Reserve Corps. The names of those honored are listed in the appendix of this book.[12]

As mentioned before, in November, 1947, a gift of 310 acres of land to the Agricultural College by the citizens of Fargo was announced by the president of the Fargo Chamber of Commerce. A sum of $31,000 had been raised among Fargo business men through the efforts of the agricultural committee of the Chamber, with J. E. Pyle, as chairman. The land, lying northwest of the campus, was to be used as a laboratory for experiments in animal husbandry, livestock nutrition, and disease control experimentation. On this land the college "barns" were re-located, new buildings replacing the old structures that the natural growth of the institution had placed in the heart of the campus. To this gift was added and incorporated on April 10, 1948 a North Dakota Agricultural College Memorial Foundation, through which future land purchases for the Experiment Station might be channeled.

The World War II period was a significant one for the Experiment Station for it was urgent that farmers everywhere go all out for production. These were years of generally good rainfall, often heavy plant growth, a condition favorable for rust development. That rust epidemics did not develop during some of these years, permitting record wheat crops to be produced, can almost certainly be credited to the resistant varieties then in extensive use. Students of the problem have estimated that the protection for the wheat crop by these varieties, in these and many other years, meant the annual savings of many millions of dollars. The appreciation of the farm people for these benefits was shown in 1949 when they voluntarily subscribed $120,000 and purchased a section farm in the Casselton area, to be known as the Agronomy Seed Farm and used for increasing new and better lines of seed.

Equally significant to variety improvement, though less striking because of the smaller acreage, had been the contribution in better flax varieties — varieties not only resistant to wilt but also highly resistant, or immune to all races of flax rust known to exist in this country and Canada. The development and introduction after 1942 of such varieties as B 5128, Victory, Sheyenne, Deoro (Golden), Marine, Norland and Bolley were to make flax a surer crop than it had been. Another important contribution to flax improvement during this period was the development of a rapid method of evaluating linseed oil quality now widely used to assist the flax breeder, and also used in industrial laboratories.

Late in July 1948, President Longwell resigned to accept the position of dean of agriculture and director of the Experiment Station at the University of Missouri, his alma mater. This action was a surprise to the campus and to the State Board of Higher Education. Dr. Longwell said that he preferred to remain in work for which he was trained and he hoped to continue agricultural research in his new post. No doubt the burden of the many administrative details of his office weighed heavily on him and his time as president was too much absorbed with matters uninteresting to one who prefers teaching and research.

An editorial in the *Fargo Forum* summarized his work:

"A vote of thanks from North Dakota is due to Dr. Longwell . . . for his accomplishments during the two years he was president of the N.D.A.C. During those two years (he) demonstrated a down-to-earth approach to the multitudinous problems attendant on administration of the college. Substantial strides were made in enhancing the general public esteem for the diverse activities of the college which so intimately enmesh with the economics and social welfare of the people of North Dakota." [13]

FOOTNOTES

[1] Minutes of the State Board of Higher Education, Mar. 5, 27, 1946.

[2] *Spectrum*, May 2, 1946.

[3] *Spectrum*, May 9, 1946.

[4] *Spectrum*, May 16, 1946.

[5] *Spectrum*, May 23, 1946.

[6] Minutes of the State Board, June 11, 1946.

[7] Minutes of the State Board, July 16, 24, 1946. The Board interviewed five candidates, then met with the advisory committee, who favored Longwell.

[8] *N.D.A.C. Alumni Review*, VIII, No. 4, July–Sept., 1946, 1.

[9] Minutes of the College Council, Dec. 17, 1947.

[10] *N.D.A.C. Alumni Review*, X, No. 8, Sept., 1948, 3.

[11] *Spectrum*, Sept. 17, 1948.

[12] *N.D.A.C. Alumni Review*, IX, No. 3, Apr.–June, 1947, 13–14.

[13] *The Fargo Forum*, Aug. 1, 1948.

◄ CHAPTER XII ►

New Advances and New Strifes, 1945-1955

D R. LONGWELL submitted his resignation in July, 1948, to go into effect September 18, 1948. Commissioner A. F. Arnason instructed President Longwell to name a campus committee to aid the State Board of Higher Education in choosing a new president. The committee named consisted of H. L. Walster, Dean of the School of Agriculture and Director of the Experiment Station, Professor A. Glenn Hill and Dr. A. D. Whedon of the School of Arts and Sciences, R. E. Dunbar, Dean of the School of Chemistry, R. M. Dolve, Dean of the School of Engineering, Professor Minnie Anderson of the School of Home Economics, W. F. Sudro, Dean of the School of Pharmacy, and E. J. Haslerud, Director of the Extension Service. The State Board reviewed a number of possible candidates for the presidency. Three of the candidates were personally interviewed by both groups. The choice was unanimous on the part of the Board and the faculty committee. On August 24, 1948, Dr. Fred S. Hultz was named president of the North Dakota Agricultural College.

Dr. Fred S. Hultz was born and educated in Ames, Iowa. He earned the bachelor's, master's and doctor's degrees at Iowa State College, with a major in animal husbandry and a minor in agricultural economics. From 1917 to 1922 he taught animal husbandry at Pennsylvania State College, except for service with the Y.M.C.A. in World War I. In 1922 Dr. Hultz became head of animal production at the University of Wyoming, where he also served as university editor and director of public relations. He was the author of three books on animal husbandry, of numerous articles in regard to livestock, and for many years was one of the editors for the *Wyoming Stockman-Farmer*. He was a 33rd Degree Mason and a member of the Lions Club, having served as president and district governor in Wyoming and later in North Dakota.

It is interesting to note that Dr. Hultz and Dr. Coulter were the only presidents of the College chosen in consultation with a committee of the staff and both came from outside the State. Presumably the others, being already connected with the College or the State, were well known.

On September 15 he arrived on the campus, and the same week he addressed the College faculty and presented the following program:

"In addition to solving research problems, to teaching young people, to carrying the message of good husbandry to the four corners of the state, we owe ourselves, and each other, an additional activity: the activity of inspiring confidence in our work on the part of the citizens of North Dakota ... The selling of this great college, and its services to our people, is one which must not be neglected. Each of you is, and should be, an emissary of good will and a source of technical information from this college to the public ...

"It is my hope that before many months have passed, we may join together in a study of the college ... The study should be helpful in: providing and maintaining adequate salaries; establishing policies for faculty rank and promotions; evaluating the services of the staff; setting up a policy for staff tenure; appraising curricula, and surveying the physical needs of the college.

"It is our pleasure to have been selected to work with you in one of the soundest most respected land grant colleges in the country. It is my hope that Mrs. Hultz and I may meet your friendliness with equal measure, and demonstrate to you our desire to be not only colleagues, but personal friends as well." [1]

On October 27, 1948, the Fargo Chamber of Commerce honored President Hultz at a dinner at the Elks Club. He was introduced by Ralph Trubey, past president of the State Board of Higher Education, and gave an address entitled "Agriculture and Business." In it he said that he had found Fargo "most progressive, most friendly, keenest for business and best humored," and a true examplar of "western hospitality." He stated further that the College was playing a leading role in the commercial and agricultural development of North Dakota and asked for strong support in the years ahead if it was to improve adequately its services and equipment to meet its share of the problems of the future.

At this dinner a deed to a half-section of land just west of the campus was presented to the College by various Fargo business firms to provide better facilities for livestock feeding and breeding. The dinner was attended by three hundred farmers from the Red River Valley and by Fargo business and professional men, who had raised $31,000 to buy the farm.

The first time President Hultz met with the deans, they suggested to him having an inaugural ceremony, such as his two predecessors had, and which was customary at other institutions in the State and in the nation. But Dr. Hultz "asked them to consider the Chamber of Commerce party as marking his official induction into office, which they accepted graciously and gladly."

President Hultz' general conception of the Agricultural College is summarized at its best in a statement which he and the College staff later prepared for the Legislative Research Committee in May, 1951:

"The Land-Grant colleges and universities, one in each state in the Union, are not only unique in the field of education. They are completely and entirely 'made in America.' These Land-Grant institutions, many of them now nearly one hundred years old, were not dreamed up by a paternalistic government. They do, in fact, stem from the grass roots, draw their nurture from the same source, and return to their sponsors, our rural citizens, a thousand fold of benefit and service.

"The Land-Grant institution is not, and cannot be, limited only to the teaching of elementary agriculture. The trained technician in agriculture today is no longer only a tiller of the soil with a horse-drawn plow. He is a planner, a soil specialist, an agronomist, a chemist, an engineer, a linguist, a stockman, an entomologist, a specialist in plant and animal disease control, a writer, a public speaker, and an economist. Most of all, especially in North Dakota, he must be prepared for citizen leadership." [2]

President Hultz soon recognized that the rejuvenation of the College depended upon a program of publicity and out of his experiences in previous positions he was adept at that type of promotion. He was able to accomplish in that line what previous administrations were less fitted or unable to obtain. A good example of it is a statement which he made in his first address to legislators:

"I have endeavored to understand the lack of financial support which the Agricultural College has had in past years. I attribute much of this lack to public relations on the part of the college. This is no specific criticism of any individual or person, but it does indicate a failure to understand the necessity of keeping our citizenry informed regarding the college." [3]

Another ability in which Dr. Hultz excelled was his mastery of the budget and his skill in gaining legislative support and appropriations for the College. In February, 1949, he appeared before the appropriations committees of both houses, to whom he remarked that "of the land-grant colleges in the United States, he didn't know of one as ill-equipped and so rundown as that of North Dakota." This was the first time that a president of the College had addressed the committees of appropriations. President Hultz had presented a ten-year program and had asked for a substantial contribution toward its eventual completion. In March, 1949, the College was granted the largest biennium appropriation that it had ever received. Appropriations were made for an engineering building, for a maintenance building, for the president's residence, for library equipment, for a beef and a hog barn, for the remodeling of the veterinary building, for acousticizing the Field House, for power house equipment, and for moving the football stadium from the center of the campus to an area north, in order to make room for new buildings. The salaries of the staff were materially increased. For the Experiment Station a new poultry plant, a new seed house, a new storage building, a new modern greenhouse and the remodeling of the farm house were made possible.

A special convocation was held on March 13, 1949, to express the school's gratitude to the Legislature and to outline to the staff and student body the projected use of the funds voted, and also to explain a proposed ten-year plan for the future of the College. Special guests included Governor Aandahl, Senator Shure, Representative A. C. Johnson and Roy Johnson, president of the State Board of Higher Education. Much enthusiasm was expressed for what the new president of the College had accomplished in his first few months in office, and for the prospects for the College.

In March, 1949, a department of public relations was set up. Merle Nott, a graduate of the College, was appointed publicity director with a secretary as assistant. But President Hultz did not rest on his laurels; soon he was making plans for the next meeting of the Legislature in 1951. In accordance with his suggestion to the faculty in 1948, early in 1949 he inaugurated a comprehensive developmental study of the College by the staff. Its main purposes were: self-analysis for the general improvement of the College; provision of useful information in securing more satisfactory financial support; establishments of goals for the future development of the College.

Following this suggestion a steering committee was appointed, consisting of Ray Wendland, chairman, C. O. Anderson, Clifton Miller, Joseph Schultz, and C. A. Sevrinson. Almost sixty topics of study were assigned to various members of the staff, who were named reporters. Fields of study included the various schools and departments, the Experiment Station, and the Extension Service. In addition, more general features of the College, such as size, organization, research, teaching load, student organizations, housing, health, etc., were also studied. About two thirds of the reports placed emphasis on existing needs, rather than constructive recommendations for the future. The study was valuable as a measure of self-appraisal, but furnished little effective material for securing more adequate appropriations.

Since the College developmental study did not accomplish its chief purpose, President Hultz turned to an interested group of citizens of the State for help. This was the Council for Agricultural Education and Research, a voluntary organization formed in 1946, composed of farmers, which gave support to the College; it was an example of grass-roots co-operation between the College and citizens of the State. Periodically Dr. Hultz met with this group in their home communities and gave reports of the College's accomplishments. Annual meetings occurred at the College in connection with a tour of the campus and acquaintance with research projects. To this council was given much credit for the increased interest of the Legislature in the welfare of the College.

On October 6, 1950, the new library was dedicated. It cost, fully equipped, $500,000. The original appropriation for the library by the State legislature in 1945 was $200,000; another of $200,000 was made in 1947, and $100,000 in 1949 for equipment. A modern, functional building, the library is equipped with the latest in lighting, heating and ventilation. On the first floor are a reading room, a student lounge, classroom, two seminar rooms, stack area, toilets, and stairways. The second floor has a reading room, faculty lounge, office, card catalog, periodical room, and stack area. The basement has space for 200,000 volumes, in addition to a place for permanent records. The total book capacity of the library is 300,000 volumes.

At the dedication ceremonies, Dr. Ralph Ellsworth, director of the Library of the University of Iowa, said: "I hope you North Dakotans understand the full significance of this building, because if you do, you will be very proud of it. North Dakota has two public buildings that command national attention, this library and the capitol. This is the first truly modular library, utilitarian and functional."[4]

1950 marked the sixtieth anniversary of the College. A profusely illustrated booklet was published. It briefly treated the history of the institution from its earliest beginning and traced the growth through the sixty years. The six schools, the Experiment Station and the Extension Service were described. The military and air sciences, athletic, and musical programs were described. New buildings were mentioned. The slogan, "It's 60 in '50," was used as a theme for homecoming. With sixty years of accomplishments the College was ready to go on to greater attainments.

In December President Hultz addressed a special convocation of the student body in which he emphasized the value of the institution to the State and to the students. He mentioned the needs for a Student Union, for dormitories, for street paving, and appealed for aid from the students during the coming holidays, when at home they might contact their legislative representatives.

In 1951 the president was successful in advancing another step in the ten-year program. Although there was uncertainty as to student enrollment and an avowed attitude of economy on the part of the legislators, appropriations were secured for added maintenance costs, for heating plant renovations, for paving on the campus, and for a new home economics building. In his report the president attributed much of the credit for these grants to the North Dakota Council for Agricultural Education and Research, to the North Dakota Homemakers' Council, to Phi Upsilon Omicron, home economics sorority, and to the Alumni Board. The Experiment Station was given another greenhouse and additional funds for wheat breeding and the study of wheat rust.

Pursuant to a resolution of the Legislature of 1951 calling "for a detailed study of the state supported institutions of higher learning . . . for the purpose of ascertaining . . . a better degree of unification and coordination, and improved standards of education," President Hultz in May presented a statement to the legislative research committee. This survey briefly treated the following topics: achievements of land-grant colleges; achievements of N.D.A.C.; N.D.A.C. expenditures; N.D.A.C. buildings; future demands on education, North Dakota income, N.D.A.C. needs; and N.D.A.C. and North Dakota. The survey emphasized the "continued and growing need for young people trained in science, in government, in home making, and in agriculture — if North Dakota's economy is to go forward competitively with an assurance of wealth and prosperity." [5]

In 1953 the North Dakota Legislature granted an increase over the previous year's budget, which was less than half of the increase recommended by the State Board of Higher Education. However, in it money was appropriated for additional paving, for sidewalks, and for landscaping the north campus, for a storm sewer, for a football stadium (a part of the old stadium had suffered damage by fire), for a cereal technology building, and for operating expenses sufficient to carry on for the biennium. Dr. Hultz published a statement in the April, 1953, issue of the *N.D.A.C. Alumni Review* in which he mentioned the reluctance of the last two Legislatures to appropriate for major college and university buildings, and that consequently a new pharmacy building for N.D.A.C. had not been allowed.

On October 22, 1954, the new home economics building was dedicated. At the ceremonies Miss Christine Finlayson, state supervisor of home economics education, presided. Representatives of the faculty, the State Board of Higher Education, and the North Dakota Legislature presented greetings and congratulations. President Hultz, one of the speakers, said those present were there "to dedicate this building to the uses of family living and the home, to the betterment of North Dakota people, and to the purposes of teaching, research, and extension." Mrs. R. L. Olson, who had served as acting dean while the building was being planned and constructed, gave the main address, "Looking Forward in Home Economics." She outlined a series of visions that would make home life satisfying, that would supply the demand for homemakers, teachers and research workers that would serve the State in many ways. The new dean of home economics, Miss Caroline Budewig, accepted the building from President Hultz.

This modern $400,000 building, fully equipped, is a "home economist's dream come true." On the first floor are offices of the dean and professor of home economics education, a social lounge, clothing and costume laboratories. On the second floor are the food laboratories and a large weaving room. On the ground floor are other offices and rooms for applied arts, ceramics and home furnishings.

The next two sessions of the Legislature, in 1955 and 1957, made appropriations for an adequate operation and maintenance of the three divisions of the College, although funds for much needed new buildings were not provided. However, in 1959 the Thirty-sixth Legislature appropriated funds for two major buildings and provided for some salary improvements and new positions to take care of an expanding enrollment. The sum of $550,000 was granted for a new pharmacy building, to be supplemented by a grant of $110,000 from the National Institutes of Health for construction and fixed equipment and an additional $15,417 for movable scientific equipment. The sum of $750,000 was appropriated for an agricultural science building, the amount including equipment and landscaping. Meanwhile, staff salaries had been increased about an average of 100 percent since 1948. At last President Hultz was able to realize the completion of his plan announced in 1948.

Another attempt to solve a perennial financial problem was undertaken in 1958. At Dr. Hultz' suggestion the various state institutions of higher learning sought to secure through an initiated measure a one-mill levy to provide funds for a permanent building program. Robert Crom, the publicity director of the North Dakota Agricultural

College, was in general charge of the campaign but the measure was defeated in the November election, along with all the other initiated measures.

A new policy initiated by President Hultz was that of renaming the campus buildings. Up to his time a few buildings had already been designated by name, for example, Morrill Hall, for the agricultural building; Ceres Hall, for the women's building; Francis Hall, at first a dormitory, later used for offices of the Extension Service, and more recently assigned to pharmacy. The other buildings were known as science hall, the library, the mechanic arts or engineering building, the men's dormitory, chemistry, the mill, and the music hall.

When the College music department learned that the old library building would be its new home, there was an immediate request that it be named Putnam Hall. The suggestion was sent to the State Board of Higher Education and received unanimous approval. The rededication ceremony took place May 17, 1951, immediately following Honors Day Convocation. Mrs. Putnam and two sons were present at the unveiling of a memorial plaque. A large portrait of Dr. Putnam was hung inside the lobby, given by many friends and former members of the band.

As a part of the Commencement in June, 1951, Science Hall was rededicated and named Minard Hall in honor of Dean A. E. Minard, who gave 46 years of service to the College. The College hymn, the words of which were written by Dean Minard, was sung at this time. A bronze plaque was placed at the entrance. Plans were made for a memorial shelf for books on philosophy to be placed in the library in his honor.

On June 2, 1952, the chemistry building was rededicated and named Ladd Hall in honor of President Ladd, who was also the first dean of the School of Chemistry and the planner of the chemistry building. Mrs. Ladd and her son, D. Milton, were present at the ceremony.

A week later, in connection with the meeting of the Veterinary Medical Association of North Dakota, the recently remodeled veterinary science building was rededicated as Van Es Laboratory in honor of Dr. Leunis Van Es, who served the College for fifteen years as head of the veterinary science department. Dr. T. O. Brandenburg, state veterinarian, was master of ceremonies. Other speakers were President Hultz, Dr. J. W. Robinson of Garrison, representing the State Livestock Sanitary Board, Dean H. L. Walster, Dr. C. H. Hofstrand of Leeds, representing the State's practicing veterinarians, and William Plath of Davenport, representing the North Dakota livestock interests.

New Advances and New Strifes, 1945–1955 201

In the late summer of 1952 the newly completed livestock arena, which had already been used for the March hog show, was named the Shepperd Arena. President J. H. Shepperd's chief interest had been animal husbandry.

At Honors Day Convocation, May 20, 1954, the home management house was renamed Alba Bales House in honor of Miss Alba Bales, dean of the School of Home Economics from 1920 to 1942. The house, first occupied in September, 1923, was originally called the practice house. In 1936 the name was changed to Home Management House. Miss Bales had planned the house and made it her home for years.

At Commencement in June, 1954, the new engineering building was named Dolve Hall in honor of the retiring dean. This new building was to provide quarters for civil and mechanical engineering. Dean Dolve had been connected with the College since his graduation in 1905 and had served as dean of the School of Engineering since 1929.

The Commencement in 1957 included naming ceremonies for two student dormitories. The men's residence hall completed in 1931 was named Churchill Hall in honor of Omar O. Churchill, a member of the School of Agriculture from 1904 to 1910 and from 1915 to 1950, and a long time faculty member on the athletic board of the North Central Conference. The new women's residence hall completed in 1954 was rededicated and named Dinan Hall in honor of A. Pearl Dinan, dean of women, who had been on the faculty since 1911. At Homecoming in the fall of 1957 the new men's residence hall was named Stockbridge Hall in honor of the first president of the College.

In the fall of 1957 a portion of old Dakota Hall was remodeled and rededicated as Casey Finnegan Hall, to be used as a dormitory exclusively by students in the athletic department. The former barracks were divided into individual rooms, redecorated and furnished by funds amounting to $4,500, given by the Alumni Association.

With the announcement of the appropriations in 1959 the College administration included names for the new buildings. The pharmacy building was to be called Sudro Hall in honor of its first dean, who had retired in 1955. The new agricultural science building was to be named Walster Hall in honor of Dr. H. L. Walster, former dean of agriculture, whose special interest was agronomy. Two new dormitories were to be called Robert B. Reed Hall in honor of the first graduate of the North Dakota Agricultural College and Jessamine S. Burgum Hall in honor of the first woman student.

Campus beautification was an important objective of the administration of Dr. Hultz. When he arrived at the College, he found a hodge-podge of barns and other buildings and a dusty campus which became gumbo-muddy in wet weather. Although there had been a number of architectural plans in the first years of the College, the administration had not adhered to them. The new administration, supported by the State Board of Higher Education, employed a firm of landscape architects to draw up a plan. This called for a central mall facing Thirteenth Street with the men's residence hall on the north and the practice house on the south. This change required the removal of the athletic field to the far northern end of the campus. The mall was surrounded, as time passed, with the Student Memorial Union on the west, a women's residence hall on the south, and the new home economics building on the north, west of the men's residence hall. The former corner entrance was closed to vehicular traffic and the old roadway seeded to lawn. A new entrance way for official business south of Ceres Hall, leading past the administration building and post office was named Administration Avenue. Farther north, between the men's dormitory and the Field House was Campus Avenue. Another entrance on Twelfth Avenue, named College Street, passed Minard Hall, Morrill Hall, Ladd Hall and the dairy building. Still another road, named Service Drive, led from Twelfth Avenue to the new maintenance building, past the greenhouses, the cereal technology building, and the State Seed Department building. In time all of these roads were paved. Within the last few years the grounds have been planted with new trees, shrubs, and perennial and annual flowers under the supervision of the superintendent of buildings and grounds and the college gardener, Karl Oveson. Although the 1957 tornado damaged many of the trees, new ones have been planted; one thousand evergreens from the nursery of Clarence Jensen, class of 1923, were donated for this purpose. In the summer the plantings of flowers, trees and shrubs make the campus a thing of beauty.

Although the College appeared to be adequately staffed in 1948, in the next few years some changes occurred on account of resignations or retirements. Dean Minard, since 1919 head and later dean of the School of Arts and Sciences, resigned in April, 1949. He was succeeded by Dr. G. Ernst Giesecke, with degrees from Leland Stanford University, who had recently served as assistant dean of the Galesburg division of the University of Illinois. Dean Davy of the School of Home Economics, resigned in 1951, and was temporarily succeeded by Lucile Horton as acting dean. In August, 1951, Clara Cerveny, a graduate of Central State College, Edmond, Oklahoma, with a master's degree from the University of Alabama, was named dean of the School of Home Economics.

New Advances and New Strifes, 1945–1955

In June, 1951, Harry Dixon resigned as chairman of the department of electrical engineering. Robert N. Faiman, assistant professor, was promoted to associate professor and named chairman of the department. In 1952 Hale Aarnes, with a Ed.D. from the University of Missouri, was chosen chairman of the department of education and psychology to succeed P. J. Iverson, deceased. In the same year Leo Hertel, with a Ph.D. degree from the University of Munich, was appointed professor of philosophy and history; in 1953 he became chairman of the department of modern languages. In 1952, also, three of the veteran professors retired, A. G. Arvold, of the department of speech; W. C. Hunter, of the department of social science; and A. D. Whedon, of the department of zoology. Frederick G. Walsh, with a Ph.D. from Western Reserve University and a M.A. in drama from the University of North Carolina, was appointed chairman of the department of speech. His main interest is in the outdoor commemoration drama and he has been closely associated with the development of the community theater. Norman I. Wengert, with a Ph.D. from the University of Wisconsin, was named chairman of the department of social science. In 1953 J. F. Cassel, with a Ph.D. from the University of Colorado and a former member of the faculty, was appointed chairman of the department of zoology.

A. H. Parrott, who retired as registrar in 1952, was chosen alumni secretary. Merlin W. Miller, M.S. of the class of 1947 and for two and a half years assistant registrar, was appointed director of Admissions and Records.

In 1953 Dean H. L. Walster retired as dean of the School of Agriculture but continued on limited service with an office on the campus. Dr. Glenn C. Holm, a member of the department of veterinary science since 1949, succeeded as dean of the School of Agriculture and director of the Experiment Station. After four years of service at the College Dean Giesecke resigned to accept the vice presidency of Texas Technological College at Lubbock. Seth W. Russell, with a Ph.D. from the University of Pittsburgh and assistant dean of the School of Liberal Arts at Pennsylvania State College, was chosen as his successor. Dr. J. Alexander Munro, head of the department of agricultural entomology, resigned to continue research with the United States Department of Agriculture.

At first relations between the administration and the faculty were most cordial. Dr. Hultz took the Council and the students into his confidence and informed them of his plans. Later in the years of continuing prosperity for agriculture and the State some of the staff were inclined to feel that the president was stressing buildings and the physical plant at the expense of salaries, although salary increases had been fairly continuous. Some of the staff felt that the policy of the president's use of counsel with a cabinet consisting mainly of deans in place of the constitutional advisory committee, on which the faculty was represented, was unwise. The local chapter of the American Association of University Professors became their spokesman. Its attitude was criticized by the president for being more concerned with the economic status of the staff than with the proper improvement of instruction and standards.

The first sign of a rift in the administration-faculty relations came late in April, 1953. At this time there appeared in the local newspaper a news item mentioning that with the approval of the State Board of Higher Education there was to be a graduate division at the North Dakota Agricultural College with Dr. Hale Aarnes, professor of education and psychology, as the dean. This action of the president and the Board seemingly was taken without consultation with the advisory committee or with the existing graduate committee. Protests came from representatives of all the schools of the College to Dean Dunbar, chairman of the graduate committee, who passed them on to the president. Dr. Hultz replied that the approval of the advisory committee had not been obtained in previous appointments of the deans of Agriculture, Arts and Sciences, and Home Economics, and that therefore approval by the Council was assumed as being valid. On May 1, however, President Hultz issued a statement according to which the establishment of a graduate school had been postponed and that the proposal had been placed in the hands of the graduate committee for study.

A second point of difference between the president and faculty began to develop at the next meeting of the College Council in May, 1953, when President Hultz urged the Council to approve immediately his recommendation to establish a director of instruction at the College to serve as executive of the teaching staff, similar to the directors of the Experiment Station and the Extension Service. The College Council, however, voted to place the proposal for further study in the hands of a committee of eighteen, three from each school, including the deans. On November 11, 1953, this committee reported its opposition to the president's proposal. On January 6, 1954, President Hultz addressed the College Council at length. He felt that education under state or Federal jurisdiction was at an important crossroad. At a recent meeting of the land-grant institutions, some speakers expressed their awareness of a growing distrust of higher education among the populace, because of the attitude of some teachers toward communism, because of the poor bargaining position of the teaching profession, and because of continued monetary inflation. Even Federal grants for teaching might be withdrawn by July 1, 1955. There was necessary a need for singleness of purpose, effort, and unselfishness on the part of the teaching staff of institutions if higher education was to advance.

As to the situation in North Dakota, Dr. Hultz feared that the adoption of a proposal for a single board responsible for all educational activities, elementary, secondary and higher, would adversely affect the College. He made the suggestion that the College Council, if it is to be representative, should probably also include assistant professors. There was also need for a director of resident instruction to correlate the various academic curricula. A graduate division should be created, with a dean who might also serve as director of resident instruction.[6]

On March 5, 1954, Professor Glenn S. Smith, unanimously recommended by the graduate committee and by the president's advisory committee, was named dean of the Graduate School by the State Board of Higher Education. The appointment was to become effective on July 1, 1954.

Another indication of a difference of opinion between the administration and the faculty came into the open in March, 1954, when the State Board of Higher Education decided to terminate geology as a major curriculum of the College. President Hultz was informed about it and the two members of the department were notified of the termination of their positions. At a College Council meeting on April 14, Dr. Wengert moved that a committee of five be elected from the Council to "wait on the Board for such counsel and advice as the Board can give with respect to the policy significance of this action." The Council passed the motion and elected Professors Wengert, Jensen, Cassel, Treumann and Posin to the committee.

The Board, with one member of the commission absent, met the committee on April 27, gave close attention to their presentation and said that they would discuss the entire problem with Dr. Hultz before making a final decision. Subsequently, on May 20, the Board held a public hearing in regard to the geology situation at the Gardner Hotel in Fargo. Sixty staff members of the College attended as well as a delegation from the Fargo Chamber of Commerce and State Senator Arthur C. Johnson, all of whom were opposed to the elimination of geology as a field of study. The North Dakota Farm Bureau and the North Dakota Council for Agricultural Research and Education also wired their objections.

However, later the Board affirmed its earlier decision to eliminate the geology major at the College. A long time Board member, Roy Johnson, resigned in protest. Dr. Pye was allowed to continue on the faculty to teach service courses in geology and associated fields. Although President Hultz was not in sympathy with the elimination of geology as a major by the Board, the decision made was a factor in increasing the dissatisfaction among faculty members, especially those who were members of the American Association of University Professors. And some members of that group purported to believe that the action in regard to the elimination of geology was initiated by President Hultz.

At the meeting of the College Council on October 13, 1954, lengthy discussions between these faculty members and the president as to faculty tenure and academic freedom at the College took place and led to a subsequent meeting of the local chapter of the American Association of University Professors on October 26 at which the issues were discussed again. Dr. Cecil B. Haver, assistant professor of agricultural economics, introduced a resolution accusing the president of intimidation and requesting his resignation. The chapter failed to pass his motion but did not interfere with publicity given to this meeting in the local newspaper. Later the group did approve a resolution that called for an "investigation of the general condition of academic freedom and tenure on the N.D.A.C. campus, with particular emphasis on the use of intimidation as an instrument of administration policy." [7]

Dr. Hultz welcomed an inquiry into his administration but suggested that the investigation be made by the national office of the American Association of University Professors. The national office refused a request to act unless it came from the local chapter. At another meeting the chapter recommended that the investigation be made by its own local committee on academic tenure.

On November 23, 1954, the State Board of Higher Education directed Commissioner Arnason to engage an attorney "to visit N.D.A.C. and to bring a full report to the Board." William R. Pearce of the Bismarck law firm of Cox, Pearce and Engebretson was employed. On December 1 he began his appraisal of the situation at the College with Robert McClure from the faculty of the School of Law at the University of Minnesota, as a national representative of the A.A.U.P., and Commissioner A. F. Arnason as observers. At his arrival Mr. Pearce said that he was available to all who wanted to be heard and assured them that their statements would be held secret.

Mr. Pearce interviewed over 90 individuals, among them over 60 members of the College staff, five members of the Alumni Board, five students and twenty-five businessmen from Fargo and North Dakota.

Many letters, petitions and telegrams were received by him. A transcript of nearly 400 pages was prepared by Mr. Pearce for the State Board of Higher Education, which met in secret session on January 8, 1955. Robert McClure, A.A.U.P. representative, was also present at this meeting. After considering all the evidence, the Board released Mr. Pearce's and the Board's own statements for publicity.

Mr. Pearce's report is quoted here in an abbreviated form in its main points:

"It seems quite clear that the greater number of the faculty are in accord with the administration of Dr. Hultz, but there are a number who believe that the president is dictatorial and does not consult or advise with the faculty on decisions affecting the college ...

"I might say here that I found nothing in the entire investigation that would lead me to a suspicion that any member of the faculty of the college is a Communist, nor any person who advocates communism.

"I did not find any evidence that the administration of the college interferes with academic freedom in the sense that academic freedom is the right to present a subject matter in the manner which the teacher believes is right.

"There was no complaint that anyone in the administration was directing a teacher as to what could or could not be taught, nor the manner in which the subject was presented ...

"As to whether 'intimidation as an instrument of administration policy' is being used, that is entirely a matter of judgment which must be based upon the record as a whole.

"While I do not undertake to exercise a judgment on the record which has been made, I do have the suggestion that one step which I believe would reduce future difficulty would be to clearly delineate spheres of authority of the college, probably through the constitution, so that there would be a clear spelling out of the functions of the various faculty members and faculty groups in their relationship with the general administration of the college." [8]

At the same time the State Board of Higher Education issued a statement of its position, which is likewise given in excerpts:

"The president is the administrative head of the institution. It is his responsibility to see that the institution functions, that all the deparments are correlated and given the proper place and that the faculty and the physical plant made to fit in the proper place to the benefit of the institution as a whole.

"... that we believe the administration has been honest and firm, and on the whole, very efficient and conducive to the development of a great institution.

"However, there has been a tendency to act precipitously, and without seeking advice and assistance from those qualified to be of help.

"We believe that good faculty relationships can best be secured through full discussion of problems with the college council, as well as other committees, and the careful consideration of the views and advice of the faculty, and through adherance to the rules in effect at the institution ...

"The faculty should never forget that the rules of tenure, of academic freedom and similar matters, are not established for their benefit alone. They are for the protection and promotion of the welfare of the students ...

"Administration and faculty alike must remember that this institution is created and exists for the students. They must not allow personal feelings, jealousies, or personality conflicts to interfere with this primary function."[9]

At the same meeting on January 8, 1955, the Board, by a vote of six to one, requested the resignation of Dr. Cecil B. Haver, assistant professor of agricultural economics; of Dr. Baldur J. Kristjanson, associate professor of agricultural economics; of Dr. Daniel Q. Posin, professor and chairman of the department of physics; and of Dr. William B. Treumann, professor of chemistry.

The four professors rejected the Board's request that they resign, and continued to meet their classes. At a special meeting on January 19, 1955, the Board discharged them with pay subject to a public hearing before the College advisory committee, which consisted of the president of the College, the six academic deans, the dean of men, the dean of women, two council members elected by the faculty, the director of the Experiment Station, and the director of the Extension Service, with a substitute for the president to be chosen from the staff.

An early hearing was set in March and attorneys were engaged by the State Board of Higher Education and by the four professors. At this time four members of the Board, Whitney, Wang, Calnan and Donnelly, were holding interim appointments, owing to deaths and resignations, and had not been approved by the State Senate. Four new members, Haas, Kruse, Mrs. Jestrab and Byrne, were nominated by the governor and approved by the Senate. The new Board, consisting of Dr. A. D. McCannell, Mrs. Vernon Johnson, D. W. Westbee in addition to the new appointees, set the hearing for April 12. The advisory committee elected Frank C. Mirgain, the new dean of the School of Engineering, to act as chairman and Dr. Walsh to serve in place of President Hultz. The hearing was postponed when Mr. Pearce, engaged as attorney for the Board, withdrew, since he had conducted the previous investigation and therefore had knowledge of the transcripts. Another attorney, E. T. Conmy, Jr., was chosen to represent Dr. Hultz. The hearing was resumed on May 17.

Dr. Hultz, president of the College, formally charged the professors individually and together with trying to undermine his way of running the College. He also requested that the professors should be fired in order to keep the College's affairs running smoothly, affairs which appeared to be handicapped on account of their lack of cooperation. The professors denied any allegations of "undermining" the authority of the president and said that any "bickering or dissension" at the College has been caused by President Hultz in his relations with the faculty. They also asserted that the privilege of academic freedom in teaching and thinking had been violated in some cases.

The hearing continued from May 16 to June 1, 1955. The prosecution attorney, E. T. Conmy, Jr., presented Dr. Hultz and a considerable number of the staff who appeared in the defense of the president's position. Dr. Hultz presented examples of discourtesy encountered at a College Council meeting during a discussion regarding the elimination of geology as a major curriculum, and accused Posin, Kristjanson, and Treumann of sneering attitudes and heckling. Several faculty members verified this and supported the president in his statement that academic freedom and tenure were not violated.

The attorneys for the defense, J. F. X. Conmy of Bismarck for Dr. Posin and Philip R. Bangs of Grand Forks for the other three professors, maintained that there was insufficient proof of the charges against their clients and asked for dismissal of the accusations by the committee, but the request was denied. Later Dr. Posin took the stand in defense of his position and was followed by Dr. Kristjanson, who denied insubordination. They were followed by several faculty members defending the accused professors. In summary there seems to have been no definite evidence of violation of academic tenure by the president or actual insubordination on the part of the professors. At the end of the hearing the advisory committee cast secret ballots in regard to the guilt of each of the four professors and sent them, sealed, to the State Board of Higher Education. At the meeting of the State Board on June 6 they were opened and showed the following tally:

for Dr. Posin	11 yes	2 no
for Dr. Kristjanson	9 yes	4 no
for Dr. Treumann	10 yes	3 no
for Dr. Haver	12 yes	1 no

The State Board of Higher Education, by a five to two vote, sustained the recommendation of the advisory committee and voted dismissal of the four professors. After the decision of the State Board the professors asked the Supreme Court to take jurisdiction and to order a review of the case. The Court refused the request, saying that the professors "were not public officers but only employees of the Board of Education." [10] On December 28, 1955, the four professors filed an appeal for review with District Judge John Sad, in Valley City, and a hearing was scheduled in the Cass County District Court for January 31, 1956. Judge Sad denied the review, on the ground that the court would have no authority to pass upon the decisions of the Board.

In the meantime, the four professors had also requested an investigation by the national American Association of University Professors, which was made September 22-26, 1955, by a committee of three, Professor Frederick K. Beutel of the University of Nebraska, Professor Thomas C. Geary of the University of South Dakota and Professor Horace M. Gray of the University of Illinois. Their report was a lengthy document going into the history of gradual development of friction between the administration and a group of faculty members, and containing a criticism of the makeup of the advisory committee, "overweighted with administrative officers and without genuine faculty representatives. Academic freedom and tenure had been violated in the removal of the professors by the State Board." [11] The chief blame for the internal strife at the College was placed by the A.A.U.P. on President Hultz. In reply Dr. Hultz sharply criticized the report as "biased, distorted, and partisan." With funds donated by friends of the College his response to the report by the A.A.U.P. committee was printed and widely circulated. Later, on April 7, 1956, at the national meeting of the American Association of University Professors, the administration of the North Dakota Agricultural College at Fargo, North Dakota, was censured. The censured list, published in the summer 1956 issue of the *Bulletin of the American Association of University Professors*, was published for the "sole purpose of informing members, the profession at large, and the public that unsatisfactory conditions of academic freedom and tenure have been found to prevail at these institutions." [12]

At a meeting of the State Board of Higher Education on August 3, 1956, President Hultz reviewed the campus situation. He reported that "people were trying to annoy and discredit the administration, often through anonymous statements, that no staff members had been lost solely because of the controversy, that his relations with the staff were courteous and easy, and that it would require two or three years for conditions to settle down." [13]

Meanwhile, the four discharged professors went off to other posts. Dr. Posin became professor of physics at DePaul University in Chicago and a television lecturer in science. Dr. Kristjanson took a post with the Canadian government in Ottawa. Dr. Haver took a research assignment at the University of Chicago. Dr. Treumann became a Fargo businessman and eventually returned to teaching at Moorhead State College. Back at the College, a small group of members of the staff began work on the long process of attaining the removal of the College from the censure list of the A.A.U.P.

FOOTNOTES

[1] Fred S. Hultz, papers, September 16–18, 1948, Library, N.D.A.C.
[2] Hultz, papers, May 1951, Library, N.D.A.C.
[3] Hultz, papers, Jan. 1949, Library, N.D.A.C.
[4] *Fargo Forum*, Oct. 7, 1950.
[5] Hultz, papers, May 1951, Library, N.D.A.C.
[6] Minutes of the Council, Jan. 6, 1954.
[7] Chapter of the A.A.U.P. minutes, Nov. 21, 1954.
[8] *Fargo Forum*, June 9, 1955.
[9] *Fargo Forum*, June 9, 1955.
[10] *Fargo Forum*, Feb. 1, 1956.
[11] American Association of University Professors, *Bulletin*, XLII, No. 2 (Spring, 1956). 130–60.
[12] A.A.U.P. *Bulletin*, XLII, No. 2 (Summer, 1956), 409.
[13] Minutes of the State Board of Higher Education, Aug. 3, 1956.

◂ CHAPTER XIII ▸

Growth in the Fifties, 1955-1960

WHEN Dr. Hultz took over the presidency of the College in 1948, student registration had reached an all time high of 2,733, partially due to the arrival of G. I. veterans from World War II. In the next four years, there was a gradual decline, with a low of 2,026 in 1951–52. From then on a gradual rise led to considerable increases until in 1960 a high of 3,408 was reached for the regular college and 4,161 with the inclusion of the summer session and evening extension courses. The increases occurred in all schools, but especially in engineering, which registered 1,211 in 1958–59. The campus disturbance over the dismissal of the four professors seemed to have had little effect on student attendance, which increased rapidly, with a greater demand for trained graduates, especially in engineering. Registration in the fall quarter of 1960 totaled 3,419, among them 2,646 men and 778 women. By classes the enrollment was 1,055 freshmen, 782 sophomores, 604 juniors, 615 seniors, 310 graduates, 53 special students.

During the later fifties staff changes occurred due to increased enrollment and to replacements for members who had reached the age of retirement or who resigned to take other, sometimes more satisfactory positions with other institutions.

In the School of Agriculture Arlon G. Hazen, with an M.S. from Iowa State College, was appointed dean to succeed Glenn C. Holm, who resigned in 1957. At the same time John A. Callenbach with a Ph. D. from the University of Wisconsin was named associate dean and Peder A. Nystuen, with an M.S. from North Dakota Agricultural College, was named assistant dean. Enoch B. Norum, with a Ph. D. degree from Iowa State College, was appointed chairman of the department of soils in 1960. In 1955 Fred R. Taylor, with a Ph. D. from the University of Minnesota, was named chairman of the department of agricultural economics to succeed Perry V. Hemphill, who had been serving as acting chairman since the resignation of Dr. Rainer Schickele in 1954. James R. Dogger, with a Ph. D. from the University of Wisconsin, was named chairman of the department of agricultural entomology in 1958. A. Paul Adams, with a Ph. D. from Iowa State College, was named chairman of the department of bacteriology in 1954. E. P. Lana, with a Ph. D. from the University of Minnesota, was appointed chairman of the department of horticulture in 1956. In 1960 Jack F. Carter, with a Ph. D. from the University of Wisconsin, succeeded T. E. Stoa, who retired, as chief of the division of plant industry and chairman of the department of agronomy. In the same year R. L. Kiesling, with a Ph. D. from the University of Wisconsin, was named chairman of the department of plant pathology to succeed W. E. Brentzel, who had retired.

In the School of Arts and Sciences in 1951 Ernst van Vlissingen was appointed chairman of the department of music. In 1954 Rudolf Ottersen, who joined the faculty in 1923, and Dr. E. W. Pettee, who came in 1928, were named rotating chairmen of the department of the social sciences in 1955 to succeed Norman Wengert, who resigned. John Hove, with a Ph. D. from the University of Minnesota, was appointed chairman of the department of English and philosophy to succeed Kenneth Kuhn, who retired in 1959.

In the School of Chemistry F. L. Minnear, with a Ph. D. from Ohio State University, and chairman of the department of organic chemistry was named acting dean of the School of Chemical Technology in 1960, to succeed R. E. Dunbar, deceased. Harold J. Klosterman, with a Ph. D. from the University of Minnesota, was appointed chairman of the department of agricultural biochemistry in July, 1957. Alfred E. Rheineck, with a Ph. D. from the University of Wisconsin, was appointed chairman of the department of protective coatings in 1958 to succeed Wouter Bosch, who resigned. In 1948 C. W. Fleetwood became professor of analytical chemistry, and in 1959 F. H. Rathmann became professor of organic chemistry.

In the School of Engineering Frank C. Mirgain, with an M. A. from Rutgers University, in 1954 was named dean to succeed R. M. Dolve, who retired. E. M. Anderson, with an M. S. from the University of Denver, was appointed chairman of the department of electrical engineering in 1958. Marion B. Richardson, with an M. E. from Pennsylvania State College, was named chairman of the department of industrial engineering in 1957. E. H. Weinberg, with a Ph. D. from the University of Iowa, was appointed chairman of the department of physics in 1958.

In the School of Home Economics Caroline Budewig, with an M. S. from the University of Minnesota, and an Ed. D. degree from George Peabody College for Teachers, in 1954 was named dean to succeed Miss Cerveny, deceased. Kathryn M. Weesner, with an M. A. from the University of Minnesota, was appointed chairman of the department of related art in 1953. Emily Reynolds, with an M. S. from the University of Tennessee, was named acting chairman of textiles and clothing in 1957 to succeed Minnie Anderson, who retired. Mavis C. Nymon, with an M. S. from Cornell University, was named chairman of the department of food and nutrition in 1960 to succeed Elvira Smith, who retired. In the same year Josephine Bartow, with an Ed. D. from Pennsylvania State University, was appointed chairman of the department of home economics education to succeed Lucile Horton, who retired.

In the School of Pharmacy Clifton E. Miller, with a Ph. D. from the University of Washington, was named dean in 1955 to succeed W. F. Sudro, who retired. Martin J. Blake, with a Ph. D. from Ohio State University, was appointed chairman of the department of pharmaceutical chemistry in 1957. Leo J. Schermeister, with a Ph. D. from the University of Illinois, was appointed chairman of the department of pharmacognosy in 1958. Max A. Heinrich, with a Ph. D. from Jefferson Medical College, was appointed chairman of the department of pharmacology in 1957. Muriel C. Vincent, with a Ph. D. from the University of Washington, was appointed chairman of the department of pharmacy in 1958.

With an enlarged staff social relations became more limited to different schools and departments. A Who's New Club was organized as a rallying group for staff members newly arrived at the College. An annual round-up was held in the Field House at which Mrs. Hultz introduced the new staff members, and President Hultz described the work and the plans of the College.

The efforts to secure a satisfactory constitution, already started in the forties, continued in the fifties. In September, 1949, President Hultz reported to the Council that the State Board of Higher Education recommended some minor changes in the 1948 draft of the constitution which the Council had approved on May 12, 1948 and which by a secret ballot had been accepted by the entire staff of the College on February 25, 1949. A new ballot of the general staff in November, 1949, adopted this constitution by a large majority.

Further discussion arose in 1953 over Article IV of the constitution, which provided for the election of faculty members to the advisory committee by the Council instead of by the general staff. On April 13, 1955, a committee composed of Dr. C. Jensen, Prof. William Promersberger, Dr. Frank Cassel, Dr. Parker Green, Christine Finlayson and E. J. Haslerud was elected by the Council to prepare an amendment in regard to the election of members to the advisory committee. At the next Council meeting, in May, the committee proposed that two members of the Council be elected by the teaching faculty and a third member be chosen by the staff of the Experiment Station and Extension Service.

On Dec. 11, 1955, Dr. Hultz appointed a new committee with Assistant Dean Hazen as the chairman, to review the whole constitution of the College. The other members were Miss Finlayson, Director Haslerud, Dr. Hertel, Prof. McCauley, Dr. Minnear, Prof. Promersberger, and Professor Street. At the Council meeting on March 14, 1956, the approval by the staff of the proposed amendment to the previous constitution of the Jensen committee was announced. On March 13, 1957, the Council received copies of a revised constitution from the Hazen committee which the Council adopted at its May meeting. At the meeting of the Council on October, 1957, President Hultz announced that he had submitted this constitution to the State Board of Higher Education for approval.[1] However no action had been taken by the Board in regard to it by Dec. 31, 1960.

The Graduate School became a reality for the College in 1954. With the approval of the State Board of Higher Education, on request of President Hultz, the School was formalized on July 1, 1954, and at the same time Dr. Glenn S. Smith was named dean. In previous years graduate work in general was administered by a graduate committee of which Dean Minard served as chairman. He was succeeded by Dean Dunbar who served as chairman of a later graduate council. The first Master of Science degree was awarded by the College in 1899, the second in 1903 and the third in 1918. Since 1921 a number of master's degrees had been awarded every year except in 1945; the largest number being 69 in 1958. Up to the end of 1960 a total of 668 master's degrees have been awarded by the College.

Upon recommendation of the graduate faculty, and at the request of President Hultz, the State Board of Higher Education on January 16, 1959, authorized the offering of the degree, Doctor of Philosophy, in plant science, animal science, pharmacy and entomology. On February 27, 1959, the Ph. D. degree in chemistry was also authorized.

On January 30, 1959, the institution was awarded four Ph. D. fellowships in plant science under the National Defense Education Act of 1958. Since then three more fellowships have been awarded under the same act. Three additional fellowships have been established by the National Science Foundation, and deans of the schools appointed candidates for the doctorate to assistantships in teaching or research. In

1960 three candidates for the Ph. D. were working in the botany department, three in agronomy (crops), three in entomology, two in coatings technology, and one each in soils, animal husbandry and pharmaceutical chemistry; a total of fourteen candidates working for a doctor's degree.

The new graduate faculty is composed of deans, heads of departments in which graduate programs are offered, and faculty members who are actively assisting in the graduate programs, or serving as major advisors to the graduate students. They meet on call, usually once a quarter. The graduate council is composed of the six academic deans, and the dean of the Graduate School, who serves as chairman. In 1960 the faculty was conducting a self study of the whole institution, in order to facilitate institutional accreditation in granting Ph.D. degrees.

On account of a steady increase in enrollment housing became a continuing problem. In 1951 a new women's dormitory was completed. A new men's residence hall, with rooms for 250 men, was finished in 1957. A double row of permanent homes for married students and faculty was constructed northwest of the Field House in 1956. After the tornado of 1957 wrecked "Silver City" (prefabricated homes for faculty on Thirteenth Street), that space was converted into a parking lot and more permanent units added to the previous group. Nevertheless, North Court, a group of temporary frame houses, remained still in use by the end of 1960. From private funds five new sorority houses were built at Thirteenth Avenue at the corners of Twelfth and Thirteenth Streets. A new Sigma Alpha Epsilon house was located on Twelfth Avenue west of Kruse Park.[2] A Farmers Union Cooperative House was built at the corner of Twelfth Avenue and Twelfth Street.

During this period finally a Student Union was built. According to alumni records, the first contribution to such a building was made in 1943 in memory of Paul R. Rowe. Other contributions brought the sum to $1,000. At the same time students voted to assess themselves a fee of $5.00 per term, an assessment still in effect. By January, 1948, the fund stood at about $38,000. A governing board was chosen consisting of four faculty members, four students, and four alumni, with the president of the College serving ex officio. Professor Glenn Hill was named president of this board. The building was also financed by the sale of bonds to be retired over twenty years. A 1,000 club was formed, with each member pledging $1,000.[3]

The Memorial Student Union was officially opened Thursday, October 29, 1953, as a part of the Homecoming activities. It was hailed as a complete answer to all the social needs and desires of the College community. The ground floor, a semi-basement, housed the Bison

Room, a lunch room and snack bar: in addition the book store, which continued to be operated for a while by EmilyDakin; a barber shop; a men's clothing store and an eight-lane bowling alley. On the first floor is the common lounge, 45 x 75 feet, including a large fire place, lounge chairs, davenports and rugs. Also, the directors' offices, a game room, a small lounge, conference rooms, are on the main floor. On the second floor are the ballroom, a dining room with kitchen facilities, a campus radio station, rooms for the board of publications and offices for the alumni secretary and for the student employment bureau. The ballroom is 45 x 80 feet, with a stage and projection booth, and has a seating capacity of 500. Increased enrollment required additional space. Early in 1959 an annex to the south of the Union building provided for an addition to the bowling alley. The space vacated on the ground floor was added to the Bison Room to supply the need for more dining accommodations.

In 1950, a College Placement Service was set up with Oscar Gjernes, representative of the North Dakota State Employment Service, in charge. Mr. Gjernes advised local, State and national offices as to the availability of graduates and former students for employment. His office was at first located in the basement of the Administration Building, was moved to the new Library in 1950, and is now on the second floor of the Memorial Union. Gale Smith, a graduate of the College, succeeded Mr. Gjernes in 1957.

The student personnel office, located in the northeast corner of the first floor of Old Main, became manned by a staff of experts in counseling. Carl H. Schmidt, who succeeded Dr. Beyers as counselor, had studied at the Universities of Iowa and Nebraska, where he majored in education and psychology; his specialties are testing and counseling. In 1958 Quentin C. Stodola, with a Ph. D. from the University of Wyoming, was appointed director of counseling and testing; L. P. Nelson, with a Ph. D. from the University of Wyoming, became assistant director in the same year. The personnel office is primarily a counseling agency, but it also aids in placement of seniors. In its files are records of all students who have attended the College since 1939. Students failing scholastically are channeled to this office to be offered aid in order to overcome any psychological difficulties that may exist.

The constitution of the student body was under consideration by the student commission in 1951–1952. A revised constitution was presented in April, 1952, which provided for a legislative policy-making body, called the Student Senate. Administrative officers were to be appointed by the chief executive with the approval of the Senate. In the election on April 7, the constitution was adopted by a vote of 260 to 194, and later approved by the College Council and the State Board of Higher Education. In May, 1953, the Student Senate organized a student-faculty committee which as a liaison group would make recommendations to improve student-faculty relations. In the last few years the new constitution seems to be functioning satisfactorily. During the controversy between President Hultz and the "four professors" the students as a whole maintained an impartial attitude.

Beginning in 1957, President and Mrs. Hultz entertained the presidents of the student organizations whose membership were collegewide in scope. Meetings of this group, named Council of Student Presidents, are held quarterly and are considered a forward step in student-administration relationship.

In 1950 the athletic program was in charge of C. C. Finnegan, director; Ervin E. Kaiser, chairman of the department of physical education for men; Mac P. Wenskunas, football coach; Ben Charles Bentson, basketball coach. During this period football had its difficulties, owing to a dearth of first-class material. But in spite of it in 1952 the football team won second place in the North Central Conference. In 1953–1955 the team failed to have a good season. L. Leslie Luymes was chosen director in 1956 and that year served also as football coach. In 1957 Robert E. Danielson was appointed football coach, but the team still was unable to better its record. The basketball team, coached by "Chuck" Bentson, made a better record, gaining first place in the North Central Conference in 1952 and 1954. Physical education for women in 1950 was in charge of Beatrice M. Wartchow, who was succeeded in 1957 by Beulah F. Gregoire, assisted by Elsie Raer.

In the fifties two Rhodes Scholarships were awarded to students of the North Dakota Agricultural College, the first to Mancur Olson in 1954, the second to Gordon Kepner in 1958. Since 1953, seventeen N.D.A.C. graduates have received Fulbright Grants for graduate study in foreign countries. An outstanding testimonial to the reputation of the School of Agriculture in more recent days was the winning of the Intercollegiate Livestock Judging Contest at the International Livestock Exposition in Chicago by the team from the College in 1960. For its success this group of students has access to and experience with the highest quality herds and flocks of purebred livestock to be found in the United States.

The religious needs of the students received increasing attention during this period. The Fargo School of Religious Education continued to function under the supervision of a nondenominational board, in the main financially supported by the Fargo United Fund. In 1960 Corwin C. Roach, with a Ph. D. from Yale University, was chosen director.

The College YMCA suffered the loss of its building by the tornado in June, 1957. Its work is carried on in the Library by Rev. Leo Johnson as executive secretary, with the understanding that its activities, as well as those of the YWCA, in the future will be housed in a new chapel building on the campus.

The Lutheran Student Association, under the direction of its campus pastor, the Rev. Arne Kvaalen, obtained a new home at the corner of Thirteenth Avenue and Twelfth Street. The House was financed by the National Lutheran Council and dedicated in 1958. St. Paul's Chapel, the Newman Club center, located at the corner of Thirteenth Street and Twelfth Avenue, was dedicated on January 9, 1959. The center, under the direction of Father W. J. Durkin, is designed to serve the 600 Catholic students at the College and was built at a cost of $250,000, raised in all parishes of the diocese of Fargo. On October 30, 1959, announcement was made that the Methodists were planning to build a $60,000 structure to meet the needs of the 250 Methodist students on the College campus. Rev. Robert Ouradnick announced that the funds would come from the Wesley Foundation and would be supported by North Dakota Methodist churches.

In the same year, the students of four churches — the United Presbyterian Church in the U.S.A., the United Church of Christ (Congregational Christian and Evangelical and Reformed), the Evangelical United Brethren, and the Disciples of Christ — organized in order to carry on their religious work. In the summer of 1960 they purchased a house located at 1130 College Street for use as a religious center for faculty, staff and students. Rev. Robert Siberry is the director of the United Campus Christian Fellowship.

In the spring of 1959 an all-college festival, "Sharivar," was held for the first time on the campus on May 8 and 9. The purpose was to show parents, alumni, taxpayers, legislators, prospective students and Fargo-Moorhead residents various facets of the College. In March of every year College students visit high schools in North Dakota to advertise the festival. Every year a special May 1 issue of the *Spectrum* carries a schedule of events, pictures, write-ups of all phases of college life, classes, labs, athletics, and extra-curricular activities. The affair has been voted by all participants as a huge success.

In the last decade a number of changes and improvements have taken place in some of the administrative offices of the College. At the turn of the century Professor McArdle served at the same time as instructor in mathematics and as registrar. In 1904 a separate and independent office was set up and A. H. Parrott was assigned to the new office as registrar. Mr. Parrott as registrar was instrumental in organizing a national conference of college and university registrars to examine the duties of a registrar and to unify the transcript procedure for students transferring from one institution to another. Out of this meeting there developed later the American Association of Collegiate Registrars and Admission Officers. After a long and successful term as registrar, Mr. Parrott retired as director of admissions and records in 1952 and was elected executive secretary of the N.D.A.C. Alumni and Former Students Association. He retired from this position in 1956.

C. E. Nugent was secretary and business manager of the College during its earlier years. In 1909 he was succeeded by W. A. Yoder, who in 1916 gave way to Addison Leach. He, in turn, was succeeded by H. W. McArdle in 1918, who continued in the office until his death in 1933. The appointment and resignation of Steve Hagan, his successor, in the thirties has been described in a previous chapter. After 1939 F. F. Skinner, business manager, was in charge of the office, except for the period of World War II when R. C. Reinhart was acting secretary. The present business manager is Miss Edythe Toring.

The first mention of a maintenance department at the College appeared in the catalog of 1909–1910. At that time Richard Kraft was named custodian of buildings; later he was called superintendent of buildings and grounds. He had come to the College as janitor in 1897. The following tribute to "Dick" Kraft is found in the pages of the Faculty Record: "Dick"— Richard Kraft, a son of an immigrant, came from Illinois. He had heard about the West. He wanted to see it — he journeyed to Fargo,— hired out as a laborer on the College farm during the summer months and in the late fall and winter, became a sheepherder on a ranch in Emmons County. He did his work so well that when he returned in the spring he was given charge of one building — then another, and another until finally the buildings and grounds were placed under his supervision. His interest in what he did, his generous heart, his willingness to lend a helping hand, his manhood, and his smiling countenance will be long remembered by thousands who called him "Dick." [4]

At the death of "Dick" Kraft in 1944, Erling "Bob" Thorson was named superintendent of buildings and grounds, and was still serving in 1960. In 1950 the construction of a new maintenance building was a great improvement for his important department. The work of Karl Oveson, the College gardener, as shown by the beautiful blooming annuals and perennials on the campus, deserves credit and appreciation.

The practice of recognizing local and national leaders at Commencement time, started by President Eversull, was continued under President Hultz. In June, 1949, Dr. Frederick L. Hovde, president of Purdue University, was the Commencement speaker and received the honorary degree of Doctor of Laws. He had received his elementary and high school education at Devils Lake. A well-known Fargoan, John Eliot (Jack) Pyle, at the same time was given the honorary degree of Doctor of Laws. Mr. Pyle, manager of the West Fargo branch of Armour and Co., had been with the company thirty-five years and had served as president of the Red River Valley Fair Association for a long time. He was largely responsible for promoting, among the members of the Fargo Chamber of Commerce, the gift of the livestock farm west of the campus to the College.

At the 1950 Commencement Dr. John Lee Coulter, former president of the College, was given an honorary degree of Doctor of Science. Since 1929 he had served as economic advisor to the Federal Tariff Commission and later advised several international trade corporations. He died in 1959. Alex Lind, one of the pioneer homesteaders of North Dakota, was awarded an honorary degree of Doctor of Laws for outstanding accomplishment in agriculture. He had given staunch support to farm cooperative organizations and to agricultural education. As State senator from Williams County he was active in urging legislative assistance to farmers in the drouth areas in the 1930's.

At the president's luncheon following Commencement of the same year Fred O. Olsen and Thomas R. Heath were presented fifty-year alumni awards. Mr. Olsen after graduation had joined his father in developing a grain, feed and coal business in Sanborn, N. Dak. In 1939 he and his brother came to Fargo and established the Olsen Fuel Company. He was mayor of Fargo for thirteen years, a member of the Fargo Board of Education and president of the Alumni Association. Mr. Heath, with earlier experience in the sale of real estate and with graduate work in engineering at the University of California, later joined the Ehrsam Manufacturing Company at Enterprise, Kansas. As its vice-president and director for thirty years he built up a three million dollar business. He married Marie Senn, who had been head of the domestic science department of the College for eight years. He also had served as mayor and a member of Board of Education in Enterprise, Kansas.

The Commencement speaker in 1951, Dr. Clyde M. Bailey, dean of the Department of Agriculture at the University of Minnesota, and a world figure in cereal chemistry, was awarded the honorary degree of Doctor of Science. He had received a B.S. from the North Dakota Agricultural College in 1913 and a Ph. D. from the University of Maryland in 1921. From 1907 until 1911 he served as scientific assistant with the United States Department of Agriculture, and at this time was stationed at the College Experiment Station. In 1911 he joined the staff of the Division of Agricultural Chemistry of the University of Minnesota, engaging in teaching and research. In 1947 he was listed among the "Ten Ablest Agricultural and Food Chemists" in the United States.

In 1952 at the June Commencement D. Milton Ladd gave the address and was awarded the honorary degree of Doctor of Laws. At this occasion he participated also, with his mother, in the naming of the chemistry building "Ladd Hall" in honor of his father, who had served many years as professor of chemistry and as president of the College. Milton Ladd is distinguished in his own right as chief assistant in the Bureau of the Federal Board of Investigation, after receiving a law degree from George Washington University. In 1952 Bernard (Ben) F. Meinecke and Harold Bachman received alumni achievement awards. Mr. Meinecke, '99, a Fargo construction engineer, had been active in College, community and professional affairs, and was a chief contributor to the Memorial Student Union. Mr. Bachman, '16, achieved national recognition as a musician, composer, band leader and educator; at one time he organized and conducted a touring concert band widely known as "Bachman's Million Dollar Band."

Dr. Harlow L. Walster, who was retiring as Dean of Agriculture and Director of the North Dakota Agricultural Experiment Station gave the Commencement address in June, 1953, and was granted the honorary degree of Doctor of Science. Outstanding achievement awards were given to Jessamine Slaughter Burgum, Percy J. Donnelly and Dr. Carl H. Hofstrand. Mrs. Burgum, the first girl to enroll at the College, an active member of the Daughters of the Revolution, an "outstanding mother" chosen by the Homemakers Clubs of North Dakota, is the author of regional books such as *Zezula*, *Dakota Ballads*, and *Stars Over the Prairies*. Mr. Donnelly, enrolled at the College from 1908 to 1910, a potato and sugar beet farmer near Grafton, was president of the North Dakota Farm Bureau and was active in the Rural Electrification Association and in community activities. Dr. Hofstrand, '11, an outstanding veterinarian and livestock breeder, a member of the North Dakota House of Representatives, and of the legislative research committee, had played an important part in State and local education.

In 1954 Dean R. M. Dolve of the School of Engineering was given the honorary degree of Doctor of Science. Achievement awards went to Arnold M. Christensen of the Class of 1916, Paul Horn, Robert R. Reed, '95, and Dr. L. R. Waldron, '99. Mr. Christensen was employed at the Dickinson Branch Experiment Station and at the Experiment Station in Fargo while doing his undergraduate work. After graduation

Growth in the Fifties, 1955–1960

he served as Pierce County extension agent and as seed extension specialist for the University of Minnesota. Later he carried on a successful wholesale seed business in Minot. Mr. Horn had been successful in business in Moorhead and as a farmer. He had served as president of the Fargo-Moorhead Executives Club and of the Northwest Farm Managers Association. Mr. Reed, the first graduate of the College in 1895, was for years treasurer of the Amenia and Sharon Land Company, founded by his grandfather, E. W. Chaffee, and later was an operator of a portion of the holdings. Dr. Waldron, '99, with a master's degree from the University of Michigan and a Ph. D. from Cornell University, served as superintendent of the Dickinson Branch Station and since 1916 as plant scientist for the Experiment Station, specializing in plant breeding and in research for high quality rust-resistant wheats. Special fifty-year recognitions were given to C. Ross Fowler, to James McGuigan, to Mrs. Edith Fowler Slocum and to Mrs. Mary Hope Darrow Weible, all of the class of 1894.

In 1955 Newell P. Beckwith, of the Class of 1936, vice president and general manager of the Rinshed-Mason Paint Company of Canada, president of the Federation of Paint and Varnish Production Clubs, gave the address at the June Commencement. He and W. F. Sudro, the retiring dean of the School of Pharmacy, were awarded the honorary degree of Doctor of Science.

Dr. E. P. Rian, president of Jamestown College, addressed the graduating class of 1956. Mr. Roy Johnson of Casselton was given the honary degree of Doctor of Science. Mr. Johnson, a graduate of the University of Minnesota, was a member of the North Dakota State Legislature for three terms and served as speaker of the House in 1923. He was appointed a member of the State Board of Higher Education in 1938 and served until 1954, twice as its president. He was also a past president of the Northwest Farm Managers Association.

Two College graduates received the distinguished alumni awards at the same time. Edwin Traynor of Starkweather, Class of 1911, was an instructor in agricultural economics following his graduation. Later he joined his father as manager of the Ramsey County family farm. He was in the State Legislature from 1923 to 1939 and served as speaker of the House in 1929. Clarence Jensen of Esmond, '23, became a teacher in the Benson County Agricultural School until 1950, when he retired to devote full time to his tree nursery. He later was chosen president of the North Dakota Horticultural Society.

In 1957 John Haw was Commencement speaker and was given the honorary degree of Doctor of Science. After attending the University of Minnesota, Mr. Haw had been for a number of years a county extension agent in North Dakota, a county agent leader from 1918 to 1924. He was an agricultural development agent for the Northern Pacific Railway from 1924 to 1927 and director after that time. He became an honorary life member of the National Reclamation Association.

Those receiving alumni achievement awards were Jorgen M. Birkeland, '27, and Patrick Henry Costello, '17. Mr. Birkeland earned an M.S. degree in bacteriology and a Ph. D. from the University of Chicago. He joined the staff of Ohio State University and became chairman of its department of bacteriology. He spent a year at the Rothamsted Experiment Station in England and for a year was attaché for the United States Department of State in Stockholm, Sweden. He is the author of "*Microbiology in Man*" and other scientific publications. Mr. Costello operated his own pharmacy for 23 years in Cooperstown. During this time he was mayor of that city, president of the National Association of Boards of Pharmacy and trustee of U. S. Pharmacopoeia. He has served as president of the American Pharmaceutical Association and of the American Council on Pharmaceutical Education, serving the latter as secretary since 1948.

In 1958 the Commencement speaker, Dr. Melvin Brodshaug, dean of the Boston University School of Public Relations and Communications, was awarded the degree of Doctor of Letters. Dean Brodshaug, who is a native of North Dakota, received the bachelor of science degree from North Dakota Agricultural College in 1923 and a Ph. D. from Columbia University. Louis, Duke of Vallambrosa of Paris, son of the Marquis de Mores and donor of the de Mores Chateau at Medora to the North Dakota Historical Society, was granted the honorary degree of Doctor of Laws.

Lieutenant General Verne J. McCaul, '25, Assistant Commandant of the U. S. Marine Corps for Air and Director of Aviation, was given an alumni achievement award. He had served in World War II and in Korea; he holds the Legion of Merit and many other awards. Milo Hoisveen, who attended the College from 1926 to 1929, State engineer at Bismarck, was another recipient of an achievement award; he has served as engineer with the Northwestern Bell Telephone Company, the Rural Rehabilitation Corporation, the Farm Security Administration and the U. S. Bureau of Reclamation.

In 1959 two men received the honorary degree of Doctor of Science, Donald G. Fletcher, a graduate of the University of Minnesota and executive secretary of the Rust Prevention Association of Minneapolis, and James C. Konen, a graduate of the College and vice president of the Archer-Daniels-Midland Company of Minneapolis. He had received his bachelor's and master's degrees in paint chemistry from the College, after which he specialized in protective coating research. Mr. Konen also gave the Commencement address in 1959.

Alumni achievement awards in this year went to Palmer L. Foss, Rear Admiral Harry G. Hanson, Harold Schafer and Dr. David E. Sonquist. Mr. Foss, a 1911 graduate of the School of Pharmacy, served in the North Dakota Legislature from 1941 to 1959, acting as president pro tem of the senate in 1959. He owns a drug store in Valley City, where he has been active in civic affairs. Admiral Hanson, '36, received a master's degree from Harvard University in 1940. He is an assistant United States Surgeon General and is president of the Conference of Federal Sanitation Engineers. Mr. Schafer, who attended the College for one year, founded the Gold Seal Company in Bismarck in 1942. In 1953 he was the youngest person to receive the Horatio Alger Award given by the Association of American Schools and Colleges for achieving success by overcoming obstacles through hard work and diligence. Dr. Sonquist, '41, a native of Fargo, worked with the YMCA and taught at several colleges; in the early 1950's he founded Senior Achievement, Inc., a corporation which employs retired persons.

At the Commencement exercises in May, 1960, the honorary degree of Doctor of Science was conferred upon T. E. Stoa, retiring chief of the division of plant industry, and the honorary degree of Doctor of Laws was given to Robert Parrott, son of A. H. Parrott, longtime registrar of the College. Dr. Parrott is a graduate of the College who worked for the Cargill Company of Minneapolis for over twenty years and then joined the Central Soya Company of Fort Wayne, Ind., of which he is now the executive vice president.

J. Allen Clark, Lyle W. Phillips, Vernon O. Trygstad and Mrs. Mary Darrow Weible received alumni achievement awards in 1960. Mr. Clark, a native North Dakotan, of the Class of 1910, formerly principal agronomist in charge of Western Wheat Investigation for the United States Department of Agriculture, is now executive secretary of the Maize Committee, and a member of the National Academy of Science and the National Research Council, Washington, D. C. Mr. Phillips, '32, with a Ph.D. from the University of Illinois, is project director of Special Projects in Science Education for the National Science Foundation, Washington, D. C. He had taught at the University of Illinois and the University of Buffalo and worked for the Armstrong Cork Company. Mr. Trygstad, '36, director of pharmacy service, Veterans Administration, Washington, D. C., served in the Navy as a narcotics agent. Mrs. Weible, '04, widow of the late Dr. Ralph E. Weible, has been an active leader in educational, civic and cultural activities in Fargo. She aided in organizing the first community lecture series, adult classes in English, the first kindergarten, and helped secure the first nurse and the first police matron in Fargo.

FOOTNOTES

[1] Minutes of the Council, Apr. 13, 1955–Oct. 8, 1957.

[2] The area formerly called the "slough," used for years for faculty gardens, between Twelfth Avenue and the Great Northern Railway, is now called Kruse Park as an acknowledgement of the effort of Martin Kruse, member of the State Board of Higher Education, to secure Board aid in purchasing this piece of land for the College.

[3] In honor of the "1,000 Club" a plaque is placed at the entrance to the Student Union which reads: "This building became a reality through the imagination and integrity of these citizens and organizations who had faith in a greater land grant college."

[4] Faculty Record, "C" 582, May 11, 1944.

◀ CHAPTER XIV ▶

College and State

FROM the very beginning North Dakota's land-grant college has been a State institution. When the Legislature of North Dakota accepted the Federal land grant providing for a College in the State, it assumed the administration and control of the College. And so the College belongs to the people of the State, who delegate their power to the governor and the legislative body, who in turn designate the members of a board to administer the affairs of the institution.

From 1890 to 1916 the governor was authorized to appoint local boards for each institution of higher education in the State. From 1916 to 1920 all the institutions of higher education were under an appointive Board of Regents. From 1920 to 1939 State educational institutions were added to the charitable and penal institutions and managed by a Board of Administration composed of three appointed and two ex-officio members. Since 1939 the supervision of the institutions of higher education has been in the hands of the State Board of Higher Education appointed by the governor from nominations made by the president of the North Dakota Educational Association, the chief justice of the North Dakota Supreme Court and the superintendent of public instruction.[1] The function of all these boards was to administer efficiently the funds provided by the Federal government and also those appropriated by the State Legislature.

The original Morrill Act of 1862 allotted to each state 30,000 acres of land for each senator and representative in Congress. In 1890, therefore, North Dakota was to receive 90,000 acres of land, the income from which could be used for maintenance of a college. The second Morrill Act of 1890 provided $15,000 a year for the first year. This sum was to be increased by annual increments of $1,000 until each state received $25,000. The Nelson amendment to the second Morrill Act, passed in

1907, provided $5,000 a year in 1908, $10,000 in 1909, $15,000 in 1910, $20,000 in 1911, $25,000 in 1912 and $25,000 thereafter. The Smith-Hughes Act of 1917, passed to promote vocational education in agriculture, industry and home economics, gave additional aid to the preparation of teachers in agriculture and home economics. The Bankhead-Jones Act of 1935 provided for resident instruction additional amounts apportioned according to population.

In North Dakota the income from land was called the Interest and Income Account and was managed by a State committee. It provided for the North Dakota Agricultural College $392.96 in the biennium 1894–1896, $5,929.19 in the biennium of 1900–1902, over $46,000 in the biennium of 1904–1906, and $129,016.83 in the biennium of 1916–1918.

In order to provide a working figure for the operation of the College in the following years, the estimated income for the decade of 1921–1930 was set at $80,000 a year. However, the actual income was far less than that, resulting in a total deficit of over $96,000 by the end of the decade. In March, 1929, this amount was borrowed from the Bank of North Dakota at six per cent interest. In this year Dr. Coulter operated on a budget of $80,000 from this fund and maintained that the State was obligated to pay the deficit. Dr. Shepperd, in the biennial report of July 31, 1930, urged that the State appropriate $100,000 to meet the deficit plus interest. In 1931 the Legislature did appropriate $113,035.75 to meet the deficit in the Income and Interest Account. Since 1942 the amount received from this account has varied from $53,500 in 1943–1944 to $87,000 in 1957–1958, averaging $65,000 for the years from 1940 to 1960, the average for the last few years being $80,000.

The income from the Bankhead-Jones Act of 1935, passed to provide aid during the depression, provided in 1959–1960 for resident instruction $26,180.98. In the same year the Smith-Hughes Act furnished $29,607.00 for vocational agriculture and home economics education. Federal grants in total, therefore, provided in 1960 $105,787.98 a year,[2] which is quite inadequate for the financial needs of the College.

Student fees in the College budget were negligible at first, but by 1916–1917 had amounted to over $17,000 a year. During the next fifteen years student fees varied from $14,500 in 1917–1918 to $63,000 in 1930–1931, averaging $35,000 a year. In the forties and fifties student fees increased from $28,500 in 1943–1944 (World War II) to $343,000 in 1957–1958, and to $440,894.75 in 1959–1960. But it must be realized by the reader that legislative appropriations included estimates of student fees.

In March, 1960, an opportunity for private donations in any amount for the use of the College was provided by the First National Bank and

Trust Company of Fargo. A North Dakota Agricultural College Foundation was formed "to advance and promote the best interests of the College, its students, faculty and program" and "to provide a vehicle through which individuals and corporations can contribute financially to the College." All funds would be invested by the trust department of the bank, subject to the direction of a board of trustees including President Hultz, President W. F. Graves of the First National, and ten other members. In launching the foundation the First National Bank and Trust Company of Fargo contributed $5,000. Dr. Hultz termed the organization "a pioneering effort in this area, reflecting the concern that citizens have for the problems faced by higher education."

However, the main source of revenue for buildings and educational maintenance had to come from State appropriations. The preceding chapters have shown how limited these appropriations have been in the earlier decades. In the appendix is a list of buildings erected with the help of State appropriations since 1890, a list which illustrates this situation, although the initial expense for buildings is not the main item in college expenditure.

The first appropriations by the State Legislature in the nineties were chiefly for buildings; presumably costs of maintenance were to come out of Federal funds. In 1901 provision for maintenance was based on a mill tax for the state institutions of higher education, one fifth of a mill being allotted to the Agricultural College. This arrangement lasted until 1913, when the act was repealed; during that time the biennial amount for maintenance varied from $24,500 in 1901 to $104,000 in 1911. In addition, during 1901–1913 appropriations were made for five new buildings. In the next decade appropriations for maintenance were made "in lieu of the repealed mill tax" and for one new building, Morrill Hall. In the twenties biennial appropriations for maintenance increased from $500,000 to $741,000 and appropriation was made for another new building, the Field House. During the depression years of the thirties, State appropriations declined from $880,000 in 1931 to $339,000 in 1933, to $404,000 in 1935, to $389,000 in 1939, and to $381,000 in 1941. Since 1947, State legislative biennial appropriations have increased considerably and amounted to almost two and one half million in 1947, to over three million in 1949 and in 1951, to over five million in 1959.

How all of these appropriations and contributions have contributed to the effectiveness of instruction and teaching in the College itself has been discussed in previous chapters. But what has the Federal Government and the State done for the agricultural research division of the College — the Experiment Station? Were its records and achievements similar? The Hatch Act passed in 1887 provided $15,000 a year for research and investigation in a land-grant college. In 1906 Congress passed the Adams Act which authorized an additional sum of $5,000, and it also authorized an increase of $2,000 each year until a total of $15,000 was reached. From 1914 to 1925 the North Dakota Experiment Station received $30,000 a year. The Purnell Act passed in 1925 increased this amount by $20,000 and provided for annual increases of $10,000 until June, 1930, when the amount from all Federal sources reached $90,000.

In 1935 the Bankhead-Jones Act authorized a national total of $1,-000,000 for 1935–1936 and an increase of $1,000,000 a year until the annual appropriation came to $5,000,000. 60 per cent of this amount was allotted to Experiment Stations according to rural population and had to be matched by equal state appropriations. By 1950–1951 the North Dakota Agricultural Experiment Station was receiving over $28,000 from the Bankhead-Jones Act. In the rest of the decade this amount increased to $277,800 in 1957–1958, averaging $147,700 for the period. So the Experiment Station was receiving from the Federal Government by 1957–1958 a total of $367,817.21. State appropriations for the Station totaled $1,013,533 for the biennium, 1957–1959.

In 1903 the State began to appropriate money for sub-stations to the main Experiment Station, in 1907 for demonstration farms, in 1909 for enforcement of pure food and paint laws, in 1911 fixed amount of $50,000 for the main Station. By 1925 the combined amount came to $255,000. In 1933 this amount was reduced to $34,000 and for 1935–1943 remained under $200,000. In 1947 the State biennial appropriation was over $600,000, in 1949 almost $1,900,000 and in 1959 $2,700,000; the last sum including appropriations for new buildings.

In addition to the contributions to the Station, what have the Federal Government and the State done to carry the work of the Experiment Station to the general public in form of the Extension Service? Federal aid for the Extension Service began in 1914 when the Smith-Lever Act provided $10,000 for each state and additional amounts prorated on the basis of rural population from a Federal fund, which had to be matched by state or local funds raised or contributed within the state. In 1928 the Capper-Kitchen Act authorized an annual appropriation of $20,000 to each state, plus a sum of $500,000 prorated on a basis of rural population and to be matched by state and local funds. The Bankhead-Jones Act of 1935 authorized $8,000,000 to $12,000,000 prorated on the basis of farm population, with no provision for matching. Other supplementary funds later were voted by Congress as a part of the Agricultural Appropriation Act. In 1937 North Dakota received $294,974 for the Extension Service from the Federal Government and

$163,365 from sources within the State. The distribution of funds for North Dakota in 1937 was from Federal funds, 60 per cent; from the State and College, 1.3 per cent; from the county, 28.4 per cent; and from farmers' organizations, 10.3 per cent.[3]

State legislative appropriations for the Extension Service began in 1921 with $35,000, averaged about $100,000 for the bienniums of 1923–31, only $10,000 for 1933 and 1935, $42,000 in 1937, $60,000 in 1939–43, $150,000 in 1947 and over $250,000 in 1949 and 1951, $376,000 in 1953 and 1955, over $500,000 in 1957 and 1959.

What are now the contributions the Experiment Station and the Extension Service have given to the State and its people? In chapter IV we gave an account of the research done by the College staff during the first quarter century of its history. Of those early scientists one of the most influential, Edwin F. Ladd, became president of the College and later United States Senator. Another, Henry L. Bolley, continued his investigations in flax and served as State seed commissioner. C. B. Waldron, in his later years less active in research, served as dean of the School of Agriculture from 1916 to 1923 and as head of the department of horticulture after that year. John H. Shepperd, head of the department of animal husbandry from 1916 to 1929 and after that president of the College, still found time to write bulletins for the Station and to furnish numerous articles for livestock journals.

L. R. Waldron did his best work after 1916 as plant breeder until his retirement in 1952. Through scientific breeding he developed and made available new varieties of wheat. Dr. Walster gives the following evaluation of his research: "Farmers of the United States grew 84,931,000 acres of all kinds of wheat (including durums) in 1949. Waldron's wheats, including Ceres, Komar, Rival, Vesta, Mida and Premier, accounted for 12.95% of that acreage, or 11,001,351 acres. Farmers of the United States grew 17,690,458 acres of hard red spring wheat in 1949, of which Waldron's six varieties totaling 11,001,351 acres, accounted for 62.1%"[4]

Dr. Waldron was a prolific writer for both agricultural and scientific publications. He wrote extensively about alfalfa, forage crops, grasses, weeds, and especially wheat. He was an omnivorous reader and had an encyclopaedic knowledge of many subjects outside his own field.[5] He was elected a Fellow of the Linnean Society of London, England. He planned the 1954 wheat breeding program pursued so efficiently by his successor, Dr. Glenn S. Smith.

In the thirties and forties other members of the College and Station have proved to be worthy successors of the earlier investigators. One of these, Orin A. Stevens, came to the College in 1909 as botanist and seed analyst. Besides his professional work in the seed laboratory, his distinguished teaching career, and his voluminous correspondence with thousands of persons, who in many fields of natural history turned to him for assistance and information, he has been a prolific writer about birds, bees, weeds and wild flowers. Dr. Walster describes him as the "modern Audubon of the Plains," a modern natural philosopher.[6] His publications include articles in the *American Bee Journal*, the *American Botanist*, the *American Journal of Botany*, the *Dakota Farmer*, *Bulletins* of the Experiment Station, and the *Seed World*. To his credit are two books: *Handbook of North Dakota Plants* (1950) and *Wild Flowers for your Garden* (1952).

Dr. H. L. Walster, who came to the College as an agronomist in 1919 remained with the College until his death in 1957, serving as dean of the School of Agriculture from 1924 to 1954, as director of the Experiment Station from 1934 to 1954 and as director of the Extension Service from 1933 to 1937. Dr. Walster did some original research in his field of agronomy and soils and is co-author of a text book on soils. His published works include a biography of George F. Will in the *North Dakota Historical Quarterly* and numerous articles about the Red River Valley, North Dakota agriculture, and the history of the Experiment Station, all in different professional magazines. He gave numerous addresses on a wide range of subjects, including the Agricultural Adjustment Act, tax research, land use, science and agriculture, soils, water, and irrigation, wheat, and many other subjects. He also spoke about his church, the Plymouth Congregational Church of Fargo, and of historic figures, such as Washington and Jefferson, and their contributions to agriculture and to other fields. After he retired, in addition to the writing of his autobiography, he prepared articles dealing with the scientific contributions of the Waldron brothers, of Bolley, of Ladd and of Shepperd.[7] He collected and compiled an extensive bibliography of agricultural history, and collected material on the Missouri Basin and Latin America.

Casper I. Nelson, who came to the College in 1914 as assistant bacteriologist for the College and the Experiment Station, secured his Ph. D. from the University of Chicago in 1926. He carried on experiments on the nature of wilt resistance in flax, in the use of industrial waters involved in treatment of sewage, in the effectiveness of heat penetration in the canning of meat by pressure cooker, and experiments concerned with the public health. He was active in faculty activities, especially in the promotion of student health. As an avocation, with Mrs. Nelson, he was an enthusiastic gardener; he specialized in peonies, dahlias and lilacs, Mrs. Nelson in African violets. He and Dr. A. F. Yeager, together with W. H. Schultz, founded the Fargo Garden Society. After his retirement in 1954, the Nelsons returned to River Falls, Wisconsin, purchased a five acre plot and started a nursery for perennial flowers and shrubs.

A. F. Yeager came to the College in 1919 as horticulturist and acquired an international reputation as a plant breeder before he resigned in 1937. He was given the title "plant wizard of the North" by men in other college experiment stations. He developed Sunshine and Golden Gem sweet corn, Bison and Red River tomatoes, Buttercup squash, Pixwell, Perry and Abundance gooseberries, Dryweather Everbearing strawberry, Zephyr cantaloupe, Red River crabapple, and unnamed plant material in his breeding programs from which later named varieties were selected after he had left the State. To eliminate sunscald he advocated a bush fruit tree. He earned his doctor's degree in genetics at Iowa State College, and served as secretary of the North Dakota Horticultural Society from the time of its organization in 1923 until his resignation from the College; he was also a founder of the Fargo Garden Society.

Theodore E. Stoa has given his whole life to the North Dakota Agricultural College. He graduated in 1915, received a master's degree in 1921 and served on the staff from that date until he retired in 1960. His work for the Experiment Station has been in the fields of breeding and crop production, the coordination of plant research as related to crop improvement, including evaluation of new lines to determine their relative suitability for this area. Along with this research he has been influential in the creation and administration of a system of increase and distribution of new seeds in order to make the program of plant improvement most effective. He has an impressive list of publications in the field of agronomy.

Other contributors to the work of the Station in the twenties and thirties include A. H. Benton in the field of marketing, T. H. Hopper and L. L. Nesbit in agricultural chemistry, Wanda Weniger and W. E. Brentzel in grain diseases and A. F. Schalk, L. M. Roderick and H. L. Foust in animal diseases.

The significance of the work of the department of agronomy in the Experiment Station in the development of rust resistant varieties in the late thirties and early forties — varieties which came to be grown extensively during the years 1940 to 1950 — cannot be over-estimated. This was the war period, and it was urgent that farmers everywhere increase production. These were years of generally good rainfall, often of heavy plant growth, a condition favorable for rust development. That rust epidemics did not develop during some of these years, but permitted wheat crops to be produced, can almost certainly be credited to the resistant varieties then in extensive use. Students of the problem have estimated that the protection of the wheat crop by these varieties meant the annual savings of many millions of dollars.

Equally significant to the improvement of wheat varieties, though less striking because of the smaller acreage, has been the contribution in the growing of better flax varieties — varieties not only resistant to wilt but also highly resistant or immune to all races of flax rust known to exist in this country and Canada. The development and introduction after 1942 of such varieties as B 5128, Victory, Sheyenne, Deoro (Golden), Marine, Norland and Bolley, many of them still widely grown, were to make flax a surer crop than it had been. Another important contribution to flax improvement during this period was the development of a rapid method of evaluating linseed oil quality now widely used to assist the flax breeder, also used in industrial laboratories.

Dr. Edgar Painter and associates in the department of agricultural chemistry were much interested in the chemistry of linseed oil and studied in detail the deposition and formation of the oil and the influence of the weather on the amount and quality of the oil. Later his successor, Dr. Carl Clagett, and his associates, in cooperation with the department of agronomy were to make an exhaustive study of the relative nutrient requirements of flax and some other North Dakota crops. The result of this study was to contradict the common notion that flax was hard on land. Actually it showed that the withdrawal from the soil, of the principal nutrients, by a good crop of flax was less than with a good crop of wheat, oats or barley.

The North Dakota Agricultural Experiment Station has, over the years, secured an increasing understanding of its efforts to improve the welfare of the people of the State, and in doing so has gained a larger interest in and acceptance of the importance of its research. The increasing legislative appropriations and private gifts have evidenced this interest. In 1949 the Legislature provided money for a new seedhouse, and a modern greenhouse to serve the plant breeding program. Subsequent Legislatures appropriated funds for more greenhouses — amounting to ten in all.

At the same time the Agronomy Seed Farm, purchased from individual statewide subscriptions provided an increase in foundation seed. It is a self-supporting unit and out of its earnings later improvements, including a new processing plant, were made. In the last ten years the Seed Farm has provided and distributed new varieties of hard red spring wheat, durum wheat, oats, barley, flax, soybeans, grass and sweet clover.

In 1952 the new livestock pavilion was completed and named Shepperd Arena. In May of the same year the remodeled veterinary building was dedicated as Van Es Laboratory. The 320-acre farm west of the campus, bought by popular subscription of Fargo business men, provided a new location for sheep, hog, and cattle barns and a poultry plant, where livestock research could be properly carried on.

The discovery of oil in the Williston Basin in 1951 caused the city of Williston to expand its boundaries beyond the Williston Branch Experiment Station. The old Station was sold, a new site was purchased on August 23, 1954, and two buildings were erected on it. The program of the new Williston Station included testing of oats, wheat, barley, potatoes, corn and soybeans for forage. A tillage experiment involving summer fallow management was undertaken. The new and larger Station also provided a limited seed source for the area.[8]

A new branch of the North Dakota Experiment Station was established in Minot, in Ward county, in 1945 by the Legislature and named the North Central Agricultural Experiment Station. Ward county contributed to it the county poor farm and 480 acres of land. The legislative act defined its functions as making "experiments with grains and grasses, native and other forage plants, including corn, sunflowers, sorghums and millets, garden and orchard crops, shelter belt and ornamental trees and shrubs, livestock and poultry;" it should "become a center for the increase and dissemination of purebred seeds, poultry and livestock."[9]

After 1946 the Dickinson Branch Experiment Station became a center for livestock research for western North Dakota. Annually a field day was held, which attracted an attendance of 700 to 1,000, at which the program consisted of tours, of feeding trials, reports of the Dickinson Station staff, a talk by the director of the North Dakota Agricultural Experiment Station, and a panel discussion on "Feeding Livestock for the Market."

The completion of the Garrison Reservoir and the development of the Garrison Diversion Program increased the interest in North Dakota in irrigation. In 1957 the legislative assembly authorized the establishment of a new irrigation station in the potential area planned for utilizing water from the Garrison Reservoir. After inspection of twelve possible sites, in 1958 a section of land near Carrington was purchased for $54,000. Plans were made to raise grain and to maintain livestock on the land. [10]

Without question, the activities of the Experiment Station at Fargo have brought national attention to the research work of its personnel. Increased appropriations have come from the State, and the United States Department of Agriculture has assigned ten research workers to the Experiment Station on cooperative problems. After 1950 the wheat crop in North Dakota was threatened again by stem rust. A new and more virulent race of stem rust came into the area, and no variety had adequate resistance. Agronomists and plant breeders had foreseen this possibility and in previous years had begun the introduction of the Khapli emmer resistance into the durum breeding program. By using modern greenhouse facilities provided by the Legislature, by growing three crops a year — and the opportunity to increase the seed supply in the South during the winter — new resistant varieties of durum, Langdon, Ramsey, Towner and Yuma, were made available in 1956. These quickly came into general use. Canadian breeders were more successful in breeding for resistance in the hard red spring wheat. Because of the fine cooperation among the plant researchers, North Dakota shared in the increase and early release of the resistant variety of Selkirk, just as other states and Canada shared in the early release of the resistant durum developed in North Dakota. More recently an annual grant of the Malting Improvement Association amounting to $50,000 has been made to the Experiment Station for barley improvement.

The basic factors which make one variety resistant to rust and another susceptible have long been a puzzling matter to the plant scientist. The work of Dr. H. H. Flor on the genetics of flax and flax rust was to show a gene for gene relationship in the host and the parasite. Later Flor and John Doubly, bacteriologists, in serologic studies found that a race of flax rust was able to attack a variety containing its specific rust antigen, but was not able to do so if the variety lacked the antigen. The information is perhaps another lead or break through to a better understanding of what resistance is; knowledge of which could be of great help to the plant breeder.

Corn hybrids developed in North Dakota are now in common use, as well as a malting barley, Traill, developed by the Experiment Station. More recently two new durum varieties were released, Wells and Lakota, which offer still more rust protection and insurance against a sudden change in the rust race picture.

Cereal technologists, devising new or modifying old techniques for evaluating quality in cereals, so necessary in a breeding program, have recently developed a micro-method for testing the malting characteristics of barley. Early gem potato, developed by the Station, is grown more commonly in some other states, but North Dakota produces much of the certified seed needed by out-of-State growers. Nodak, Norland, and Norgleam, all high quality potato varieties, were introduced a few years ago, with Norland, a red skinned variety with fine field, culinary and processing characteristics, proving of particular value. A new potato variety, Snowflake, a smooth, white skinned variety with some resistance to virus is scheduled for release.

Investigating the minor constituents in linseed meal by the department of agricultural biochemistry led to the discovery and identification of four new compounds. One of these has already come into use in medical research and found to be involved in the formation of cholesterol. Another has been found to have an antagonistic effect on Vitamin B.

A recent contribution from the department of animal husbandry, which is now in wide use, is the pelleting of barley, making for better utilization of this feed crop in the feeding of pigs. This is providing an increased outlet for barley, a crop grown more extensively in North Dakota than in any other state.

An important contribution from the department of veterinary sciences is its work on listerellosis in sheep. Department researchers found that the responsible organism affects the reproductive system, causing abortion. To overcome this heavy loss to the sheep industry a successful vaccine was developed which is now in wide use. Another research contribution has resulted in the development of more effective means of controlling worms in sheep by an alkaline drench now in common use.

When the sugar beet root maggot threatened the beet industry, a research contribution from the department of agricultural entomology, including a biological study of the pest, made possible recommendations for control which have proved very effective.[11]

Soil scientists have developed modified procedures for testing North Dakota soils for phosphorus availability. These have yielded results that correlate with field response and have provided a basis for establishing a soil testing service that is now widely used by North Dakota farmers.

These are a few of the more recent contributions from the Experiment Station. As problems to be met become increasingly complex, the research sponsored by the Experiment Station is less and less a matter of individual experimentation. More and more it has become a matter of each scientist contributing from his specialized training and talents. This is true not only at this Station but may also extend to workers in other institutions in the United States, Canada and even foreign countries. The experimental work of the Station was further aided by a bequest in 1959 from the John S. Dalrymyple estate through a donation of a half section of land located near Mapleton, to be known as the "Dalrymple Experimental Plot."

Just as the contributions from research over the past 60 years have been considerable, there are good reasons to expect that, with an increasingly competent and larger staff, and under the leadership of the chairmen of the following departments even larger contributions can be expected in the future. Those departments and their chairman as of 1960 are: in agricultural biochemistry (formerly agricultural chemistry) Dr. Harold Klosterman; in agricultural economics, Dr. Fred R. Taylor; in agricultural engineering, Wm. Promersberger; in agronomy (crops) Dr. J. F. Carter; in animal husbandry, Prof. M. L. Buchanan; in bacteriology, Dr. Paul Adams; in botany, Dr. E. A. Helgeson; in cereal technology, Prof. K. A. Gilles; in dairy technology, Dr. Christen Jensen; in entomology, Dr. J. R. Dogger; in horticulture, Dr. E. P. Lana; in plant pathology, Dr. Richard Kiesling; in poultry husbandry, Dr. Reece L. Bryant; in soil science, Dr. E. B. Norum; and in veterinary technology, Dr. D. F. Eveleth.

Agricultural information resulting from the research done by the staff of the Experiment Station is disseminated among the people of the State and outside in many ways, including bulletins, circulars, news stories, radio, television, and by field days and other meetings conducted by Experiment Station and Extension Service staff members. The Station has published bulletins since 1891, numbering 430 altogether, which describe results of individual projects. A bi-monthly publication, known originally as the *Bimonthly Bulletin* and now called *Farm Research,* contains progress reports of projects of general interest, and has been published regularly since 1938. Seventy-three *Circulars* were published between 1914 and 1946.

According to the Smith-Lever Act of 1914, the Cooperative Extension Service was charged with the responsibility of disseminating research and other useful information pertaining to agriculture and home economics. By 1960 this responsibility was being fully met, for farm families were assisted in making needed adjustments in farm organization and operation and in family living. During the last twelve years farm families in North Dakota were faced with the following problems: 12,300 fewer farms (an average loss of 1,200 per year); increased average size of farm from 630 to 755 acres; increased average farm capital investment of $18,000 ($52,000 in 1960); increased farm expenses and lower prices for farm produce; loss of acres in wheat (North Dakota's most profitable cash crop) through farm program allotments; need for more mechanization and specialization to compete profitably; modernization of farm homes to provide conveniences and a higher standard of living.

The staff of the Extension Service has conducted an intensive educational and training program in farm and home management in order to help farmers to reorganize their individual farm operations and to utilize their resources more efficiently. In 1960 for example Extension specialists and county extension agents gave assistance to 9,966 farmers and to 20,359 different farm families. With the cooperation of other State livestock organizations the Extension Service has carried out an intensive livestock production and feeding program; greater returns have been obtained from feed and forage, family labor has been utilized, and a consequent increase of farm income has resulted. North Dakota farmers have increased their average net farm income in the last five years by sixteen per cent over the years of 1949 and 1950 and they did this with ten to twelve per cent fewer harvested acres.

The North Dakota Extension Service program is carried out by the director of Extension, a state administrative-supervisory staff, 71 county extension agents and assistant agents located in every county in the State, 22 home demonstration agents and assistants in nineteen counties, nineteen agricultural extension specialists, six home economics specialists, and five full-time staff members in the 4-H and YMW programs. Much of the success of the Extension Service is due to the support and assistance of voluntary local leaders. In 1960 there were 13,024 such voluntary leaders assisting Extension staff members in organizing, planning, and conducting the North Dakota Extension program. This total includes 11,006 Homemakers Club leaders, 1,986 4-H club leaders, 111 leaders in YMW work and 441 agricultural program leaders.

The Extension Service has made a major contribution in assisting rural families in North Dakota to modernize the home and provide a more satisfying family life through the organization of Homemakers Clubs. Project lessons and training have been provided in foods, clothing and home management areas. In addition, Homemakers Clubs participate in health, safety, family life, citizenship, civil defense, gardening, and home and yard beautification activities.

The 4-H Club program, in which boys and girls are given training in agriculture, home economics, leadership, citizenship, health, public speaking and related projects is an important part of the Extension Service. Voluntary local leaders are responsible for the success of the community 4-H Club, leadership training and project material being provided by the Extension Service. 4-H Club enrollment increased from 12,435 in 1948 to 17,507 in 1960.

Another program is for young men and women (YMW) from 18 to 30 years of age. It emphasizes leadership training, career guidance, preparation for adult life, and participation in community activities. A majority of the twenty International Farm Youth Exchange delegates from North Dakota to foreign countries have been YMW members.

The main Extension methods used by the members of the Extension staff include personal contacts, meetings, demonstrations, organized club programs and mass communication media. Local planning committees determine the educational work to be stressed in the State program. Extension subject matter and assistance to the people of North Dakota is provided by the information department. In 1960 this department prepared 950 articles for newspapers, 3,120 radio programs for 19 stations, television programs for five stations, 8,163 slides and seventeen films for the use of agents and specialists. Club literature for 17,507 4-H Club members and for 21,144 Homemakers has been prepared and 200,000 bulletins and circulars have been distributed.

The Extension Service has also made its contributions to the improvement of agriculture and home life by means of the work of the county extension agents and home agents. During the depression years of the thirties the Extension Service played a major role in relief work, and organized the wheat allotment plan of the Agricultural Adjustment Administration. Emergency problems of national defense, scarcity of labor and increased demand for food during World War II were handled by Extension Service personnel and trained local leaders. The entire program of the Extension Service emphasizes the development of local leadership in farm and, of late years, in urban, communities.

The personnel of the Extension Service as of 1960 include the director, Edwin J. Haslerud, three district supervisors, Stanley W. Bale, Byron W. Berntson and Merrill S. Burke, a program planning supervisor, Russell B. Widdifield, a county agent leader, Paul R. Kasson, a home demonstration leader, Mrs. Naurine Higgins, who succeeded Grace DeLong, longtime state leader, in 1960; a 4-H and YMW leader, Craig R. Montgomery, an associate 4-H and YMW leader, Dr. Kenneth S. Olson; an agricultural economist, Harry G. Anderson; an agricultural engineer, Arthur H. Schulz; an agronomist, L. A. Jensen; a forester, John J. Zaylskie; a dairyman, Clarence C. Olson; an entomologist, Wayne J. Colberg; a horticulturist, Harry A. Graves; a nutritionist, Ruth Dawson; a soil conservationist, Irvine T. Dietrich; and state agents: for clothing, Marian D. Tudor; for home management, Irene Crouch; for marketing, Herbert W. Herbison; for livestock, George E. Strum; and editor, Thomas W. Gildersleeve.

In 1955 five extension workers of long service were honored at the State Extension Conference: J. C. Russell, agricultural engineer, for

College and State

31 years of service; N. D. Gorman, county agent leader, for 31 years; Julia E. Brekke, clothing agent, for 35 years; Grace DeLong, home demonstration leader, for 31 years, and Pauline Reynolds, rural young people leader, for 30 years.

Important contributions to the State and its people, however, came also from the research in other schools of the College. In the field of paint chemistry Dr. Wouter Bosch, a native of The Netherlands and a graduate of the University of Utrecht, encouraged research in coatings technology. Forty-two graduate students finished their master's degrees under his direction, and he taught 22 paint short courses which were attended by students from all over the world. He was succeeded in 1958 by Dr. Alfred E. Rheineck who continues the work of his predecessor. Research in other fields of chemistry has been made possible through grants from the National Science Foundation, from the Freeman Chemical Company, from the American Zinc Institute, from the Hercules Powder Company, from the Archer-Daniels-Midland Company, and from the National Institutes of Health.

In the field of electrical engineering on November 1, 1949, a first contract amounting to $450 monthly was signed by the National Bureau of Standards and the department of engineering to monitor and record data in the area of radio propagation. On May 7, 1951, with a grant of $24,000 the two parties contracted to provide equipment to study radio propagation by means of ionospheric scatter. Later contracts in 1957 and 1958 provided additional funds to determine if it was feasible to provide a communications system which would rely on the presence of meteors and meteor trails for its success. These projects of the department of engineering and its station were under the direction of Professors Faiman, E. M. Anderson, E. G. Anderson and L. L. Melanson.

Two students receiving their M.S. in electrical engineering have also been directed in their research by the department of physics. An educational grant of $24,642 from the Atomic Energy Commission was made in support of the nuclear engineering program. The Atomic Energy Commission in addition contributed $8,000 for the purchase of pharmaceutical equipment; the National Institutes of Health has provided $7,000, the North Dakota Cancer Society, $12,000 and the North Dakota Heart Association $4,090, which grants are utilized for investigation by members of the staff of the School of Pharmacy. A new building housing the School of Pharmacy, completed in the summer of 1960, facilitates all the research done in pharmacy.

Altogether since 1954 the National Institutes of Health have provided over $267,000 for use in research by the departments of bacteriology, biochemistry, entomology and veterinary science. The National Science Foundation has made grants of over $535,000, to be used in the departments of biochemistry, botany, chemistry, entomology and zoology. Miscellaneous grants for bacteriology and graduate fellowships amount to $28,800. Grants in the field of pharmacy research and education amounted to $15,350.[12]

As one phase of the 60th anniversary of the College in 1950 Dean Giesecke of the School of Applied Arts and Sciences, with the approval of President Hultz and the cordial support of his school, initiated a program which became known as the North Dakota Institute for Regional Studies. Seven members of the staff were chiefly responsible for its founding: Dean Giesecke; H. Dean Stallings, librarian; W. C. Hunter, chairman of the department of social sciences and professor of history; O. A. Stevens, professor of botany; Kenneth Kuhn, chairman of the department of English; E. A. Helgeson, chairman of the department of botany; and Rudolf Ottersen, professor of history. The purpose of the Institute was to encourage research and writing by providing a collection of books, maps, manuscripts, plants and animals and providing a center for information on the life and culture of the Northern Plains and particularly of the State of North Dakota.

As time passed, other faculty members were elected to the board of directors. Dean Stallings has continued as chairman of the board; Leonard Sackett, associate professor of English, became executive secretary, who personally and through correspondence secured the majority of the historical collections; Dr. O. A. Stevens is curator in charge of scientific collections and museum specimens; Dr. Hunter is archivist in charge of manuscripts and documentary records; Dr. Leo Hertel is editor of its publications; Dean Seth Russell is director in charge of its general policies. The other members of the board in 1960 were Dean Glenn S. Smith, and Professors Hale Aarnes, Glenn Fisher, Richard Lyons, Rudolf Ottersen and Jesse Parsons.

The first publication of the Institute, in 1950, was the *Handbook of North Dakota Plants,* written by O. A. Stevens. Other books published in the meantime have been *Measure of My Days* by Aagot Raaen in 1953; *Modern Sagas, the Story of the Icelanders in North America* by Thorstina Walters in 1953; *North Dakota, a Human and Economic Geography* by Melvin E. Kazeck in 1956; *God Giveth the Increase, the History of the Episcopal Church in North Dakota* by Robert P. and Wynona H. Wilkins in 1959. *An Appraisal of Conservation Purpose and Policy* by G. B. Gunlogson was published in 1954 and a reference book *Aberdeen Angus Bloodlines* by C. J. Christians in 1959. A social science monograph, *Income in North Dakota, 1929–1956,* by Glenn

Fisher came out in 1958 as well as a collection of poems by Richard Lyons under the title *One Squeaking Straw*. Several pamphlets have also been printed in addition to a series of social science reports, which were mimeographed. A very popular pamphlet was *Waterfowl of North Dakota*, by Paul A. Johnsgard.

A number of exhibitions of regional art were sponsored by the Institute. In 1952 the paintings, oil and water colors of Elmer H. Halvorson from Wheelock, in Williams County, were shown. Another group of paintings by Einar H. Olstad, a rancher-blacksmith of Sioux Falls, S. Dak., was exhibited in 1953. In the next year there was a memorial exhibition of the paintings of Paul E. Barr, the former head of the art department of the University of North Dakota. Willis Nelson, social studies teacher in the Valley Junior High School of Grand Forks, exhibited his paintings, water colors, and pastels in 1956.

In February, 1955, a group of interested persons met with Miss Wilbur Armistad, a faculty member of the School of Home Economics, in order to organize a North Dakota Craftsmen Guild under the auspices of the Institute for Regional Studies. As a result, a traveling exhibit of about 100 pieces was shown at the College Library and later at Minot and at Bismarck. Categories included ceramics, wood carvings, violins, puppets and dolls, baskets, beadwork, hand weaving, embroidery and lace, hooked rugs, leather, etc.

One main purpose of the Institute is to collect books, diaries, atlases and personal manuscripts relating to the history, geography and natural history of North Dakota and the Northern Plains as a basis of research for faculty and students. It already has over eleven hundred records of source materials; it has one of the largest collections of information regarding "bonanza farming," indexed and available for use by scholars.

In order to promote graduate research by the staff of the School of Arts and Science, Dean Russell appointed Courtney B. Cleland, G. B. Comita, Glenn W. Fisher, D. Ross Moir and Warren C. Whitman as a committee in order to pass on summer research proposals and to advise him, as director, how to allot travel expenses and subsidies to various members of the staff for the purpose of research and study.

As a result of a bequest made to the College by the late Adolph J. Wiesbach a series of lectures by various members of the faculty has been presented to the public annually. The selection of the lecturer is done by a committee of the faculty in consultation with the different schools on the campus. The first lecture was entitled "Grass on Our Prairies" and was given by Dr. Warren C. Whitman in 1957. A second lecture, by Dean Ralph E. Dunbar, given in 1958, was entitled "Research or . . . ?" The third lecture, given in 1959, was presented by Dr. Gabriel Comita, whose subject was "Life in Lakes." The subject of the fourth, in 1960, was "The New Look in Mathematics" by Prof. A. Glenn Hill. The last one was due to a bequest from the estate of Adrian Butts.

A series of lectures in memory of Dr. P. J. Iverson, financed by his friends, was given annually from 1957 to 1961. The first of these was presented by Dr. Frank Cyr of Columbia University, speaking on the subject, "Future of Education in the Great Plains." The second address, in 1958, entitled "New Opportunities in Education," was given by Dr. J. D. Weeks, president of the University of South Dakota. In 1959 Dr. Harvey Wright, president of Macalester College, spoke on the "Future of Teachers' Education." The next year Dr. Paul Dressel, director of research, Michigan State University, gave an address on "General Education in a Land-Grant College."

The increase in enrollment of undergraduate students from 375 in 1920 to 1,993 in 1941 was quite spectacular. World War II interrupted this trend and reduced enrollment to 550 in 1945. By 1948 an attendance record was reached, due to the return of veterans. A decrease occurred as the number of veterans declined. In the last decade enrollment again reached a new high of 2,562 in 1950, dropped to 1,026 in 1952, gradually rose to 3,060 in 1956 and to 3,624 in 1959. The enrollment in the fall of 1960 numbered a total of 3,141.[12]

Although the fluctuation of farm income in the forties and fifties would be expected to have affected enrollment in institutions of higher education, its effect has been rather limited in North Dakota. While gross farm income dropped 72 per cent from 1929 to 1932, student enrollment dropped only 12 per cent from 1930 to 1933, and recovered quickly to the 1930 level by 1935. The fact that in spite of depression and drought during this period the fluctuation in student enrollment varied only little can perhaps be explained by two factors. In the first place, employment opportunities during depression are extremely scarce, and many people who otherwise would go into farming, business or employment went to school. Further, in proportion to the general population of the State, college enrollment is relatively small. During this time most of the students came from the economically more secure families who had savings to draw upon or whose income was less deflated than that of the average family.

In the last few years there is observable a sharp trend toward increased attendance in institutions of higher education from all levels of the population. Whereas only four per cent of the college-age group attended colleges and universities in 1904, the national average now stands above 40 per cent, and is increasing at an annual rate of one per cent.

The relation of college enrollment to population, however, might have a bearing on the future of the institution. The population of the State of North Dakota reached a peak in the late twenties. Since 1930 there has been a decline of about 27 per cent due to the drought and depression of the thirties, the rapid mechanization of agriculture resulting in an increase in the size of farms, a decrease in the number of farms, and the migration of workers to industries. This trend in the population of the State is still indicated in the 1960 census, which represented only a two per cent increase in comparison to the 1950 census.

Fortunately in spite of this decline of population, there seem to be increasing incentives for students to attend institutes of higher education and as graduates to remain in the State. Higher incomes and living standards require more services that will absorb a larger part of the North Dakota youth. Irrigation and electric power development resulting from the harnessing of the waters of the Missouri River will create new opportunities for many workers. The opening up of new oil fields in the State, together with the probable exploitation of lignite, may very well in the future affect the growth of population and an increase of employment.

An important factor in attracting students to educational institutions in the State and causing them to stay is the constantly increasing number of scholarships awarded to deserving students. The number of recipients of these scholarships has increased from 50 in 1943, the first year on record, to 290 in 1960, with a corresponding increase in the total cash value.

For financial aid to students, several loan funds are made available. The National Defense Student Loan Program of 1958 has funds supplied by the Federal Government from which superior students who are in need may borrow up to $1,000 a year for educational purposes. Qualified North Dakota students may borrow up to $500 a year from the North Dakota Loan Fund, administered by the Department of Public Instruction in Bismarck. The College itself maintains a modest loan fund for the benefit of worthy students who are in need of a short time loan.

Freshman scholarships ranging from $150 to $200 are provided by various private organizations. The State of North Dakota scholarships equivalent to institutional fees are awarded to students from the State on the basis of academic aptitude, financial need and character. 4-H Club members are eligible for scholarships provided by the

North Dakota Homemakers Council, the J. R. Watkins and the Occident Flour companies. The Elks Lodge sponsors local, state and national prizes to high school graduates who intend to enroll in a college and who are in need of financial assistance.

The various schools on the campus also have at their disposal scholarships ranging from $50 to $800 a year; the funds in general are furnished by fraternal and service groups, by student organizations, by private individuals, and by professional and business firms. The Fulbright Grants, the Rhodes Scholarships and the Sparks Memorial Fellowships of Phi Kappa Phi have been awarded to superior students of the College for a number of years. Also a long list of awards and accompanying trophies, each ranging in value from $10 to $25, is annually presented at a special Honors Day Convocation. In 1960 the number of awards amounted to 290, with a total value of $40,000. At first the Honors Day Convocation was sponsored by Phi Kappa Phi. Since 1941, when there were only 53 awards, Blue Key Fraternity and Senior Staff have been in charge of the program, supported by a faculty committee, on which Dean Sudro, Dean Thompson, Professor Van Vlissingen and Dr. Hertel have been long-time members.

FOOTNOTES

[1] A list of the governing boards from 1890 to 1960 is found in the appendix.

[2] Figures from the College business office.

[3] George A. Works and Barton Morgan, *The Land Grant College* (Washington, 1939), 66.

[4] H. L. Walster, mss. "Five for the Land," in the North Dakota Institute for Regional Studies, Library, N.D.A.C.

[5] This knowledge was illustrated often enough, when he and the author were on a radio program, "Stump the Professors." Dr. Waldron could answer many more questions than any one of the rest of the group.

[6] H. L. Walster, papers, in the North Dakota Institute for Regional Studies, Library, N.D.A.C.

[7] H. L. Walster, papers, in the North Dakota Institute for Regional Studies, Library, N.D.A.C.

[8] *Bi-Monthly Bulletin, XVIII*, 5, 151–159.

[9] *Laws of North Dakota*, 1944–1945, Chap. 48, 97.

[10] *Bi-Monthly Bulletin*, Nov.–Dec., 1959, 10–13.

[11] *Bi-Monthly Bulletin*, Mar.–Apr., 1956, 116–120.

[12] Figures from the College Business Office.

◄ CHAPTER XV ►

The College Becomes a University

By the legislative act of 1890 the name "North Dakota Agricultural College," had been given to the newly established institution in Fargo. In the seventy years of its history many attempts were made to change the name on the ground that the name was not a true designation of the educational work of the institution. One of the first of such complaints is found in the *Spectrum* of February 15, 1900, only ten years after the establishment of the College:

"It is difficult to realize what an idea a large number of people in this state — yes, even in this city, — have of our institution. Their idea seems to be that the Agricultural College is an institution where a lot of young men learn how to plant corn, hoe potatoes, care for stock, and raise grain in the most approved scientific manner. It is often amusing to hear the expressions of surprise from visitors here for the first time, when, instead of a lot of hot-houses, barns and other mechanisms designed expressly for the farm and farmer, they find a thoroughly equipped, modern institution for the higher learning. While the right idea is being rapidly disseminated throughout the state, yet we feel the name will continue to injure the work of the institution by preventing the attendance of a larger class of students desiring a regular collegiate education, by the false impression which it conveys. While this misunderstanding does not affect the efficiency of the institution, it tends to cause many seeking a professional education, to go to other places, no better than this and perhaps not so well equipped. All this is in a name, and as the name is such an important factor why not change it to one that will give the people of the state for which it is supported, the true idea of its character. It is true the agricultural sciences are taught here, but this might easily be indicated and the institution shown in its true light by calling it the State College and School of Agriculture."

The next reference to a change of name is found in the *Weekly Spectrum* of October 8, 1919, about twenty years later, in an editorial under the title, "Shall It Be Changed?"

"A matter of the utmost importance to every student on the campus was a recent one discussed at the Student Commission meeting on Thursday. Shall we or shall we not vote and act to recommend the change in the name of our college? This is an old question with the student body of this school, and one discussed in many of the organizations on the campus. It is a vital question because it affects the welfare of our institution and its future growth. Its present name, The North Dakota Agricultural College, is not inclusive enough — it names Agriculture as if it were the only course offered at the institution. And because it names this course only, many excellent high school students from every part of the state are lost to us, thinking they must go elsewhere to get courses in the Sciences and Arts.

"The name proposed for the school is one used by many other states in naming their schools of Agriculture: 'The State College of Agriculture and Mechanic Arts', this name naturally becoming: 'The State College.' The proposed name has the advantage of being short and terse; it gives no particular course, and because of that fact invites investigation; and even were the entire title applied to the school the name would tell the high school students they could obtain more than the one course at the institution."

Two weeks later another editorial in the *Spectrum* of October 23, 1919, expressed itself as follows:

"The campaign to change the name of the institution has been definitely determined upon by the Student Commission. It has been decided to petition for the change of the post office name to that of 'State College, N. Dak.' and, using that for the opening lever to prevail upon people and legislature to alter the name given us by the constitution to that of 'The State College of Agriculture and Mechanic Arts.' It is, of course, expected the name 'The State College' will be reverted to popularly, when designating our institution.

"This action on the part of the student governing body is merely the expression of a change long desired by the thinking students of the College. Its purpose is apparent to even the casual observer: — a neater, shorter and more concise name, yet carrying as great dignity as does the present one. 'State College' while denoting no special courses, has an invitation to investigation of our curriculum attached to it. The change has not the least slight of the term 'Agricultural' in mind, but argues that since agricultural courses are by no means the only courses given in our schools, this one science should not be named at the expense of others. The number of students who should be added to our roll because of this one change should be large."

One year later the arguments for changing the name are summed up in an article in the *College and State* of Jan.-Feb., 1920, as follows: "Full title gives more information as to courses offered here than does the title Agricultural College; Short title while naming no courses invites investigation, students are going elsewhere at present because agriculture is apparently the only work taught here; names no course at the expense of others; short title is much handier for correspondents of the college; changing of name will not lose the support of the farming population, since agriculture will still be a major subject taught here; State College is name used in large percentage of like institutions in the country."

An editorial in the *Spectrum* of March 3, 1922, which attributed the suggestion to President Coulter, started another attempt to change the name of the College. The editorial stated that the objectives of a land-grant college as laid down by congressional statute, should be the teaching of "such branches of learning as are related to agriculture and the mechanic arts, not excluding other scientific and classical studies, and including military tactics, in order to provide the liberal and practical education of the industrial classes in the several pursuits and professions in life." The author admitted the importance of tradition and sentiment for the name, North Dakota Agricultural College, but said that tradition has its limitations. He believed the institution had been hampered in its growth by its name.

A test ballot conducted by the *Spectrum* of March 31, 1922, resulted in a vote of 234 favoring North Dakota State College, eight favoring North Dakota A. and M. College, 14 for A. and M., six for N.D.A.C. To be official the change of name had to go before the Legislature, be passed twice and then voted on by the people. One of the minority questioned the appropriateness of the new name, as 70 per cent of the State was classified as rural and this was the only institution of its kind in the State.

A later issue of the *Spectrum,* May 5, 1922, stated that Patterson's *American Educational Directory* did not list North Dakota Agricultural College or Michigan Agricultural College as colleges, but did list Pennsylvania State College and Iowa State College. The only mention of North Dakota Agricultural College in the directory was under a list of schools of domestic science, agriculture, pharmacy and veterinary medicine.

Since no action was taken at this time, the controversy remained dormant but was revived in 1926. An "inquiring reporter" conducted a column in the *Spectrum* of March 2, 5, 9, 12, 1926, which carried statements in favor of a name change from representative students and staff members, including Professor Waldron, Athletic Director Cortwright, and Registrar Parrott. Mr. Parrott stated that "of the fifty-one land-grant institutions in the country, only Colorado, Oregon, South Carolina and North Dakota retained the name *Agricultural College* and these had not developed strong curricula in the sciences, notably in chemistry, as we had."[1] One of the students asked "why the College should be named after a course which embraces only 13 per cent of the total college enrollment . . . Statistics obtained from the registrar's office reveal the fact that of 843 students taking college courses, only 114 are enrolled in the School of Agriculture." [2]

A student election on March 12, 1926, showed a vote of 331 in favor of changing the name from "North Dakota Agricultural College" to "North Dakota State College of Agriculture and Mechanic Arts," while only three dissented. This, however, was a light vote, for less than 25 per cent of the total enrollment voted. At the June meeting of the Alumni Association it was recommended that steps be taken to change the name of the college. The result of a questionnaire based on this recommendation sent to every alumnus was as follows: 303 votes received, 245 in favor of change, 58 against, 167 voted for North Dakota State College. The legislative committee of the Alumni Association, consisting of R. W. Lumry, Amos Ewen and H. E. Dixon, heartily recommended the change.

In June, 1926, the students of the College of Mechanic Arts began the publication of a quarterly which they called the *"State College Engineer."* In commenting on this title President Coulter wrote:

"I could not help but note at once the title which you have given your publication. I appreciate the fact that in nearly all of the states the state land grant college established under the Morrill Act is technically called "State College of Agriculture and Mechanic Arts." The short title generally is "State College." In North Dakota our State College is technically known as the North Dakota Agricultural College. However, since the people of the nation and of the State have decreed that Civil, Electrical, Chemical, Agricultural and Architectural Engineering are proper subjects for the land grant colleges, and since most of the land grant colleges have developed along these lines, while all of us officially responsible for the management of this institution feel that we should use the regular technical designation "North Dakota Agricultural College," I have felt that it was hardly our responsibility to try to tell students or their parents or former students and alumni or taxpayers in general that they should not use the short title "State College" or that they should not use the longer, more official title "State College of Agriculture and Mechanic Arts." [3]

In 1929 when the new field house was dedicated letters instead of numerals were used on the clock to spell "State College." A branch of the Fargo post office called Agricultural College Station had been on the campus for quite a while. When in 1925 the city of Fargo annexed a part of the campus, Mr. Parrott, who was acting College postmaster, went to President Coulter and suggested that the College station be named State College Station. Dr. Coulter was in favor of it; after following the proper procedure the branch was called the State College Station thereafter.

Another reference in the *Spectrum* of October 3, 1930, to the question of the name change occurred in the following editorial:

The College Becomes a University

"For the past several years, there has been difficulty over the name of the institution. The *Spectrum,* the athletic department, and other organizations on the campus feel that the name North Dakota State suits us much better than the Agricultural College. Accordingly all the publicity that comes from these sources is put out under the State heading. On the other hand the Agriculture offices and the offices of Registrar use the Aggie cognomen.

"We feel that there is some dissension concerning the name. Apparently the entire alumni body is behind the name State, newspapers in every corner of North Dakota are calling us State in their sport columns. The credit for this goes to Jack Stewart, Bison publicity agent. The local papers, however, still cling to the old name.

"We feel that we are North Dakota State College. . . . Most of the state's newspapers are behind us. With the aid of the entire student body and the press our aim will be realized."

During the depression and war years little was said on the campus about changing the name of the College. But on April 25, 1952, an editorial in the *Spectrum* claims that "of the 48 land-grant colleges established by an act passed in 1862, only 3 are called Agricultural Colleges. They are North Dakota, South Carolina and Utah. Of the remainder, 27 are combined with the State Universities, 8 are called Agricultural and Mechanic Arts Colleges, 5 are called State Colleges, and 2 are called Polytechnical Colleges." The student writer suggested as a new name, "North Dakota State College of Agricultural and Mechanical Arts." According to the editorial, students graduating from professional schools, such as engineering, chemical technology, pharmacy and home economics were at certain disadvantages by graduating from an "agricultural" school.

Editorials in the *Spectrum* of October 8, 1954, suggested a change of the name of the College in order to meet the new industrial changes in the State. "Towering oil derricks in western Dakota, lignite mines, light industry near the larger cities, the Garrison Dam, powerful television transmitters; all these signify the beginning of a new age for our state." In the last decade the Schools of Engineering and Arts and Sciences have greatly outnumbered the School of Agriculture in enrollment.

In November, 1957, a student committee was appointed by the president of the student body to discuss the advisability of changing the name of the College. At its organizational meeting one of the committee members stated that the name university is applicable for an institution if a number of colleges are brought together under one administrative head. North Dakota Agricultural College qualifies for that name since it offers curricula in the fields of engineering, agriculture, pharmacy, home economics, chemistry, and arts and sciences.

In January, 1958, the students of the College prepared and paid for the following leaflet which was distributed over the state:

Who is Proposing This Name Change?

The student body of North Dakota Agricultural College with hope of gaining support from the administration and faculty, alumni and former students, the State Board of Higher Education, the Legislature, and the people of North Dakota.

Why?

NDAC needs a name that accurately describes the scope of its educational offerings. It is not a "single-purpose" institution.

Why University?

Because NDAC is actually a university! A university is a grouping of colleges under one administration with courses that place common reliance on a broad base of instruction in the sciences and the arts.

A college, on the other hand, usually confines its instruction to one field or a group of fields that are closely related.

On the NDAC campus there are seven "colleges" covering a wide range of studies with more than 3,000 students enrolled. These colleges, now called schools, are:

The School of Agriculture, which serves the state through its classroom courses, agricultural research, and allied agricultural extension programs.

The School of Applied Arts and Sciences, which provides training in more than a dozen fields, including speech, psychology, philosophy, English, music, physiology, the natural, social, and library sciences, and the teaching profession.

The School of Pharmacy, which is the largest in this immediate five-state area, holds the nation's highest accreditation rating.

The School of Engineering, which has the largest enrollment on campus, provides training in eight vital branches of engineering.

The School of Chemical Technology, which includes the oldest and best regarded department of paint, varnishes and lacquer in the world.

The School of Home Economics, which graduates homemakers, dietitians, home extension agents, and educators for North Dakota.

The Graduate School, which offers advanced degrees in the fields cited above.

When the name change is authorized, these "schools" will be known as "colleges." The school of agriculture will be designated College of Agriculture, thus continuing a 68-year agricultural college tradition.

A name change in no way lessens the importance and contribution of the present agricultural facilities of the institution to the people of North Dakota. Many outstanding colleges of agriculture are parts of state universities. Examples are Michigan State University, Purdue University and the Universities of Minnesota, Wisconsin, Illinois, and Nebraska.

In fact, the College of Agriculture, as well as other colleges on the NDAC campus, will gain added and deserved prestige by being part of a North Dakota State University.

Eighty-three percent of the present students at NDAC are majoring in non-agricultural curricula. A name change to North Dakota State University is highly desirable in order to appropriately accommodate these students, who

The College Becomes a University 253

make up the vast majority of NDAC enrollment, as they apply for jobs throughout the world in their specialized fields.

The name change proposal is no sudden action in response to institutional vanity. It involved the same extended study that prompted 83 percent of the other separated *land-grant* colleges in the United States to seek and officially receive a name change.

In the spring of the next year, the president of the student body submitted a petition to President Hultz to be presented to the State Board of Higher Education. The petition, signed by 84 percent of the student body, asked that the name of the North Dakota Agricultural College be changed to North Dakota State University. The State Board was asked to place the name change before the 1959 Legislature. On April 21, 1958, the State Board of Higher Education by a six to one vote turned down the student request, stating that the Board is "dedicated to a program built around the continued strengthening and advancement of agriculture." In a reply Dr. A. E. Mead, commissioner, also indicated that it was doubtful if the name could be legally changed without a constitutional amendment, and that a change of name should be decided by a vote of the entire citizenry of the State.

After the action of the Board the students decided to initiate an amendment to the constitution changing the legal name from the "Agricultural College of Fargo" to the "North Dakota State University of Agriculture and Applied Science." Sufficient signers for the measure were secured through the support of many organizations all over the State, and it was placed on the ballot for the general election on November 4, 1958. In the election the initiated measure was defeated by a narrow margin; the total "Yes" vote was 61,470, the "No" vote 71,960.

However, campus leaders were not discouraged by the defeat of the initiated measure. On the front page of the next *Spectrum*, on November 7, 1958, appeared the following editorial:

Look For . . .
A Silver Lining

"The people have spoken.

"The votes have been cast and the ballots counted. And at first glance it would be easy to come to the conclusion that the North Dakota Agricultural College has suffered a serious defeat.

"But let us not look lightly at the election result. Let's examine the score and see what the score really is.

"Rather than having suffered a serious defeat, we have been offered by the voters of North Dakota an encouraging response. And this is not semantic doubletalk.

"The fact is that the proposal to change the name of the college was defeated by a relatively small number of votes. At last count, before all returns were in, the decision was rendered by as few as eight persons per precinct. When this is viewed in its proper perspective, alongside the overwhelming "No" votes cast against the other amendments, it becomes apparent that the defeat was registered by voters who, bewildered by an overly long ballot, cast a consecutive string of negative votes on all amendments.

"We can be encouraged by the great number of votes cast in favor of the name change. This suggests that we have made a favorable impression in the minds of the voters of North Dakota. It suggests that the present has had its moment of darkness but that the future is a bright one and the path from here is one lighted by optimism.

"Let us not be downcast. Instead, let us thank the voters of North Dakota for their wise encouragement. Let us thank them for their recognition that we are, have been, and will continue to be a University in our actions, in our service, in our purpose, and in our devotion to the people of this great state."

In October, 1958, a report of a *"Survey of Higher Education in North Dakota"* was published in Washington, D.C., Department of Health, Education and Welfare. This survey had been requested by the North Dakota Legislative Research Committee and by the State Board of Higher Education. An intensive study of the existing institutions of higher education in the State, including the social and economic setting for higher education in North Dakota, was made by a committee of educators from outside of the State. In it were studied the programs of instruction, research and service, the training, teaching loads and salaries of the faculties of the various institutions and their physical facilities.

As to the North Dakota Agricultural College the survey approved the contemplated change of the institution to a university. However, in connection with the survey of the College it also made some suggestions in regard to the growth and expansion of the School of Arts and Sciences. A true university structure would include geology, physics and chemical technology in addition to its existing departments. A School of Education should include agricultural and home economics education and library science, and the College should be given approval to train elementary school teachers and to grant degrees in elementary education. Library holdings should be expanded in the arts and sciences, particularly in the fields of psychology and education. If the Agricultural College is given the authority to grant the doctorate degree, the first step should be in the field of chemistry, in which there is a very strong staff. However, the staffs in mathematics and physics should be strengthened and increased expenditures made for equipment and the library. As to physical facilities, an auditorium-classroom building, a pharmacy building, a new chemistry building, a

The College Becomes a University

men's dormitory and a branch experiment station were needed, according to this survey.[4]

In January, 1959, the State Board of Higher Education authorized the North Dakota Agricultural College to award the degree of Doctor of Philosophy to qualified candidates in the fields of plant science, animal science, pharmacy and entomology; later chemical technology was added to the list. Although 18 master's degrees had been granted by the College before 1954, it was in that year that the College set up a graduate program at the master's level, with Dr. Glenn S. Smith as dean of the Graduate School.

In May, 1959, students and alumni were laying the foundation for another appeal by vote to change the name of the College in 1960. Robert L. Owens, president of the Cass-Clay Chapter of the Alumni Association, spearheaded the preliminary work. By December, 1959, a committee of 15 members from all sections of North Dakota was chosen, with Robert and Shirley Nasset of Regent, N. Dak., as co-chairmen. Chairmen in all the 53 counties in the State were appointed in order to secure signatures for another amendment to the constitution of the State. In August, 1960, petitions with more than 34,000 signatures were submitted to the secretary of State.[5]

The name-change proposal was placed on the ballot to be voted on by North Dakotans on November 8, 1960. The advocates of the change were cheered by the news that four more land-grant institutions, Iowa State College, Kansas State College, Washington State College, and Alabama Agricultural and Mechanical College, had become universities within the past year. The students as well as the alumni deserve much credit in organizing and presenting the facts which they believed justified the change. This was done voluntarily in most of the communities in the State.

At the November election, the proposal to change the name of the North Dakota Agricultural College to North Dakota State University of Agriculture and Applied Science was approved by a two to one margin, the vote being 153,409 "Yes" and 73,827 "No." This recognition by the voters of the State corrected a misleading conception which had existed for a number of years and so in December 1960 the College became a University in name as in fact.[6]

In the November election of 1960 William L. Guy, a graduate from the North Dakota Agricultural College in 1941, was elected governor of the State of North Dakota on the Democratic ticket. Mr. Guy after receiving his master's degree in agricultural economics in 1946 had also been a part-time instructor in agricultural economics at the College for several years. When elected governor he was farming near Amenia in Cass County

These developments end the successful campaign to change the name of North Dakota's Agricultural College. They are in line with a new conception of the future function of land-grant institutions in general. In 1959 President Hannah of Michigan State University appointed a committee on the "Future of the University." This committee found four major precepts as characterizing the educational philosophy of land-grant institutions.

"A fundamental assumption of the philosophy underlying the land grant university is the desirability of equality of educational opportunity at the university level. In part, this assumption is based upon the democratic philosophy epitomized by Abraham Lincoln. In part, it is based on the equally tenable basis that modern society needs many highly trained individuals. Originally the Land-Grant College Act provided for institutions of higher learning that would devote themselves to the education of the agricultural and industrial classes. Furthermore, the land-grant institution presented the opportunity to those who were not necessarily rich and well-born to become educated and to perform a variety of useful roles in society.

"A second precept of the land-grant philosophy is the desirability of providing a broad liberal education for students who are also interested in technical or professional training. This has often been overlooked by proponents of the land-grant philosophy, but it was clearly expounded by the early leaders of the movement. Moreover, it is increasingly clear that education for citizenship and for a full and satisfying life requires far more than a good technical or professional education. A university that does not enable its graduates to understand their own culture must count itself a failure. In addition, in the world today, a university must enable its graduates to grasp the significance of events in the world outside of their immediate culture.

"The third feature of the land-grant philosophy is that the university should use its knowledge and facilities for solving the significant problems of society. At the point in time when the land-grant system was founded, the major needs of society were related to the development of agriculture. Shortly thereafter, the development of mechanic arts became a necessity to support an expanding industrial society. *The true genius of the land-grant institution is that it relates itself to the developing major needs of a society rather than being frozen to a particular pattern of emphasis which may be increasingly less relevant.* Another facet of this third characteristic is the recognition of the university's responsibility to carry knowledge to the people through extension and continuing education programs.

"A fourth precept of the land-grant philosophy is that the university ought to be a mechanism for change in society. Land-grant universities must not become so oriented to the problems of today that they do not look toward to the solution of the problems of tomorrow. In the present day, the land-grant institution must recognize that society has changed and that the agricultural and industrial urban portions of our society are no longer separate. No longer is our society largely aloof from the rest of the world. Thus, the land-grant institution must continue to modify its emphasis to include new developmental needs and to find new ways to serve the needs of society, for no group in our modern society can be reached in quite the same way as the agricultural group was in the past."[7]

Already most of the early land-grant colleges attempted to combine liberal and vocational education at the college level. A study of the catalogs of North Dakota Agricultural College during the nineties shows that its curriculum also included a large proportion of courses in the liberal arts. No doubt this was necessary because the technical and scientific fields were not sufficiently developed to provide course work.

The land-grant institutions in the present day which remain dedicated solely to an agricultural, veterinary, home economics and engineering orientation would be archaic and would find themselves shortly relegated to a minor educational role. Our society and our economy have changed and the land-grant institutions can serve their original purpose not only by adhering to it but also by changing with the advancing times.

The future of the North Dakota State University of Agriculture and Applied Science will depend on the combined efforts of its administration, its staff of teachers and experimenters, its students and its alumni. And their efforts will have to rest upon the support given by the people of North Dakota through its Legislature. The amount and nature of the research, the quality of its teaching, the character of the distribution of information through extension, will depend upon the popular understanding of the function of a university. May this institution, which has been a beacon across the prairie, shine with greater clarity and intensity in the years to come. May the youth educated at North Dakota State University serve the State and nation with devotion and steadfastness far into the future.

FOOTNOTES

[1] *Spectrum*, Mar. 5, 1926.
[2] *Spectrum*, Mar. 12, 1926.
[3] *State College Engineer*, I, 1, June, 1926, 4.
[4] Office of Education, Department of Health, Education and Welfare. *Higher Education in North Dakota* (Washington, 1958).
[5] The initiative petition for a constitutional amendment reads as follows:

FOR CONSTITUTIONAL AMENDMENT

"We, the undersigned, qualified electors of the State of North Dakota, consisting of more than twenty thousand of the electors at large, hereby propose to initiate and enact the following amendment to the Constitution of the State of North Dakota, and we request that the same be placed upon the ballot in the manner and form provided by law, and submitted to the qualified electors of the State of North Dakota, for their approval or rejection at the General Election to be held in November 1960, in accordance with the provisions of Section 202 of Article XV of the Constitution of the State of North Dakota, as amended.

As such petitioners, we hereby present and propose the following Ballot Title and amendment to the Constitution as follows, to wit:

An Initiative Petition to amend and reenact the Third Paragraph of Section 215 of Article XIX of the Constitution of the State of North Dakota to change the name of the Agricultural College to "The North Dakota State University of Agriculture and Applied Science."

BE IT ENACTED BY THE PEOPLE OF THE STATE OF NORTH DAKOTA:

Paragraph Third of Section 215 of Article XIX of the Constitution of the State of North Dakota, as amended, is hereby amended and reenacted to read as follows:

Third: The North Dakota State University of Agriculture and Applied Science at the city of Fargo, in the county of Cass.

[6] The North Dakota Legislature of 1961 passed House Bill 117, introduced by its members Stockman, Baldwin, Boe, Idso, Aamoth, Otis and Trom. It was designated as an Act to amend and reenact Sec. 15-12-01 of the North Dakota century code relating to the location and official name of the North Dakota State University of Agriculture and Applied Science.

[7] Paul Dressel, *"General Education in a Land-Grant College."* Address given on Jan. 14, 1960 at N.D.A.C., copy in the Library.

Appendices, Bibliography, and Index

Appendices

I – FIRST MORRILL ACT

An Act donating Public Lands to the several States and Territories which may provide Colleges for the Benefit of Agricultural and the Mechanic Arts.

Be it enacted by the Senate and House of Representatives of the United States of America in Congress assembled, That there be granted to the several States for the purposes hereinafter mentioned, an amount of public land, to be apportioned to each State a quantity equal to thirty thousand acres for each senator and representative in Congress to which the States are respectively entitled by the apportionment under the census of eighteen hundred and sixty: *Provided,* That no mineral lands shall be selected or purchased under the provisions of this act.

SEC. 2. *And be it further enacted,* That the land aforesaid, after being surveyed, shall be apportioned to the several States in sections or subdivisions of sections, not less than one-quarter of a section; and whenever there are public lands in a State subject to sale at private entry at one dollar and twenty-five cents per acre, the quantity to which said State shall be entitled shall be selected from such lands within the limits of such State, and the Secretary of the Interior is hereby directed to issue to each of the States in which there is not the quantity of public lands subject to sale at private entry at one dollar and twenty-five cents per acre, to which said State may be entitled under the provisions of this act land scrip to the amount in acres for the deficiency of its distributive share: said scrip to be sold by said States and the proceeds thereof applied to the uses and purposes prescribed in this act and for no other use or purpose whatsoever: *Provided,* That in no case shall any State to which land scrip may thus be issued be allowed to locate the same within the limits of any other State, or of any Territory of the United States, but their assignees may thus locate said land scrip upon any of the unappropriated lands of the United States subject to sale at private entry at one dollar and twenty-five cents, or less, per acre: *And provided further,* That not more than one million acres shall be located by such assignees in any one of the States: *And provided further,* That no such location shall be made before one year from the passage of this act.

SEC. 3. *And be it further enacted,* That all the expenses of management, superintendence, and taxes from date of selection of said land, previous to their sales, and all expenses incurred in the management and disbursement of the moneys which may be received therefrom, shall be paid by the States to which they may belong, out of the treasury of said States, so that the entire proceeds of the sale of said lands shall be applied without any diminution whatever to the purposes hereinafter mentioned.

SEC. 4. (original). *And be it further enacted,* That all moneys derived from the sale of the lands aforesaid by the States to which the lands are apportioned, and from the sales of land scrip hereinbefore provided for, shall be invested in stocks of the United States, or of the States, or some other safe stocks, yielding not less than five per centum upon the par value of said stocks; and that the moneys so invested shall constitute a perpetual fund, the capital of which shall remain forever undiminished, (except so far as may be provided in section five of this act,) and the interest of which shall be inviolably appropriated, by each State which may take and claim the benefit of this act, to the endowment, support, and maintenance of at least one college where the leading object shall be, without excluding other scientific and classical studies, and including military tactics, to teach such branches of learning as are related to agriculture and the mechanic arts, in such manner as the legislatures of the States may respectively prescribe, in order to promote the liberal and practical education of the industrial classes in the several pursuits and professions in life.

SEC. 4. (as amended March 3, 1883). That all moneys derived from the sale of lands aforesaid by the States to which the lands are apportioned, and from the sales of land-scrip hereinbefore provided for, shall be invested in stocks of the United States or of the States, or some other safe stocks; or the same may be invested by the States having no State stocks, in any other manner after the legislatures of such States shall have assented thereto, and engaged that such funds shall yield not less than five per centum upon the amount so invested and that the principal thereof shall forever remain unimpaired: *Provided,* That the money so invested or loaned shall constitute a perpetual fund, the capital of which shall remain forever undiminished (except so far as may be provided in section five of this act), and the interest of which shall be inviolably appropriated, by each State which may take and claim the benefit of this act, to the endowment, support, and maintenance of at least one college where the leading object shall be without excluding other scientific and classical studies, and including military tactics, to teach such branches of learning as are related to agriculture and the mechanic arts, in such manner as the legislatures of the States may respectively prescribe, in order to promote the liberal and practical education of the industrial classes in the several pursuits and professions in life.

SEC. 5. *And be it further enacted,* That the grant of land and land scrip hereby authorized shall be made on the following conditions, to which, as well as to the provisions hereinbefore contained, the previous assent of the several states shall be signified by legislative acts:

First. If any portion of the fund invested, as provided by the foregoing section, or any portion of the interest thereon, shall, by any action or contingency, be diminished or lost, it shall be replaced by the State to which it belongs, so that the capital of the fund shall remain forever undiminished; and the annual interest shall be regularly applied without diminution to the purposes mentioned in the fourth section of this act, except that a sum, not exceeding ten per centum upon the amount received by any State under the provisions of this act, may be expended for the purchase of lands for sites or experimental farms whenever authorized by the respective legislatures of said States.

Second. No portion of said fund, nor the interest thereon, shall be applied, directly or indirectly, under any pretense whatever, to the purchase, erection, preservation, or repair of any building or buildings.

Third. Any State which may take and claim the benefit of the provisions of this act shall provide, within five years, at least not less than one college, as described in the fourth section of this act, or the grant to such State shall cease; and said State shall be bound to pay the United States the amount received of any lands previously sold, and that the title to purchasers under the State shall be valid.

Fourth. An annual report shall be made regarding the progress of each college, recording any improvements and experiments made, with their cost and results and such other matters, including State industrial and economical statistics, as may be supposed useful; one copy of which shall be transmitted by mail free, by each, to all the other colleges which may be endowed under the provisions of this act, and also one copy to the Secretary of the Interior.

Fifth. When lands shall be selected from those which have been raised to double the minimum price, in consequence of railroad grants, they shall be computed to the States at the maximum price, and the number of acres proportionately diminished.

Sixth. No State while in a condition of rebellion or insurrection against the Government of the United States shall be entitled to the benefits of this act.

Seventh. No State shall be entitled to the benefits of this act unless it shall express its acceptance thereof by its legislature within two years from the date of its approval by the President.

SEC. 6. *And be it further enacted,* That land scrip issued under the provisions of this act shall not be subject to location until after the first day of January, one thousand eight hundred and sixty-three.

SEC. 7. *And be it further enacted,* That the land officers shall receive the same fees for locating land scrip issued under the provisions of this act as is now allowed for the location of military bounty land warrants under existing laws; *Provided*, their maximum compensation shall not be thereby increased.

SEC. 8. *And be it further enacted,* That the Governors of the several states to which scrip shall be issued under this act shall be required to report annually to Congress all sales made of such scrip until the whole shall be disposed of, the amount received for the same, and what appropriation has been made of the proceeds.

Approved, July 2, 1862.

II – HATCH ACT

An Act to establish agricultural experiment stations in connection with the colleges established in the several States under the provisions of an act approved July second, eighteen hundred and sixty-two, and of the acts supplementary thereto.

Be it enacted by the Senate and House of Representatives of the United States of America in Congress assembled, That in order to aid in acquiring and diffusing among the people of the United States useful and practical information on subjects connected with agriculture, and to promote scientific investigation and experiment respecting the principles and applications of agricultural science, there shall be established, under direction of the college or colleges or agricultural department of colleges in each State or Territory established, or which may hereafter be established, in accordance with the provisions of an act approved July second, eighteen hundred and sixty-two, entitled "An act donating public lands to the several States and Territories which may provide colleges for the benefit of agriculture and the mechanic arts," or any of the supplements to said act, a department to be known and designated as an "agricultural experiment station:" *Provided,* That in any State or Territory in which two such colleges have been or may be so established the appropriation hereinafter made to such State or Territory shall be equally divided between such colleges, unless the legislature of such State or Territory shall otherwise direct.

SEC. 2. That it shall be the object and duty of said experiment stations to conduct original researches or verify experiments on the physiology of plants and animals; the diseases to which they are severally subject, with the remedies for the same; the chemical composition of useful plants at their different stages of growth; the comparative advantages of rotative cropping as pursued under a varying series of crops; the capacity of new plants or trees for acclimation; the analysis of soils and water; the chemical composition of manures, natural or artificial, with experiments designed to test their comparative effects on crops of different kinds; the adaptation and value of grasses and forage plants; the composition and digestibility of the different kinds of food for domestic animals; the scientific and economic questions involved in the production of butter and cheese; and such other researches or experiments bearing directly on the agricultural industry of the United States as may in each case be deemed advisable, having due regard to the varying conditions and needs of the respective States and Territories.

SEC. 3. That in order to secure, as far as practicable, uniformity of methods and results in the work of said stations, it shall be the duty of the United States Commissioner (now Secretary) of Agriculture to furnish forms, as far as practicable, for the tabulation of results of investigation or experiment; to indicate, from time to time such lines of inquiry as to him shall seem most important; and, in general, to furnish such advice and assistance as will best promote the purposes of this act. It shall be the duty of each of said stations, annually, on or before the first day of February, to make to the governor of the State or Territory in which it is located a full and detailed report of its operations, including a statement of receipts and expenditures, a copy of which report shall be sent to each of said stations, to the said Commissioner (now Secretary) of Agriculture, and to the Secretary of the Treasury of the United States.

SEC. 4. That bulletins or reports of progress shall be published at said stations at least once in three months, one copy of which shall be sent to each newspaper in the States or Territories in which they are respectively located, and to such individuals actually engaged in farming as may request the same, and as far as the means of the station will permit. Such bulletins or reports and the annual reports of said stations shall be transmitted in the mails of the United States free of charge for postage, under such regulations as the Postmaster-General may from time to time prescribe.

SEC. 5. That for the purpose of paying the necessary expenses of conducting investigations and experiments and printing and distributing the results as hereinbefore prescribed, the sum of fifteen thousand dollars per annum is hereby appropriated to each State, to be specially provided for by Congress in the appropriations from year to year, and to each Territory entitled under the provisions of section eight of this act, out of any money in the Treasury proceeding from the sales of public lands, to be paid in equal quarterly payments, on the first day of January, April, July, and October in each year, to the treasurer or other officer duly appointed by the governing boards of said colleges to receive the same, the first payment to be made on the first day of October, eighteen hundred and eighty-seven: *Provided, however,* That out of the first annual appropriation so received by any station an amount not exceeding one-fifth may be expended in the erection, enlargement, or repair of a building or buildings necessary for carrying on the work of such station; and thereafter an amount not exceeding five per centum of such annual appropriation may be so expended.

SEC. 6. That whenever it shall appear to the Secretary of the Treasury from the annual statement of receipts and expenditures of any of said stations that a portion of the preceding annual appropriation remains unexpended, such amount shall be deducted from the next succeeding annual appropriation to such station, in order that the amount of money appropriated to any station shall not exceed the amount actually and necessarily required for its maintenance and support.

SEC. 7. That nothing in this act shall be construed to impair or modify the legal relation existing between any of the said colleges and the government of the States or Territories in which they are respectively located.

SEC. 8. That in States having colleges entitled under this section to the benefits of this act and having also agricultural experiment stations established by law separate from said colleges, such States shall be authorized to apply such benefits to experiments at stations so established by such States; and in case any State shall have established under the provisions of said act of July second aforesaid, an agricultural department or experimental station, in connection with any university, college or institution not distinctively an agricultural college or school, and such State shall have established or shall hereafter establish a separate agricultural college or school, which shall have connected therewith an experimental farm or station, the legislature of such State may apply in whole or in part the appropriation by this act made, to such separate agricultural college, or school, and no legislature shall by contract express or implied disable itself from so doing.

SEC. 9. That the grants of moneys authorized by this act are made subject to the legislative assent of the several States and Territories to the purposes of said grants: *Provided,* That payment of such installments of the appropriation herein made as shall become due to any State before the adjournment of the regular session of its legislature meeting next after the passage of this act shall be made upon the assent of the governor thereof duly certified to the Secretary of the Treasury.

SEC. 10. Nothing in this act shall be held or construed as binding the United

States to continue any payments from the Treasury to any or all the States or institutions mentioned in this act, but Congress may at any time amend suspend or repeal any or all the provisions of this act.

Approved, March 2, 1887.

III – SMITH-LEVER ACT

An Act to provide for cooperative agricultural extension work between the agricultural colleges in the several States receiving the benefits of an Act of Congress approved July second, eighteen hundred and sixty-two, and of Acts supplementary thereto, and the United States Department of Agriculture.

Be it enacted by the Senate and House of Representatives of the United States of America in Congress assembled, That in order to aid in diffusing among the people of the United States useful and practical information on subjects relating to agriculture and home economics, and to encourage the application of the same, there may be inaugurated in connection with the college or colleges in each State now receiving, or which may hereafter receive, the benefits of the Act of Congress approved July second, eighteen hundred and sixty-two, entitled "An Act donating public lands to the several States and Territories which may provide colleges for the benefit of agriculture and the mechanic arts" (Twelfth Statutes at Large, page five hundred and three), and of the Act of Congress approved August thirtieth, eighteen hundred and ninety (Twenty-sixth Statutes at Large, page four hundred and seventeen and chapter eight hundred and forty-one), agricultural extension work which shall be carried on in cooperation with the United States Department of Agriculture: *Provided,* That in any State in which two or more such colleges have been or hereafter may be established the appropriations hereinafter made to such State shall be administered by such college or colleges as the legislature of such State may direct: *Provided further,* That, pending the inauguration and development of the cooperative extension work herein authorized, nothing in this Act shall be construed to discontinue either the farm management work or the farmers' cooperative demonstration work as now conducted by the Bureau of Plant Industry of the Department of Agriculture.

SEC. 2. That cooperative agricultural extension work shall consist of the giving of instruction and practical demonstrations in agriculture and home economics to persons not attending or resident in said colleges in the several communities, and imparting to such persons information on said subjects through field demonstrations, publications, and other-wise; and this work shall be carried on in such manner as may be mutually agreed upon by the Secretary of Agriculture and the State agricultural college or colleges receiving the benefits of this act.

SEC. 3. That for the purpose of paying the expenses of said cooperative agricultural extension work and the necessary printing and distributing of information in connection with the same, there is permanently appropriated, out of any money in the Treasury not otherwise appropriated, the sum of $480,000 for each year, $10,000 of which shall be paid annually, in the manner hereinafter provided, to each State which shall by action of its legislature assent to the provisions of this Act: *Provided,* That payment of such installments of the appropriation hereinbefore made as shall become due to any State before the adjournment of the regular session of the legislature meeting next after the passage of this Act may, in the absence of prior legislative assent, be made upon the assent of the governor thereof, duly certified to the Secretary of the Treasury: *Provided further,* That there is also appropriated an additional sum of $600,000 for the fiscal year following that in which the foregoing appropriation first becomes available, and for each year thereafter for seven years a sum exceeding by $500,000 the sum appropriated for each preceding year, and for each year thereafter there is permanently appropriated for each year the sum of $4,100,000 in addition to the sum of $480,000 hereinbefore provided: *Provided further,* That before the funds herein appropriated shall become available to any college for any fiscal year plans for the work to be carried on under this Act shall be submitted by the proper officials of each college and approved by the Secretary of Agriculture. Such additional sums shall be used only for the purposes hereinbefore stated, and shall be allotted annually to each State by the Secretary of Agriculture and paid in the manner hereinbefore provided, in the proportion which the rural population of each State bears to the total rural population of all the States as determined by the next preceding Federal census: *Provided further,* That no payment out of the additional appropriations herein provided shall be made in any year to any State until an equal sum has been appropriated for that year by the legislature of such State, or provided by State, county, college, local authority, or individual contributions from within the State, for the maintenance of the cooperative agricultural extension work provided for in this Act.

SEC. 4. That the sums hereby appropriated for extension work shall be paid in equal semiannual payments on the first day of January and July of each year by the Secretary of the Treasury upon the warrant of the Secretary of Agriculture, out of the Treasury of the United States, to the treasurer or other officer of the State duly authorized by the laws of the State to receive the same; and such officer shall be required to report to the Secretary of Agriculture, on or before the first day of September of each year, a detailed statement of the amount so received during the previous fiscal year, and of its disbursement, on forms prescribed by the Secretary of Agriculture.

SEC. 5. That if any portion of the moneys received by the designated officer of any State for the support and maintenance of cooperative agricultural extension work, as provided in this Act, shall by any action or contingency be diminished or lost, or be misapplied, it shall be replaced by said State to which it belongs, and until so replaced no subsequent appropriation shall be apportioned or paid to said state, and no portion of said moneys shall be applied, directly or indirectly, to the purchase, erection, preservation, or repair of any building or buildings, or the purchase or rental of land, or in college-course-teaching, lectures in colleges, promoting agricultural trains, or any other purpose not specified in this Act, and not more than five per centum of each annual appropriation shall be applied to the printing and distribution of publications. It shall be the duty of each of said colleges annually, on or before the first day of January, to make to the governor of the State in which it is located a full and detailed report of its operations in the direction of extension work as defined in this Act, including a detailed statement of receipts and expenditures from all sources for this purpose, a copy of which report shall be sent to the Secretary of Agriculture and to the Secretary of the Treasury of the United States.

SEC. 6. That on or before the first day of July in each year after the passage of this Act the Secretary of Agriculture shall ascertain and certify to the Secretary of the Treasury as to each State whether it is entitled to receive its share of the annual appropriation for cooperative agricultural extension work under this Act, and the amount which it is entitled to receive. If the Secretary of Agriculture shall withhold a certificate from any State of its appropriation, the facts and reasons therefor shall be reported to the President, and the amount involved shall be kept separate in the Treasury until the expiration of the Congress next succeeding a session of the legislature of any State from which a certificate has been withheld, in order that the State may, if it should so desire, appeal to Congress from the determination of the Secretary of Agriculture. If the next Congress shall not direct such sum to be paid, it shall be covered into the Treasury.

SEC. 7. That the Secretary of Agriculture shall make an annual report to Congress of the receipts, expenditures, and results of the cooperative agricultural extension work in all of the States receiving the benefits of this Act, and also whether the appropriation of any State has been withheld, and if so, the reasons therefor.

SEC. 8. That Congress may at any time alter, amend, or repeal any or all of the provisions of this Act.

Approved, May 8, 1914.

IV – CONSTITUTIONAL AMENDMENT ESTABLISHING A STATE BOARD OF HIGHER EDUCATION

(Submitted by Initiative Petition:)

1. A board of higher education, to be officially known as the State Board of Higher Education, is hereby created for the control and administration of the following state educational institutions, to-wit:
    (1) The State University and School of Mines, at Grand Forks, with their substations.
    (2) The State Agricultural College and Experiment Station, at Fargo, with their substations.
    (3) The School of Science, at Wahpeton.
    (4) The State Normal Schools and Teachers Colleges, at Valley City, Mayville, Minot and Dickinson.
    (5) The Normal and Industrial School, at Ellendale.
    (6) The School of Forestry, at Bottineau.
    (7) And such other State institutions of higher education as may hereafter be established.

2. (a) The State Board of Higher Education shall consist of seven (7) members, all of whom shall be qualified electors and taxpayers of the State, and who shall have resided in this State for not less than five (5) years immediately preceding their appointment, to be appointed by the Governor, by and with the consent of the Senate, from a list of names selected as herein-

after provided. There shall not be on said board more than one (1) alumnus or former student of any one of the institutions under the jurisdiction of said State Board of Higher Education at any one time. No person employed by any institution under the control of the board shall serve as a member of said board, nor shall any employee of any such institution be eligible for membership on the State Board of Higher Education for a period of two (2) years following the termination of his employment.

On or before the 1st day of February, 1939, the Governor shall nominate from a list of three names for each position, selected by the unanimous action of the President of the North Dakota Educational Association, the Chief Justice of the Supreme Court, and the Superintendent of Public Instruction, and, with the consent of a majority of the members-elect of the Senate, shall appoint from such list as such State Board of Higher Education seven (7) members, whose terms shall commence on the 1st day of July, 1939, one of which terms shall expire on the 30th day of June 1940, and one on the 30th day of June in each of the years 1941, 1942, 1943, 1944, 1945, and 1946. The term of office of members appointed to fill vacancies at the expiration of said terms shall be for seven (7) years, and in the case of vacancies otherwise arising, appointments shall be made only for the balance of the term of the members whose places are to be filled.

(b) In the event any nomination made by the Governor is not consented to and confirmed by the Senate as hereinbefore provided, the Governor shall again nominate a candidate for such office, selected from a new list, prepared in the manner hereinbefore provided, which nomination shall be submitted to the Senate for confirmation, and said proceedings shall be continued until such appointments have been confirmed by the Senate, or the session of the legislature shall have adjourned.

(c) When any term expires or a vacancy occurs when the legislature is not in session, the Governor may appoint from a list selected as hereinbefore provided, a member who shall serve until the opening of the next session of the legislature, at which time his appointment shall be certified to the Senate for confirmation, as above provided; and if the appointment be not confirmed by the thirtieth legislative day of such session, his office shall be deemed vacant and the Governor shall nominate from a list selected as hereinbefore provided, another candidate for such office and the same proceedings shall be followed as are above set forth; provided further, that when the legislature shall be in session at any time within six (6) months prior to the date of the expiration of the term of any member, the Governor shall nominate his successor from a list selected as above set forth, within the first thirty (30) days of such session, and upon confirmation by the Senate such successor shall take office at the expiration of the term of the incumbent. No person who has been nominated and whose nomination the Senate has failed to confirm, shall be eligible for an interim appointment.

3. The members of the State Board of Higher Education may only be removed by impeachment for the offenses and in the manner and according to the procedure provided for the removal of the Governor by impeachment proceedings.

4. The appointive members of the State Board of Higher Education shall receive seven dollars ($7.00) per day and their necessary expenses for travel while attending meetings, or in the performances of such special duties as the

board may direct; provided, however, no member shall receive total expense money in excess of five hundred dollars ($500.00) in any calendar year.

5. The legislature shall provide adequate funds for the proper carrying out of the function and duties of the State Board of Higher Education.

6. (a) The State Board of Higher Education shall hold its first meeting at the office of the State Board of Administration at Bismarck, on the 6th day of July, 1939, and shall organize and elect one of its members as president of such board for a term of one year. It shall also at said meeting, or as soon thereafter as may be practicable, elect a competent person as secretary, who shall reside during his term of office in the City of Bismarck, North Dakota. Said secretary shall hold office at the will of the board. As soon as said board is established and organized, it shall assume all the powers and perform all the duties now conferred by law upon the Board of Administration in connection with the several institutions hereinbefore mentioned, and the said Board of Administration shall immediately upon the organization of said Board of Higher Education, surrender and transfer to said State Board of Higher Education all duties, rights and powers granted to it under the existing laws of the State concerning the institutions hereinbefore mentioned, together with all property, deeds, records, reports and appurtenances of every kind belonging or appertaining to said institutions.

(b) The State Board of Higher Education shall have full authority over the institutions under its control with the right, among its other powers, to prescribe, limit, or modify the courses offered at the several institutions. In furtherance of its powers, the State Board of Higher Education shall have the power to delegate to its employees details of the administration of the institutions under its control. The said State Board of Higher Education shall have full authority to organize or re-organize within constitutional and statutory limitations, the work of each institution under its control, and do each and everything necessary and proper for the efficient and economic administration of said State educational institutions.

(c) Said board shall prescribe for all of said institutions standard systems of accounts and records and shall biennially, and within six (6) months immediately preceding the regular session of the legislature, make a report to the Governor, covering in detail the operations of the educational institutions under it control.

(d) It shall be the duty of the heads of the several State institutions hereinbefore mentioned, to submit the budget requests for the biennial appropriations for said institutions to said State Board of Higher Education; and said State Board of Higher Education shall consider said budgets and shall revise the same as in its judgment shall be for the best interests of the educational system of the State; and thereafter the State Board of Higher Education shall prepare and present to the State Budget Board and to the legislature a single unified budget covering the needs of all the institutions under its control. "Said budget shall be prepared and presented by the Board of Administration until the State Board of Higher Education organizes as provided in Section 6 (a)." The appropriations for all of said institutions shall be contained in one legislative measure.

(e) The said State Board of Higher Education shall have the control of the expenditure of the funds belonging to, and allocated to such institutions and also those appropriated by the legislature, for the institutions of higher edu-

Appendices

cation in this State; provided, however, that fund appropriated by the legislature and specifically designated for any one or more of such institutions, shall not be used for any other institution.

7. (a) The State Board of Higher Education shall, as soon as practicable, appoint for a term of not to exceed three (3) years, a State Commissioner of Higher Education, whose principal office shall be at the State Capitol, in the City of Bismarck. Said Commissioner of Higher Education shall be responsible to the State Board of Higher Education and shall be removable by said board for cause.

(b) The State Commissioner of Higher Education shall be a graduate of some reputable college or university, and who by training and experience is familiar with the problems peculiar to higher education.

(c) Such Commissioner of Higher Education shall be the chief executive officer of said State Board of Higher Education, and shall perform such duties as shall be prescribed by the board.

8. This constitutional provision shall be self-executing and shall become effective without the necessity of legislative action.

Approved June 28, 1938.

V – MEMBERS OF THE GOVERNING BOARDS OF NORTH DAKOTA AGRICULTURAL COLLEGE

DIRECTORS, 1890–1896

O. W. Francis, Cass County, 1890–96, president, 1890–92
J. B. Power, Richland County, 1890–96, secretary
S. S. Lyon, Fargo, treasurer, 1890-96
E. M. Upson, Traill County, 1890–92
M. J. Sanderson, LaMoure, 1890-92
J. D. Wallace, Pembina, 1890-92
Jacob Lowell, Fargo, 1892-96
Peter McKenna, Fargo, 1892-96
H. F. Miller, Fargo, 1892-96, president, 1892-96
A. M. Tofthagen, Lakota, 1892-96
Joseph Deschenes, Grafton, 1892–96

TRUSTEES, 1896–1916

W. H. Robinson, Mayville, 1896-1903, 1905-07, president
J. O. Smith, Casselton, 1896-97, secretary
N. A. Lewis, treasurer, 1896-1901
H. J. Rusch, secretary, 1897-1904
L. R. Casey, Jamestown, 1896-1901
E. H. Dikes, Minot, 1896-97
Alex Stern, Fargo, 1896-1907, 1913-16
George E. Olsgard, Fargo, 1896-1903
Roger Allin, Grafton, 1897-1901
Edward M. Warren, LaMoure, 1897-1901
Maynard Crane, Cooperstown, 1901-05
B. N. Stone, LaMoure, 1901-09
S. S. Lyon, Fargo, 1901-07

L. B. Hanna, treasurer, 1901-04
Addison Leach, Warren, 1903-07
Chas. McKissick, Mayville, 1903-05
G. S. Barnes, Fargo, 1905-05
Eric B. Ramstad, Minot, 1905-06
T. B. Kulaas, Minot, 1906-07
L. R. Wallin, Washburn, 1905-09
Geo. H. Hollister, Fargo, 1907-16
C. N. Nelson, Mayville, 1907-09
Clark W. Kelley, Devils Lake, 1907-16
C. E. Nugent, secretary, 1907-09
James Radford, Warren, 1907-12
H. R. Hartman, Page, 1907-12
L. A. Ueland, Edgeley, 1909-11
Frank Sanford, Valley City, 1909-13
R. J. Bowen, Mohall, 1909-12
W. A. Yoder, secretary, 1909-16
W. P. Porterfield, treasurer, 1909-13
H. D. Mack, Dickey, 1911-13
C. E. Nugent, Fargo, 1912-16
Peter Elliot, Fargo, 1912-16
John Donnelly, Grafton, 1912-13
Eugene Weigel, Hebron, 1913-16
J. Fred Jensen, Westhope, 1913-16
Fred Irish, treasurer, 1913-16

REGENTS, 1916–20

Lewis F. Crawford, Sentinel Butte, 1916-20, president, 1916-19
Dr. John D. Taylor, Grand Forks, 1916-19
Frank White, Valley City, 1916-17
Emil Scow, Bowman, 1916-17
J. A. Power, Leonard, 1916-17
Chas. Brewer, Bismarck, secretary, 1916-18
Robert T. Muir, Sarles, 1917-20, president, 1919-20
George A. Totten, Bowman, 1917-20
Chas. E. Vermilya, Bismarck, 1918–20, vice-president
E. B. Craighead, Bismarch, commissioner
Chas. Liessman, Bismarck, secretary, 1918–20
Roscoe W. Beigle, Sawyer, 1919-20

BOARD OF ADMINISTRATION, 1920–39

P. M. Casey, Fargo, 1920-21
Robert T. Muir, Bismarck, 1920-23, president, 1922-23
Geo. A. Totten, Bismarck, 1920-25, president, 1920-22
Minnie J. Nielson, superintendent of public instruction, 1920-27
John N. Hagen, commissioner of agriculture and labor, 1920-22, 1938-39
Chas. Liessman, executive secretary, 1920–23
J. J. Cahill, Leith, 1921
J. A. Kitchen, Sentinel Butte, 1922-33
F. S. Talcott, Fargo, 1922-25

R. B. Murphy, Grafton, 1922-33, chairman, 1924-30
Ernest G. Wanner, executive secretary, 1923
H. P. Goddard, Bismarck, 1923-25
F. E. Deihl, Bowman, 1924-19
W. J. Church, York, 1926-31
Bertha R. Palmer, Bismarck, superintendent of public instruction, 1928-33
J. E. Davis, Fargo, 1930-35, chairman, 1930-32
Nelson Sauvain, Devils Lake, 1932-37, chairman, 1932-36
R. M. Rishworth, Jamestown, 1932-37
Laura B. Sanderson, LaMoure, 1932-37
A. E. Thompson, Washburn, superintendent of public instruction, 1933-39
John Husby, Finley, 1933-35
Mrs. Jennie Ulsrud, Bismarck, 1934-39, chairman, 1937-38
Theodore Martel, Bismarck, 1935-39
J. D. Harris, Bismarck, 1936-37
R. A. Kinzer, Bismarck, 1938-39
M. J. Forkner, Langdon, 1939, chairman, 1939
R. H. Sherman, La Moure, 1939
Math Dahl, commissioner of agriculture and labor, 1939

VI – MEMBERS OF THE STATE BOARD OF HIGHER EDUCATION SINCE 1939

P. J. Murphy, Grafton, 1939–42, president, 1939–41
Howard J. Henry, Westhope, 1939–1949, president, 1942–43
Merle Kidder, Towner, 1939–56
Mrs. Matt Crowley, Hebron, 1939–42
Lars W. Fredrickson, Pekin, 1939–51
F. J. Traynor, Devils Lake, 1939–52
Roy Johnson, Casselton, 1939–54, president 1941–42
R. B. Murphy, secretary, 1939–44
R. A. Trubey, Fargo, 1942–51, president, 1948–49
A. S. Marshall, Forbes, 1942–57
A. F. Arnason, commissioner, 1944–57
Dr. A. D. McCannel, Minot, 1949–, president, 1946–47, 1951–52, 1949–58
Frank P. Whitney, Dickinson, 1951–55, president 1954–55
D. W. Westbee, Grand Forks, 1951–58, president, 1956–57
Mrs. Mildred Johnson, Wahpeton, 1952–   , president, 1952–53, 1958–59
Gilman Wang, Cartwright, 1950–55
John W. Calnan, Bismarck, 1951–55
P. J. Donnelly, Grafton, 1953–55
Albert Haas, New Rockford, 1955–   , president, 1956–57
Martin G. Kruse, Kindred, 1955–60, president, 1959–60
M. L. Byrne, Bowman, 1955–
Mrs. Elvira Jestrab, Williston, 1955
A. E. Mead, commissioner, 1957–
C. W. Baker, Minot, 1957–
Fred R. Orth, Grand Forks, 1959
Ralph A. Christensen, Minot, 1960–
Ray Schnell, Dickinson, 1960–

VII – PRESIDENTS AND DIRECTORS OF THE NORTH DAKOTA AGRICULTURAL COLLEGE

Presidents:

Horace E. Stockbridge....1890–93
(J. B. Power............1893–95)
John H. Worst.........1895–1916
Edwin F. Ladd...........1916–21
John Lee Coulter........1921–29

John H. Shepperd........1929–37
(John C. West..........1937–38)
Frank L. Eversull........1938–46
John H. Longwell.......1946–48
Fred S. Hultz............1948–61

Directors of Experiment Station:

H. E. Stockbridge.........1890–93
J. B. Power...............1893–95
J. H. Worst.............1895–1913
Thomas Cooper...........1913–17
L. Van Es................1917–18

P. F. Trowbridge..........1918–34
H. L. Walster.....1934–37, 1939–53
H. C. Hanson.............1937–39
Glenn C. Holm...........1953–57
Arlon G. Hazen..........1957–

Directors of Extension Service:

Thomas Cooper...........1914–17
E. F. Ladd (acting).......1917–18
Gordon W. Randlett.......1918–26

Charles F. Monroe........1926–34
H. L. Walster............1934–37
George J. Baker (acting)..1938–39
E. J. Haslerud..........1939–1961

VIII – BLUE KEY – DOCTORS OF SERVICE

1930	"Doc" C. S. Putnam	1946	Prof. Ernst Van Vlissingen
1931	Professor H. L. Bolley	1948	Prof. A. Glenn Hill
1932	Professor O. O. Churchill, Richard Kraft	1950	Ben F. Meinecke
		1951	Percy F. Donnelly
1933	Dr. C. I. Nelson	1952	Roy Johnson
1934	Dean H. L. Walster	1953	Alfred H. Parrott
1935	Dr. L. R. Waldron	1954	Dean R. M. Dolve
1936	Prof. A. G. Arvold	1955	Dean W. F. Sudro
1937	Dr. W. C. Hunter	1956	William H. Euren
1938	Dean A. E. Minard	1957	Dean A. Pearl Dinan
1939	Dean C. B. Waldron	1958	Prof. T. E. Stoa
1940	Prof. O. A. Stevens	1959	Dr. Hale Aarnes
1941	Dean W. F. Sudro	1960	Dean R. E. Dunbar

IX – FACULTY AND STAFF MEMBERS WHO HAVE SERVED TEN YEARS OR MORE

(Stars indicate members who served 25 years or more)

A

Abrahamson, Paul K., county extension agent, 1934–46
Alberts, Howard C., herdsman, 1929–48
Altenburg, Martin E., county extension agent, 1934–45
*Anderson, A. W., mechanical engineering, 1934–

Appendices 275

Anderson, C. O., mechanical engineering, 1948–
Anderson, Edwin M., electrical engineering, 1949–
Anderson, Ernest G., electrical engineering, 1947–
Anderson, George E., carpenter, buildings, 1918–37
*Anderson, Harry G., extension agricultural economist, 1928–
*Anderson, Minnie, home economics, 1921–57
Anderson, Neva M., physical education, 1948–60
Andrews, Ethel, clerk, 1921–43
Andrews, Ralph, extension secretary, 1918–33
Armour, Herbert, painter, 1940–
*Arvold, A. G., speech, 1907–52

B

Bakken, Stewart E., mechanical engineering, 1946–
Bale, Stanley W., extension service supervisor, 1939–
Bales, Alba, dean, home economics, 1920–37, 1940–42
*Barrett, Ben, county extension agent, 1927–59
*Barton, O. A., poultry, 1918–52
Batt, Max, modern languages, 1902–16
Bell, Wm. B., zoology, 1906–16
Benton, Alva H., marketing, 1922–34
Bentson, Ben Charles, basketball coach, 1949–
*Berntson, Byron, extension district supervisor, 1934–
Bolin, Donald W., animal nutrition, 1945–
Bolin, F. M., veterinary science, 1938–
Bolin, Margaret, economics, 1946–
*Bolley, H. L., biology, 1890–1946
*Borderud, Viola, assistant registrar, 1919–60
Bosch, Wouter, paint chemistry, 1947–58
*Brekke, Julia E., extension clothing, 1927–58
Briscoe, C. A., night watchman, 1911–42
*Bruegger, Ruth Shepard, associate 4-H club leader, 1933–
*Brush, Harper J., extension district supervisor, 1921–55
Bryant, Reece L., poultry husbandry, 1946–
Bryn, Milo F., mathematics, 1947–
Buchanan, M. L., animal husbandry, 1945–
Buddmeyer, Ella, secretary, experiment station, 1918–37
Burke, Merrill S., extension district supervisor, 1937–
Butcher, F. Gray, extension entomologist, 1936–50

C

Calhoun, E. A., county extension agent, 1925–44
*Calnan, T. X., county extension agent, 1914–45
*Carey, Ethel, secretary, speech, 1914–52
*Carlson, Elsie, clerk, 1926–
Carrick, L. L., dean, chemistry, 1920–43
Cassel, Frank, zoology, 1950–
*Challey, A. M., extension district supervisor, 1921–59
Chapman, James E., soils, 1922–34
*Chisholm, Haile, blacksmith, 1902–37

*Christensen, F. W., animal nutrition, 1917–46
*Churchill, O. O., agronomy, 1904–51
Cleland, C. B., sociology, 1950–
*Cleveland, Elizabeth, recorder, 1929–
*Cobb, Thomas P., modern languages, 1933–58
Cole, Dorothy, physical education, 1925–36
Cook, J. Earl, extension poultryman, 1934–47
Corbett, Roy A., physics, photographer, 1911–31
Couey, Worth, seed analyst, 1919–34
Craig, Alice, library, 1939–49
Currie, Lyle W., county extension agent, 1936–

D

*Dahl, Joey, bookkeeper, 1928–
*Dahl, Julian, technician, botany, 1942–
*Dakin, Emily, bookstore, 1921–58
Danielson, H. R., specialist, farm management, 1918–32
*Dawson, Ruth M., extension nutritionist, 1930–
Day, Florence P., extension agent, home management, 1938–53
DeAlton, E. L., agricultural education, 1936–
*DeLong, Grace, extension home demonstration leader, 1921–60
Delphia, John M., zoology, 1950–
*Dice, James R., dairy, 1920–45
*Dinan, A. Pearl, dean of women, English, 1910–58
Dinusson, Wm. E., animal nutrition, 1949–
*Doerr, L. O., mechanical engineering, 1929–60
*Dolve, R. M., dean, engineering, 1908–58
Dolve, Winston, agricultural education, 1945–
Doneghue, R. C., agronomy, 1909–19
Doubly, John A., bacteriology, 1948–
Douglas, Raymond, superintendent, Dickinson Branch Station, 1928–38, 1950–
*Dubetz, Emma, modern languages, 1924–
Dunbar, R. E., dean, chemistry, 1937–60
Dynes, Roy C., county extension agent, 1918–31

E

Edhlund, Nora, laboratory assistant, 1944–
Engleking, Reuben, statistical clerk, 1942–
*Erickson, M. B., mechanical engineering, 1910–41
Estenson, Ernest, psychology, 1946–
Euren, William, music, 1948–
Evanson, Eleanor, secretary, 1938–
Eveleth, D. F., veterinary science, 1943–

F

Fields, Mary E., administrative assistant, experiment station, 1928–39
*Finlayson, Christine, home economics supervisor, 1922–1960
*Finnegan, C. C. (Casey), director, athletics, 1928–55
Fleetwood, C. W., chemistry, 1946–

Appendices

Flynn, Merritt N., education, 1948–
Foust, Harry L., veterinary science, 1916–31
Franke, Max, janitor, 1937–
Friese, Charles R., mathematics, 1943–44, 1946–50, 1954–
Fuller, Orville M., agricultural economics, 1923–33

G

*Geiken, Dirk H., herdsman, 1906–39
*Geiszler, G. N., superintendent, Northern Great Plains Station, Minot, 1930–
*Gildersleeve, Thomas W., extension editor, 1929–
Goodearl, Geo. P., poultry husbandry, 1928–44
Gordon, Emma, clerk, 1944–
*Gorman, N. D., county agent leader, 1919–52
Grasse, Edythe, music, 1907–19
Graves, Harry A., extension horticulturist, 1936–
Gregory, E. M., extension supervisor, 1928–40
*Grimes, Ruby, mathematics, 1925–60
Griswold, D. J., animal husbandry, experiment station, 1921–33
*Gronaas, Olaf M., technician, agronomy, 1916–54
Guy, William, superintendent, county agents, 1916–26

H

*Haine, Jacob, dairy herdsman, 1923–54
Hanson, Herbert C., botany, director, experiment station, 1930–40
Harris, Rae H., cereal chemistry, 1936–60
Hartwell, Leon, English, 1931–44
*Haslerud, E. J., director, extension service, 1927–
Haw, John, county agent leader, 1914–24
Hawkins, Mildred, home economics, 1940–
Hay, Donald G., speech, rural sociology, 1926–36
Hazen, Arlon G., dean, agriculture; director, experiment station, 1946–
Hedin, Dagmar, library, 1950–
*Heggeness, Olaf, flax investigator, 1914–54
*Heldt, W. O., machine shop, 1912–47
*Helgeson, E. A., botany, 1935–
*Hemphill, Perry, agricultural economics, 1935–
*Henning, Knute, architecture, 1930–
*Herbison, H. W., extension, marketing specialist, 1928–
*Hill, A. Glenn, mathematics, 1927–
Hitt, A. L., assistant multilith operator, 1948–
Hitt, Lillian, clerk, 1942–
Hoag, Donald G., horticulture, 1947–
Hoeft, Lena, cashier, 1938–59
Hoffman, H. M., physics, 1923–37
Holt, John G., laboratory mechanic, 1948–
Hopper, T. H., agricultural chemistry, 1920–40
*Horton, Lucile, home economics, 1929–60
Hosted, E. G., mechanical engineering, 1946–

*Householder, F. C., mathematics, 1904–44
Hultz, Fred S., president, 1948–
*Hunsaker, A. F., social science, 1919–36
*Hunter, W. C., history, 1923–52

I

*Iverson, P. J., education, 1920–52

J

*Jensen, Christen, dairy husbandry, 1926–
Johnson, Ross, horticulture foreman, 1946–60
Johnson, Tracy W., journalism, 1925–38
Jones, E. H., agricultural education, 1921–38
Jones, Paul W., architecture, 1928–38
Jongeward, Mattys, pharmacy, 1918–20, 1925–42

K

Kaiser, E. E., physical education, 1942–
Kaslow, C. E., chemistry, 1930–41
*Kasson, Paul R., county agent leader, 1935–
*Kasson, Verne E., county extension agent, 1932–58
*Kastet, Olga, secretary, 1928–
Kaufman, E. E., dairy, 1892–1905
*Keene, E. S., dean, engineering, 1892–1928
*Keidel, Roman B., multilith operator, 1920–
Kelsey, Elizabeth, matron,   –1926
Kirk, Monroe, farm foreman, 1927–38
Kirst, Mildred, social director, 1938–
Kjenstad, Don, plot and seedhouse assistant, 1949–
Klosterman, Harold J., agricultural chemistry, 1946–
*Koel, J. P., mechanical engineering, 1918–54
*Kraft, Earl, night watchman, 1930–
*Kraft, Richard, custodian of buildings, 1898–1944
Kristjanson, Theodore, county extension agent, 1910–32
Krueger, Augusta, steonographer, 1921–45
*Kuhn, Kenneth, English, 1922–59

L

*Ladd, E. F., chemistry, president, 1890–1921
Lamb, Frances, English, 1922–35
Lanxon, W. R., superintendent, Hettinger branch station, 1909–17
*Larsen, Paul, heating plant, 1916–46
Lawrence, W. J., 4-H club assistant agent, 1933–55
Lawritson, Glenn, education, 1927–42
*Leeby, Constance, home economics, 1923–53
Light, Merle R., animal husbandry, 1948–
Long, Harry D., seed analyst, 1910–29
Lovering, Majore, home economics education supervisor, 1949–
Lowe, Robert, athletics, 1925–45
Luptak, Charles, technician and shop foreman, 1949–

M

*McArdle, H. W., mathematics, business manager, 1891–1933
McCaul, Benj., agricultural enconomics, 1926–37
McCormick, Ada, assistant to secretary, 1920–33
McGrath, Jane, clerk, 1947–60
McGrath, Wm., janitor, 1933–52
McMahon, Don, extension veterinarian, 1918–30
*McVeety, Ethel, librarian, 1897–1945
Mangels, C. E., cereal chemistry, 1921–36
Martin, Joe, herdsman, 1925–43
Mattson, Harold, horticulture, 1937–51
Mattson, Lydia, secretary, 1940–
Melanson, Lawrence, electrical engineering, 1949–
*Metzinger, Leon, modern languages, 1915–47
*Mickelson, J. H., steam fitter, 1921–53
*Miller, Cap E., agricultural economics, 1918–51
Miller, Clifton E., dean, pharmacy, 1939–
Miller, Geo. E., zoology, 1910–30
Millette, Rose Ann, library, 1940–58
*Minard, A. E., dean, applied arts and sciences, 1904–50
*Monson, Gladys, secretary, 1923–
*Montgomery, Craig R., 4-H club leader, 1934–
*Moomaw, Leroy, superintendent Dickinson branch station, 1919–30
Moore, Frank E., poultry husbandry, 1931–41
Munro, J. A., entomology, 1926–46

N

*Nelson, C. I., bacteriology, 1914–54
Nelson, Doris, accountant, 1941–
Nesbitt, L. L., chemistry, 1923–43
Nessett, Oscar J., administrative assistant, extension service, 1943–54
*Newcomer, Ralph C., county extension agent, 1919–48
Norum, Enoch, soils, 1947–
Nystuen, Peder A., assistant to dean of agriculture and assistant director of experiment station, 1946–

O

Oakey, John A., civil engineering, 1946–
Olson, Olaus, fireman, 1941–
Olson, P. J., agronomy, assistant to dean of agriculture, 1924–39
*Otterson, Rudolf, history, 1923–
*Oveson, Karl, gardener, 1929–
Owen, Shubel, agricultural education, 1938–

P

Page, Wm. R., county extension agent, 1927–50
*Palmer, W. C., editor, 1910–47
*Parizek, E. C., assistant county agent leader, 1918–48

*Parrott, A. H., registrar, 1903–56
Parsons, Jesse L., bacteriology, 1949–
Pearce, W. T., dean, chemistry, 1916–36
Pearson, Harriet, library, 1914–33
Peet, Ethel Jones, extension clothing, 1936–50
Perry, Mary S., agricultural education, 1941–
*Pettee, E. W., economics, 1928–
*Phillips, Jessie, English, 1929–
Pinckney, A. J., agricultural chemistry, 1927–41
Plath, Emily May, laboratory technician, dairy, 1943–55
Poseley, Clare, messenger, 1943–
Promersberger, Wm., agricultural engineering, 1938–
*Putnam, C. S., music, 1903–44

R

Raer, Elsie, physical education, 1945–
*Randlett, Gordon W., director, extension service, 1908–37
Redman, Kenneth, pharmacy, 1930–47
Remington, Roe, food chemist, 1908–18, 1921–27
Rehn, Harriet, mimeograph operator, 1942–
Reynolds, Emily, home economics, 1948–
Reynolds, E. S. botany, 1912–27
*Reynolds, Pauline M., extension young people, 1923–60
*Rilling, Harry, 4-H club leader, 1920–50
Rinde, Audrey, secretary, 1943–
Roen, Mrs. L. W., cafeteria manager, 1936–
Rose, P. S., engineering, 1901–11
Rotzein, Courtney R., extension information assistant editor, 1942–
*Rush, Harry, electrical engineering, 1920–45
*Russell, J. Clayton, county extension agent, agricultural engineering, 1920–51

S

*Sackett, Leonard, English, 1929–
*Sanderson, Thomas, miller, 1907–39
Sands, Frederick H., chemistry, 1946–
Sands, Mary Green, business office, 1918–36
Schaffner, LeRoy, agricultural economics, 1947–
Schalk, A. F., veterinary, 1910–30
Schmidt, Carl H., counseling, 1943–
Schneider, Hugo, veterinary assistant, 1907–51
Schoff, Francis G., English, 1937–
Schollander, E. G., superintendent demonstration farms, 1907–14, 1918–35
Scott, Geo. M., technician, 1942–
Secord, Alfred, agronomy assistant, 1923–53
Severson, Al, animal husbandry, 1920–43
Severson, Nettie, extension home economics, 1944–
*Sevrinson, Charles A., dean of students, 1928–

Appendices

*Shelton, Norman, technician, 1935–
Shepperd, Adele, chemistry assistant, 1900–19
*Shepperd, John H., agriculture, president, 1892–1939
Sibbitt, L. D., cereal chemist, 1939–
Simmons, Abbie, English, 1908–28
Skinner, Forrest F., business office, 1939–41, 1943–55
Skogen, Madeline Kaiser, assistant to dean of arts and sciences, 1937–
*Slocum, Roy H., civil engineering, 1907–52
*Smith, Elvira, home economics, 1923–59
*Smith, Glenn S., principal plant breeder, dean, graduate school, 1929
*Smith, I. W., mathematics, 1909–37
Solem, Andrew, carpenter, 1907–49
Sommerfeld, Edna, home economics, 1923–36
Stallings, H. Dean, librarian, 1948–
Stefanson, Haldor, county extension agent, 1929–30, 1936–55
*Stevens, O. A., botany, seed analyst, 1909–56
Stickney, Bertha, library, 1922–32
*Stoa, T. E., agronomy, 1921–60
Strand, Oliver, horticulture foreman, 1919–31
Strum, George, extension animal husbandman, 1941–2, 1945–
*Sturlaugson, Victor, superintendent, Langdon branch station, 1925–
*Sudro, W. F., dean, pharmacy, 1907–55
Sullivan, Margurette, library, 1947–
Sunde, C. J., chemistry, 1926–42
Swallers, Clarence, agronomy, 1931–57
Swanson, Karl, county extension agent, 1923–44
Swisher, Chas. L., physics, 1924–46

T

Tarbell, Olivia E., music, 1920–32
Tesdell, Angelina, library, 1931–47
Tewksbury, W. M., county extension agent, 1934–
*Thompson, E. J., animal husbandry, 1910–40
*Thompson, Matilda, mathematics, dean of women, 1923–
*Thompson, Oscar A., superintendent, Edgeley station, 1903–30
Thordarson, T. W., supervised study, 1923–39
Thorfinnson, H. B., county extension agent, 1934–44
Thorfinnson, Snorri, county extension agent, 1934–47
*Thorson, Erling Q., superintendent of buildings and grounds, 1927–
Tibert, George, superintendent of buildings and grounds, 1902–16
Toring, Edythe, business manager, 1938–
*Traynor, Jean, secretary, 1911–52
Trowbridge, P. F., director, experiment station, 1918–37
Turn, Jenny, technical assistant, veterinary, 1949–

U

Ulio, James, military, 1901–11

V

*Vancura, Edward W., county extension agent, 1921–48
Van Es, Leunis, veterinary, 1902–20
Van Vlissingen, Ernst, music, 1938–
Virgin, Eleanor, home economics, 1946–
Vogel, Sebastian, extension agricultural engineer, 1947–59

W

*Waldron, C. B., horticulture, dean of agriculture, 1890–1940
*Waldron, L. R., plant breeder, 1899–1952
Walrath, Glenn, mathematics, 1946–
*Walster, H. L., agronomy, dean of agriculture, director of experiment station and extension service, 1919–54
Wartchow, Beatrice M., physical education, 1940–55
*Weeks, A. D., dean, education, 1907–37
Wenger, W. R., chemistry, 1929–42, 1946–7
Wentz, Mrs. John B., library, 1942–55
West, Constance, speech, 1945–56, 1960–
*Whedon, A. D., zoology, 1923–52
White, Richard D., military, 1929–47
Whitman, Ruth, library, 1918–53
Whitman, Warren C., botany, 1938–
Widdifield, Russell B., program planning coordinator, extension service, 1938–
*Wiidikas, Wm., agronomy, 1933–
Willard, Rex, farm management, 1918–31
Williams, Charlotte, secretary, 1938–
Williams, Minerva, stenographer, 1923–33
Willson, E. A., rural sociology, 1919–33
Wiseman, J. Scott, agricultural engineering, 1939–54
Witz, Richard L., agricultural engineering, 1945–
Wolla, Chester W., county extension agent, 1934–44
*Woodley, W. L., mathematics, 1937–
Worst, John H., president, 1895–1916

Y

Yeager, A. F., horticulture, 1919–37
Yott, Geo. F., mechanical engineering, 1927–37
Young, Ralph A., soils, 1948–

Z

Zaylskie, John J., extension forester, 1942–
Zerby, Paul E., economics, 1928–43
Ziegenhagel, Emmeline, clerk, 1948–
Zubriski, Joseph C., soils, 1950–

Appendices

X – EDITORS AND MANAGERS OF THE YEARBOOKS

		Editor	Business Manager
Agassiz	1907	Genevieve Holkesvig	John Thysel
	1908	W. O. Whitcomb	Leo P. Nemzek
	1910	Peter J. Olson	Howard B. Darling
	1911	Chas. H. Ruzicka	H. M. Dodge
	1912	Ben Barrett	Edwin Evingson
	1913	Chas. W. Hammond	Edgar I. Olson
	1914	Arthur Ogaard	Jack Nolet
	1915	George Stewart	August Berg
	1916	William Guy	Halvor Aakhus
	1917	Sidney Hooper	Stephen K. Bjornson
	1918	Robert R. Lewis	F. W. Powell
			Walter Stockwell
	1919		
	1920		
by Class of	1921	Ralph W. Baker	Roy C. Reis
	1922	Matthew E. Tindall	E. Vernon Ladd
	1923	W. Philip Balsley	Earl J. Heising

BISON YEARBOOK

			Editor	Business Manager
Class of	1924		Arthur Ostman	Donald Peet
	1925		E. Verle Deach	Philip H. Boise
	1926		Stewart Schlipf	Byron Hanson
	1927		Carrie Dolphin	Emery Putnam
	1928		Richard C. Hackenberg	F. Ralph Hollands
Students	1929		Everett J. Wallum	F. Ralph Hollands
	1930		Jessie McLachlin	Frank Hannaher
	1931		Amos Wallum	Adolph Pahl
	1932		Elene Weeks	Floyd Viel
Jr. class	1933		Mart Vogel	Edgar L. Crewe
	1934		Donald R. Fredrikson	William E. Heller
	1935		Paul Deal	Gordon Strong
	1936	(pub. '35)	Cathryn Ray	Chester Perry
Students	1937	(pub. '36)	William Murphy	Warner Litten
	1937		Katherine Kilbourne	Maurice Benidt
	1938		James H. Critchfield	Archie Seebart
	1939		James H. Critchfield	Myrle Anderson
	1940		Connie Taylor	Leland Stenchjem
	1941		Bill Guy	Gorman King
	1942		Richard Crockett	George Koch
	1944		Polly Carter	Maxine Schlagel
	1945		Sue Stenerson	Laura Jane Hugelen
	1946		Doris Oliver	Darlene Jones
	1947		Alex MacGibbon	Donna Jean Nellermoe
	1948		Iona Jean Bolton	Daly King
	1949		Anne Stegner	Gerald Bolmeier
			Ed Graber	
	1950		Waldemore Klundt	LeRoy Johnson

	1951	Waldemore Klundt	Gordon Badger
	1952	Patricia Carlson	Gordon Badger
		Marilyn Hunter	
	1953	Dave Bartholomew	Ed Boerth
	1954	Gary Hart	Bob Kubas
		Wesley Ray	Nick Roster
	1955	Gary Hart	Nick Roster
	1956	Mel Ostby	Jon Dewey
	1957	Reg Gorder	Kerry Murphy
	1958	Judy Hammer	Sharon Shepard
	1959	Pat Larson	Sharon Shepard
		Mitzi Mallarian	
	1960	Al Hart	Kathy Shepard
	1961	Mary Wallum	Willis Kingsbury

XI – EDITORS AND MANAGERS OF THE SPECTRUM

		Editor	Business Manager
Monthly	1896–1897	C. O. Follett	Thomas H. Heath
	1897–1898	Lawrence R. Waldron	Thomas H. Heath
	1898–1899	Edeth L. Hill	Lawrence R. Waldron
	1899–1900	Thos. H. Heath	Chas. J. Phelan
	1900–1901	James McGuigan	T. W. Osgood
	1901–1902	T. W. Osgood	James McGuigan
	1902–3	E. M. May	Arthur Peterson
	1903–4	William H. Westergaard	Fred G. Birch
	1904–5	A. M. Mikkelson	Norman Ellison
	1905–6	E. G. Schollander	F. Birch
	1906	C. I. Gunness	Harry Carpenter
	1907	C. I. Gunness	Harry Carpenter
Weekly	1908	Victor C. Parker	Wilfred P. Heath
	1908–1909	Levi M. Thomas	S. V. Anderson
	1910	LeRoy D. Gifford	J. Allen Clark
	1911	Cal M. Hennis	Harold M. Dodge
	1912	Alfred Anderson	
	1913	Arthur Ogaard	Jack Nolet
	1914	Homer E. Dixon	Reuben Larson
	1915	George Dixon	Winney Crouch
	1916	Percy Beals	Winney Crouch
	1917	A. R. Matters	A. P. Beals
	1918	Glenn E. McLellan	Frank Henning
	1919	Ethel B. Tousley	
		Mayre Healy	
		Edwin Falkenstein	
	1920	Edwin Falkenstein	Herbert Zimmerman
		Stuart Kelly	Vernon Ladd
	1923	Herbert W. Herbison	Fred D. Wilkinson
	1924	Herbert W. Herbison	
Spectrum	1925	Edward Yocum	

Appendices 285

1926	Eugene Fitzgerald	Paul Revell
1927	Wallace Matson	Earl Hendrickson
1928	Richard G. Hackenberg	Lester E. Thompson
1929	Henry Sullivan	Harold Phillips
1930	Henry H. Presler	Ralph K. Welch
1931	Anthony Faber	Earl Hodgson
1932	Margery Archer	Glenn Reichert
1933	Robert M. Connolly	William P. MacDonald
1934	Gale Monson	Robert B. Parrott
1935	Maxine Rustad	James Golseth
1936	John B. Spalding	Francis Walters
1937	Orville Goplen	Francis Ladwig
1938	George Putz	James Elwin
1939	John F. Lynch	Richard Cook
1940	Don Bloomquist	Abner O. Selvig
1941	Jane Blair	Bill Borderud
1942	James Ford	Reo Carr
1945	Nathan Crosby	Darlene Jones
1946	Adelaide Dinwoodie	Edward Murphy
1947	Richard C. Olson	Betty Sue Armstrong
1948	Dan Chapman	Ardyce Toohey
1949	Wallace Anderson	Warren Jacobsen
1950	Robert A. Johnson	Gordon Kartenson
1951	Ed Sveinson	Stan Lunde
1952	Betty Lou Danielson	Dick Kloubec
1953	Dorothy Morrow	Dick Hill
1954	Renée Baker	Dean Johnson
1955	Leon Johnson, Jr.	Peter Mark
1956	Leon Johnson, Jr.	Peter Mark
1957	Jerry Bender	Jim Feeny
1958	Neal Bjornson	Jim Feeny
1959	Loretta Struble	David Graben
1960	Bob Thompson	Jack Brush
1961	Evanne Grommesh	Ruth Brakel

XII – PRESIDENTS OF STUDENT COMMISSION

1917	William W. Mendenhall		1932	Leonard Luther
1921	George Hansen		1933	Erling Thorson
1922	Hamlet Larson		1934	Donald Arthur
1923	Harvey E. Hoffman		1935	Carmen Hunt
1924	Louis Duerner		1936	Earl Jennings
1925	Harry A. Swanson		1937	Walter McGrath
1926	Philip H. Boise		1938	Robert Sanders
1927	Cyril Arnold		1939	Theodore Whalen
1928	William H. Gray		1940	James Critchfield
1929	F. Ralph Hollands		1941	Arthur Lahlum
1930	M. Foss Narum		1942	John Fisher
1931	Lawrence Parsons		1943	Clark Haggeness

1944	James Love		1953	John Dean
1945	John Slingsby		1954	Mancur Olson
1946	Gil Spooner		1955	Duane Anderson
1947	Russell Heine		1956	Merlin Ludwig
1948	Daly King		1957	John "Tip" Miller
1949	Paul Bibelheimer		1958	Eldon Mclain
1950	Kenny Olson		1959	Noel Estenson
1951	Vern Freeh		1960	Allyn Hart
1952	Robert Schnell			

XIII – STUDENT ORGANIZATIONS IN 1960

Agricultural Economics Club	local	technical
Agronomy Club	local	technical
Alpha Gamma Delta	national	social
Alpha Gamma Rho	national	social (agriculture)
Alpha Phi Omega	national	service
Alpha Tau Omega	national	social
Alpha Zeta	national	honor (agriculture)
American Institute of Architects	national	technical
American Institute of Electrical Engineers	national	technical
American Society of Agricultural Engineers	national	technical
American Society of Civil Engineers	national	technical
American Society of Mechanical Engineers	national	technical
American Pharmaceutical Association	national	technical (pharmacy)
Angel Flight	national	social (military)
Arnold Air Society	national	social
Association of United States Army	national	social
Associated Women Students	national	service
Baptist Student Union	local	religious
Blue Key	national	service
Business Economics Club	local	professional
Canterbury Club	local	religious
Ceres Hall Club	local	social
Chemistry Club	local	technical
Christian Fellowship	local	religious
Dinan Hall Club	local	social
Edwin Booth Dramatic Club	local	honor (dramatics)
Engineering Council	local	technical
Eta Kappa Nu	national	honor (electrical engineering)
Farmers Union Cooperative Association	national	technical (agriculture)

Appendices

Farmers Union Local	local	social (agriculture)
Farmhouse Fraternity	national	technical (agriculture)
4-H Club	national	technical (agriculture)
Future Farmers of America	national	technical (agriculture)
Gamma Delta	national	religious
Gamma Phi Beta	national	social
Gold Star Band	local	professional (music)
Guidon	national	social (military)
Independent Student Association	local	social
Institute of Aeronautical Sciences	national	technical
Institute of Industrial Engineers	local	technical
Inter-Dormitory Council	local	service
Inter-Fraternity Council	local	service
Inter-Religious Council	local	religious
International Relations Club	local	service
Kappa Alpha Theta	national	social
Kappa Delta	national	social
Kappa Delta Pi	national	honor (education)
Kappa Epsilon	national	professional (pharmacy)
Kappa Kappa Gamma	national	social
Kappa Kappa Psi	national	professional (band)
Kappa Psi	national	professional (pharmacy)
Kappa Tau Delta	local	honor (architecture)
Letterman's Club	local	(athletics)
Lincoln Debate Society	local	(speech)
Lutheran Student Association	national	religious
Memorial Union Board	local	service
Newman Foundation	national	religious
Orchesis	national	honor (dance)
Panhellenic Council	local	service
Junior Panhellenic Council	local	service
Phi Kappa Phi	national	honor
Phi Mu	national	social
Phi Upsilon Omicron	national	professional (home economics)
Physical Education Club	local	professional
Pi Tau Sigma	local	honor (mechanical engineering)
Rahjah Club	local	athletic
Rho Chi	national	honor (pharmacy)
Saddle & Sirloin Club	national	(agriculture)
Scabbard and Blade	national	honor (military)
Senior Staff	national	honor (service)
Sigma Alpha Epsilon	national	social
Sigma Alpha Iota	national	professional (music)
Sigma Chi	national	social
Sigma Nu	national	social

Sigma Phi Delta	national	professional (engineering)
Ski Club	local	social
Student Union Activities Board	local	service
Tau Beta Pi	national	honor (engineering)
Tau Beta Sigma	national	honor (band)
Tau Kappa Epsilon	national	social
Theta Chi	national	social
Tryota Club	national	professional (home economics)
United Campus Christian Fellowship	local	religious
Vet's Club	local	social
Pre-Veterinary Medicine Club	local	professional
Wesley Foundation	national	religious
Women's Athletic Association	local	professional
YMCA	national	religious
YWCA	national	religious

XIV – STUDENTS WHO GAVE THEIR LIVES IN WORLD WAR II

Sidney C. Aamodt
Robert L. Aas
Hale Fuller Abbott
Alan Bernard Anderson
Reuben Clarence Anderson
Vernon E. Anderson
Robert William Arhart
Warren Harris Badewell
Leo F. Baumgartner
Clarence Victor Beckley
Bernard S. Bennison
Donald James Bettschen
Donovan Blade
Elmer Bollmquist
Bernard C. Boepple
Eugene Joseph Bolger
Russell James Botsford
Charles Frederick Bowers
Robert T. Boyle
Frederick W. Braa
Conrad B. Brakke
Melvin G. Brastad
Robert W. Brown
Ford H. Browne
William Earl Bryans
Alf Lennard Burman
Ralph Calkins
Gerald John Callahan
Lorne McNab Campbell
Terrance John Carey
Bill E. Cates
James M. Cathcart
Kermit Edward Chapman
Edward J. Church
Wilfred Phelps Comrie
David William Conlon
Willard Coulter
William Kenneth Crawford
Robert Cross
Donn W. Cummings
Harold William Dalby
Russell David Danielson
John McCoy Davenport
Ernest Peter Deutsch
Sam Dobervich
Robert Ervin Docktor
Robert Ferdinand Drier
Frederick Dyke
Robert H. Earhart
Dale H. Ellingson
Henry Elvik
Harold Charles Forsberg
Orville J. Fossum
James Emmett **Fox**

Appendices

George Robert Fredericks
Aubrey John Freeman
John Vincent Fryslie
Carlyle R. Fuglie
Robert Gage
Athniel Gebhard
Frederick John Gerlich
Ernest Lynn Gray
Warren Cecil Gray
Harvey R. Grenier
James Andrew Guy
Robert L. Haley
Former Hansen
Edward Hasenmueller
Robert Henry Hegg
Wilbur William Hindemith
Lee L. Hinschberger
Ronald Charles Hockeng
Dwight True Hunkins
Norman Lewis Hunsaid
William Ingalls
Paul S. Johnson
Robert Daniel Kaercher
William Joseph Kelly
Richard John Knapp
Ernest Floyd Kruger
Joseph Francis Kufner
Arthur B. Kuntz
Pius Gregory Kuntz
Robert William Kvenmoen
Loren R. Ladwig
Donald Robert Landeck
Owen T. Langen
George LaPage
Harold J. Larson
John F. Lavelle
Benton Lee Lawrence
Glenn Lawritson
Roy M. Lee
Earl H. Leland
Jack Lepird
Ernest Otto Lidstrom
Floyd R. Lien
Sylvan R. Lucier
William O. Lund
Gene Lundwall
William H. Magill
Lee Roos Malmo
Elroy Louis Marion
Eugene P. Marquart

Edward G. Meath
John R. Mendenhall
Lloyd Mergenthal
Einar Mickelson
Alven E. Moe
Jack Moore
Frank Harriman Mumm
George Lawrence Murray
Maurice McCormick
James Lyle McCreary
Dennis Burdine McDonough
Robert Dale McDougall
James McGrath
Donald Richard McDay
Norman J. McKendry
William T. McMahon
Earl G. Naumann
David E. Nelson
Norman H. Nelson
Leslie W. Neumann
George R. Newgard
Ardell Axel Nord
Marvin E. Nurnberger
Emmett P. O'Day
Kenneth D. Olson
Norman Edward Olson
Orville Olson
Carrol Nels Osterdahl
Charles M. Page
Harold W. Parker
Carl Victor Person
John Woodrow Pehrson
Marion Richard Petrick
Sidney A. Petrie
Robert Peyton
William K. Pflugrath
Robert B. Pfusch
Noel John Pineur
Gordon Potter
Lance Albin Pousette
Marvin P. Quamme
John W. Powell
Joseph S. Pyle
Darwin H. Raatz
George Vernon Rasmusson
Gladwin L. Roberts
Donald Curtis Robbins
Charles Ben Robinson
Robert Fillmore Rohs
John Alexander Ross

Paul Robert Rowe
Helmer Olie Rude
Lewis F. Ruffcorn
Kermit P. Rufsvold
Reuben Palmer Ruud
Albert A. Schneider
Donald A. Schollander
Charles L. Scouten
Blair E. Seitz
Allen Duane Severson
Verne Leslie Skjonsby
William Forrester Smith
Arthur Solow
Ralph C. Specht
Alvin Stocking
Francis Herman Stoeber
Maurice Alfred Strand
Gordon J. Strom
John Svenningsen
Hubert Paul Sweeney
Donald Juill Swenson

Rueben Stanley Tastad
Arthur Tarlor
Clarence A. Thompson
Nickolie J. Thompson
Philip E. Thompson
Albert Oliver Thorwaldson
Donald R. Thue
William Tolin
Robert A. Ulland
Clarence van Ray
Carl E. Vettel
Harry Marvin Walen
Ira L. Walla
William R. Weir
Frank Welch
Lewis Dale Wilson
William R. Winn
Adolph Winther
Elwood Wylie
Clarian Carl Wysocki
Desmond M. Yetter

XV – THE BUILDINGS ON THE CAMPUS

1891....Administration building, $25,155; boilerhouse and greenhouse
1892....
1892....Francis Hall; Engineering building; farm house and barn
1894....
1895....
1896....
1897....Festival Hall
1898....
1899....
1900....
1901....Science Hall
1902....
1903....
1904....
1905....Chemistry building, $50,000; Library (aided by Carnegie grants)
1906....
1907...."New" Engineering building
1908....
1909....Chemistry building burned
1910....Ceres Hall
1911....Chemistry building, $65,000; Veterinary building, $30,000
1912....
1913....Dairy building
1914....
1915....

Appendices

1916....
1917....Army barracks, now Dakota Hall
1918....Science Hall addition
1919....
1920....
1921....Morrill Hall, $103,000
1922....Home Management House
1923....
1924....
1925....
1926....
1927....
1928....
1929....
1930....Field House, $155,650
1931....Men's Residence hall (Fowler-Hamilton Dormitory law, not an appropriation)
1932....
1933....
1934....
1935....
1936....
1937....
1938....Stadium (WPA project)
1939....Health Center
1940....
1941....
1942....
1943....
1944....
1945....
1946....
1947....
1948....
1949....Sheep barn, $45,000; Grain storage building, $10,000; Corn seed house, $85,000; Poultry plant, $75,000; President's house, $40,000
1950....Maintenance building, $120,000; Library, $400,000; Power house equipment; moving the stadium; Field House remodeling; hog barn $30,000; beef barn $50,000; greenhouse $40,000.
1951....Veterinary Science building remodeled $43,000; Agricultural Engineering building remodeled $115,000; Engineering building $400,000; Livestock Arena $260,000; second greenhouse $45,000.
1951–53.Home Economics building $450,000; Memorial Union, including equipment $600,000; dairy barn $95,000; herdsman's house $14,000; heating plant remodeled $194,000.
1951–55.Cereal Technology building; stadium.
1959....Pharmacy building, $550,000 ($110,000 for equipment); Agricultural Science building, $750,000

Bibliography

MANUSCRIPTS AND CORRESPONDENCE

David Baglien, "The McKenzie Era," Unpublished Master's Thesis, North Dakota Agricultural College, 1955, Library, N.D.A.C.

Henry L. Bolley, correspondence, 1891–1931, North Dakota Institute for Regional Studies, Library, N.D.A.C.

Ernest L. DeAlton, "The Historical Development of Vocational Agriculture in North Dakota," Fargo, 1940 (typed), Library, N.D.A.C.

Paul Dressel, "General Education in a Land Grant College," Speech on January 14, 1960 (mimeographed), North Dakota Institute for Regional Studies, Library, N.D.A.C.

Faculty Record, 1890–1916, Office of Director of Admissions, N.D.A.C.

Norbert D. Gorman, "Some Cooperative Agricultural Extension History of North Dakota," (typed), Office of Director of Extension Service, N.D.A.C.

Archie E. Minard, papers, North Dakota Institute for Regional Studies, Library, N.D.A.C.

Minutes of the College Council, 1917–1960, Office of Director of Admissions, N.D.A.C.

Harriet Pearson, "N.D.A.C. Library History," 1928 (typed), North Dakota Institute for Regional Studies, Library, N.D.A.C.

Wesley E. Peik, "Training of Teachers in North Dakota, a survey," Bismarck, 1930, North Dakota Institute for Regional Studies, Library, N.D.A.C.

James B. Power, correspondence with Horace Stockbridge, May–August, 1890, North Dakota Institute for Regional Studies, Library, N.D.A.C.

Samuel G. Roberts, letter to his daughter, Mrs. G. W. Haggart, 1921, Library of the *Fargo Forum.*

John H. Shepperd, papers, 1893–1939, North Dakota Institute for Regional Studies, Library, N.D.A.C.

Burleigh Folsom Spaulding, Autobiography, North Dakota Institute for Regional Studies, Library, N.D.A.C.

Clare B. Waldron, "North Dakota Agricultural College, history, 1940 (mimeographed), North Dakota Institute for Regional Studies, Library, N.D.A.C.

Harlow L. Walster, "Horace Edward Stockbridge," address before N.D.A.C. Quarter Century Club, May 13, 1957, North Dakota Institute for Regional Studies, Library, N.D.A.C.

Harlow L. Walster, "Five for the Land," (unpublished mss.) North Dakota Institute for Regional Studies, Library, N.D.A.C.

John H. Worst, correspondence, Carnegie Library, 1902–1905. Library, N.D.A.C.

A. F. Yeager, correspondence, 1919–1937. North Dakota Institute for Regional Studies, Library, N.D.A.C.

Bibliography

PUBLIC DOCUMENTS

Dakota Territory, *Journal of the Council*, 1882-1889, Yankton, 1889.
Dakota Territory, *Laws of the Fifteenth Session*, Yankton, 1883.
Dakota Territory, *Laws of the Eighteenth Session*, Bismarck, 1889.
North Dakota, *Journal of the Constitutional Convention*, Bismarck, 1889.
North Dakota, *Laws*, Bismarck, 1890-1959.
North Dakota, *Journal of the Senate of the Legislative Assembly*, Bismarck, 1889-1960.
North Dakota, *Annual Reports of the Board of Administration to the Governor*, Bismarck, 1919-1938.
North Dakota, *Biennial Reports of the State Board of Higher Education*, Bismarck, 1938-1960.
North Dakota, *Biennial Reports of the State Board of Regents*, Bismarck, 1916-1919.
North Dakota, *Minutes of the State Board of Administration*, Office of Commissioner, Bismarck, 1920-1939.
North Dakota, *Minutes of the State Board of Higher Education*, Office of Commissioner, Bismarck, 1939-.
United States, Office of Education, Department of Health, Education and Welfare, "*Higher Education in North Dakota*", a report of a survey, October, 1958, Washington, D.C.

NORTH DAKOTA AGRICULTURAL COLLEGE PUBLICATIONS

Agassiz, Fargo, 1907-1923.
Alumni Review, Fargo, October 1939-1959.
Bison, Fargo, 1924-1942, 1944-1960.
Bison Briefs, Fargo, 1959-1960.
Bison Boundaries, hand book, Bulletin XLI, 4, Fargo, 1950.
Bison Furrows, Fargo, 1938-1950.
North Dakota Agricultural Experiment Station, *Bulletins*, Fargo, 1891-1960.
North Dakota Agricultural Experiment Station, *Bi-Monthly Bulletins*, 1938-1958.
North Dakota Agricultural Experiment Station, *North Dakota Farm Research*, 1958-1960.
North Dakota Farmers' Institute Annual, Fargo, 1900-1916.
Catalogs and Bulletins, N.D.A.C., Fargo, 1891-1960.
College and State, Fargo. Jan.-Feb. 1917-Mar.-Apr., 1933.
Directory, Fargo, 1925-1960.
The Extension, Fargo, 1908.
Papyrus Ebers, Fargo, 1944-1952.
Prospectus, Fargo, June, 1891.
Seventeenth Annual Commencement, Fargo, 1911.
Spectrum, I-XI, Fargo, Dec., 1896-June, 1907; *XXI-LVIII*, 1924-1960.
Weekly Spectrum, XII-XX, Fargo, 1907-1915.
State College Engineer, Fargo, 1926-1960.

STATE HISTORY

Crawford, Lewis F. *History of North Dakota*. Chicago: American Historical Society, 1931. 3 vols.
Hennesy, William B. *History of North Dakota*. Bismarck: Bismarck Tribune Publishing Co., 1910.
History of the Red River Valley, Past and Present. Grand Forks: Herald Printing Co., Chicago: C. F. Cooper and Co., 1909. 2 vols.
Hyde, C. W. G. and William Stoddard ed. *History of the Great Northern and Its Men of Progress*. Minneapolis: Minneapolis Journal, 1901.
Kingsbury, George W. *History of Dakota Territory*. Chicago: G. J. Clarke Publishing Co., 1915. 2 vols.

Lounsberry, Clement A. *Early History of North Dakota.* Washington, D.C.: Liberty Press, 1919.
Lounsberry, Clement A. *North Dakota History and People.* Chicago: The S. J. Clarke Publishing Co., 1917.
Federal Writers' Project, *North Dakota, a Guide to the Northern Prairie State.* New York: Oxford University Press, 1950.

NEWSPAPERS, PERIODICALS, ANNUALS

Better Farming Association, Annual Reports, Fargo, 1912–1914.
Bismarck Daily Tribune, Bismarck, N. Dak.
Bulletin of the American Association of University Professors, XLII, nos. 1 and 2, Spring, Summer 1950, Easton, Pa.
Christian Science Monitor, Boston, Mass.
Fargo Daily Argus, Fargo, N. Dak.
Fargo Weekly Argus, Fargo, N. Dak.
Fargo Courier News, Fargo, N. Dak.
Fargo Daily Forum, Fargo, N. Dak.
Grand Forks Daily Herald, Grand Forks, N. Dak.
North Central Association Quarterly, Menosha, Wis.
N.D.A.C. *Purge,* newspaper clippings compiled by Grace DeLong, July 1937–Aug. 1939 in North Dakota Institute for Regional Studies, Library, N.D.A.C.
N.D.A.C. *Four Professors,* newspaper clippings, Oct. 1954–Apr. 1956, in N. D. Institute for Regional Studies, Library, N.D.A.C.
Normanden, Fargo, N. D.
North Dakota Farmer, Lisbon, N. D., 1902–1918.
Renville County Farmer, Lisbon, N. D.
Richland County Farmer-Globe, Wahpeton, N. D.
St. Paul Dispatch, St. Paul, Minn.
Sanitary Home, Fargo, N. D., 1899–1901.
The Leader, Bismarck, N. D.
The Record, I-IX, May 1895–Mar. 1905, Fargo, N. D.

BOOKS AND MONOGRAPHS

Arvold, Alfred G. *The Little Country Theater.* New York: Macmillan, 1923.
Brittain, Marion L. *The Story of Georgia Tech.* Chapel Hill, N. C.: University of North Carolina Press, 1948.
Chaffin, Nora C. *Trinity College, 1839–1892, The Beginnings of Duke University,* Durham, N. C.: Duke University Press, 1950.
Curti, Merle E. and Vernon Carstenson, *The University of Wisconsin, A History.* Madison, Wis.: University of Wisconsin Press, 1949.
Department of the Interior, Bureau of Education, Andrews, Benjamin F. *"The Land-Grant Act of 1862 and the Land-Grant Colleges."* Bulletin 1918 No. 13, Washington, D. C.: Government Printing Office, 1918.
Dunaway, Wayland F. *History of the Pennsylvania State College.* State College, Pa.: The Pennsylvania State College, 1946.
Eddy, Edward D. *Colleges for Our Land and Time.* New York: Harper and Brothers, 1959.
Gaston, Herbert E. *The Nonpartisan League.* New York: Harcourt, Brace, and Howe, 1920.
Geiger, Louis G. *University of the Northern Plains.* Grand Forks: University of North Dakota Press, 1958.
Goldberg, Ray, *The Nonpartisan League in North Dakota.* Fargo: Midwest Printing & Lithographing Co., 1948.
Gray, James, *Open Wide the Door, The Story of the University of Minnesota.* New York: Putnam, 1958.

Bibliography

Hale, Harrison, *University of Arkansas, 1871–1948*. Fayetteville, Ark.: University of Arkansas Alumni Association, 1948.

Hicks, John D., *The Populist Revolt, a History of the Farmers Alliance and the People's Party*. Minneapolis: University of Minnesota Press, 1931.

James, Edmund J., *The Origins of the Land-Grant Act of 1862*. University of Illinois Studies, vol. 4, No. 1, Urbana, Ill.: University of Illinois Press, 1910.

Kandel, Isaac L., *Federal Aid for Vocational Education*. Report to the Carnegie Foundation for the Advancement of teaching. Bulletin No. 10, New York: Carnegie Foundation, 1917.

Kuhn, Madison, *Michigan State, The First Hundred Years, 1855–1955*. East Lansing, Mich.: Michigan State University Press, 1955.

Murray, Stanley N., Railroads and Agricultural Development of the Red River Valley of the North, 1870–1890. *Agricultural History*, XXXI, (Oct. 1957), 57–66.

Parker, William B. *The Life and Public Service of Justin Smith Morrill*. Boston: Houghton, Mifflin Co., 1924.

Rolfsrud, Erling N., *Lanterns over the Prairies*, II. Brainerd, Minn., 1953.

Ross, Earle D., *Democracy's College, The Land-Grant Movement in the Formative Stage*. Ames, Iowa: Iowa State College Press, 1942.

Russell, Charles E. *Story of the Nonpartisan League*. New York: Harper and Bros., 1929.

Saloutos, Theodore and John D. Hicks, *Agricultural Discontent in the Middle West*. Madison: University of Wisconsin Press, 1951.

Saloutos, Theodore. *Rise of the Nonpartisan League in North Dakota*. Agricultural History, XX (1946), 43–44.

Smith, Clarence B., and Meredith Chester Wilson, *The Agricultural Extension System of the United States*. New York: John Wiley and Sons, Inc., 1930.

True, Alfred C., *A History of Agricultural Education in the United States*. United States Department of Agriculture. Miscellaneous Publication No. 36. July, 1929, Washington D. C.: Government Printing Office, 1929.

True, Alfred C., *A History of Agricultural Experimentation and Research in the United States, 1607–1925, including a History of the United States Department of Agriculture*, United States Department of Agriculture, Miscellaneous Publication No. 251; Washington D.C.: Government Printing Office, 1937.

True, Alfred C., *History of Agricultural Extension Work in the United States, 1785–1923*, United States Department of Agriculture, Miscellaneous Publication No. 15, Oct. 1928, Washington, D.C.: Government Printing Office, 1928.

Viles, Jonas, *The University of Missouri, a Centennial History*, Columbus, Mo.: University of Missouri, 1939.

Willard, Julius T., *History of the Kansas State College of Agriculture and Applied Science*, Manhattan, Kans.: Kansas State College Press, 1940.

Works, George N., and Barton Morgan, *The Land Grant College*, Staff Study No. 10 prepared for the Advisory Committee on Education, Washington, D.C.: Government Printing Office, 1939.

PERSONAL INTERVIEWS

Alfred G. Arvold, Fargo, N. D.
Mrs. William B. Bell, Washington, D. C., (Feb., 1949).
J. Allen Clark, Washington, D. C., (Feb., 1949).
Dr. John Lee Coulter, Washington, D. C., (June 20, 1950)
Robert N. Dolve, N.D.A.C.
Ralph E. Dunbar, N.D.A.C.
John W. Haw, (May 22, 1951)
A. Glenn Hill, N.D.A.C.
Lucile Horton, N.D.A.C.
Fred S. Hultz, N.D.A.C.

Cap. E. Miller, N.D.A.C.
Casper I. Nelson, N.D.A.C.
Ole A. Olson, New Rockford, N. D. (Oct. 10, 1951)
Alfred H. Parrott, N.D.A.C.
O. A. Stevens, N.D.A.C.
H. L. Walster, N.D.A.C.
John C. West, Pres., U.N.D.

(Names without a date indicate several interviews over an extended time.)

Index

Aandahl, Fred, 196
Aarnes, Hale, 203, 204, 242
Abbott, John, 166
Accreditation, 153
Adams, A. Paul, 213, 238
Adams Act, 230
Administration Avenue, 202
Administration Building, 34, 35, 202, 217
Administrative Committee, 157
Advisory Committee, 110, 128, 182, 184, 204, 205, 208, 209, 214
Agassiz, 70, 74, 116, 118
"Aggies," 116, 251
Agricultural Adjustment Act, 139, 140, 146, 232, 240
Agricultural Building, 105, 115
Agricultural College. *See* North Dakota Agricultural College
Agricultural Economics, 107, 108, 113, 186, 206, 208, 212, 233, 238
Agricultural Education, 107, 108
Agricultural Entomology, 107, 109, 186, 203, 213, 238, 242
Agricultural Science Building, 199
Agriculture, School of, 90, 107, 108, 131, 144, 168, 176, 193, 201, 203, 204, 212, 218, 222, 232, 251, 252
Agronomy, Department of, 39, 107, 213, 233, 238
Agronomy Seed Farm, 191, 234
Airheart, Walter Lee, 168–70
Alba Bales House, 106, 201
Alma Mater, 80
Alpha Gamma Rho, 83, 180
Alpha Mu, 82–3
Alpha Zeta, 83, 167
Alumni, 118–19, 148, 190, 221, 222, 223, 224, 225, 248
Alumni Association, 118, 132, 136, 146–49, 154, 165, 182, 183, 198, 206, 220, 250, 255
American Association of University Professors, 110, 126–27, 129, 204, 206, 210
American Federation of Teachers, 91, 98, 129
American Pharmaceutical Association, 224
American Student Union, 141
American Youth Foundation, 168
Anderson, Albert W., 187
Anderson, Clifford O., 196
Anderson, Edwin M., 213, 241
Anderson, Ernest G., 241
Anderson, Harry G., 240
Anderson, Minnie, 107, 110, 193, 214
Animal Husbandry, Department of, 107, 137, 153, 201, 237, 238
Animal Industry, Division of, 168, 185
Applied Arts and Sciences, School of, 90, 131, 193, 202–204, 213, 242, 251–52, 254
Appropriations, 23, 26, 31, 35–6, 77, 88, 105, 106, 115, 125, 127, 140, 183, 189, 195–99, 229–31, 234
Arbor Day, 68
Architecture, Department of, 107, 109
Armistad, Wilbur, 243
Armory, 34, 35, 36, 71, 73, 100, 123
Army Administration School, 180
Army Specialized Training Program, 180
Arnason, Albert F., 182, 184, 188, 193, 206
Arnason, R. Gordon, 155
Arnold, Cyril, 115
Arvold, Alfred G., 39, 48, 58, 75–78, 108, 142, 157, 203
Athenian Literary Society, 29, 75, 76, 118
Athletic Association, 69, 72, 251
Athletic Board of Control, 69, 164
Athletics, 69, 70, 72, 115–16, 123, 166, 189,

218; baseball, 73; basketball, 71-3, 115, 166, 189, 215, 218; football, 70-1, 115, 166, 189, 218; track, 73, 115; women's 72, 116, 218; bowling, 217
Atomic Energy Commission, 241
Audit, 35, 152-53

Babcock, Ray, 81
Bachman, Harold, 222
Bacteriology, *See* Biology
Bailey, Clyde L., 185, 221
Baird, R. O., 103
Baker, George J., 149-50, 176
Bale, Stanley N., 240
Bales, Alba, 106, 107, 110, 144, 150, 152, 161, 173-74, 201
Balke, Frank T., 190
Bangs, Philip R., 209
Bank of North Dakota, 87, 228
Bankhead-Jones Act, 132, 136, 141, 228, 230
Barr, Paul E., 243
Barrows, Thomas, 153
Barton, Orla A., 186
Bartow, Josephine, 214
Baseball, *See* Athletics
Basketball, *See* Athletics
Batt, Max, 37
Bawden, William T., 88
Beckwith, Newell P., 223
Bell, William B., 39, 42, 72
Benidt, Maurice, 155
Benton, Alva H., 112, 113, 233
Bentson, Ben Charles (Chuck), 218
Berntson, Byron, 240
Better Farming Association, 58-61
Beutel, Frederick K., 210
Beyers, Otto J., 165, 217
Biology, 18, 22, 40, 108; bacteriology, 40, 91, 108, 109, 232, 238, 241; botany, 18, 22, 46, 91, 108, 150, 238; zoology, 40, 91, 108, 203, 213, 232, 238
Birch, Fred, 71, 72
Birkeland, Jorgen M., 224
Bismarck, 7, 9, 10, 11, 12, 14, 65, 77, 136
Bison, 74, 115, 116, 118
Bison Furrows, 167, 168
Bjornson, B. K., 146
Black Maria, 65
Blake, Martin J., 214
Blakely, Harry E., ("Red"), 115
Blue Book, 43, 92, 99, 110, 157, 160, 188
Blue Key, 118, 246
Board of Administration, 85, 96-9, 102-04, 106-07, 108, 111, 120, 123-41, 144-55, 159-60, 164, 227

Board of Public Speaking Control, 76, 160
Board of Publications, 118
Board of Regents, 44, 62, 86, 88, 90, 92, 94, 188, 227
Board of Trustees (or Directors), 16-18, 19, 27-28, 40, 42, 54, 61, 87
Bolley, Henry L., 18, 19, 22, 24, 26, 27, 28, 42, 46-7, 58, 61, 62, 64, 65, 68, 69-70, 72, 90, 91, 99, 103, 108, 124-25, 176, 177, 231, 232
Borderud, Viola, 161
Borke, Millard, 155
Borleske, Stanley, 108, 115
Bosch, Wouter, 213, 241
Botany, Department of, *See* Biology
Bottenfield, L. S., 25, 27, 36, 42, 68
Bottineau, 12, 121, 152
Brandenberg, T. O., 200
Brannon, Melvin A., 70
Brekke, Julia, 176, 241
Brentzel, W. E., 213, 233
Brodshaag, Melvin, 224
Brostrom, Paul ("Red"), 189
Brumbaugh, A. J., 153
Bryan, William Jennings, 76
Bryant, Reece L., 186, 238
Buchanan, M. L., 185, 238
Budewig, Caroline, 199, 214
Buildings and Grounds, 25, 26, 34, 35, 36, 65, 105, 106, 123, 167, 172-3, 196, 197, 199, 200, 202, 216-17, 220
Burchard, F. F., 152
Burgum, Jessamine Slaughter, 35, 65, 201, 222
Burke, Andrew H., 19
Burke, John, 76
Burke, Merrill S., 240
Byrne, M. S., 208

Cahill, Judson, 102
Callenbach, John A., 212
Calnan, John W., 208
Campus, 201-02, *See also* Buildings and Grounds
Campus Avenue, 202
Capper-Kitchen Act, 230
Carnegie Library, 36
Carrick, L. L., 107, 109, 131, 150, 157, 173
Carrithers, F. B., 116
Carter, Jack F., 213, 238
Casey, P. M., 96, 102
Cass County, 8, 11, 13, 14
Cassel, J. Frank, 203, 205, 215
Catalogs, 24, 65, 74, 80
Catholic students, 219
Cereal Technology, 198, 202, 236, 238

Index

Ceres Hall, 35, 83, 111, 180, 200, 202
Cerveny, Clara, 202, 214
Chaney, George A., 134
Chapel, 67-8
Chemistry Building, 35, 200
Chemistry, 18, 21, 22, 24, 26; Department of, 50; School of, 90, 107, 109, 131, 150, 173, 193, 200, 213; Chemical Technology, 252; Agricultural Chemistry, Department of, 107, 233, 238; Biochemistry, Department of, 107, 213, 238, 242; Inorganic Chemistry, Department of, 107; Organic Chemistry, Department of, 107; Physical Chemistry, Department of, 107; Protective Coatings, Department of, 213
Chernick, M. H., 152
Chisholm, Haile, 37, 52, 177
Christians, C. J., 242
Christensen, A. M., 178, 222
Christensen, Fred W., 91, 110, 112, 114
Church, Louis K., 12
Church, W. J., 126
Churchill, O. O., 40, 52, 107, 187, 201
Churchill Hall, 201
Clagett, Carl, 234
Clark, J. Allen, 72, 225
Clason, John, 155
Claxton, P. P., 88
Cleland, C. B., 243
Cochems, Eddie, 70
Coffman, Lotus D., 88, 132
Colberg, Wayne J., 240
Cole, Dorothy, 116
Cole, Myrtle Gleason, 111, 114
College and State, 104, 118-19, 248
College Council, 92, 110-11, 157, 188, 203-06, 209, 214-15, 218
College Farmers' Union, 141
College Hall, 25, 26, 34, 65, 67, 77
College hymn, 73
College placement service, 217
College Street, 202
Comita, Gabriel W., 243, 244
Commencement, 29, 68, 187, 200, 201, 220-26
Commissioner of Agriculture and Labor, 96, 104, 126
Committee of 100, 166
Communism, 132, 207
Conmy, E. T., 151, 208, 209
Conmy, J. F. X., 209
Constitution, College, 43, 92, 99, 110, 157, 160, 188, 204, 210, 214-15
Cook, Glenn, 146
Cooper, Thomas P., 58, 59, 61, 62, 86, 91

Cortright, Ion, 115, 249
Cosgriff, Ed, 134
Costello, Patrick H., 224
Coulter, John Lee, 103-120, 123, 125, 168, 171, 188, 194, 221, 228, 249, 250
Council, College. *See* College Council
Council for Agricultural Education and Research, 197, 198, 205
Crack squad, 73
Craighead, Edwin B., 88, 89
Crawford, Lewis F., 62, 88, 93
Crom, Robert, 199
Crouch, Irene, 240
Crowley, Mrs. Matt, 161
Cyclone Circus, 75-6
Cyr, Frank, 244

Dacotah Field, 71, 164, 166
Dahl, Math, 159, 160
Dairy Building, 25, 36, 202
Dairy Department of, 54, 107, 238
Dakin, Emily, 217
Dakota Hall, 94, 166, 167, 180, 190, 201
Dakota Territory, 3, 7, 8
Dalrymple Experimental Plot, 237
Danforth Foundation, 168
Danielson, Robert E., 218
Darling, Elmer C., 174, 187
Darrow, Frank, 72, 73
Darrow, Kent, 72
Darrow, Mary, 68. *See* also Mary Darrow Weible
Davy, Leita, 174, 202
Dawson, Ruth, 240
Deans, *See* names of individual deans.
Dean of men, 39, 131, 144, 150, 154, 157, 166, 181, 184
Dean of women, 40, 111, 112, 201
Debating, 75
Degrees: M.S., 42, 215; Ph.D., 215-16, 255; honorary, 176-77, 184, 187, 221-25
DeLong, Grace, 176, 240, 241
Delta Phi Beta, 83
Demonstration farms, 53-54, 230
Depressions, 27, 124, 126, 130, 135, 138, 139, 229
Development survey, 196
Devils Lake, 12, 14, 48, 77
Dewey, George, 115
Dice, James R., 107, 128
Dickinson Teachers College, 134
Dietrich, Irvine T., 240
Dillman, A. C., 46
Dinan, A. Pearl, 40, 100, 112, 157, 187, 201
Dinan Hall, 201

300   *Beacon Across the Prairie*

Dinwoodie, Florenz, 155
Dinwoodie, J. T. E., 137, 140
Disciples of Christ, 219
Dispensary, 172
Dixon, Harry, 203, 250
Dobie, Gilmour ("Gil"), 70–71, 72
Doctors of Service, 118, Appendix VIII
Dogger, James R., 213, 238
Dolve Hall, 201
Dolve, Robert M., 39, 110, 131, 144, 150, 152, 161, 193, 201, 213, 222
Doneghue, R. C., 39, 83
Donnelly, Percy J., 208, 222
Dormitories, 26, 34, 35, 68, 111, 123, 171, 180, 200, 201, 202, 216
Doubly, John, 236
Dramatics, 75, 77–8, 142
Dressel, Paul, 5, 244
Drought, 27, 29, 31, 85, 124, 126, 135, 138, 139, 140, 141
Dunbar, Ralph E., 173, 193, 204, 213, 215, 244
Duplication, 88, 108, 133, 144, 205–06
Durkin, W. J., 219
Dworak, Mayme, 92
Dynes, C. R., 81
Dynes, O. W., 81, 118

Eddy, Edward D., 3
Edgeley Branch Station, 53
Education, Department of, 7, 108, 111, 174, 187, 203, 204; School of, 39, 40, 90, 108, 131, 187, 254
Edwards, Major Alonzo W., 8, 9, 11, 19
Edwin Booth Club, 75, 77
Elks Club, 194; Lodge, 246
Ellendale, 12, 48, 121, 152
Ellsworth, Ralph, 197
El Zagal Shrine, 142
Employment service, *See* Student employment
Engineering, Department of, 25; School of, 131, 144, 193, 196, 201, 208, 212, 213, 222, 251; Agricultural Engineering, 39, 189, 238; Civil Engineering, 107, 108, 109, 187; Electrical Engineering, 109, 203, 213, 241; Industrial Engineering, 213, *see also* Mechanic Arts.
English, 25, 36, 39, 40, 108, 213
Enrollment, *See* Student enrollment
Entrance requirements, 23, 24, 41, 66
Erickson, O. E., 126
Evangelical United Brethren students, 219
Eveleth, D. F., 238
Eversull, Frank L., 158–161, 163–66, 168, 170, 172, 173, 175, 176, 179, 181, 182, 183–84, 188, 220
Eversull, Harry K., 164
Ewen, Amos, 250
Experiment Station. *See* North Dakota Agricultural Experiment Station
Extension Service. *See* North Dakota Agricultural Extension Service

Faculty, 16, 23, 25, 27, 29, 36–40, 41–43, 64, 90–92, 93, 98–9, 102–03, 108–11, 126–32, 134, 164–65, 173–75, 180–83, 188, 203–10, 212–14
Faculty Women's Club, 100
Faiman, Robert N., 202, 241
Fallis, M. H., 81
Fancher, F. B., 12
Fargo, 8, 9, 10, 11, 12, 13, 14, 15, 28, 89, 102, 119, 127, 147, 148, 150, 180, 183, 186, 191, 194, 205–06
Fargo Chamber of Commerce, 120, 145, 147, 149, 151, 163, 165, 191, 194–95, 205, 221
Fargo College, 10, 18, 23, 64, 71, 102
Fargo Courier News, 95
Fargo Daily Argus, 8, 9, 19
Fargo Daily Forum, 27, 89, 133, 134, 137, 192
Fargo Daily Republican, 8
Fargo Garden Society, 232, 233
Fargo Kiwanis Club, 132
Fargo Park Board, 48
Fargo Rotary Club, 119
Fargo School of Religious Education, 169–70, 218
Fargo United Fund, 218
Fargo, Y.M.C.A., 71
Fargo-Moorhead Executives Club, 183, 223
Farm Credit Administration, 140
Farm Folk School, 166–68
Farm Research, 238
Farmers' Alliance, 12, 27
Farmers Equity Union, 59
Farmers' Excursions, 55
Farmers' Institutes, 25, 54–55
Farmers Union. *See* North Dakota Farmers Union
Farrell, George E., 140
Federal Crop Insurance, 150
Federal Emergency Relief Administration, 131
Federal Government, 5, 6, 19, 149, 227–29, 230–31
Fees. *See* Student fees
Festival Hall, 36, 73, 123, 180, 185

Index 301

Field, Merton, 29
Field House, 180, 190, 196, 202, 214, 229, 250
Fine, C. W., 141
Finlayson, Christine, 109, 110, 199, 215
Finley, Charles, 153
Finnegan, Casey C., 115, 189, 201, 218
First National Bank and Trust Company, 228-229
Fisher, Glenn W., 242-243
Fleetwood, C. W., 213
Fletcher, Donald G., 224
Fletcher, Jim, 166
Flor, Harold H., 236
Foley, James W.,
Football. *See* Athletics
Forkner, Mark I., 160
Fort, Abercrombie, 7; Buford, 7; Union, 7
Foss, Palmer L., 225
Founding of North Dakota Agricultural College, 3-19
4-H Institute, 57, 94, 239, 240, 245
Foust, H. L., 233
Fowler, Arthur W., 68, 120, 123, 134
Fowler, C. Ross, 223
Francis, O. W., 16, 17, 19
Francis Hall, 26, 34, 35, 36, 55, 68, 81, 106, 200
Fraternities, 82-83, 118, 180, 216
Frazier, Lynn, 92, 103, 126
Fredrikson, Lars O., 161
Fulbright Grants, 246

Garrison dam, 235, 251
Gastman, Louis, 37
Gay Cat Day, 118
Geary, Thomas C., 210
Geiken, Daddy, 52
Geology, 108, 187, 205-06, 209, 254
Giesecke, G. Ernst, 202, 203, 242
Gilbertson, H. W., 149
Gildersleeve, Thomas W., 240
Gilles, K. A., 238
Gillette, John M., 92
Gillig, E. M., 125, 158
Gjernes, Oscar, 217
Good Government League, 154
Gooden, Psyche, M., 117
Goplen, Orville, 155
Gorman, Norbert D., 140, 144, 146, 150, 152, 161, 241
Gottschalk, C. A., 107
Government Insurance (G.I.) Bill, 189, 212
Graduate School, 204, 205, 215-16, 252, 255

Grand Forks, 12, 13
Grand Forks Herald, 11, 28, 122
Grasse, Edythe A., 78
Grasshoppers, 48
Graves, Harry A., 240
Graves, William F., 229
Gray, Horace M., 210
Great Northern Railway, 7, 17, 48, 53, 55, 56, 77
Green, Parker, 215
Gregoire, Beulah F., 218
Grimes, Ruby, 109
Grimm Alfalfa Association, 51
Griswold, D. J., 113
Gunkelman, Ralph, 120
Gunlogson, G. B., 242
Gunvaldson, O., 146, 153
Gustafson, George W., 81
Guy, William, 146
Guy, William L., 255

Haas, Albert, 208
Hagan, John, 96, 102, 128, 137, 144, 145, 149, 158, 159, 160
Hagan, Steve W., 128, 136, 145, 155-156, 175, 220
Haggart, John, 9, 12, 14, 15, 19
Halbeisen, J. G., 146
Haley, Alice, 150, 157
Hall, Charles M., 29, 38, 70, 73
Hall, J. B., 8
Halland, J. G., 37
Hallenberg, Victor, 71
Halvorson, Elmer H., 243
Hance, R. T., 108
Handbook of North Dakota Plants, 242
Hanna, Louis B., 62, 88, 92
Hannah, John, 256
Hanson, Fritz, 189
Hanson, Harry G., 225
Hanson, Herbert C., 137, 149, 150, 161
Hanson, Thomas L., 173
Hardaway, Elliot, 175-176, 187
Harrell, W. F., 108, 116
Harris, J. D., 134, 145, 159, 160
Harrison, John, 70
Haslerud, Edwin J., 140, 176. 193, 215, 240
Hatch, Dorothy, 110
Hatch Act, 6, 17, 230
Haver, Cecil B., 206, 208, 209, 210
Haw, John, 59, 103, 223
Hayden, W. H., 25, 73
Hays, W. M., 24, 65
Hays, Mrs. W. M., 24, 65
Hazen, Arlon G., 212, 215

Heath, Thomas R., 221
Heinrich, Max A., 214
Helgason, Arni, 177
Helgeson, Earl A., 150, 238, 242
Hemphill, Perry V., 213
Henning, Knute, 173
Henry, Howard I., 161, 184
Herbison, Herbert W., 240
Hertel, Leo, 203, 215, 242, 246
Hettinger Branch Station, 53
Higgins, Naurine, 240
High School, 40–41, 187
Higher Education, 8, 12–14, 15, 135, 156, 161, 182, 227, 254
Hilborn, John W., 29
Hill, A. Glenn, 174, 193, 216, 244
Hill, Edith, Club, 82
Hinebauch, Theries D., 18, 22, 24, 26, 65, 70
History, 37, 108, 170
Hjelmstad, J. H., 108
Hofstrand, C. H., 200, 222
Hogoboom, Dale, 155
Hoisveen, Milo, 224
Holes, James, 17
Hollis, A. P., 58
Hollister, George H., 62
Holm, Glenn C., 203, 212
Home Economics building, 198, 199
Home Economics, 24, 56; Department of, 26, 34, 35, 37, 68; School of, 90, 107, 110, 131, 144, 173–74, 199, 201, 202, 214, 243, 252; Applied Art, Department of, 107, 214; Clothing and Textiles, Department of, 107, 110, 214; Foods and Nutrition, Department of, 107, 214; Home Economics Education, Department of, 214
Home Makers Clubs, 114, 239, 240
Home Management House, 106, 173, 201
Honors Day, 200, 201, 246
Hooper, Sidney W., 95
Hopper, T. H., 107, 114, 138, 233
Horn, Paul, 222
Horne, John, 81
Horticulture, Department of, 21, 48, 68, 107, 108, 150, 186, 213, 231, 233, 238
Horton, Lucile, 110, 174, 202, 214
Householder, Fred C., 174
Housing, 26, 34, 35, 123, 180, 181–82, 190, 201, 216
Hovde, Frederick L., 221
Hove, John, 213
Hoverstad, A. T., 55
Hubbard, N. K., 11
Huey, S. Lynn, 146

Hughes, Max, 146
Hult, Gottfried, 36
Hultz, Fred S., 193–97, 198, 199, 200, 201, 203, 204, 206, 207, 208, 209, 210, 212, 214, 215, 218, 221, 229, 242, 253
Hultz, Mrs. Fred S., 214, 218, 242
Hunsaker, Andrew F., 108
Hunter, William C., 109, 170, 203, 242
Huntoon, Homer B., 109

Inaugurations, 164, 168, 185, 194
Influenza epidemic, 171
Initiative and referendum, 86
Initiated measures, 86, 127, 154, 159, 199, 253, 255
Intercollegiate Live Stock Judging Team, 51, 218
Interest and income account, 228
International Relations Club, 141
Intrastate Student Conference, 183
Iverson, Peter J., 187, 203, 244

Jamestown, 10, 12, 13, 14
Jensen, Christen, 205, 214, 238
Jensen, Clarence, 202, 223
Jensen, Katherine, 68, 90, 91, 98
Jensen, Lars A., 240
Jestrab, Mrs. Elvira, 208
Johnson, Arnold ("Swede"), 166
Johnson, Arthur C., 196, 205
Johnson, Leo, 219
Johnson, Roy, 120, 161, 184, 196, 206, 223
Johnson, Mrs. Vernon, 208
Jones, Edward H., 107, 108, 174
Jones, Paul, 172

Kaiser, Ervin E., 218
Kappa Kappa Gamma, 83
Kasson, Paul R., 240
Kaufman, E. E., 25, 26, 54, 73
Kazeck, Melvin E., 242
Keene, Edward S., 25, 26, 28, 42, 73, 83, 90, 91, 102, 107, 109, 110, 116, 168
Kellogg, C. E., 128
Kelley, Clark, 77
Kepner, Gordon, 218
Kidder, Merle, 161
Kiesling, R. L., 213, 238
Kildee, Henry H., 177
Kinzer, R. A., 137, 144, 145, 149, 152, 159, 160
Kitchen, Joseph A., 104, 126
Klostermann, Harold, 213, 238
Knight, S. Fred, 169
Konen, James C., 224
Kostka, Stan, 189

Index 303

Kraft, Richard (Dick), 69, 220
Kristjanson, Baldur J., 208, 209, 210
Kruse, Martin G., 208
Kruse Park, 216
Kuhn, Kenneth, 109, 213, 242
Kvallen, Arne, 219

Ladd, Edwin F., 18, 19, 22, 23, 25, 26, 28, 29, 42, 48–51, 52, 56, 61, 62, 64, 83, 85, 86, 90–100, 102, 103, 200, 222, 231
Ladd, D. Milton, 200, 222
Ladd Hall, 200, 202, 222
LaMoure, Jud T., 11, 14
Lana, E. P., 213, 238
Land-Grant College, 3, 4, 5, 6, 34, 133, 195, 227, 249, 250, 251, 256–57
Langdon Branch Station, 53
Langer, William, 126, 128, 134, 135, 136, 142, 145–48, 152, 156, 158
Langer, Mrs. William, 135
Larsen, Spencer A., 133
Latzke, Esther, 114
Lawrence, Aubrey, 92
Leach, Addison, 14, 70, 220
Leader, The, 89, 127–28, 133, 135, 147, 155
Lee, Ida Bisek Procop, 177–78
Leeby, Constance, 110, 114
LeFor, Adam, 135
Legislation, 5, 15–16, 19, 85–6, 125, 127, 130, 134
Legislative Research Committee, 195, 198, 254
Legislature. *See* North Dakota Legislature
Lemke, William, 103
Lettermen's Club, 115
Lewis, Adah, 107
Library facilities, 23, 26, 34, 36, 108, 141, 175–76, 187, 189, 197, 200, 217, 219, 254
"Limited Service," *See* Retirement, 182
Lincoln, Abraham, 4, 256
Lind, Alex, 221
Lindley, Walter C., 156
Literary societies, 74, 75, 76
Little All American, 189
Little Country Theater, 67, 77–78, 106, 142
Longwell, John H., 168, 181, 184–88, 189, 191, 192, 193
Lounsberry, Clement A., 34, 84
Lowell, Jacob, 17
Lum, E. D., 132
Lumry, R. Worth, 146, 250
Lutheran Student Association, 219
Luymes, L. Leslie, 218
Lynch, John, 155

Lyon, S. S., 17, 28
Lyons, Richard, 242, 243

McArdle, Harry W., 22, 25, 26, 27, 42, 48, 78, 95, 99, 171, 219, 220
McCannell, A. D., 208
McCaul, Verne J., 224
McCauley, Prof., 215
McClure, Robert, 206, 207
McCulloch, Clarence, 135
McDonald, May C., 61
McDowell, J. C., 39
McGregor, James, 155
McGuigan, James, 223
McKenzie, Alex, 8, 9, 10, 11, 14
McMahon, Don, 103
MacPherson, Hector, 103
McVeety, Ethel, 36, 108, 175
Maintenance Building, 189, 196, 202, 220
Mall, 202. *See* Buildings and Grounds
Manns, T. F., 72, 81
Martel, Theodore, 95
Master's degrees, *See* Degrees
Mathematics, 22, 89, 108, 144, 254
May, Emily, 72
Mayville Teachers College, 12, 134, 152
Mead, A. E., 253
Meadows, Ada, 91
Mechanic Arts, School of, 90, 102, 107, 109, 110, 117, 166, 250
Mechanical Building, 26, 34, 35, 73, 106, 200
Meinecke, Bernard F. ("Ben"), 68, 120, 222
Melanson, L. L., 241
Mendenhall, Dean, 81
Men's Residence Hall. *See* Dormitories
Mercer, W. H., 91
Metcalf, H. E., 94
Methodist students, 219
Metzinger, Leon, 108, 110
Michigan Agricultural College, 4, 22, 299; State University, 256
Milbraith, D. G., 91
Military training, 73, 108, 116, 141–42, 180–190
Mill tax, 36, 229
Miller, Cap E., 91, 107
Miller, Claudie, 115
Miller, Clifton E., 196, 214
Miller, George E., 171
Miller, H. F., 12, 14, 27
Miller, John, 15
Miller, Merlin W., 203
Minard, Archie E., 39, 79, 92, 94, 99, 103,

108, 109, 110, 118, 120, 122, 128, 131, 157, 200, 202, 215
Minard Hall, 86, 200, 202
Minnear, F. L., 213, 215
Minot Teachers College, 48, 77, 134
Mirgain, Frank C., 208, 213
Modern Languages, 25, 37, 108, 203
Moir, D. Ross, 243
Monroe, Charley F., 114, 131, 139, 140
Montgomery, Craig R., 240
Moodie, Thomas H., 135
Morrill, Justin, 4, 6, 15, 164
Morrill Act, 3, 4, 5, 6, 15, 16, 33, 227
Morrill Hall, 105, 106, 115, 189, 200, 202, 229
Morris, Mercedes, 155
Moses, John, 159, 160, 161, 165
Muir, Robert T., 93, 96, 102, 103, 110
Mumford, F. B., 103
Munro, J. Alex, 109, 186, 203
Murphy, Dr., 94
Murphy, P. J., 161
Murphy, R. B., 126
Music, 78–80, 108
Music Hall, 35, 106, 200

Name change, 102, 247–255
Nasset, Robert and Shirley, 255
National Defense Education Act, 215, 245
National Institutes of Health, 199, 241
National Science Foundation, 215, 241, 242
National Youth Administration, 141, 166
Nelson, Casper I., 40, 91, 92, 98, 99, 103, 107, 108, 110, 112, 157, 171, 232
Nelson, DeLawrence, 155
Nelson, L. P., 217
Nemzek, Leo, 71
Nesbit, L. L., 233
New Salem Breeding Circuit, 51
Newman Club, 219
Newton, Julia D., 58, 61
Nickeus, Johnston, 8, 9
Nielson, Minnie, 96, 102, 104
Nonpartisan League, 59, 86–87, 92, 96, 99, 102, 106, 123, 126, 128, 155
Normanden, 153
North Central Association of Colleges, 153–56, 158, 159, 160, 163, 165, 176
North Central Conference, 102, 115, 123, 166, 201, 218
North Court, 190, 216
North Dakota, 3, 4, 6, 8, 34, 37, 46, 47, 58, 85, 99, 105, 112, 135, 164, 183, 197, 199, 205, 227, 238, 253, 257
North Dakota Agricultural College, 3, 5, 6, 11–15, 21–23, 31–34, 87–89, 93–95, 102, 104–05, 108, 114, 123–24, 132–37, 144–48, 163–65, 179, 183, 228, 248
North Dakota Agricultural College *Alumni Review,* 198
North Dakota Agricultural College Memorial Foundation, 191, 229
North Dakota Agricultural Experiment Station, 16–18, 26–7, 46–53, 91, 112–113–14, 124, 138–39, 191–92, 229–30, 231–38
North Dakota Agricultural Extension Service, 54–58, 60, 61, 86, 114, 139–41, 145–46, 230–31, 238–41
North Dakota Bar, 165
North Dakota Boys' and Girls' Institute, 57
North Dakota Cancer Society, 241
North Dakota Constitutional Convention, 12–14
North Dakota Council for Agricultural Education and Research, 198
North Dakota Educational Association, 156, 165, 227
North Dakota Experimental Union, 52
North Dakota Farm Bureau, 187, 205, 222, 223
North Dakota Farmers' Union, 116, 129, 216
North Dakota Government Survey Commission, 133
North Dakota Heart Association, 241
North Dakota Holiday Association, 137
North Dakota Homemakers' Council, 198, 246
North Dakota Horticultural Society, 178, 223, 233
North Dakota Institute for Regional Studies, 242–243
North Dakota Legislative Committee, 195, 254
North Dakota Legislature, 15, 19, 26, 27, 31, 36, 43, 49, 85–6, 87, 96, 125, 127, 130, 140, 141–42, 180, 189, 198–99, 229–31, 257
North Dakota Livestock Association, 122
North Dakota Loan Fund, 245
North Dakota State Employment Service, 217
North Dakota State University of Agriculture and Applied Science, 251–255
North Dakota Supreme Court, 135, 156, 227
North Dakota Taxpayers' Association, 126, 127, 133
Northern Pacific Railway, 7, 12, 17, 28, 48, 53, 55, 56

Index

Northwest Farm Managers' Association, 223
Northwest Ordinance of 1787, 5
Norum, Enoch B., 212, 238
Nott, Merle, 190, 196
Nugent, Claude, 62, 70, 220
Nygaard, Cliff, 166
Nymon, Mavis C., 214
Nystuen, Peder A., 212

Oakey, J. A., 187
Officer Candidates School, 180
Ohio Company, 5
Old Main, 25, 34, 43, 67, 189, 217
Oldfather, Charles H., 160
Olsen, Edgar I., 53, 103, 146
Olsen, Fred, 68, 120, 221
Olson, Clarence C., 240
Olson, Kenneth S., 240
Olson, Mancur, 218
Olson, Ole, 135
Olson, Peter J., 131, 144, 150–51, 152, 161
Olson, R. C., 150
Olson, Mrs. R. L., 199
Olstad, Einar H., 243
Omnibus Bill, 12
Ostman, Arthur, 116
Ottersen, Rudolf, 109, 213, 242
"Our State is Our Campus," 104, 119
Ouradnik, Robert, 219
Oveson, Karl, 202, 220
Owens, Robert L., 255

Painter, Edgar P., 234
Palmer, Bertha, 126
Palmer, W. C., 56, 58, 103, 176
Parizck, E. G., 176
Parrott, Alfred H., 39, 69, 72, 127, 144, 150, 152, 161, 187, 190, 203, 219–20, 225, 249, 250
Parrott, Robert, 225
Parsons, Jesse, 242
Pearce, W. T., 91, 107
Pearce, William R., 206, 207, 208
Pearson, Harriet, 175
Peik, W. E., Report, 132, 157
Pembina, 7
Peoples' Party, 27
Pettee, Eugene W., 213
Pharmacy, School of, 40, 107, 110, 131, 149, 150, 193, 214, 225, 241, 242, 252
Pharmacy Building, 198–199, 201
Phi Kappa Phi, 118, 246
Phi Upsilon Omicron, 83, 198
Phillips, Lyle W., 225
Philomathean Literary Society, 75, 76

Philosophy, Doctor of, *See* Degrees
Physical Education, 26, 36, 73, 108, 115, 116, 123, 124, 218
Physics, Department of, 107, 109, 208, 213, 241, 254
Pi Gamma Mu, 118
Pierce, Gilbert A., 11
Plant Pathology, Department of, 213, 233, 238
Plath, William, 200
Polytechnic Society, 43
Populism, 27, 31
Posin, Daniel Q., 205, 208, 209, 210
Post Office, 250
Post, R. L., 186
Post War Education Planning Conference, 181
Poultry Husbandry, 238
Power, James B., 7, 17, 27, 28–9, 31
Power, James A., 62, 90
Power machinery, 37, 75
Practice House, 106
Preparatory department, 24, 41, 67
Presidents. *See* individual names: Stockbridge, Worst, Ladd, Coulter, Shepperd, Eversull, Longwell, Hultz
President's house, 196
Priscilla Club, 100
Progressive Era, 31, 55, 85–86
Promersberger, W. J., 167, 214, 215
Prospectus of the North Dakota Agricultural College, 22, 23
Public Relations, 163, 164, 165, 183, 194, 195, 196, 199, 219
Purdue University, 22, 47
Purge, 144–61, 188
Purnell Act, 230
Putnam, Dr. Clarence S. ("Doc"), 38, 78–80, 108, 168, 200
Putnam Hall, 200
Pye, Willard D., 187, 206
Pyle, John E. ("Jack"), 191, 221

Quarter Century Club, 187

Raaen, Aagot, 242
Raer, Elsie, 218
Ralston Purina Mills, 168
Randlett, Gordon W., 56, 58, 86, 99, 103, 114
Rathman, F. H., 213
Record, The, 34
Red River Valley, 7, 17, 28, 104, 194, 232
Reed, C. P., ("Chalky"), 189
Reed, Robert B., 29, 65, 70, 120, 201, 222
Reed Hall, 201

Regents, *See* Board of Regents
Regulatory Division, 50, 103, 129
Reinhart, R. C., 220
Religion, 67, 78, 80–2, 166, 168–70, 218–19
Remington, Roe E., 107
Reorganization of the College, 90, 131
Republican Party, 8, 27, 28, 31, 32, 87, 88, 123, 126
Research, 26–7, 46–53, 112–14, 137–38, 231–38
Reserve Officers Training Corps, 108, 116, 141–142, 180, 190
Retirement, 182, 185, 201, 203, 213, 214, 220, 222, 225
Reynolds, E. S., 91, 92, 108
Reynolds, Emily, 214
Reynolds, Pauline, 241
Rheineck, Alfred E., 213, 241
Rhodes Scholarships, 218, 242, 246
Rian, E. P., 223
Rice, Elizabeth, 72
Richards, W. B., 39
Richardson, George, 71
Richardson, Marion B., 213
Richland County Farmer Globe, 132, 133
Riebe, Evelyn H., 107
Rilling, Harry E., 114, 176
Rishworth, Robert M., 128, 134, 137
Roach, Corwin C., 170, 218
Roberts, Samuel G., 8, 9, 11, 13, 14
Robinson, J. W., 200
Rockefeller Institute, 82
Roderick, L. M., 112, 131, 151, 233
Rolfsrud, Erling, 48
Rose, P. S., 37, 177
Ross, Earle D., 108
Rothrock, Clifford, 189
Rowe, Paul R., 216
Rueber, Arthur, 72
Rush, H. S., 109, 150, 157, 161
Russell, J. C., 240
Russell, John Hale, 160
Russell, Seth W., 203, 242, 243

Saalwechter, Leonard, 115, 123
Sackett, Leonard, 242
Sad, John, 209
Saddle and Sirloin Club, 51, 138
Salaries, 16, 29, 42, 97, 98–99, 126, 127, 128, 129–31, 135, 136, 140, 185, 196, 199, 204
Sales tax, 128
Sanderson, M. J., 17
Sanderson, Thomas, 49, 52
Sanitary Home, 56
Satterthwaite, S. T., 17

Sauvain, Nelson, 123, 124, 125, 128, 134
Scabbard and Blade, 141, 190
Schaetzel, Murray, 166
Schafer, Harold, 225
Schalk, Arthur F., 103, 107, 112, 233
Schermeister, Leo J., 214
Schickele, Rainer E., 186, 213
Schmidt, Carl H., 181, 217
Scholarships, 218, 245–246
Schollander, E. G., 53
Schollander, O. A., 146
School of Agriculture, *See* Agriculture
School of Applied Arts and Sciences. *See* Arts and Sciences
School of Chemistry or Chemical Technology. *See* Chemistry
School of Education. *See* Education
School of Engineering. *See* Engineering
School of Home Economics. *See* Home Economics
School of Mechanic Arts. *See* Mechanic Arts
School of Pharmacy. *See* Pharmacy
School of Science and Literature, 39, 108, 109
School of Veterinary Science. *See* Veterinary Science
Schulz, Arthur H., 240
Schultz, Joseph H., 186, 196
Schultz, W. H., 232
Schweitzer, Richard E., 166
Science Hall, 35, 86, 96, 106, 115, 124, 180, 200
Scow, Emil, 62
Sears-Roebuck and Company, 167, 168
Selective Service Act, 179
Senior Staff, 118, 246
Senn, Marie, 25, 26, 37, 68
Service Drive, 202
"Service to the State," 164
Sevrinson, Charles A., 150, 154, 157, 166, 181, 184, 196
Shafer, George F., 134
Sharivar, 219
Shepperd, John H., 24, 25, 26, 28, 29, 37, 39, 51–2, 68, 122–26, 128, 129, 130, 132, 134, 136, 142, 144–45, 146, 150, 153, 201, 228, 231
Shepperd, Mrs. Adele, 72, 142
Shepperd Arena, 201, 234
Sherman, R. H., 160
Shortridge, Eli, C. D., 27, 28
Shure, W. H., 196
Siberry, Robert, 219
Sigma Alpha Epsilon, 216

Sigma Alpha Iota, 102
Sigma Theta, 102
Sigma Xi, 174
Silver City, 216
Simmons, Abbie L., 40
Sixtieth Anniversary, 197
Skinner, F. F., 220
Slocum, Edith Fowler, 223
Slocum, Roy H., 39, 92, 98, 103, 107, 109, 110
Smith, Elvira, 110, 214
Smith, Gale, 217
Smith, Glenn S., 186, 205, 215, 231, 242, 243, 255
Smith, Irvin W., 39, 108, 131, 144, 150, 152, 161, 174
Smith, R. N., 126
Smith, Stanley A., 107
Smith-Hughes Act, 95, 228
Smith-Lever Act, 61, 86, 176, 230, 238
Social Sciences, 108, 203, 213, 243 (Sociology)
Soil Science, 212, 237, 238
Soil Survey, 38, 139
Sonquist, David E., 81, 225
Sons of American Revolution, 132
Sorlie, A. G., 115
Sparks Memorial Fellowshops, 246
Spaulding, Burleigh F., 9, 10, 11, 12, 13, 14, 90
Spectrum, 67, 68, 70, 72, 73, 74, 115, 118, 119, 247, 248, 249, 250, 251, 253
Speech, Department of, 108, 203
Stadium, 71, 164, 166, 190, 196, 198
Stallings, H. Dean, 187, 242
State Board of Higher Education, 154, 156, 159, 161, 181, 182, 183, 184, 189, 192, 193, 194, 196, 198, 199, 202, 204, 205, 206, 207, 208, 209, 210, 214, 215, 218, 223, 227, 253, 254
State College, 102, 247, 248, 250, 251
State College Engineer, 167, 250
State College Station, 250
State Department of Education, 174
State Livestock Sanitary Board, 200
State Mill and Elevator, 86, 87, 106, 128, 129
State School of Science, 133, 134
State Seed Commissioner, 47, 124–26, 137
State Superintendent of Public Instruction, 96, 104, 126, 134, 145, 156, 227
State Supreme Court, 93, 135, 156, 209
Stevens, Orin A., 38, 40, 125, 186, 187, 231–32, 242
Stewart, George, 81

Stoa, Theodore E., 57, 81, 119, 131, 213, 225, 233
Stockbridge, Horace E., 18, 19, 21, 22, 23, 26, 27, 28, 31, 64, 65
Stockbridge Hall, 201
Stodola, Quentin C., 217
Strayer, George D., 97
Street, John Paul, 215
Strum, George E., 240
Studer, Stafford, 170
Student Army Training Corps, 94, 167, 170
Student Commission, 67, 70, 74, 117, 118, 131, 182, 183, 217
Student employment, 117, 166, 217
Student enrollment, 24, 31, 36, 66, 90, 114, 116–17, 123, 166, 168, 179, 185, 189, 212, 216–17, 244–45
Student-faculty relations, 117, 142
Student fees, 66, 172, 190, 216, 228
Student government, 64, 66, 67, 74, 117, 142, 217
Student guidance, 116, 117, 142, 165, 181, 217
Student health, 170–73; Health Center, 170, 172–73
Student housing. *See* Housing
Student Life Special, 77
Student registration, 24, 116, 117, 179, 212
Student senate, 217, 218
Student trust fund, 172, 198
Student Union, 182, 189, 190, 202, 216–17
Students, 40, 64–83, 114–18, 123–24, 154, 166, 167, 183, 188, 189, 198, 203, 208, 217, 251, 252
Substations, 53, 230; Dickinson, 48, 53, 186, 235; Hettinger, 53; Minot, 48, 53, 77, 235; Williston, 235
Sudro, William F., 40, 107, 110, 131, 150, 157, 193, 201, 213, 223
Sudro Hall, 201
Summer School, 40, 111
Supervised Study, 111
Surveys, 88–89, 233, 254
Sweetman, Ray, 81
Sweitzer, Richard E., 166
Swisher, Charles L., 109

Tainter, E. J., 137
Tanberg, Larry, 166
Taylor, Fred R., 212, 238
Taylor, H. C., 103
Taylor, J. D., 62
Teachers' Union, 102

Theta Chi, 83, 180
Thompson, A. E., 134, 144, 145, 149, 158, 159, 160
Thompson, Elmer J., 107
Thompson, Eric, 118
Thompson, Matilda, 109, 174, 246
Thompson, O. A., 53
Thordarson, T. W., 111, 119
Thorfinnson, Matt, 81
Thorfinnson, T. S., 119
Thorson, Erling ("Bob"), 220
Tibert, George W., 37
Toring, Edythe, 220
Totten, George A., 93, 96, 102, 103, 110
Townley, Arthur C., 86–87
Track, 73. *See* Athletics
Traynor, Edwin, 223
Traynor, Jean, 145, 152, 161
Traynor, F. J., 161
Treumann, William B., 205, 208, 209, 210
Trowbridge, Perry F., 91, 99, 104, 112, 125, 128, 131, 138, 141
Trubey, Ralph, 194
Trullinger, R. W., 149
Trustees. *See* Board of Trustees
Trygstad, Vernon O., 225
Tudor, Marian D., 240
Tuesday Sewing Circle, 100

Ulio, Capt. James, 73, 76, 180
Ulsrud, Jennie, 128, 134, 137, 145, 148, 149, 151, 159, 160, 164
United Church of Christ, 219
United Presbyterian Church, 219
United States Armed Forces Institute, 181
United States Department of Defense, 184
University Christian Mission, 166
University of Minnesota, 70, 104, 123, 132
University of North Dakota, 6, 9, 10, 11, 12, 14, 15, 70, 71, 72, 82, 88, 92, 104, 126, 128, 132, 134, 137, 148, 156, 164, 166, 189
University of Wisconsin, 70, 104
Upson, E. M., 17

Vallambrosa, Louis, Duke of, 224
Valley City, 11, 12, 13, 134
Van Es, Leunis, 37, 38, 53, 90, 91, 184, 200
Van Es Laboratory, 200, 234
Van Vlissingen, Ernst, 213, 246
Vermilyea, C. E., 93
Veterans, 94–95, 181–83, 189, 190, 212
Veterinary Building, 35, 196, 200
Veterinary Medical Association, 184, 200

Veterinary Science, 18, 22, 24, 26, 53, 90, 91, 107, 108, 112, 131, 151, 203, 233, 234, 237, 238, 242
Vincent, Muriel C., 214

Wahpeton, 12, 13, 71
Waldron, Clare B., 18, 19, 21, 24, 26, 27, 28, 48, 68, 90, 91, 94, 99, 105, 107, 108, 176, 178, 186, 231, 232, 249
Waldron, Lawrence R., 48, 62, 68, 112, 177, 222, 231, 232
Wallace, J. D., 16
Walsh, Frederick G., 203, 208
Walsh, George H., 8, 9, 11
Walster, Harlow L., 46, 50, 91, 103, 109, 112, 131, 138, 140, 145, 151, 157, 161, 166, 167, 168, 176, 184, 185, 187, 193, 200, 201, 203, 222, 231, 232
Walster Hall, 201
Walter, Clarence, 81
Walters, Thorstina, 242
Wang, Gilman, 208
Warburton, C. W., 149, 150
Ward, Ralph D., 29, 70
War Training Programs. *See* S.A.T.C., R.O.T.C., Officer Candidate School, Army Administration School, A.S.T.P.
Wartchow, Beatrice M., 218
Washington Bicentennial, 142
Watt, William, 120
Webster, R. L., 107, 186
Weeks, A. D., 39, 56, 90, 92, 94, 99, 108, 111, 131, 174
Weeks, J. D., 244
Weesner, Kathryn M., 214
Weible, Mary Darrow, 68, 223, 225
Weinberg, E. H., 213
Welch, A. B., 145, 146
Welford, Walter, 135
Wendland, Ray, 196
Wengert, Norman L., 203, 205, 213
Weniger, Wanda (Brentzel), 233
Wenskunas, Mac P., 218
Wesley College, 169
Wesley Foundation, 219
West, John C., 132, 137, 144, 145, 146, 148, 149, 150, 153, 154, 155, 157
Westbee, D. W., 208
Weston, Eli, 132
Whalen, W. H., 25, 65
Whedon, Arthur D., 109, 193, 203
Wheeler, Ernie, 166, 189
White, Frank, 62, 93
Whitman, Warren C., 243
Whitney, Frank P., 208
Who's New Club, 214

Index

Widdifield, Russell B., 240
Wilcox, E. Mean, 103
Wilkins, Robert P. and Winona H., 242
Will, George F., 177, 232
Willard, Rex E., 113
Williams, Clarence A., (Bill), 81, 120, 154
Williams, Joseph R., 4
Willson, Edwin A., 128
Wilson, M. L., 177
Winship, George B., 11
Wolstad, Clarence, 81
Women's Athletics, *See* Athletics
Wood, Howard, 71
Works, George A., 153
Works, Progress Administration, 164, 172, 175
World War I, 83, 93, 102, 109, 114, 124, 170, 171
World War II, 166, 179–83, 189, 190–91
Worst, John Henry, 29, 31, 36, 39, 40, 43, 44, 46, 54, 61, 62, 68, 76, 77, 83, 85, 92, 96, 187, 220
Wright, Harvey, 244

Yankton, 7, 9, 10
Yeager, A. F., 114, 150–51, 232, 233
Yellow and Green, 78–80, 200
Yerrington, Carl, 81
Yoder, W. A., 220
YMW, Young Men and Women, 239–240
Young Men's Christian Association, 80–82, 118, 166, 169, 180, 182, 190, 218
Young Women's Christian Association, 76, 82, 166, 169

Zaylskie, John J., 240
Zoology, *See* Biology

Campus View in 1960